WHAT I LEARNED ABOUT INVESTING FROM DARWIN

WHAT I LEARNED ABOUT INVESTING FROM DARWIN

PULAK PRASAD

Columbia University Press
Publishers Since 1893
New York   Chichester, West Sussex
cup.columbia.edu

Library of Congress Cataloging-in-Publication Data
Names: Prasad, Pulak, author.
Title: What I learned about investing from Darwin / Pulak Prasad.
Description: New York : Columbia University Press, [2023] | Includes index.
Identifiers: LCCN 2022040465 | ISBN 9780231203487 (hardback) |
    ISBN 9780231555074 (ebook)
Subjects: LCSH: Investments. | Evolution (Biology) and the social sciences.
Classification: LCC HG4515 .P73 2023 | DDC 332.6—dc23/eng/20220913
LC record available at https://lccn.loc.gov/2022040465

Columbia University Press books are printed on permanent and
    durable acid-free paper.
Printed in the United States of America

Cover design: Noah Arlow
Cover images: Shutterstock (finch), Getty Images (branch)

For Deepa and Ansh ❧

CONTENTS

ACKNOWLEDGMENTS

I may have written this book, but *I* am the result of innumerable interactions and influences since my birth, the vast majority of which I cannot recall. But there are a few I *do* recall, and this section is written for them.

I am supremely grateful for the stellar team at Nalanda—Anand Sridharan, Ashish Patil, Ayalur Seshadri, Gaurav Kothari, and Mukund Dhondge. Without them, there would be no Nalanda and so there would be no book. In their own separate and unique ways, they have made Nalanda what it is today. Anand's brilliant suggestion that I add a summary at the end of every chapter has made this book (I hope) much more readable. I am also grateful to our support staff Choon San Soh, Christina Tan, Henrietta Pereira, and Oi Bek Soh for ensuring that we stay focused on investing (and writing the occasional book!).

The idea of the book started taking a concrete shape at a Chinese restaurant in Singapore in February 2020 where I was meeting my investors (and friends) Lisa Pattis and Mark Pattis. Since the founding of Nalanda in 2007, I have been drawing investing analogies and lessons from evolutionary theory in my quarterly letters. But writing an entire book is a different ball game from penning brief pontifications in a letter. I knew that it would be a long and arduous journey. Without the initial encouragement and guidance from Lisa and Mark, I doubt this book would have seen the light of day.

All of us need some luck in our lives—mine came in the form of my insightful and knowledgeable agent John Willig. John didn't have much to go on when I first contacted him since I had written only one chapter (chapter 7). Thankfully, it didn't deter John. With his deep reserve of patience and persistence, John helped me prepare a book proposal that I could never have done on my own.

Which brings me to my publisher Myles Thomson at Columbia University Press. When Myles responded favourably to the book, given his stature in the publishing world and his focus on long-term investing, I was overjoyed to have hit the jackpot. My initial reaction wasn't misplaced. My interactions with Myles over the past couple of years have solidified my admiration for his intellect, investing acumen, and generosity. My investing strategy is "sleep well at night"; little did I know that with Myles, it would also apply to getting this book published. I am also grateful for his brilliant colleague Brian Smith whose thoughtful inputs and suggestions have made this book infinitely more readable and dare I say enjoyable.

I am also grateful to Kalie Koscielak, Kara Cowan, and Laura Bowman at KnowledgeWorks Global for helping produce the book. Their thoroughness and attention to detail has been truly exemplary.

My journey into investing was an accident. I will forever be grateful to Dalip Pathak and Chip Kaye, my bosses at Warburg Pincus, for convincing me to make the switch from consulting, and then giving me the free hand to learn from my mistakes. It is impossible for me to overstate the value of their mentorship and guidance.

I want to thank my parents Upendra and Veena for (literally) everything and my siblings Roli and Rahul for their undying support and love. This fantastic life journey would not have been possible without the two biggest loves of my life: my wife Deepa and my son Ansh. Thank you for being you.

WHAT I LEARNED ABOUT INVESTING FROM DARWIN

INTRODUCTION

With such moderate abilities as I possess, it is truly surprising that thus I should have influenced to a considerable extent the beliefs of scientific men on some important points.

Charles Darwin, last sentence of The Autobiography of
Charles Darwin: 1809–1882, *August 3, 1876*

Ben Graham taught me forty-five years ago that in investing it is not necessary to do extraordinary things to get extraordinary results.

Warren Buffett, annual letter to shareholders, 1994

Evolutionary biology, as the name suggests, is the study of the causes and nature of the evolution of organisms since the beginning of life on Earth. Investing, unlike the name suggests, is all too often a euphemism for gambling in which the practitioners rarely do better than dart-throwing primates.

Superficially, there are many other differences between the two fields. Evolutionary biology is practiced by serious professionals, and the investment field is dominated by amateurs who take themselves too seriously. Knowledge and the quest for truth motivate evolutionary biologists; for most investors, knowledge and truth be damned so long as their 2/20[1] is protected. Evolutionary biologists perform a tremendous amount of research in narrow fields (e.g., "Secondary Contact and Genomic Admixture Between Rhesus and Long-Tailed Macaques in the Indochina Peninsula"[2]). Investors, on the other hand, make confident pronouncements (e.g., "I think the markets will rise 10 percent this year") based on spurious spreadsheets, flawed assumptions, and inflated egos.

The biggest difference, though, is that the two are moving in opposite directions. Evolutionary biologists continue to become better at their craft, whereas investors continue to get worse.

In recent years, biologists have used Darwin's evolutionary theory to explain things like the origin of the human hepatitis virus, the consequences of sexual selection acting on female animals, the effect of microbiomes on the evolution of animals, the link between cultural inheritance among the great apes and Darwinian evolution, and the effect of gene flow on evolution of species.[3] If you explore the "evolution" section of any scientific journal (for example, *Proceedings of the National Academy of Sciences*, available at www.pnas.org), you will be dazzled by the range of research topics and the stunning advances being made by scientists.

But the investment community? It doesn't matter how you look at it—the data are ugly. Really ugly. And it shows that we, the fund managers, are idiots.

According to a 2021 S&P report on the U.S. equity market (called the SPIVA U.S. Scorecard), across periods of five, ten, and twenty years, 75 to 90 percent of U.S. domestic funds underperformed the market.[4] Let that fact sink in before you read any further. About *75 to 90 percent* of fund managers, most of whom have graduate degrees, including MBAs, from elite schools and manage trillions of dollars, fail to beat the market. If you are part of the financial services community, you may believe that it is easier to outperform the small-cap market benchmarks. Not true. The market outperformed about 93 percent of small-cap funds during the ten-year period from 2011 to 2021.

That is bad enough, but the dismal news does not end there. Not only are most U.S. funds underperforming, but they have also gotten *worse* over time. According to the same S&P report, in 2009,[5] over three- and five-year periods (ten- and twenty-year periods were not reported), "only" 55 to 60 percent of U.S. domestic funds had underperformed the market.

This phenomenon is not unique to the United States. In the Indian equity market, as of 2017, 43 to 53 percent of large-cap funds had underperformed benchmarks over three- and five-year periods.[6] However, as of 2020,[7] those numbers had become much worse: About 70 to 80 percent of large-cap funds had been unable to beat their benchmarks over periods of three, five, and ten years.

No wonder passively managed funds have been growing at a much faster pace than active mutual funds. According to a 2020 Deloitte report,[8] since 2009, U.S. passive funds, valued at $6.6 trillion in 2018, had grown by more than four times, whereas U.S. active funds, valued at $11.4 trillion, had grown by less than 1.7 times. The reason? The performance of U.S. passive funds handsomely beat that of U.S. active funds during that period.

I know you may now be asking the following questions: How in the world can an obscure field like evolutionary biology be a solution to this problem? What is it that investors' overpriced and overvalued MBA educations did not teach them that a study of Darwinian evolution could? What can the folks who worship abstractions like cash flow, price/earnings (PE) ratios, and capital asset pricing models learn from the people who spend decades digging up fossil specimens, argue whether Neanderthals had sex with humans, and accord a godlike status to a nineteenth-century Englishman who studied earthworms, pigeons, and barnacles? A lot, I will argue.

But before we get there, who am I, and why did I write this book?

Who Am I?

I am an equity fund manager. In 2007, I founded an investment firm called Nalanda Capital, which currently manages a little more than US$5 billion invested in listed Indian securities. Nalanda's investment philosophy can be summarized in ten words: *We want to be permanent owners of high-quality businesses.*

Let me repeat that: We want to be *permanent* owners. We don't invest unless we think we can own a business forever. A bad business that is dirt cheap? Pass. A mediocre business at a low price? Thanks, but no thanks. A high-quality business at a fair price? Give me more so I can never let go.

We invest almost exclusively in businesses owned and run by entrepreneurs of which the entrepreneur is typically the largest shareholder, and we are usually the second largest.

Nalanda's approach to investing comprises three straightforward, *sequential* steps:

1. Avoid big risks.
2. Buy high quality at a fair price.
3. Don't be lazy—be *very* lazy.

That's it.

This straightforward investment process has led to the following outcome. One rupee (INR 1) invested in Nalanda's first fund at its inception in June 2007 would have been worth INR 13.8 in September 2022. The same amount invested in India's Sensex (the country's large-cap index) would have been worth INR 3.9, and if invested in the Midcap Index would have been worth only INR 4. Over a little more than fifteen years, based on actual cash inflows and outflows, the annualized rupee return for this fund was 20.3 percent (after all our fees), and the fund beat both the Sensex and the Midcap Index by 10.9 percentage points. That is not a bad track record.

Before founding Nalanda, I worked for almost nine years at the global private equity firm Warburg Pincus. Before that, I spent six years at the management consulting firm McKinsey & Company, serving clients in India, South Africa, and the United States. My consulting clients ranged from a South African retail bank, a U.S. technology company, and a Swiss insurer to an Indian conglomerate. As an investor, I have been on the board of an Israeli services company, a Singaporean food company, and an Indian telecommunications company, among a couple dozen others. My investments have been across early-stage companies (through which I lost money) to late-stage ones (through which I made some money).

As you can see, I haven't *done* anything. I haven't been responsible for meeting production deadlines, managing a sales team, turning around troubled companies, or launching and managing brands. What I *have* done, though, for almost three decades of my consulting and investing career is observe. Not being in a day-to-day operational role has afforded me the luxury of stepping back to think about what works in the corporate world and what doesn't.

This experience across industries, companies, and continents may qualify me to pontificate on the peculiarities of a pizza delivery business model, but I will not begrudge you for questioning my authority to speak on matters of evolution when I do not have a degree in evolutionary theory. My defense is the same as the one given by Mary Jane West-Eberhard in her stunningly original book *Development Plasticity and Evolution*: I can read.[9]

I blame my passion for investing on luck (I stumbled on this profession in 1998) and for evolutionary theory, oddly enough, on Charlie Munger, Warren Buffett's longtime friend and confidant. Munger was the chair of Wesco Financial until Berkshire Hathaway bought it in 2011. Like Buffett at Berkshire's legendary annual meetings, Munger held forth on a wide range of subjects at Wesco's annual meetings. In 2000, in response to a question about his favorite books, Munger recommended *The Selfish Gene* by Richard Dawkins.[10] I read the notes of this meeting in 2002 and decided to buy the book. My life hasn't been the same since.

I found the subject of Darwinian evolution extraordinarily fascinating and enriching. Thanks to Amazon and Borders (oh, I miss you so), I have been reading books on the subject for about two decades now. These include popular books, esoteric books, and graduate course books; books on insects, vertebrates, and humans; books that deal with highly specialized areas such as genetics and books on the general theory of evolution; books on the philosophy of evolution and books that deal only with mathematical concepts applied to evolution (yes, there is a lot of math in biology).[11] I can't say that I am an expert in evolutionary theory, but I think I can hold a reasonably coherent conversation on the subject with an expert. By the way, I can't say I am an expert even in investing; I can admit only to being a passionate practitioner.

Why This Book?

It was only after I had read dozens of books on evolution that I realized why I was so deeply absorbed in the subject. Almost every topic I studied in evolutionary biology has parallels to investing in general and to the Nalanda way of investing in particular. The more I studied Darwinian evolution, a new hobby, the more I learned about investing, an old passion.

This book is about how we can derive the core investment principles of long-term and patient investing from the basic concepts of evolutionary biology, the very epitome of a long-term process.

While this is a book on investing, it is not an "investing 101" book. I will not be discussing depreciation methods, lease accounting policies, or valuing intangibles—you can learn those things from hundreds of other sources. I will not be dissecting valuation ratios or commenting on off-balance sheet accounting. I also will not reveal any new investing techniques.

This book is about adopting a new *mindset* for investing—about *reimagining* investing by applying the time-tested principles of biological evolution. I will deliberate the counterintuitive Darwinian evolutionary principles that can be called upon to understand the business world, thereby helping investors excel at their craft.

What you will discover in the following pages is a description, not a prescription. It's a description of our strategy of investing at Nalanda and its uncanny parallels to evolutionary theory. Instead of saying, "This is what *you* should do," this book says, "This is what *we* have done." As mentioned, most investors have a poor long-term track record. The implication of this is obvious: Most investment methods don't work over the long run. Ours has. And so here I am, sharing my thoughts with you.

This book is for many types of readers. If you are an amateur investor, this book should intrigue you as you discover exciting parallels between the natural world and the world of money. Second, this book is for professional investors who are Buffett fans. (Okay, agreed, everyone is a Buffett fan.) This book is for Buffett fans who try to invest the way he does. While you may not learn any new tricks here, you will learn to visualize Buffett's core investment principles in an entirely new light as you peer through the lens of evolutionary biology.

The third group who may find this book interesting is science buffs. Most people of science avoid thinking about money like the plague, but the opportunity cost of not investing well can be substantial. For those individuals, this book may nudge you toward thinking more actively about investing your money well, especially because the concepts discussed here will resonate with you.

This book is also for readers with eclectic taste who are looking for something interesting to read. You may not find this book to be an Agatha Christie-esque page-turner, but hopefully your gray cells will be tickled.

If you are an expert on investing, you may not agree with many (or all) of the investing-related topics I discuss. And if you are an evolutionary biologist, you may scoff at some (or all) of the themes I present. But the great thing about these two vast areas of knowledge is that there are almost no fixed "laws" in biology[12] or in investing, in contrast to the many immutable laws in physics and chemistry. Just as scientists can't agree on the definition of what constitutes a species or a gene,[13] investors have wildly different opinions on calculating something as simple as a business's value.

The Three Elements of Nalanda's Investment Strategy

In this book, I describe one method of long-term investing and its parallels with Darwinian evolutionary biology: the way we invest at Nalanda as permanent owners. I have organized the book into three sections that mirror the three elements of our strategy:

Section I. Avoid Big Risks
Section II. Buy High Quality at a Fair Price
Section III. Don't Be Lazy—Be *Very* Lazy

Section I highlights the most basic investing lesson of all: Avoid big risks. Don't lose money. Like most deceptively simple things in life, this is easier said than done. Yes, *not* losing money is a skill, maybe a skill harder to learn than making money. As Warren Buffett has famously said, "Rule number 1: Never lose money. Rule number 2: Don't forget rule number 1."

Have you noticed that almost every book on investing provides strategies and tactics that encourage you to *do* things a certain way? Some advise you to trade based on market signals, some recommend buying value stocks, and some urge you to bet on AI and biotech start-ups. These books are about *making* money. You do not see books telling you how not to *lose* money. The sad reality is that unless an investor learns to avoid losses, their investment career is likely to be short and brutal.

Section II sums up Nalanda's second mantra: Buy high quality at a fair price. It focuses on the nuts and bolts of Nalanda's buying process as seen from the perspective of Darwinian evolutionary theory. Chapters 2 to 4 deal with *what* to buy, and chapters 5 to 7 explore *how* to buy.

Section III covers the third area of Nalanda's investment approach: Don't be lazy—be *very* lazy. We buy rarely, and we sell even more rarely. In this world of nonstop action where Nike's slogan "Just do it" seems to be the core mantra of a successful life, our core tenet of "Just *don't* do it" may seem out of place. In this section, I describe the logic of our laziness by invoking three concepts from evolutionary theory.

I then conclude by drawing a lesson from an intriguing creature that even Darwin could not understand: the honeybee.

✳ ✳ ✳

In the following pages, you will encounter many facets of Darwinian evolutionary theory that have laid the groundwork for our investing philosophy at Nalanda. This book is a compendium of analogies. As you may have discovered while persuading or being persuaded by someone, analogies can be useful for making a case. *Any* case. So be careful. Treat the evolution lessons for what they are: a plea for investors to think long term. *Very* long term.

SECTION I

AVOID BIG RISKS

This section has only one chapter, but it is the most important one in this book. If, for some reason, you lose the book after reading chapter 1, I believe you still will have more than gotten your money's worth.

The problem with our investment community is that we don't take investing seriously. Seriously. Those of you who are in the investing profession are probably bristling with indignation right now. You travel two hundred days a year, work sixty to eighty hours a week, deal with irate and demanding clients, attend excruciatingly boring conferences, your spouse and kids rarely see you, and the stress of beating the markets is making you look ten years older than your actual age. And I have the temerity to tell you that you are not taking your job seriously? Well, if you are so angry, answer this question for me: Would you bet your life on your next investment?

In this chapter, I discuss how "betting your life" is a remarkably sound strategy for investing and how adopting this approach has led to the spectacular success of *all* living organisms over millions of years.

All the investment advice from well-known books, investment gurus, and finance academics centers on making investments. This chapter is about *not* making investments. I will argue that learning the skill of *not* investing is harder and more important than learning how to invest.

CHAPTER 1

OH, TO BE A BUMBLEBEE

On the other hand, in some cases, as with the elephant and rhinoceros, none are destroyed by beasts of prey; even the tiger in India most rarely attacks a young elephant protected by its dam.

Charles Darwin, On the Origin of Species, *chapter 3, "Struggle for Existence"*

We have written in past reports about the disappointments that usually result from purchases and operation of "turnaround" businesses. Literally hundreds of turnaround possibilities in dozens of industries have been described to us over the years and, either as participants or observers, we have tracked performance against expectations. Our conclusion is that, with few exceptions, when a management with a reputation for brilliance tackles a business with a reputation for poor fundamental economics, it is the reputation of the business that remains intact.

Warren Buffett, *annual letter to shareholders, 1980*

hen you start reading a book on investing, I assume you want to be dazzled by the author's brilliance. It won't happen this time. I will begin this journey by profiling my stupidity.

After spending six years at McKinsey, I joined Warburg Pincus, a global private equity firm. After a few years of investing, I had learned the basics. Or at least I thought I had. They appeared simple: Invest in a high-quality entrepreneur running a growth business, and don't overpay. I had lucked out on a couple of investments by then and so was flying high.

An entrepreneur running a successful business approached us to raise funds for expansion in the early 2000s. The business had a reasonable scale by Indian standards, and the company had many marquee clients, including one of India's largest businesses. Notably, this company had also made inroads in overseas markets. It wasn't common to see Indian companies outside the software services industry build a thriving export business in those days.

I started our diligence process and did the usual: spent time with the founder and senior managers to understand their strategy and competitive differentiation, visited the company offices, talked to several customers in India and Europe, employed a firm specializing in forensic diligence to assess governance issues, hired the leading legal and accounting firms in India to perform diligence, and quizzed some industry experts on the company's potential for growth and value creation. Everything was looking good, and I didn't even have to haggle much on valuation or the legal documents.

I communicated my enthusiasm to my bosses and got the green light. The company raised $50 million—a big sum of money for a private equity investment in India at the time—and I enthusiastically led the investment. Warburg Pincus's return on this investment? Zero. The firm lost all its money.

It was entirely my fault. I had screwed up. Big time.

Before Making Money, Learn Not to Lose Money

The next time you are in a bookshop, go to the section with investing books. Many of you below the age of thirty probably don't know what a bookshop is. No worries—go to Amazon and type in "investment books." Do you notice anything common across titles that scream things like *Investing 101* or *One Up on Wall Street* or *You Can Be a Stock Market Genius* or *New Era Value Investing*? All of them are about how to make money. Duh. What else is an investing book supposed to teach? I hope to convince you that an essential prerequisite for *making* money is the ability *not to lose* money.

Almost everyone—and I say "almost" because this statement does not apply to my wife—makes mistakes. These errors fall into two broad categories: We do things we are not supposed to, and we don't do things we are supposed to. For me, buying a hot fudge sundae at McDonald's falls into the first category, and not keeping in regular touch with my school and college friends falls into the second.

All investors, too, make these two mistakes. Let me borrow from the field of statistics to describe them. The first kind—dubbed a type I error[1] by statisticians who can never be blamed for being creative—occurs when I make a bad investment because I erroneously think it is a good one. It is the error of committing self-harm and is also called a false positive or error of commission. A type II error occurs when I reject a good investment because I erroneously think it is bad. This is the error of rejecting a potential benefit and can be termed a false negative or error of omission. Every investor, including Warren Buffett, makes these two errors on a regular basis. They either harm themselves or walk away from a great opportunity.

As any statistician will tell you, *the risk of these two errors is inversely related.*[2] Minimizing the risk of a type I error typically increases the risk of a type II error, and minimizing the risk of a type II error increases the risk of a type I error. Intuitively, this seems logical. Imagine an overly optimistic investor who sees an upside in almost every investment. This individual will make several type I errors by committing to bad investments but also will not miss out on the few good investments. On the other hand, an overly cautious investor who keeps finding reasons to reject every investment is likely to make very few bad investments but will lose out on some good investments.

Investors can't have their cake and eat it, too! They need to choose to be more sensitive to making one type of error while living with the consequences of making more errors of the other kind. What should one do? What should *you* do?

In other words, which of the following investment strategies should you use: (1) making a lot of investments so as not to lose out on some good opportunities and, as a result, living with some failed investments, or (2) being highly selective to avoid making bad investments, thereby missing out on some good investments?

Let's turn to evolution to seek the answer.

The goal of *all* animals is to survive for as long as possible, at least until they reproduce. In the animal world, everyone is both prey *and* predator. Yes, even we, the *Homo sapiens*. How are we prey? Remember COVID-19?

Let's start with the prey. What would be a type I error for a prey animal? It would equate to inflicting sufficient harm on itself to compromise its fitness. Let me illustrate the case of an adult male deer to explore two kinds of type I errors.

The first kind occurs when the deer is thirsty and is near a watering hole. Borne by instinct or experience or both, the deer knows that the watering hole could sound its death knell if a lion or leopard or crocodile is hiding, waiting for the opportunity of an easy meal. If the deer chooses to approach the watering hole, it slakes its thirst quickly and then moves away. And if it mistakenly draws near while a predator is ready and waiting, its life ends.

From the fossil record, we know that the deer that we see today evolved from ungulates about fifteen to thirty million years ago.[3] They have survived millions of years amid ferocious predators by being *very* sensitive to making type I errors—errors of not being too careful. If they weren't so, the species would have become extinct. Obviously, some individual deer do end up making the fatal error of commission by drinking at watering holes when predators are present, but the species as a whole has done remarkably well.

If you have seen African wildlife videos or gone on a safari, you will have noticed how vigilant wildebeests, antelopes, zebras, and other herbivores are. They seem to see danger where there is none. But it is this alertness that has allowed them to survive and thrive for millions of years. A type I error of underestimating a threat could be the last error one of these animals makes.

The second kind of type I error that the deer can commit is seen in mating rituals. One fascinating sight in the wild for me, and dare I say for the female deer, is two adult male deer fighting over the exclusive control of a harem. Let me describe the mating behavior of the red deer found in many parts of Europe and in western and central Asia.[4] The males are called stags, and the females hinds. The hinds live in groups called harems. Stags, armed with impressively large antlers, "fight" with one another to gain exclusive mating rights to the harem females. I have put the word "fight" in quotation marks because the stags rarely end up fighting physically. A type I error, or the error of commission, in this scenario would be the mistake of committing to fighting, thereby risking becoming injured or disabled. Although the prize of a harem is quite substantial, the stags show extreme sensitivity to the type I error by dueling very rarely. Here is how it works.

Stags are capable of mating when they reach the age of about sixteen months, but they don't usually mate for the first time until they are at least six years old. This is because they don't develop large and powerful antlers before this age. They could fight and take a chance, but *none* do. They could get seriously hurt, which could compromise their fitness for future mating or even their life.

When they do reach mating age, they approach the rutting grounds where hinds have gathered. But they don't start fighting immediately. Scientists have observed that locking antlers is almost always the last resort, and a rutting stag will typically fight only five times during the three weeks of the rut. A series of highly choreographed rituals that serve to actively *discourage* physical contact precedes the locking of horns. When two stags challenge each other, one emits an impressive roar. The other then responds with seemingly equal vigor, because sound quality is a reliable indicator of the strength of one's rival. The roaring may go on for more than an hour, with the number of roars peaking at three to four per minute. At this stage, based on the quality of roars, one of the stags typically withdraws.

If they are unable to decide their relative strengths based on roars, they move on to the next stage of the "fight" by walking with stiff legs parallel to each other. Yes, they threaten their opponent by walking! This parallel walking spectacle lasts many minutes during which time the rivals assess each other's strength and physical condition from a distance of about two meters. During this period, they also thrash the vegetation and roar to appear more intimidating to their rival. Again, one may choose to withdraw at this stage. Only if both stags refuse to back down do they choose to clash antlers. To me, it seems more like a push-and-shove match. This "show"—most of these interactions don't look like a real brawl—can last several minutes, at the end of which one stag admits defeat and runs away.

If this were a human boxing match, the crowd would trash the arena because the boxers would be screaming and hitting the ground instead of each other! Stags have found great evolutionary success because at each stage of the contest, they minimize the error of committing self-harm: They do not even attempt to duel until they have big enough antlers, and even after acquiring their deadly weapons, they refuse to engage until they believe they have more than a fair chance of winning. Even their duel is not deadly—scientists have observed that only about 5 percent of rutting stags receive permanent injuries.

The bottom line is that the stags' evolutionary success, at least in part, can be attributed to their instinct to preserve life and limb—to minimize the risk of committing a type I error.

But there is a significant trade-off to the approach of minimizing the risk of type I errors: the deer make many more type II errors. A type II error, or the error of omission, means avoiding a watering hole where no predator is waiting. Stags also too often withdraw from a rutting duel when they have a good chance of winning the harem. The cost is the lost opportunity to drink water or to mate.

In some cases, a type II error may turn out to be a fatal mistake. A thirsty deer may not be able to run quickly enough to escape a predator, and an over-cautious stag may not get to pass his genes on to the next generation. But *on average*, making this trade-off in favor of reducing the number of errors of self-harm while tolerating a higher number of errors of rejecting potential benefit has worked quite well for the species.

Committing a type I error can be and has been deadlier than the loss of a single animal—it can lead to the extinction of an entire species. The flightless dodo bird, a native of Mauritius, was first spotted by sailors in 1507 and went extinct by 1681.[5] Dodos were bigger than turkeys, and since they had no natural predators on the isolated island, they were not afraid of the human invaders. They committed the cardinal type I error—they did not avoid the humans when they should have—which led to their extinction.

Let's now turn our attention to the predator. The predator, too, can make two types of error: It can commit itself to killing prey that turns out to be too dangerous or too large or too fast (type I error), or it can refrain from attacking prey that it could easily have killed (type II error).

Which error do you think a predator makes more often?

A cheetah is the fastest mammal on Earth and routinely achieves speeds of eighty to one hundred kilometers per hour while chasing prey.[6] It sacrifices size and bulk for speed. A cheetah typically weighs 34 to 54 kilograms (75 to 120 pounds), which is significantly less than a lion, whose weight typically ranges from 170 to 230 kilograms (375 to 500 pounds). Hence, a cheetah usually preys on smaller animals like birds, rabbits, and small antelopes. A cheetah will *never* attempt to kill an adult water buffalo, a favorite prey of lions. The cheetah is simply trying to avoid getting hurt. Committing a type I error will lead either to death—water buffalos can turn on their hunters aggressively—or wasted energy—when a cheetah chases an antelope that was too far away to begin with. These mistakes, in turn, will lead to hunger and poorer hunting performance. For a cheetah mother, a type I error can also lead to the death of her offspring. The fact the species has been successful for eons demonstrates that cheetahs, as a species, have not committed too many type I errors. A type II error for a cheetah would mean not chasing prey it should have. This would leave the cheetah and maybe even her babies hungry, but they would all live to see another day.

Deer and cheetahs do not manufacture complex decision-tree diagrams with associated probabilities to make decisions in their lives. These animals do what they do because natural selection has honed their instincts over countless generations. Natural selection among animals is incessant and merciless and has produced millions of species, all of whom adhere to this simple principle: Minimize the risk of committing type I errors to curtail the risk of injury or death, and learn to live with type II errors or foregone benefits.

What about plants, the ultimate source of all life on Earth?

Plants have been immensely successful evolutionarily: The first land plants appeared in the Ordovician era about 490 million years ago, and there are about 400,000 plant species found on our green planet.[7] Unlike animals, the dramas of whose lives play out on African safaris, on wildlife TV channels, and in children's books, plants may seem uninteresting, sedate, peaceful, and "inactive." Nothing could be further from the truth. Look closely, and you will notice that the life of a plant, in many ways, is more exciting and action-packed than that of almost any animal. Paradoxically, this is because plants can't move. If they are malnourished, they can't move to a different location to feed; when attacked by herbivores, they don't have feet to run or claws to fight back; when infected by pathogens, they can't be offered treatment and cuddles like we humans can.

Plants can choose to commit resources broadly to two areas: defending against attacks or growing. As with deer and cheetahs, any error that significantly compromises life or fitness for a plant can be categorized as a type I error. Since the lack of a proper defense may prove fatal to a plant, a type I error, or an error of commission, occurs when the plant does not devote resources to protecting itself. A type II error occurs when a plant directs energy toward preservation when it should have invested in growth. This error of omission may not kill the plant but may compromise its ability to grow and reproduce relative to its competitors.

Ample evidence from nature suggests that plants avoid type I errors at the cost of committing more type II errors.[8] Let's examine how plants handle insect herbivores.

The first defense of plants against insects is physical structures like wax, thorns, and trichomes. A trichome is the layer of hairs on leaves, stems, and fruits and can be spiral, straight, hooked, or glandular. A dense trichome on a leaf impedes the movement of insects and their larvae, thereby reducing their ability to damage the leaf epidermis. Trichomes in glandular form can secrete poisonous or otherwise harmful chemicals like flavonoids and alkaloids, which repel insects. Some glandular trichomes can also trap insects.

Producing and maintaining trichomes is metabolically expensive for a plant and prevents it from making additional leaves, stems, or fruits. Thus, when there are few or no insects, we should expect trichomes to be tiny or nonexistent. But when there is an insect attack, to reduce the risk of a type I error (erroneously investing in growth instead of preparing defenses), we should expect the plant to start making trichomes. And this is what we see. For example, scientists have observed that when adult leaf beetles attack the willow plant, new leaves grown after the attack develop higher trichome density. The willow plant *redirects* its resources from growth to defense as a result of sensing a predator. Trichome density also increases in other species like pepperwort and wild radish after an insect attack. When a butterfly species attacks a black mustard plant, the trichome density of the plant's leaves increases, as does the production of pungent chemicals called glucosinolates. Within a few days or weeks following an insect attack, trichome density can increase from 25 to 1,000 percent!

A plant's defense mechanisms are not limited to trichomes, however. Lignin is a phenol compound that plays a vital role in a plant's defense against insects. Lignin does two things to the leaves: It increases their toughness, thereby making them unpalatable, and it reduces their nutritional content. A leaf with excess lignin would be anathema for insects. Just as with trichomes, it is costly to produce lignin. Also as with trichomes, the plant ramps up its lignin production after an insect attack. In addition to lignin, compounds called flavonoids, tannins, lectins, and peroxidases also serve to reduce the risk of plants committing type I errors by directing resources to defense rather than growth.

What I have described are *direct* defenses against pests. But many plants also resort to *indirect* defenses, which are rarely seen in animals.

An indirect defense works on the simple principle that "my enemy's enemy is my friend."[9] It works simply—and beautifully—like this. When a plant senses an insect attack, it releases some chemical compounds from its leaves, flowers, and fruits into the atmosphere. These chemical compounds attract predators of the insects attacking the plants. For example, plants like lima beans and *Arabidopsis* release a chemical called methyl salicylate to attract insect predators like big-eyed bugs, ladybird beetles (commonly known as ladybugs), and green lacewings. This trick is not limited to the aerial parts of plants. Roots, too, can release chemicals that attract underground predators to underground pests. For example, when western corn rootworm threatens maize plants, the maize roots release a chemical that attracts a nematode species that preys upon the rootworm.

When aphids attack, many plants emit a chemical called beta-farnesene. It does not appear to be a coincidence that when predators attack aphids, the aphids release this chemical, presumably warning other aphids to stay away. Thus, a plant releasing beta-farnesene is equivalent to a deer mimicking a lion roar when attacked by a leopard!

Plants, like animals, have found a way to their spectacular evolutionary success by focusing on reducing their errors of commission. In other words, like their animal counterparts, *they avoid taking risks to their life and well-being at the cost of giving up some potentially juicy opportunities.*

Buffett's Two Rules of Investing

As one should expect, Warren Buffett figured out this lesson from evolutionary theory before almost everyone else. He famously coined his two rules of investing as follows:

> Rule number 1: Never lose money.
> Rule number 2: Never forget rule number 1.[10]

But wait a minute. What does he mean by commanding us to "never lose money"? How can one *choose* not to lose money? Isn't that what every investor wants? Why would any investor deliberately wish to lose money?

In fact, Buffett seems to have violated his own two rules on many occasions. For example, in 1993, Berkshire bought Dexter Shoe for $433 million in Berkshire stock. As he detailed in his 2007 annual letter, "What I had assessed as a durable competitive advantage vanished within a few years. . . . That move made the cost to Berkshire shareholders not $400 million, but rather $3.5 billion. In essence, I gave away 1.6 percent of a wonderful business—one now valued at $220 billion—to buy a worthless business."

In his 2014 annual letter, he admitted his mistake in Berkshire's Tesco investment, "We sold Tesco shares throughout the year and now are out of this position. Our after-tax loss from this investment was $444 million. . . ." More recently, in the middle of the COVID-19 pandemic market meltdown, Buffett sold all his airline stocks. He had invested between $7 billion and $8 billion for large stakes in four airlines: American, Delta, Southwest, and United. Berkshire's position was worth a bit more than $4 billion at the time of his sale.[11] "It turned out I was wrong," he said.

Back to Buffett's two rules. Despite losing money occasionally, what is he asking us to do when he orders us not to lose any? Buffett has never explicitly explained this (at least I have never found an explanation), but this is what I think he means: *Avoid big risks.* Don't make type I errors. Don't commit to an investment in which the *probability* of losing money is higher than the probability of making money. Think about risk first, not return.

Before we go any further, allow me a slight digression to get the definition of "risk" out of the way. The definition I use in this book is not the same as the one defined by corporate finance theorists. Finance theory claims that risk is the chance that the actual investment return will *differ* from the expected investment return.[12] Thus, if an asset is highly volatile, it will be classified as riskier than an asset that is not as volatile.

If you think about this for a moment, you will conclude that this is nonsensical. For any investor, risk should simply be the probability of incurring a capital loss. The following example will make this clear. Let's say I am evaluating an investment in a high-quality grocery retailer. The retailer has been performing quite well, resulting in a steadily increasing stock price over the years. Let's say the market price was $90 in early 2020. After the COVID-19 crisis, the stock market became highly volatile, and the market price of this business dropped to $30. Let's also assume that you have done your work and have concluded that grocery retailers may benefit from the crisis since consumers will stock up their pantries. Which would be a riskier investment: investing in the business at $90 or at $30? If your intuition says $90, you are right. This is because the risk of losing money is greater at $90 than at $30. But, believe it or not, academics of finance would argue exactly the opposite! No, I am not kidding. They would conclude that the post-COVID-19 crisis business is riskier because the *volatility* of the stock price has increased!

We at Nalanda *never* bring stock price volatility into a risk discussion. We define "risk" as the probability of capital loss. The higher the probability of loss, the higher the risk. If my investment in Company A is likely to lose more money over my investment in Company B, I will deem Company A to be "riskier" than Company B irrespective of past or future volatility in their stock prices.

As Buffett's diktat shows, he is focused on minimizing risk and, in doing so, has become the envy of the entire investment world, which seems obsessed with running after every half-baked business idea. Buffett and the natural world are fixated on minimizing the risk of type I errors. Should we follow them blindly? Will the explicit lesson from Buffett and the implicit one from leopards and legumes work for ordinary mortals like us?

Why or why not?

A Great Investor Is a Great Rejector

Let's walk through a simple example that contrasts two different investment styles. And let's then see if Buffett's advice makes sense. According to data from the World Bank, the United States had 4,400 listed companies in 2018.[13] For simplicity, let's assume a round 4,000. First, we need to decide how many of these are "good investments." Let's keep it simple and classify a "good investment" as one that will make us a decent return over the long run. It has a competent and honest management team, a modest growth rate, makes enough money, and has low leverage. If you are a finance nerd, you are probably bristling at this moment. What in the world do I mean by vague terms like "decent," "enough," and "competent"? Don't worry, we will get into numbers shortly, but at this stage, let's just say we know a good investment when we see it.

Let's assume that 25 percent of the listed universe comprises "good investments." If you talk to practitioners—that is, actual investors—you will not get a number too far from this percentage. In any event, the exact percentage is less significant, as we will see. Thus, we can say there are 1,000 good investments and 3,000 bad investments in the U.S. listed universe by this logic. Again, don't get too pained about this strict dichotomy; it is serving a purpose that we will get to.

Let's say you encounter a savvy investor who claims that he is right 80 percent of the time in his investment decisions (it is usually a "he"; we men are evolutionarily programmed for empty exaggerations). Stated differently, if he encounters a bad investment (i.e., one in which he will not make any money), he rejects it 80 percent of the time. If he sees a good investment (i.e., one in which he will make money), he makes a favorable investment decision 80 percent of the time. Thus, his rates of type I and type II errors are both 20 percent. If this star investor makes an investment decision, what is the probability that it is a good investment? You'd say 80 percent, right? Wrong. The answer is 57 percent. But why? Isn't he right 80 percent of the time? How can we go from 80 percent to 57 percent?

Here is how.

There are 1,000 good investments in the market, and since this investor makes a type II error 20 percent of the time (i.e., he mistakenly rejects 20 percent of these), he will select only 800 companies from his list. The market also has 3,000 bad investments, and since he makes type I errors 20 percent of the time (i.e., he mistakenly accepts 20 percent of these), he will mistakenly select 600 companies from this list, *thinking* that they are good investments. Thus, his universe of what he thinks are good investments will be 1,400 companies (800 + 600). Are you with me? Good. Now to the most interesting part.

Of these 1,400 businesses that the investor *thinks* are good investments, how many do you think *are* good investments? Only 800. Hence, the probability of his making a good investment will be 800 ÷ 1,400 = 57 percent.

So here is the unfortunate conclusion. Even if an investor is endowed with the divine power of being right 80 percent of the time, the probability that he will select a good investment is only 57 percent. Even though he is "right" 80 percent of the time, 43 percent of his investments will turn out to be bad! The reason is simple, especially when we incorporate our prior knowledge of the business world: *There are very few good investments in the market.*

Let me repeat this statement, which is the bedrock of our philosophy and that of the rest of this book: *There are very few good investments in the market.*

As we have just seen, the prevalence of type I and type II errors can lull us investors into thinking that we are better than we really are. But these errors carry a deeper meaning for our profession. Given a choice, which error would you like to reduce, and why?

Let's say that our investor, Investor A, decides to become better at rejecting bad investments and reduces his rate of type I errors from 20 percent to 10 percent. Thus, from the 3,000 bad investments in the market, he will select only 300 businesses (10 percent × 3,000). As his type II error rate remains 20 percent, he will erroneously reject 200 of the 1,000 good investments, thereby selecting 800 investments. Thus, Investor A has selected 1,100 investments (300 + 800), but only 800 of these are good. In this scenario, Investor A's probability of selecting a good investment improves from 57 percent to 73 percent (800 ÷ 1,100). I assume you will admit that this is quite a dramatic improvement in his success rate.

Investor B, unlike Investor A, is more focused on not missing out on good opportunities. He chooses to reduce his rate of type II errors from 20 percent to 10 percent and keeps his rate of type I errors at 20 percent. Thus, of the 1,000 good investments, he will select 900 (90 percent × 1,000), and of the 3,000 bad investments, he will mistakenly assume that 600 are good (20 percent × 3,000). Thus, Investor B has selected 1,500 investments (600 + 900), but only 900 are good. Thus, Investor B's probability of selecting a good business improves from 57 percent to 60 percent (900 ÷ 1,500). This is an improvement—but only by 3 percentage points. Good, but not great.

The relative impact of reducing each type of error is quite stark, as shown in table 1.1.

TABLE 1.1 Type I and II errors

Type I error	Type II error	Success rate
20%	20%	57%
10%	20%	73%
20%	10%	60%

Thus, there is a 16-percentage-point improvement in investor performance by reducing the rate of type I errors from 20 percent to 10 percent. On the other hand, reducing the rate of type II errors by the same amount improves performance by only 3 percentage points.

Guess what happens if another investor, Investor C, improves his rate of *both* type I and type II errors from 20 percent to 10 percent. I was flabbergasted when I first saw the answer: 75 percent. This is barely above the 73 percent achieved by Investor A, who was focused only on reducing type I errors. A dramatic improvement in performance comes only when the rate of type I errors—errors of making bad investments—is reduced.

Thus, whereas most investment books and college curricula focus on teaching how to make good investments, everyone would be better off by learning how *not* to make bad investments. An investment career is probably among the very few that rewards the skeptic more than the optimist.

Buffett is the best investor in the world because he is the best *rejector* in the world.

How to Avoid Big Risks

It's all well and good to assert that we should learn from the evolutionary success of animals and plants to avoid big risks and become better investors. But how?

There are myriad ways of learning life lessons—parents, siblings, one's spouse, friends, books, movies, school, college, work, and leaders are a few sources that come to mind. I will never really know *why* I am what I am. But I am reasonably confident of the identity of my primary teacher and guide in the area of investing—my own mistakes.

Early in my investing career at Warburg Pincus, I committed the cardinal sin of minimizing errors of omission instead of trying to control type I errors. I was too afraid to miss out on good opportunities. I founded Nalanda after gaining more than eight years of investing experience. Our reasonable success of staying away from trouble is the result of the follies of the first three to four years of my career. In my case, nothing has succeeded like a failure.

Most investors will keep making type I errors (making bad investments) throughout their careers. At least I have, and I will. It's inevitable. So when I say that we need to avoid type I errors, I am proposing that we try to avoid the *avoidable* type I error. By not taking on big risks. What is a big risk? It is not clear to me that a definition is possible or even desirable for a practitioner. Instead of defining "big risk," let me describe the kinds of situations we avoid at Nalanda.

This is not an exhaustive list, but hopefully it will give you a good sense of the kinds of risks we don't price.

Being Wary of Criminals, Crooks, and Cheats

People don't change. Especially criminals, crooks, and cheats. As permanent owners, we at Nalanda have no interest in a business owned or run by someone who defrauds customers, suppliers, employees, or shareholders. When we come across such a person, we don't ask if the business is cheap enough for the risk to be mitigated; we don't ask if we could persuade this individual to change; we don't ask if their crimes are trivial enough to ignore. We simply walk away.

I don't know about other countries, but the Indian capital market, I am sad to admit, teems with dodgy and deceitful promoters (Indian parlance for the largest or controlling shareholders). As a result, we are highly vigilant and do not even start assessing the business fundamentals until we have convinced ourselves that the promoters have impeccable integrity. A KPMG report on the Indian private equity (PE) industry euphemistically claimed, "Many risks are common to all emerging markets—political and regulatory uncertainty and weak corporate governance among them. Many of these risks are more likely in India, even if they are not unique—such as working with family-owned businesses, navigating IPO exits and compliance risks."[14] This was a polite way of saying, "Beware of being swindled."

We employ a two-level process for this assessment. We *always* hire a forensic diligence expert to assess if the owner or senior managers have a dubious past. During this period, we conduct our parallel diligence on the promoters and managers by scouring the media, studying past annual reports, listening to their conference call recordings, reading their interviews, and talking to people who have had personal and business dealings with them. In almost half the cases, we ask the external firm to further probe issues that have arisen during our diligence (for example, money leakage for large capex contracts or a cash payment to senior managers). This dual check provided by outsourcing and insourcing has prevented a lot of heartburn for us over the years. More importantly, it has saved a lot of money for our investors.

But shouldn't this be obvious?

There is nothing extraordinarily insightful about claiming that one needs to check for promoters' integrity before committing capital. You are right. Governance checks in India should be par for the course. But they are not. Let's take an example of investing in the infrastructure and real estate sectors. In India, these two industries are highly regulated, involve a lot of cash transactions, and require a plethora of approvals; hence, over the years, they have attracted a set of entrepreneurs who can successfully "manage" the system. Looking for the proverbial needle in a haystack would be a cakewalk compared to finding infrastructure and real estate entrepreneurs who don't mistreat minority shareholders. We have chosen to avoid these industries completely.

When we launched Nalanda in 2007, it was a boom time for fundraising in the real estate and infrastructure sectors. According to a McKinsey report, from 2005 to 2008, real estate absorbed almost a quarter of all PE investments, and infrastructure's share was nearly 30 percent.[15] A relatively large portion of these ended up in a disaster, and PE and public market investors lost billions of dollars. Real estate returns on exit were only 2 percent, and only 9 percent of energy segment investments could get an exit. One key reason for this unfortunate outcome was the adverse selection of entrepreneurs by the fund management community.

But it would be hypocritical of me to complain about others when I, too, have fallen into the same trap.

Let's go back to the business for which I led the investment of $50 million from Warburg Pincus and which seemed to have ticked all the boxes. Here is what I did not tell you on the first page of this chapter: The governance check from the outsourced firm had given a clean chit to the promoter, but our internal team had heard some informal negative "buzz" about him. It wasn't strong or unequivocal, but it was buzz nevertheless. I ignored it. I am still not sure why. Maybe I trusted our outsourced provider more than I should have, maybe I had become arrogant owing to recent successes, maybe I had been too charmed by the smooth-talking promoter, maybe I was in too deep after completing many months of diligence, or maybe all of the above.

At this stage, I should have gone back to our service provider and asked them to do more work. I also should have dug deeper into the veracity of the criticisms of the promoter. I didn't do either of these things. It was too late by the time we discovered this individual's shenanigans; he had sucked the company dry, and Warburg lost almost all its money. Since this incident, I have been extra cautious, both at Warburg and at Nalanda. We never invest unless we are fully and absolutely satisfied with the governance standards. We haven't lost a single dollar at Nalanda yet on dodgy promoters, but this doesn't mean we never will. But if we ever do, it will not be because we didn't do our best.

Some investors may object that if the company's survival is not under threat owing to the bad behavior of the promoter, investing in a somewhat shady business at a very cheap valuation may be a good way of making money over the medium to long term. The fact remains that there are some well-known dodgy businesses in India whose stock prices have done reasonably well over the past few years. But we have never played this game and never will. Our philosophy of permanent ownership requires—*demands*—that we partner only with promoters of the highest integrity. And so that is what we do.

Avoiding Turnarounds

Imagine a tennis match in which Roger Federer is playing John, who is ranked 500 in the world. I ask you to bet 5 percent of your wealth on John winning the match. You refuse (I hope). But John wants you to bet on him. And so, before the match starts, in a face-to-face meeting with you, John makes an impassioned plea to ignore his ranking and recognize his innate talent. He speaks eloquently and makes a slick PowerPoint presentation on his plan to defeat Federer. John says he has been watching Federer's game very closely for the past two years, and his plan, he believes, is exemplary. To bolster his claim, John invites one of the leading tennis coaches in the world, who admits that John's plan is laudable and that he has a real chance of beating Federer. It's decision time for you. Would you bet 5 percent of your wealth on John?

This is *exactly* what happens in the world of investing. Managements that have underperformed for long periods are able to convince investors to bet on their businesses with nothing but fancy promises and McKinsey reports. I blame neither managements nor McKinsey because optimism is not a crime. But I do get baffled at investors who, despite having access to data that amply demonstrate the incompetence of incumbent management, are willing to bet their clients' money on the hope that this management will suddenly morph into an industry beater in the near future. More often than not, the dream scenario hyped up by the management morphs into a nightmare.

Occasionally, the board or the owner fires the previous CEO and brings in a new one to turn around a struggling business. The new CEO usually comes with an impressive resume, and many *are* highly qualified. But we don't bet on these turnarounds either. An exceptional CEO was impressive in a certain context with a certain business—*this* context and *this* business are different. How are we to know that the new CEO, faced with a set of challenges they have almost certainly never met before, will do what they are promising to do? We don't.

I know what you are thinking. The upside, if we *were* able to detect a genuine turnaround, would be significant. Agreed. Let's assess the following two situations.

Case 1: A company that has been very profitable over many decades has recently fallen prey to smaller and more nimble competitors. It has suffered massive losses over the past two years. The company sells its highly engineered products to medium and large businesses. The board starts searching for a new CEO and identifies a promising candidate. There are, however, a few worrying problems with this choice: The candidate does not understand technology, he does not understand how to sell to businesses because he has run a company that sells biscuits to consumers (!), and he has had no experience turning around any business, let alone a complex engineering one like this.

Would you invest in this business once this CEO takes over?

Case 2: A venerated hundred-year-old department store has been struggling with falling sales. Over the past four years, sales have fallen 10 percent from $20 billion to $18 billion, and the operating income has plummeted about 65 percent from $1.1 billion to $380 million. The stock price has crashed from $81 to $32.

The board appoints one of the world's leading retail experts as the new CEO of this business. He has had two great successes in the past few years. As VP of merchandising at one of the largest U.S. retailers, he made the store appeal to young and trendy consumers. He also struck several designer partnerships that were a huge hit with shoppers. His next job was at a large company where he was responsible for opening retail stores. He hit the ball completely out of the park. The sales per square foot at these stores now exceeds even luxury retailers like LVMH. His innovations in design and service at these stores were so popular that shoppers now need to book an appointment many days in advance in many cities across the world.

Would you invest in this business once this CEO takes over?

I would not buy the shares of the first business but would load up on the second. I assume, dear reader, that you would do the same. We would both be dead wrong. You and I would have missed out on a seven-fold increase in stock price over the next ten years in the first business. We would have been wiped out completely—yes, with a 100 percent loss—in the second.

The first business is IBM, and its famous turnaround in the late 1990s was led by Lou Gerstner, the ex-CEO of RJR Nabisco.[16] Previously called International Business Machines, IBM was a behemoth that ruled the world of technology in the latter half of the twentieth century. In the early 1990s, about half its revenues came from huge mainframe computers sold to businesses. These mainframes had hardware and software bundled into one system. The world, however, was fast shifting to smaller and midsized machines running on microprocessors. The technology universe was witnessing the unbundling of hardware and software with different vendors specializing in each segment. Companies like HP, Sun, Compaq, and Dell were eating IBM's lunch on hardware, and Microsoft and Oracle were starting to dominate software.

To make matters worse, individual consumers had started buying personal computers, in which IBM had no expertise or experience. The company also had a huge internal bureaucracy that hobbled decision-making. From being the second most profitable company in the world in 1990, IBM lost $16 billion between 1991 and 1993.

Lou Gerstner seemed like a strange choice for the board to make. But it worked wonders. Gerstner resorted to a massive cut in expenses by laying off staff, sold many assets to raise cash, transformed the organizational culture to encourage business units to cooperate and not compete, linked the compensation of senior managers to overall company performance, created a single brand message for all units of IBM, and much more. IBM's stock price jumped seven times from $13 to $77 during his tenure from April 1, 1993, to December 31, 2002. If you want to learn more about Gerstner's miracles, I urge you to read his book *Who Says Elephants Can't Dance? Inside IBM's Historic Turnaround.*

The second business is JCPenney, where Ron Johnson, credited with transforming Target and creating the iconic Apple Stores, was brought in as CEO in late 2011.[17] The stock price jumped 24 percent at the news! The market was betting that Johnson would be the miracle cure for JCPenney. He changed everything at the company—the logo, the store design, the advertisements, the pricing model, and the popular private labels. JCPenney was known for coupons and clearance sales—Johnson ended them. Big mistake. In 2012, sales dropped 25 percent, from $17 billion to $13 billion, as customers abandoned the stores en masse. More worryingly, the company suffered an operating loss of $1.3 billion. The board fired Johnson in mid-2013, just seventeen months after installing him as CEO. The stock price had dropped 60 percent during his short tenure. JCPenney never recovered from this fiasco and filed for bankruptcy in May 2020.

If we could not predict the fate of turnaround efforts at what *appeared* to be slam-dunk cases (IBM and JCPenney), what hope do we have in situations that don't seem so clear cut? The corporate world is brutally competitive. Even the best companies have to run hard just to stay in the same place. How could the probability of success at a troubled company be anything but minuscule? And if so, why would we indulge in the fantasy?

Detesting Debt

As a consultant in the early 1990s, I almost always focused on the profit-and-loss (P&L) account. Revenue, cost, profit. Almost nothing else mattered.

Remarkably, a consultant's P&L obsession remains intact. My niece is currently a consultant in London and primarily serves private equity clients. She is hyper-focused on just one aspect of P&L: EBITDA (earnings before interest, tax, depreciation, and amortization). P&L obsession is not limited to consultants. Read any analyst report or listen to conference call recordings that discuss quarterly results. You will be inundated with comments and questions on revenues, costs, and profit.

After many years of investing, I realized that I needed to focus as much, if not more, on the company's balance sheet. Receivables, inventory, payables, fixed assets. And most important of all, debt. Corporate finance theory has a thing for leverage. For those of you who are not familiar with it, finance academics claim that companies need to have an "optimal" level of leverage to improve returns.[18] If a company can borrow money to purchase assets, its return on equity and earnings per share should improve. Mathematically, this is undoubtedly true. Realistically, this is undoubtedly dangerous.

What could be more important than improving short-term return on equity and earnings per share for a business? In my view, two things.

Start with the easy one. Survival. There is no point in improving return on equity by a few percentage points if it compromises long-term survival. The COVID-19 crisis demonstrated clearly that the companies caught with their pants down were the ones with substantial leverage. In the second quarter of 2020, the following are just some of the well-known companies that announced bankruptcy: Gold's Gym, Hertz, Intelsat, J. Crew, JCPenney, Neiman Marcus, and Sur La Table.[19] Here is what is common across all these names: *All* had a large amount of debt. It is not impossible for an unleveraged business to go belly up, but it sure is quite hard. If I were to list the twenty biggest bankruptcies in the United States,[20] you would notice that *all*—with Lehman at the top and LyondellBasell at number 20—were heavily indebted.

One might argue that these businesses were unlucky and that everything would have been fine if there had been no COVID-19. One might also contend that mismanagement or other factors contributed more to their downfall than debt. And that "correlation is not causation." Maybe. But it's one hell of a correlation. As a long-term investor in a business, I don't want the company *ever* to go bankrupt—whether the times are good or bad. I can live with a slightly lower return on equity and lower earnings-per-share (EPS) growth, but at least I will live.

Not having high leverage probably makes sense to everyone. But the following may not: I am an advocate of *no* leverage. More than 90 percent of our portfolio companies have—and have always had—excess cash. Only three businesses out of about thirty in our portfolio have some debt. But even this debt is quite small—the maximum debt/equity ratio among these three is 0.3.

Why would I demand zero debt when a modest level would not compromise the survival of the business? The answer lies in the following *Business Insider* headline: "No Layoff, Asian Paints Will Give Salary Increments to Boost Employees Morale."[21]

Asian Paints is India's largest paints business and probably one of the country's best-run businesses. As an aside, it is sadly not in our portfolio. I had a chance to buy it during the global financial crisis of 2008, but I refused to pay 15 percent more for the privilege of owning this marvelous compounder. I was a fool. Anyway, let's return to a more pleasant topic.

This "no-layoff, salary increment" story would not be newsworthy in normal times. But this announcement was made on May 15, 2020. At the time, India had been under an almost complete lockdown since mid-March as a result of the COVID-19 pandemic. Every business was witnessing a catastrophic decline in revenues and profits. Also, no one had any visibility as to when the situation would improve—remember that the possibility of vaccines wasn't even on the horizon in May 2020. Asian Paints was itself going through a catastrophic quarter—during the period from April to June 2020, the company's revenue declined by 43 percent, and its net profit went down by 67 percent compared to the same period in 2019. Was the company foolish to be increasing salaries in this period? No. Just cash rich. In March 2020, at the start of the pandemic, the company had $220 million cash (its revenue for the year ended March 2020 was $2.9 billion).

Which brings me to the second reason I detest *any* debt. This answer is often underappreciated and even ignored by investors and management. It is this: Debt diminishes strategic flexibility and hence long-term value creation. For a day trader or even an investor whose holding period ranges from three to five years, a reasonable amount of leverage may not matter. But for a permanent owner like Nalanda, any constraint that prevents a business from taking calculated strategic bets is undesirable.

Asian Paints is the leader in the highly competitive Indian paints industry; its competitors can and do copy what the business is trying to do. However, every few years, the company gets an opportunity to make an investment or take a strategic bet that its competitors find hard to emulate. The salary increase was one such bet. But it did not stop there. The company sanitized its dealers' paint shops without charging any fees, offered medical insurance to its painters, gave forty-five-day extensions on payments to its dealers, and announced relief worth more than $5 million to its contractors. The CEO, Amit Syngle, pointed out, "We have been debt free for years and are quite comfortably placed even if the uncertainty goes on for the next four or five months."[22]

The impact of the company's largesse may not be felt in the short term, but the long-term impact is likely to be significant. Asian Paints was able to commit to these highly unusual actions only because—apart from their exceptional strategic vision—they had no debt.

The global pandemic is an extreme case, and one may assert that it would be foolhardy to keep excess cash on hand for a once-in-a-century event. But this premise is false. Bad things happen to businesses at remarkably regular intervals. The harsh reality of companies in any capitalist society—and the reason to always have cash—is not that things *can* go wrong, but that they *do* go wrong. Businesses suffer adversity across a wide range of situations: The macroeconomic environment can become a stiff headwind as in the global financial crisis of 2008 or a recession; the industry can suffer a cyclical downturn; a well-funded competitor can start overspending on advertising or giving discounts; the company can lose some of its best employees to competitors; one or more major customers can leave or go belly up; consumer tastes can suddenly change; a large strategic acquisition or investment may not pay off; a factory can catch fire or a supplier may get in trouble; currency can move adversely in a foreign market that contributes to significant sales; regulations can get in the way; the company can get sued for a significant amount. I could go on and on.

None of these issues is hypothetical—I have seen *all* of these happen to our portfolio companies over more than two decades of investing. Occasionally, two or more problems can arise simultaneously, putting significant pressure on businesses. While worrying about market share loss, low supplier commitment, competitor aggression, and employee dissatisfaction, the last thing management should worry about is interest payments. In my experience, only when the financial risk is low can management focus on mitigating business risks.

I have always maintained that the notion of an "optimal" capital structure that requires companies to have leverage, which is espoused by corporate finance theorists, is not just wrong but dangerous. A strong balance sheet is not the one that maximizes debt to minimize the cost of capital but the one that minimizes debt to maximize the safety of capital.

Fortunately, none of the owners of Nalanda portfolio companies studied finance at fancy business schools.

Ignoring M&A Junkies

Nothing happens in well-oiled businesses on a day-to-day basis. Sorry, a lot happens, but it's largely mundane, repetitive, uninteresting, dull, and monotonous. And this is the way it should be. Imagine the day-to-day operations of a business that sells bars of bath soap. Here is a typical day or week or month or year: The factory manufactures bars of soap in the thousands and performs quality control checks to reject defects; the packing department stacks the bars in boxes; logistics ensures timely shipping at pre-agreed costs; warehouses stock the boxes in assigned positions; last-mile delivery delivers the bars on time; and the finance department records the payments received from the retailers. No news. No excitement.

What would be the best way for such a business—or any business for that matter—to get reported on in the *Wall Street Journal* or the *Financial Times*? M&A. In industry parlance, "mergers and acquisitions." For some reason, the media love the news of one business merging with or acquiring another one. The investment bankers and financiers who make fat fees love them even more. Following such an announcement, the CEO is typically invited to a CNBC interview during which they will extol the virtues of "strategic fit," "synergies," "culture fit," and other boilerplate platitudes uttered in every single M&A. They are almost always wrong. Most mergers and acquisitions fail.

Here are the statements made by the CEOs of AOL and Time Warner when they announced their $350 billion (!) merger on January 10, 2000. Stephen Case, the cofounder of AOL, proudly proclaimed, "This is a historic moment when new media has truly come of age." Not to be left behind, Gerald Levin, the CEO of Time Warner, gushed philosophically that the internet had begun to "create unprecedented and instantaneous access to every form of media and to unleash immense possibilities for economic growth, human understanding and creative expression." The result of this bromance? The largest failed merger in the history of the corporate world.[23] Within two years, AOL took a write-off of $99 *billion* on the deal. Yes, "billion" with a "b." The market value of AOL went from $226 billion in 2000 to $20 billion in 2002. In June 2015, it was acquired for a mere $4.4 billion by Verizon.

Go ahead and blame me for cherry-picking. Guilty as charged. But think about this. AOL and Time Warner were undisputed leaders in their industries. They had highly regarded CEOs, their boards were exemplary, their financial position was rock solid, they employed supremely talented and motivated staff, they had access to the best consultants, and yet they failed. Miserably. If they couldn't hack it, what chance do most companies have? The sad fact is the disastrous AOL Time Warner saga plays out thousands of times every year. And an even sadder fact is that everyone knows about it.

There is a *lot* of literature available on the high failure rate of M&A.[24] A *Harvard Business Review* article by Clayton Christensen and others titled "The Big Idea: The New M&A Playbook" claims that 70 to 90 percent of mergers and acquisitions fail; a KPMG study claims that 83 percent of merger deals did not create value; a Cornell University research article declares that "an abundance of empirical research has examined the performance of acquirers across all industries and in general has failed to find consistent evidence of improvements in value after the acquisition"; an *Organizational Dynamics* research article by Toby J. Tetenbaum asserts that 60 to 80 percent of all mergers are financial failures; and a study by Great Prairie Group cites studies from McKinsey, Harvard Business School, Bain, and the Wharton School to state that the M&A

failure rate is over 70 percent. In all these studies, the reasons for failure include culture mismatch, overpayment, misevaluation of the opportunity, external factors, and integration problems, among many others.

But they don't point out the single biggest reason *we* detest M&A: opportunity cost. Let's visit the German giant Bayer to understand this reason.

Dr. Marijn Dekkers, the chair of Bayer AG, had every reason to be proud in 2015. During his five years as chair, this life sciences company has grown revenue from €35 billion to €46 billion, and its EPS had more than tripled from €1.6 per share to €5 per share. It continued its reign as the largest company on the German stock exchange with a market value of about €140 billion. The 2015 annual report was replete with good news. Without being boastful, Dr. Dekker's excellent commentary made it evident that the company was one of the world's leading life sciences businesses.

The only piece of bad news was tucked away on page seven of the report. Dr. Dekkers wrote, "This is my last Chairman's Letter to you as CEO of Bayer."

How bad was Dr. Dekker's revelation for Bayer? In 2020, its sales had fallen to €41 billion from €46 billion in 2015; from being a highly profitable business with a return on equity of 18 percent in 2015, it declared a net loss of €10 *billion*; and its dividend per share was 20 percent lower than in 2015. Oh, and by June 2021, less than six years after the glorious year of 2015, Bayer's market value had declined by 65 percent to €50 billion.

What happened? Within ten days of Dr. Dekker's departure, Bayer made a bid to acquire Monsanto, the U.S. agrochemical giant. Bayer ended up paying $63 billion for the acquisition, which was more than Bayer's market value in June 2021!

If you read reports on the reasons for this disaster, most will focus on Bayer losing multiple lawsuits and incurring billions in damages because plaintiffs were able to convince the U.S. courts that Monsanto's Roundup weed killer causes cancer. The reports aren't wrong, but they missed the real value destroyer invisible in the Bayer–Monsanto transaction, and the reason we abhor almost all M&A: opportunity cost. Stated simply, most analyses of M&A failure focus on the bad things that happened, rather than on the good things that *didn't* happen.

Let's see what Bayer may have missed doing by making a gargantuan acquisition. These actions (and inactions) fall into three categories: divestiture of attractive businesses, reduced focus on existing businesses, and missed opportunities.

After acquiring Monsanto, Bayer had to divest many of its core businesses for two reasons. First, regulators forced them to do so because both companies were large players in the agrochemical sector. Second, Bayer had to pay down the huge debt they had incurred to finance the deal. Bayer's net debt had gone up ten times from €3.6 billion in 2017 to €36 billion in 2018!

In 2017, Bayer divested large parts of its seed and herbicide businesses for €6 billion. In 2018, it sold its 60 percent stake in a highly lucrative business called Currenta for €1 billion and sold the consumer brands Coppertone and Dr. Scholl's. In 2020, Bayer exited its leading and highly profitable Animal Health business for €7 billion. If we add up the sale value of these divestitures, that's at least €15 billion, or about 30 percent of Bayer's market value in mid-2021. These businesses had been owned and run by Bayer for decades, and so it is possible that the market was assigning a much higher value than €15 billion to them when they were *inside* Bayer. The future benefit from these attractive businesses was lost forever. The geese laying golden eggs were slaughtered to buy a hen that refused to lay *any* eggs.

The second major opportunity cost is a reduced focus on existing businesses because of the distraction of a bad acquisition. You can see this in Bayer's annual reports of 2018, 2019, and 2020, in which a lot of ink was expended on justifying the acquisition and on steps being taken to mitigate the disaster. As usual, numbers tell a better story, as I will explain next.

Bayer has three business divisions: pharmaceuticals, consumer health, and crop science. From 2016 to 2020, the sales of its pharma division stayed flat at around €16 billion to €17 billion. (Although 2020 was the year of COVID, most global pharma companies did not experience a decline in sales.) Could this stagnation have been due to the acquisition distraction? From 2010 to 2015, pharma sales had more than doubled from €6.6 billion to €13.7 billion. From 2015 to 2020, rather than assuming a doubling of sales, let's consider a modest 50 percent increase in a scenario in which management was not being compelled to fight fires. This would have led to pharma sales of €21 billion. The actual number was €17 billion. I think it's fair to assume that Bayer's pharma division "lost" sales of €4 billion as a result of the Monsanto acquisition. The market value of global pharma companies is about three to five times sales. Let's be conservative and take a 2.5-times multiple. This is an opportunity cost of *at least* €10 billion.

The operating income of Bayer's consumer health division declined from €1.2 billion in 2015 to €0.8 billion in 2019 (let's ignore 2020, when many consumer businesses were affected by COVID). Most global consumer businesses grew their operating income during this period. Similarly, the operating income of Bayer's crop science division fell from €2.1 billion to €1.9 billion during this period while its competitors did much better. And remember that Monsanto's acquisition is counted in the crop science division, and so despite the $63 billion acquisition, the operating income of the division *fell* from 2015 to 2019!

In 2015, the operating income of the consumer health and crop science divisions added up to a little more than half the consolidated operating income of Bayer. Thus, we can conservatively assume that at least a third of Bayer's value in 2015 was derived from these two divisions. Since Bayer's value was €140 billion in 2015, we can assign a value of at least €45 billion to €50 billion to these divisions for 2015 (which was the *total* value of Bayer in June 2021). What was the opportunity cost of the underperformance of these two divisions? If the top management had not been consumed by Monsanto's unending troubles, and if they had enhanced their 2015 value by 30 to 50 percent over the next five years, we see a likely missed gain of around €15 billion to €25 billion.

Let's now come to the third, and probably the largest, opportunity cost: missed opportunities. For Bayer, this was not making a COVID-19 vaccine.

Imagine the end of 2019 at Bayer. The company's leverage has multiplied more than nine times since 2017 to €34 billion, the U.S. litigation is getting uglier and more costly by the month, the return on capital is down to less than 4 percent from the high teens a few years earlier, and the investors are as angry as hell with the stock price falling to half its peak, also a few years earlier.

And then COVID strikes in early 2020. Do you think the senior management assembled around the table at corporate headquarters and said, "Let's bet billions on developing a vaccine that we do not even know is possible"? Would the Bayer management have been willing to take a bet on an uncertain outcome given their dire operating and financial condition? We will never know for sure, and your guess is as good as mine, but a shot in the dark for an uncertain payoff by this long-suffering company? Unlikely.

Bayer's 2020 annual report mentions that they signed an agreement with a biotech company to develop and manufacture a COVID-19 vaccine that would be launched in 2022. Meanwhile, four competitors of Bayer—AstraZeneca, Johnson & Johnson, Moderna, and Pfizer—had administered about five *billion* doses by July 2021.

The COVID-19 vaccine contributes to almost all of Moderna's revenues and profits, and so Moderna is a good candidate to use to assess the notional loss for Bayer. From December 2019 (before the pandemic hit) until July 2021, Moderna added about $120 *billion* (€100 billion) to its market value. If we assume that the probability of Bayer's success would have been 50 to 75 percent (after all, it was one of the global leaders), Bayer has foregone €50 billion to €75 billion in value creation owing to its inability (or was it its unwillingness?) to develop a vaccine.

If we add up all these numbers, the opportunity cost of Monsanto's acquisition is probably in the range of €90 billion to €100 billion. In other words, instead of about €50 billion in June 2021, Bayer *could* have been valued at €140 billion to €150 billion. How do we know this is not a massive overstatement? Because Bayer's value in *2015* was €140 billion. If anything, this opportunity cost calculation is a significant understatement because it assumes almost *no* additional value creation since 2015, while every other major pharmaceutical, consumer, and agrochemical business has added significant value since 2015.

I don't know anything about Bayer's management, but presumably they are world class given their outsized success before 2016. If that's the case, how did they get lulled into making such an acquisition? Because like most acquirers across the world, they genuinely believed that *this time*, it's different. Managers—especially high-performing ones—and their advisers have a sense of invincibility and arrogance when evaluating a target. They firmly believe that *they* will buck the trend the corporate world has witnessed for a century. Most of them don't realize their folly until it's too late.

If a business is a serial acquirer, we stay away. We know we can't price the risk. If we had been evaluating Bayer as a new investment in 2016, we would have passed until we were convinced that management would not repeat its mistakes.

Some of our portfolio companies do occasionally make acquisitions. Our counsel to them is to be deeply skeptical of the potential value creation in all cases. I will admit that the success rate of our advice has not been very high. Fortunately, none of our companies is addicted to M&A, and the ones that do make acquisitions have never bet the company. I am convinced that the cost of distraction—even if it was a small one—has not been worth the effort. If any of them start becoming serial acquirers, we will promptly press the exit button.

Not Predicting Where the Puck Will Be

What do mid-nineteenth-century railways and late-twentieth-century dot-coms have in common?

Railways transformed the United Kingdom in the early nineteenth century.[25] The first passenger railway between Liverpool and Manchester was authorized by Parliament in 1826 and opened in 1830. Railways allowed people to travel farther at a much lower cost and in less time than the alternatives. They also spurred the growth of cities by enabling cheaper and faster transport of people and building materials. Many entrepreneurs jumped into the fray and by 1844 had opened more than 2,200 miles of railroad line. The stock market loved these companies, which promised growth forever. Between 1843 and 1850, 442 railway companies made a public offering of shares. Between January 1, 1843, and August 9, 1845, the index of railway stock prices doubled. But the bubble burst, as they inevitably do. The railway index fell over 67 percent from 1845 to 1850—many companies collapsed owing to incompetence, poor financial planning, or fraud.

Not unlike the railway mania of the 1840s, with the arrival of the internet in the mid-1990s for the masses, venture capitalists and public markets funded hundreds of companies in the rapidly changing landscape. This was called the dot-com boom.[26] The NASDAQ index of technology stocks jumped *five-fold* between 1995 and 2000. For the first time in recent capital market history, *losing* money seemed to be the key to success. In October 1999, just six months before the bubble burst, the market value of 199 internet stocks tracked by Mary Meeker, Morgan Stanley's internet analyst, was $450 billion. All these businesses were essentially start-ups; they had been created in the previous two to five years. More remarkably, their combined revenue was only $21 billion, and their cumulative loss was a staggering $6.2 billion. When discussing the initial public offering (IPO) of Priceline.com, a venture capitalist at Benchmark admitted, "We're in an environment where the company doesn't have to be successful for us to make money."

The year 2000 marked the end of this insanity. By the year 2005, listed Silicon Valley companies had lost two-thirds of their value from market peak; this was equivalent to a staggering $2 trillion loss of shareholder wealth. Venture capital funding collapsed from about $105 billion in 2000 to $21 billion in 2004. Nasdaq had reached its peak in March 2000. It took more than fifteen years for it to regain this level.

You can now guess the answer to the question I raised at the beginning of this section: The common thread that binds eighteenth-century railways and twentieth-century dot-coms is the potential for enormous value destruction wrought by a fast-changing industry.

There are many similar examples in India of various new and upcoming industries that catch the fancy of investors. When Nalanda was established in 2007, the infrastructure boom was at its peak, and some of the leading companies were valued at billions of dollars. The Indian government had finally begun focusing on building roads, airports, power plants, and ports, and private and public equity investors seemed to have an unlimited appetite for these companies. But the infrastructure business in India was in a fledgling state in the late 2000s, the regulations were nascent and untested, and the basis of long-term success was unclear. The ensuing value destruction assumed epic proportions. Two of the affected infrastructure businesses were Reliance Power and Jaiprakash Power Ventures, whose market values were $29 billion and $23 billion, respectively, in early 2008. Each was valued at less than $700 million at the end of 2021, a collapse of more than 97 percent.

The Indian public equity market has witnessed similar booms and busts across other rapidly evolving industries like retail, real estate, education, and microfinance. Private equity has gone wild for nonbank finance companies (NBFCs), new-age e-commerce businesses like food and grocery delivery, and software-as-a-service and digital education companies, to name just a few.

Some companies in industries that change fast ultimately do end up creating a lot of value. But *very* few companies. The only ones that have created truly significant value from the dot-com era are Amazon and Google (Facebook was founded in 2004). If you want to be charitable, you could add eBay and Priceline (now called Booking Holdings). But that's it. Just step back and think about this for a moment. Only a handful of businesses from the 1995–2000 bubble have prospered. To give you a sense of the scale of destruction, 546 IPOs successfully raised $69 billion in 1999 alone. What would have been the probability of finding the next winner?

The path to creating wealth in rapidly evolving industries is treacherous, and we refuse to walk on it. Many investors are slaves to the famous quote of the hockey legend Wayne Gretzky: "I skate to where the puck is going to be, not where it has been."[27] I am not one of them. I am just not that smart. In fast-changing industries, I have no idea who will win, when, or how. And to draw the parallel with hockey, since I don't know where the puck is going to be, I refuse to play.

We at Nalanda love stable, predictable, boring industries. Give us electric fans over electric vehicles, boilers over biotech, sanitaryware over semiconductors, and enzymes over e-commerce. We like industries in which the winners and losers have been largely sorted out and the rules of the game are apparent to everyone.

For everything else, thanks, but no thanks.

Not Aligning with Unaligned Owners

As an outside and passive owner, we at Nalanda want the company owner to align their interest with the shareholders'. We have only one objective as a shareholder of any business: long-term value creation. The company must do this in an ethical, sustainable manner that is fair to all stakeholders, including employees, vendors, suppliers, and customers. But as strange as it may sound, not every owner has the same objective. There are broadly three categories of owners that we avoid to mitigate our type I risk.

First, government-owned businesses. Unlike the Western world, India has a large number of publicly traded government-owned companies. They are almost always cheap, and, for a value investor, they have been unhappy hunting grounds for as long as I can remember. I say "unhappy" because most of these cheap businesses almost always stay cheap. Some fund managers may have figured out a way to invest successfully in government-owned businesses, but we will not invest in a government-owned enterprise at any price. The government wants to achieve multiple objectives with their businesses, some of which may have nothing to do with enhancing value and profits.

For example, the Indian state and federal governments regularly resort to farm loan waivers.[28] This involves forgiving the loans of farmers who have borrowed from government-owned banks. The loan waiver trend started in 1990 (the first waiver was for $1.4 billion) and continues today. Almost every state and federal government has gotten on the bandwagon over the past three decades. This may suit the governments and maybe even the farmers (I say "maybe" because farmers may not find it easy to borrow the next time they go to the bank). But it may be destructive for the minority shareholder.

It is not unusual for the Indian government to reward a senior bureaucrat by giving them a senior position at a government-owned business. Again, this may suit the bureaucrat but not a shareholder. We have nothing against bureaucrats, but the skill required to run a company successfully in a competitive environment is not the same as that needed to manage a district or devise a sound social policy for a state. Some businesses, especially the public sector oil companies, occasionally become cash rich, and the government then uses them as a piggy bank to manage their fiscal deficit. It suits the government, but how can this be beneficial for a shareholder? It is not that the government objectives are "wrong"—they make sense in the light of the multiple constituencies whose needs they are trying to meet. Their objectives are just different from ours.

The second category of owners we avoid religiously is the listed subsidiaries of global giants. A few decades ago, the Indian government forced all Indian subsidiaries of global multinational companies (MNCs) to list in the domestic market. Global MNCs like Cummins, Nestlé, Procter & Gamble (P&G), Siemens, Unilever, and many others have locally listed subsidiaries. Some are fairly large by Indian standards. For example, the Unilever subsidiary in India, Hindustan Unilever, is valued at about $70 billion.

At first glance, it may appear that these MNCs should be aligned with the Indian minority shareholder. But there have been many instances when they weren't. A few decades ago, a large global MNC with a listed company in India set up a *separate* fully owned subsidiary. This makes no logical sense because the global giant has only one listing in its *home* market. For a minority shareholder of the listed Indian business, this was a stab in the back because the fully owned subsidiary now does a significant amount of business. So why would the parent company do this? Isn't it interested in value creation? Yes, it is. But it is more interested in the value creation of the *parent*, not the Indian-listed child. By creating a separate fully owned business, the global MNC has ensured that value accrues to the shareholders in its home market at the cost of the Indian minority shareholder. It gets worse. My friends who have worked for many years in this MNC have told me that its best managers are sent to the privately held business, not the listed company. What can a minority shareholder do? Absolutely nothing.

Not all MNCs resort to such shenanigans, but enough do. Even if an MNC has behaved well in the past, there is no reason it wouldn't change its mind in the future. There is a *structural* problem with an arrangement in which a parent also has a listed subsidiary. We have better things to do than to participate in this inherent conflict.

Last, we are not fans of the Indian conglomerates. The best known is the Tata Group, which Jamsetji Tata established in 1868.[29] The group had twenty-nine listed businesses with combined revenues of $128 billion and a market value of $311 billion as of March 2022. They manufacture steel, gold jewelry, air conditioners, tea, and cars. Oh, and they also own and operate five-star luxury hotels from Mumbai to New York. There are many others, like Adani, Aditya Birla, L&T, Mahindra, and RP-Sanjiv Goenka. All typically run a gamut of unrelated businesses across a wide range of industries.

We believe that value creation is possible only through sustained focus. However, while focus is necessary, it does not guarantee success in a competitive world; most focused businesses *aren't* successful. So how does one achieve excellence in multiple entities across entirely different industries? It's hard but not impossible. One of the world's leading technology services businesses is a Tata Group company called TCS, whose market value of around $150 billion was about 25 percent more than that of IBM in mid-2022. You may have seen its name splashed across Manhattan in November in the years it sponsored the New York City Marathon. TCS is the exception that proves the rule.

Maybe the Indian conglomerates will succeed in creating great businesses across their entire portfolios one day. But we are unwilling to wait for that glorious future.

But You Would Have Missed Tesla!

Yup. We would have.

We eschew a very long list of risks. This is the core element of our investment strategy. We don't invest in businesses run by crooks, we detest turnarounds, we stay as far away from leverage as possible, we refuse to engage with M&A addicts, we can't figure out fast-changing industries, and we don't align ourselves with unaligned owners. Are there any businesses left for us to invest in? In India, not many. At Nalanda, our shortlist comprises seventy-five to eighty companies out of a universe of about eight hundred with a market value of more than $100 million.

Except for filial love, nothing in life comes free. Nalanda's approach has a trade-off that many of you may find unacceptable.

Imagine it's late 2017, and you are impressed with all the media coverage of Tesla. The product seems like a winner based on its vast fan following. The CEO looks as impressive as the car he makes. But in 2017, Tesla had a net debt of about $7 billion and had suffered an operating loss of $1.6 billion. The company was also burning cash very fast—it had consumed $4.1 billion during the year. The traditional car businesses like BMW, Ford, GM, and Toyota had not yet entered the electric vehicle fray, but they had announced big plans. We abhor debt in general, but debt in a loss-making company with negative free cash flow in a fast-changing industry? One can get fired at Nalanda for proposing an investment in a business like this.

If you had listened to what we had to say about the business, you would not have invested. Your opportunity loss? Ten times your money over the next three years.

When we started Nalanda in 2007, there was a lot of buzz around a company called Eicher Motors led by a young, dynamic guy called Siddhartha Lal. Lal had inherited a hodgepodge of poor-quality businesses from his father in 2004. They manufactured motorcycles, footwear, garments, tractors, trucks, auto components, and a few other products, and none was an industry leader. In a remarkably bold strategic move, Lal decided to divest thirteen of the fifteen businesses to focus on just two products: trucks and motorcycles.[30]

Almost every analyst was gung ho about the future of Eicher; they were all taken in by its dynamic leader who was aggressively culling businesses, something that Indian firms rarely did. However, in 2007, this was a turnaround story with no empirical evidence of success. The company's biggest hit, the Enfield Classic motorcycle, was launched only in 2010.

We decided not to invest in the business. By the 2010s, the company's motorcycles had taken on cult status in the Indian consumer's mind. Sales exploded from just 52,000 units in 2009 to 822,000 units in 2019: a sixteen-fold growth.

If you had listened to what we had to say about the business, you would not have invested. Your opportunity loss? Seventy times your money from 2007 until 2021.

Tesla and Eicher Motors are the kinds of type II error we will inevitably commit because we reject highly indebted businesses, rapidly evolving industry landscapes, and turnarounds. But we will not change our approach. For every Tesla and Eicher, hundreds of unproven business models and turnaround stories are unceremoniously consigned to the dustbin of history. We believe our success is contingent upon our being *comfortable* with missing out on Teslas and Eichers because *on average*, avoiding type I errors works wonders over the long term. It has done so for us.

* * *

A bumblebee is a hairy insect that barely measures an inch in length.[31] The species—there are about three hundred of them—have been around for about thirty million years. They are preyed upon by crab spiders and birds. Their survival strategy was beautifully demonstrated in an experiment conducted by Dr. Tom Ings and Professor Lars Chittka of Queen Mary University of London, whose work was published in *Science Daily* in 2008.

The scientists created a garden of artificial flowers that also contained some robotic crab spiders. They hid some spiders and made others visible. Whenever a bumblebee landed on a flower with a crab spider, the spider "captured" the bumblebee between its foam pincers. Within a few seconds, the robotic spider released the bee. The team found that the bumblebees soon started committing more type II errors: they started avoiding flowers even where there were no spiders, thereby reducing their foraging efficiency. In the wild, this instinct to avoid danger at the cost of going hungry must have played a significant role in the tremendous success of the species over millions of years.

If the bumblebee can, why can't we?

Chapter Summary

Evolutionary theory has taught me that . . .

. . . the first and probably most important step in reimagining investing is to learn how *not* to invest.

1. Living things prioritize survival over everything else. In the animal world, this applies to prey *and* predator. Plants give up on opportunities to grow by redirecting resources when survival is at stake.
2. Millions of years of evolution have programmed the organic world to minimize errors of commission in favor of errors of omission.
3. Buffett's two rules of investing (never lose money, and don't forget to never lose money) are essentially a diktat for eliminating significant risks.
4. At Nalanda, we want to be permanent owners of high-quality businesses. Hence, we want to minimize risk before maximizing returns.
5. Just like the living world, we forgo potentially juicy opportunities if the risk of losing our capital is high.
6. We do this by avoiding crooks, turnarounds, high debt, serial acquirers, fast-changing industries, and unaligned owners. I believe we can be better investors only if we are better "rejectors."
7. One downside of this approach is that we occasionally walk away from a potentially attractive investment. We are willing to live with this downside.

SECTION II

BUY HIGH QUALITY AT A FAIR PRICE

This section describes and, using evolutionary theory, justifies our buying philosophy at Nalanda. For many investors, identifying the right business to buy at the right time is almost all there is to investing. Switch on CNBC, open a financial newspaper, or read a blog, and you will witness a lot of time spent and ink spilled on companies to buy. This is unfortunate. As we have already seen in section I, *not* buying is an equally—if not more—important skill.

There is also a profound conundrum about the buying strategy advocated by most fund managers. *Everyone* seems to spout the exact same philosophy as this section's topic: Buy high quality at a fair price. I challenge you to find me a fund manager who professes to buy poor-quality businesses at high prices.

Then why does the performance of professional investors vary so widely? One reason—not the only one, but a crucial one—is that our community has wildly different opinions on the meaning of "high," "quality," and "fair." In this section, with many evolutionary theory elements as a backdrop, I will clarify the meaning of these words as they apply to Nalanda. I will discuss *what* we buy in chapters 2 to 4 and *how* we buy in chapters 5 to 7.

Let's begin. In Siberia.

CHAPTER 2

THE SIBERIAN SOLUTION

Hairless dogs have imperfect teeth; long-haired and coarse-haired animals are apt to have, as is asserted, long or many horns; pigeons with feathered feet have skin between their outer toes; pigeons with short beaks have small feet, and those with long beaks large feet. Hence, if man goes on selecting, and thus augmenting any peculiarity, he will almost certainly unconsciously modify other parts of the structure, owing to the mysterious laws of the correlation of growth.

Charles Darwin, On the Origin of Species, *chapter 1,*
"Variation Under Domestication"

An economic franchise arises from a product or service that (1) is needed or desired; (2) is thought by its customers to have no close substitute; and (3) is not subject to price regulation. The existence of all three conditions will be demonstrated by a company's ability to regularly price its product or service aggressively and thereby to earn high rates of return on capital. Moreover, franchises can tolerate mismanagement. Inept managers may diminish a franchise's profitability, but they cannot inflict mortal damage.

Warren Buffett, annual letter to shareholders, 1991

Lyudmila Trut was dumbfounded.

It had all started almost exactly five years ago when she had met Dmitri Belyaev, the famous director of the institute. When she heard about Dmitri's project from her professor, she enthusiastically volunteered. Dmitri's candor, passion, and intellect immediately enamored her. And surprisingly, in this male-dominated field in which women were treated as second-class citizens, he had talked to her as a peer, though he was a couple decades older and a renowned personality in the field.

Dmitri was trying to enlist a graduate student for a secret project, but Lyudmila had not yet even finished her undergraduate studies. He must have seen something unique in the young and talented student to recruit her after just one meeting. She remembered his warnings about the physical hardship, the long hours, and, most importantly, the uncertain fate of her budding scientific career. Dmitri's project carried a lot of risk and could come to naught. And even if the project succeeded, they could not talk about it openly because scientists had been killed for less, including Dmitri's brother.

She was grateful to Dmitri for not sugarcoating the work. But it turned out to be far more demanding than she had imagined. She was living in the middle of Siberia, and although she had grown up in Moscow, she had not yet become accustomed to the bone-chilling cold. Worse, the project required her to travel far across the Siberian wilderness on cold, dark, and dreary trains, and she desperately missed her fast-growing toddler, Marina. There were no phones, so she could not even hear her child's voice. It had been five years of unrelenting hard work and sacrifice, and she had precious little to show Dmitri.

In April 1963, as she approached one of the cages, she was stopped in her tracks. She had never seen anything like this before. Nor had any other human being. Was she really witnessing this, or was it an illusion? Had her patience and diligence paid off? She was a scientist and knew that she could not get carried away by emotion. But she could not contain the feeling when it welled up: pure joy.

Unbelievably, inconceivably, Ember was wagging his tail.

Oh, Where Do I Begin?

You have decided to become an investor in listed companies. You value your intellect and discipline, and it seems that many of your friends and cousins are successful investors. Most of them are lying, but that's another story. If they can do it, why can't you?

You choose to ignore Buffett's advice about investing in index funds[1] and launch headlong into analyzing businesses. You have read the first chapter of this book, and although you are mildly peeved at the author's degree of risk aversion, you decide that maybe he has a point (thank you!). Heeding his advice, you have done your best to reject the many categories of companies that may increase your blood pressure at a later date.

Having shot down hundreds of businesses, you are now excited about *selecting* high-quality businesses. You open your laptop, launch the application or a website with data on companies, and then . . . what? What do you do?

For every company, you see a gazillion pieces of information on tap: revenue growth, profit growth, debt level, margin profile, stock price movement, analysts' views, bond ratings, Twitter commentary, shareholder information, top management résumés, conference call transcripts, annual reports, quarterly filings, media coverage, competitor profiles, shares bought or sold by senior management, receivable and inventory levels, CEO statements, Reddit threads, hedge fund ownership, and so much more. And all this is just at the company level.

You have listened to so-called experts on TV, many of whom seem to believe that one must also consider macro factors when making a buy decision. You start wallowing in the data on historical GDP growth, projected GDP growth, inflation, inflationary expectations, interest rates, government deficit, employment levels, commodity price movement, projected demographics, money supply, political and regulatory forces, and many such readily available factors supposedly crucial for your buy decision.

Should you study all of them or only some of them? How do you start short-listing the businesses that you want to explore further? What macro factors, if any, should you consider?

In short, where do you begin? One option would be to analyze each listed business after you have cast aside the high-risk ones. The problem is that you do not have unlimited time. The number of companies may be in the hundreds, and you may need to spend months, if not years, to go through the entire list.

One alternative would be to use a two-step process that we use at Nalanda. In the first step, we use *one* selection criterion that filters out low-quality or average-quality businesses and yields a preliminary list of high-quality companies. In the second step, we do more work on this preliminary list to further whittle it down to a final list.

Our investable universe is around 800 Indian businesses (with a market value of more than $150 million). Of these, we have rejected close to 350 companies to minimize the risks outlined in the previous chapter. About 450 businesses remain. We then apply a *single* filter to cut down this list to about 150 firms. Let me call this single filter "F." Remember that F simply gives us the preliminary list on which we need to work further to reject or choose businesses. After doing this work, our final list has only about 75 to 80 businesses. F gave us an excellent head start. And it continues to do so because we don't spend any time analyzing a business unless F has cleared it.

This chapter is about the F filter: what it is and why. What, in your opinion, is F? To do its job, it needs to satisfy three criteria. First, it should be easily measurable. Second, it should remove most, if not all, low-quality businesses. Last, it should select most, if not all, high-quality businesses.

Let's start with some guesses.

A first plausible assumption would be "a great management team." Great businesses and outstanding management teams seem like tautologies. Finding an excellent set of leaders may automatically lead us to a high-quality business. Even if it does not, it *looks* like a good starting point for our filter. An exceptional management team would ensure revenue and profit growth ahead of the competition, a balance sheet that is not risky, a sustainable competitive advantage, and products or services that customers love. Easy, right? Not so fast.

How is an investor supposed to find a great management team? If you are a small investor, the best you can do is read their interviews, listen to their conference call recordings, check out their Twitter feeds, watch some of their interviews on YouTube, and peruse their annual reports. If you are a large or prominent investor, you might even be able to meet the senior leaders. However, in my experience as an investor, none of these activities helps an investor calibrate the quality of a management team.

Here is a stark example. If you have time, I suggest watching the YouTube video of the January 2000 presentation by the president of Enron, Jeffrey Skilling, and his senior management on the launch of Enron Broadband.[2] I dare you not to be impressed. The guys are poised, confident, and, at least to my eyes, extremely competent. It is hard to find fault with their strategy or vision, and their execution plan for broadband services seems spot on. However, in less than two years after this impressive presentation, Enron went bankrupt, and in 2006 Skilling was sent to prison for perpetrating a massive fraud.[3] Except for a few short sellers, no professional analysts or investors could have guessed what was going on at Enron even though the management was quite open to the media and regularly gave interviews.

I know what you are thinking. Am I building my entire case on an outlier like Enron? Let's look at it another way. I assume you have read the interviews of many CEOs or company presidents. Did any mention that they *don't* care for the customer, that they have stopped innovating, or that they hire people who have been rejected by other companies? Have you ever heard a company leader disparage their products or services or admit that their competition is doing a better job or that they are sick and tired of company politics? You will rarely—if ever—learn anything insightful from what the management says. They always say what they have been taught to say, which at best is useless and at worst is harmful, because, as with Enron, their words are persuasive. In my experience, when someone says, "This is a great management team," what they are *actually* saying is, "These guys talk so well!" The "great management team" filter thus fails the first criterion of measurability (being easily measurable).

I know that many professional investors will disagree with me. Many people in the fund management world pride themselves on their purported ability to separate the wheat from the chaff after a series of management meetings. Some of them may have this rare skill, but most are either deluded or lying. And if there *is* someone out there who can assess a company's quality by meeting management, we can applaud them from the sidelines without falling into the trap ourselves.

What about other guesses for choosing a single company trait that could point to its overall quality? Could it be revenue growth? Markets seem to love companies growing at a fast pace. The problem with a revenue growth measure is this: How do we know what went *into* achieving this growth?

In the previous chapter, I discussed the dot-com bust in the context of fast-changing industries. This period is also relevant when assessing high-growth businesses. In the late 1990s, most internet businesses were growing fast, but they were achieving this gravity-defying feat by spending millions of dollars of cash far in excess of their revenues. Predictably and unfortunately, growth did not turn out to be the blessing investors had hoped it would be. They ignored the cost of growth and suffered for it. Almost all the dot-coms went belly-up eventually.[4] By the end of 2005, the loss of market value of these newfangled businesses was almost $2 trillion.

More recently, the spectacular failure of WeWork provides a lesson in funding hyper-growth by burning cash.[5] As many of you may already know, Softbank-funded WeWork became one of the largest coworking-space companies on the planet and was once valued at $47 billion. In late 2021, its market value had fallen to about $5 billion. The company grew its revenues from $415 million in 2016 to $3.5 billion in 2019, an eight-fold jump over just three years. Also in 2019, IWG, the old-world coworking giant, had revenue of $2.7 billion, a growth of "only" 28 percent since 2016. WeWork was consuming cash as if it had a side business running a printing press for dollars; in the third quarter of 2019 alone, the company declared a loss of $1.25 billion. It had to pull its IPO in the fourth quarter.

Many high-growth companies don't burn equity for growth but rely on debt instead, which is even worse because debt holders need their money back with great regularity, unlike equity investors. Do you remember the fast-growing Lehman Brothers and Bear Stearns? Lehman grew its revenue by 36 percent annually from $17 billion in 2003 to $59 billion in 2007.[6] This incremental revenue of about $40 billion was funded by an incremental debt of almost $90 billion. Similarly, Bear Stearns grew its revenue *seven-fold* from 2003 to 2007.[7] Its incremental revenue of $3.5 billion during this period was primarily funded by an additional debt of $42 billion. When the financial crisis hit in

2008, these highly leveraged entities—which had contributed to the problem—had nowhere to hide. They both collapsed that year.

I also have a personal reason for not wanting revenue growth to be the primary selection criterion. In my experience, high-growth businesses can hide myriad problems, ranging from issues of product or service quality, employee culture, and accounting to a bloated balance sheet. According to a study conducted by the Kauffman Foundation and *Inc. Magazine*, five to eight years after the magazine had identified five thousand businesses as "fastest-growing," two-thirds of those had shut down, downsized, or been sold disadvantageously.[8] I hope you will agree that while "high growth" is easy to measure, it stumbles on our second filtering criterion (removing most, if not all, low-quality businesses).

I know, I know. You will counter me with just one word: Apple. This fantastic business grew its revenue thirty-three-fold from 2004 to 2020 at an annualized growth of 25 percent. But for every Apple, there are hundreds, if not thousands, of lemons.

Okay, let's recap. We want to use a single filter, F, to select businesses for further analysis. This should hopefully save us a lot of time and effort. We wondered if we could use "quality management teams" or "fast growth" as our starting point. We rejected both as good candidates for F because it is tough to assess the former, and the latter can end up causing heartburn.

A third guess for a criterion for short-listing businesses for further analysis could be margins. Is a high-margin business a high-quality business? Many seem to think so. Margins can mean many things: gross margin (sales minus cost of goods sold divided by sales), EBITDA margin (earnings before interest, tax, depreciation, and amortization divided by sales), or EBIT margin (earnings before interest and tax divided by sales). Which of these, if any, should we choose for F?

Let's start with gross margin, which measures the *direct* cost of producing the product or service being sold; accountants call this the "cost of goods sold." If a bar of bath soap retails for $1 and costs 30 cents to make, then the gross margin is 70 percent. Does a high gross margin tell us anything about the *quality* of the business? Not really. Several internet businesses boasted a gross margin of more than 90 percent in the dot-com era, but almost all experienced huge losses because of their marketing spends.

What about EBITDA margin or EBIT margin (also called operating margin)? Measuring EBIT margin would be more sensible because it accounts for depreciation, which is a real cost of doing business. But just because it is a better measure does not mean it is a good measure.

Take this example of two real-world businesses: Business C has had an operating margin of about 3 percent over the past fifteen years. Business T has delivered an operating margin of 19 percent over the same period. Would you reject

Business C and select Business T because T is "better" than C? If you did so, you would have spurned Costco, one of America's best-run businesses. Business T is Tiffany & Co., a reasonably well-run business but not as well run as Costco. What makes Costco at a margin of 3 percent a better company than Tiffany at 19 percent?[9] I will get to that shortly. Suffice it to say that using margins as a starting point to narrow our list of companies may lead us astray. It fails our second *and* third criteria (removing most, if not all, low-quality businesses and selecting high-quality businesses).

We haven't yet considered macro factors for building the short list. But which single piece of macro data should we consider for short-listing individual businesses? For example, if "experts" believe that inflation will rise, should we short-list only consumer goods businesses able to pass on the increased cost to their customers? If we do so, should we then completely revise the list if the inflation expectations get reversed within six months? I don't know how to account for macro factors for short-listing high-quality businesses. I am not suggesting that it is the wrong thing to do—just that I don't know how it can be done. And so, we avoid considering *any* macro factor as our preliminary filter F. What about accounting for macro factors when making our final list? More on that later.

The Evolutionary Cascade of a Single Selection Criterion

Meanwhile, we seem to be stuck. What could F be? Maybe Lyudmila and her tail-wagging Ember can help us.

But before we seek guidance from them, let's briefly visit the Russia of the 1920s and '30s. The brutal Communist regime under Joseph Stalin was forcing individual farmers to give up their land and consolidate their holdings under *kolkhozy,* or collective farms.[10] The central planners of the Communist Party had envisaged a dramatic increase in agriculture production and productivity arising from scale economies and improved control of output by the State. They expected to be able to feed the rising urban population and increase exports. The opposite happened.

The farmers strongly resisted giving up their ancestral land and property; in fact, many chose to destroy their crops and slaughter their animals instead of giving in to collectivization. Stalin sent millions of people to prison camps, and millions more died of starvation as famine set in owing to the reduction in agriculture production.

In the middle of this disaster, Trofim Lysenko, an agriculture scientist, claimed that he had invented a new technique to significantly increase agriculture production. This "new" technique envisaged that a plant's acquired characteristics could be inherited. This was in stark contrast to Mendelian genetics and Darwinism, which had demonstrated—by this time, experimentally—that genes were the unit of inheritance. Lysenko, however, promised an agricultural revolution with his unscientific techniques and got the attention of Stalin, who desperately needed a Russian hero to solve his food crisis.

Over time, as Lysenko became more powerful, he declared genetics a pseudoscience, and practicing geneticists were either executed or sent to labor camps. In this environment, the authorities fired the leading geneticist Dmitri Belyaev from his job at the Department of Fur Animal Breeding at the Central Research Laboratory. Belyaev's elder brother, who was studying the genetics of silkworms, was executed at Lysenko's behest in 1937.

Dmitri, however, kept studying genetics in secret. In 1959, with Nikita Khrushchev's ascension to power, he became the director of the Institute of Cytology and Genetics of the Russian Academy of Sciences in Novosibirsk, Siberia. Dmitri held this post for twenty-six years, until his death in 1985. And during this time, he conducted one of the most remarkable, longest-running experiments in the history of biology.[11] The investigation continues today.

Dmitri Belyaev wanted to answer two questions: (1) How had the domestication of animals (e.g., dogs, pigs, goats, and cows) started, and (2) Why did most domestic animals have similar characteristics, including floppy ears, curly tails, a piebald coloration (patches of black and white), and babyish faces? He believed that the domestication of animals resulted from underlying heritable genetic changes that had occurred during the course of selection over millennia.

The big unanswered question was, *What* was being selected? Natural and artificial selection can occur only if *something* is selected for generation after generation. For example, whereas both cheetahs and lions are ferocious predators, among many other factors, cheetahs have been selected for speed and lions for their size and strength. In other words, a slow cheetah is unlikely to leave any offspring, but a big, strong lion is likely to leave many.

Dmitri hypothesized that the key factor selected when our ancestors domesticated wild animals was *tameness*. Thus, the unit of selection was not related to an animal's physical attributes but to its *behavior*. This was an audacious guess since most scientists then assumed that physical morphology was the unit of selection. How could Dmitri test his bold theory? Only by going back to the time when animals first started becoming domesticated. For dogs, this would have meant experimenting on wild wolves. But getting a supply of wolves would have been very hard in Siberia, so he chose the silver fox. He designed a selective breeding experiment that focused *only* on tameness as the selection factor.

As described earlier, he recruited Lyudmila Trut, an undergraduate student at the prestigious Moscow University, to lead and manage the experiment in Siberia. Lyudmila would forever change the field of behavioral genetics with her tenacity and creativity.[12]

Lyudmila's first task was to select a location for breeding the foxes. She chose a large commercial farm (that sold fox fur) called Lesnoi, more than 350 kilometers from Novosibirsk, where she and her family lived. She began the experiment in the fall of 1960 with about a dozen foxes. She also hired several women from nearby villages to be caretakers and experimenters. Here is how it worked.

The experimenters gave the foxes a series of tests from the time they were one month old to their sexual maturity at six to seven months. When a fox pup was one month old, the experimenter extended her hand to offer it food while trying to stroke it. She tested the fox pup twice: once in the cage and once while the pup was roaming freely with other pups in a larger enclosure. She repeated this test monthly until the pup reached sexual maturity. To ensure that the pup's reaction to these tests was based solely on genetic selection, the pups were not trained and did not have any human contact except for their brief interactions with the experimenters. The pups were caged with their mothers until they were about two months old and then with their litter mates. At about three months of age, they were put into their own cages.

When the pups were about seven months old, the experimenters assigned them to one of three categories based on their tameness. Class III foxes were unfriendly toward the handlers and either ran away from them or were aggressive. Class II foxes behaved neutrally and displayed no emotional response toward the handlers. Class I foxes were the friendliest and seemed to want to engage with the handlers.

Lyudmila and her team selected a few of the calmest Class I foxes for mating and repeated the experiment with the next generation of pups. By the third generation in 1962, Lyudmila noticed that some of the tamer foxes had started mating a few days earlier than usual and were producing slightly larger litters than wild foxes. Otherwise, there was no indication of any significant change.

In April 1963, as Lyudmila approached the cages of the fourth generation of pups, she saw a male pup called Ember vigorously wagging his tail. This was precisely what a puppy would do. But no one had ever witnessed a silver fox—whether in a cage or the wild—wag its tail at a human. Ember wagged his tail at other humans, too. No other pup of his generation did so, but even a single fox radically altering its behavior to mimic a dog was significant news. Dmitri had told Lyudmila in their first meeting that he wanted to make a dog out of a fox. Had the process begun?

In 1966, many of the sixth-generation pups that Ember had sired started wagging their tails at the handlers. Ember had not been an anomaly—he was a trailblazer. Lyudmila had categorically demonstrated that tail wagging was genetically heritable. By this time, the researchers had to add another class of foxes called Class IE: the elites. These foxes were extremely friendly, were eager to establish human contact, and, like dogs, whimpered to attract attention. In the sixth generation, about 1.8 percent of the pups were elites. By the twentieth generation, almost 35 percent had reached elite status. After about thirty-five generations, more than 70 percent of the population had attained elite status.

This is a breakneck pace of evolution: In less than forty years, Dmitri and Lyudmila's experiment had essentially converted a population of wild foxes who avoided humans into dog-like creatures that could be kept as pets in any of our homes. These foxes were very docile, competed for human attention, and formed deep emotional bonds with their handlers. It had become hard to distinguish their behavior from that of dogs. Lyudmila and her team had erased their wildness almost completely. But don't raise your eyebrows in astonishment just yet. I haven't even told you the most interesting result of the experiment.

The experimenters noticed that the eighth generation of these tamer foxes also started displaying some novel *physical* traits. The first change was in coat color: Some of the foxes' fur had a piebald pattern, which is common among domesticated animals like sheep, dogs, horses, pigs, goats, mice, and guinea pigs. A piebald pattern forms when two colors—typically black and white—form irregular patches on the animal's skin. No wild foxes in the experiment were piebald, but as their tameness increased over the generations, they started showing this coloration. Further physical traits to appear were floppy ears and rolled tails—again, common among many domesticated species, especially dogs.

In 1974, Lyudmila decided to raise the experiment's stakes by living with the foxes in the same house. To start, she chose a friendly fox called Pushinka. One evening, Lyudmila was sitting on a bench outside her home with Pushinka relaxing next to her as usual. Suddenly, Pushinka got up as if she had heard something and started barking. It turned out to be the night guard, and Pushinka stopped her aggressive posturing and barking when she realized that the guard posed no imminent danger to Lyudmila. This guard-dog-like behavior—rushing to protect a human from a potential threat—had never been observed before by Lyudmila.

In the early 1990s, the team also started noticing that the skulls and jaws of the domesticated foxes had started diverging from those of their wild brethren. The cranial height and width of the domesticated foxes' skulls had shortened. Their snouts had become shorter and wider giving them a baby-like appearance—almost exactly mimicking the differences between a dog and a wolf.

Let's consider this for a moment. Remember, Dmitri and his team were selecting for only *one* trait: the willingness of foxes to be tamed. They weren't interested in body size, coat color, skull shape, ear stiffness, or anything else. The experimenters took great care to ensure selection based *only* on tameness. But this single filter of a *behavioral* characteristic had triggered many *physical* changes in the animals. How could this have happened?

There were no new mutations in the domesticated silver foxes, but their *gene expression* had changed owing to the selection for tameness. This is how a gene does not change but alters what it expresses: It produces more or fewer chemicals like proteins or hormones. For example, when a dog owner stares lovingly into their canine's eyes, oxytocin is released in the systems of both the dog and the owner, creating a positive feedback loop in which the two enjoy each other's company more and more. If the same owner encounters an unknown dog on the street, no oxytocin is released. Although it's the same gene in question, the gene expression is different in different situations. Scientists have demonstrated that gene expression needs to change only a little to have a significant impact on an animal's body and behavior.

As Lyudmila and her team selected tamer foxes, they unknowingly impacted the expression of a select set of genes. This selection altered the amount and timing of release of certain neurochemicals and hormones that regulated the developmental and physical traits of the foxes. For example, the hormone melatonin is known to manipulate the timing of mating in many species. The researchers found that the elite females released a lot more melatonin than their Class II and III peers and were ready for mating a few days earlier than normal. The hormonal change was so extreme that some females were ready to mate twice a year, a phenomenon never seen in the wild. Selecting for tameness had impacted the reproductive cycle of the species! A gene called HTR_2C produced much higher levels of serotonin and dopamine in the elites than in wild foxes. Serotonin is a key hormone in shaping the early development of an animal and its increase is likely to have changed the physiology and behavior of the domesticated foxes. The researchers also discovered that the tamed foxes had much lower levels of adrenaline than their wild cousins. Adrenaline regulates the production of melanin, which determines the coloration of skin and fur.

The silver fox experiment also solved the centuries-old puzzle of the numerous physical similarities among domesticated animals discussed earlier. Dmitri had rightly hypothesized that since mammals share similar hormonal and neurotransmitter regulatory systems, selecting for tameness would unleash broadly similar developmental and physical changes in them as well.

Dmitri and Lyudmila's experiment, now running for more than sixty years, has demonstrated that evolution does not occur piecemeal. The behavior and physiology of animals are intimately connected. Darwin, with his acute powers of observation, knew this. His statement at the beginning of this chapter asserts that hairless dogs have imperfect teeth and pigeons with feathered feet have skin between their outer toes. He predicted that if humans choose to select for one characteristic, they will surely also cause transformations in other characteristics owing to what he called the "mysterious laws of the correlation of growth."

Dmitri and Lyudmila had proven Darwin right.

Select One, Get Many Free

As an investor, would you not want to be in the position of selecting just *one* trait of a business but getting many high-quality attributes for "free"? As discussed earlier, this single trait should satisfy three criteria: it should be measurable, reject *most* businesses of poor quality, and select *most* high-quality businesses. Most, not necessarily all. We have seen that some factors like high-quality management, revenue growth, and margins do not serve the purpose well enough.

At Nalanda, here is what we *begin* with while short-listing businesses: historical return on capital employed (ROCE).

The first word first. *Historical.* I devote an entire chapter to this important and oft-ignored word, but for now I wanted to clarify that the ROCE number is what a business has delivered in the *past.* We don't listen to stories about how ROCE will improve in the future. We want to assess a company purely on its historically delivered ROCE.

Now let's look at some definitions. ROCE is simply the operating profit of the business as a percentage of total capital employed. As defined earlier, operating profit is earnings before interest and taxes, or EBIT. Why do we not use profit after tax (PAT) instead? Remember, we want to understand a business's *operating* performance, and mixing it with financial measures like tax and interest will muddy the waters. We do not ignore tax or interest charges in our *overall* evaluation of the business, but for calculating ROCE, we limit ourselves to operating performance.

What about total capital employed? This typically comprises two factors: net working capital and net fixed assets. In the net working capital number, we like to exclude excess cash (i.e., cash minus debt if cash happens to be much greater than debt) because extra cash is not an operating asset. Also, high-ROCE companies generate a lot of cash, and incorporating cash into the capital employed number will unnecessarily reduce ROCE. If you are uncomfortable with this, you can include a portion of cash in capital employed. For an acquisitive company, we also include the capital invested in acquiring businesses, but let's keep things simple for the moment. Thus, ROCE for nonfinancial companies can be defined as follows:

EBIT ÷ (net working capital + net fixed assets)

Do you now see why using operating margin to filter businesses may not be the best approach? Margins do not tell us what we had to *invest* to get those margins. The advantage of measuring ROCE is that it accounts for the quality of P&L (in the numerator) as well as the balance sheet (in the denominator). Let's return to Costco and Tiffany.

I claimed that Costco at an operating margin of 3 percent is a better business than Tiffany at 19 percent. If we limit our definition of "better" to the level of ROCE, then I was right. This is because Costco's average ROCE from 2014 to

2019 (pre-pandemic) was 22 percent compared to Tiffany's 16 percent. Costco is deploying its capital much more effectively than Tiffany, and this more than compensates for Costco's low margin. Let's take the example of just one important part of its capital employed: inventory. Costco keeps about 31 days of inventory in its warehouses and retail stores. Guess the same number for Tiffany. It is *521 days*, or almost a year and half! Tiffany's operating margin is impressive, but Costco's dramatically better management of its inventory and other assets ensures it earns a higher ROCE than Tiffany.

Many investors prefer return on equity (ROE). I don't. ROE is calculated after taxes and interest payments, and hence mixes operating performance with financing strategy and tax structure. As a business owner, I am much more concerned with the superior *operating* performance of a business. While taking on leverage (which will improve ROE but not ROCE) and "planning" for taxes may benefit a firm in the short to medium term, in my experience, success over the long term comes *only* by running great operations. Which brings us back to ROCE.

What does a high ROCE of, say, 20 percent tell us? A simple fact: This business earns $20 for every $100 it invests. This is equivalent to making a bank deposit of $100 and earning $20 on it after a year. No, you are not in a hyperinflationary Latin American economy but in the "normal" world. I assume you would be on the moon if you owned a high-ROCE business like that. They are rare, but they do exist, and when you find them, they will tell you a lot.

High ROCE is a lot like tameness in the Siberian silver foxes. Just as tameness brings with it a curly tail, piebald fur, and floppy ears, a high-ROCE business ushers in many attributes relevant for an owner like us at Nalanda. Here are some examples.

A Consistently High-ROCE Business Is Likely to Be Run by an Excellent Management Team

What? "Excellent management team" again? If we can't measure it directly, why am I sneaking it in indirectly?

Just because we can't measure management quality through interviews and discussions does not mean quality management teams do not exist. Of course they do. What we need is not some airy-fairy impression of an investor made over a coffee (or a Zoom call) but a quantitative measure. We don't vote for the best cricket bowler, best running back, or best marathoner based on their interviews or their ability to articulate their excellence, so why should we do it for management teams? The best bowling statistics and the best finish times determine the best bowler and the best marathoner. Similarly, in my view, an excellent—but not the only—indicator of the *quality* of the management team is their historical track record on the *quantity* of ROCE.

Sustaining high ROCE in *any* industry over *any* length of time is extraordinarily hard. Microeconomic theory states that excess returns should be driven to zero in competitive markets, which means that businesses need to run very hard simply to earn their cost of capital. This may be true for most businesses, but there are a select set of companies that defy logic and competition to earn high returns on capital year on year, decade after decade.

The median historical ROCE of our portfolio of thirty businesses—most of which are more than thirty-five to forty years old—is about 42 percent. I am obviously biased since I am an investor in these businesses, but I do think the management teams of these businesses are excellent. Are they exemplary, or am I just calling them first rate because they happen to have high ROCE? I don't know. Does it matter?

We should expect the following from a quality management team. That they deliver products and services to their customers that are superior to those of their competitors, allocate capital prudently, attract and retain quality employees, manage their cost structure (which is commensurate with their size and revenue), maintain a quality balance sheet, and continuously innovate by taking calculated risks. All this should—and does—correlate with high ROCE.

A Consistently High-ROCE Business Is Likely to Have a Strong Competitive Advantage

All long-term investors, mentored by more than five decades of Buffett's letters and annual meetings, demand that companies have a "sustainable competitive advantage" (SCA). But how does one go about assessing whether a company has an SCA? If you peruse business and investment books, the sources of SCA turn out to be the usual suspects: brand, intellectual property, network effect, economies of scale, and low cost.[13]

Let's analyze "brand" as a source of competitive advantage. Almost every investor I know justifies a consumer-focused company's stock market success by touting brand and distribution as the sources of competitive advantage. One of the great consumer-focused investment success stories began more than thirty years ago in 1988 and 1989 when Buffett purchased Coke and Gillette shares. Berkshire invested almost $600 million in Coke in 1988 and nearly the same amount in Gillette in 1989. By 1993, the combined value of these two shareholdings for Berkshire was $5.6 billion, which was equal to *all* other holdings combined, and Buffett was sitting on a gain of about $4 billion in these businesses. His commentary on Coke and Gillette in his 1993 annual letter is as follows: "The might of their brand names, the attributes of their products, and the strength of their distribution systems give them an enormous competitive advantage, setting up a protective moat around their economic castles."

Buffett, as usual, is correct. Almost three decades after this letter, Coke and Gillette continue to be enormous successes and, given their increasing market share, continue to have a solid competitive advantage. But did Buffett conclude that they had a strong competitive advantage because they had strong brands and product attributes, or was his claim based on the empirical fact that these businesses had high ROCE and an increasing market share over a long period? We will never know of course. My guess (contention?) is that it was the latter.

The reality is that most brands don't have *any*—forget about "sustainable"—competitive advantage. Depending on which source you believe, across tens of thousands of brand launches annually in the United States, the failure rate is 80 to 90 percent.[14] It's not as bad as buying a lottery ticket, but it's also not that far off. You may also think that failure is limited to small and untested businesses and that the likes of Coke and Pepsi do very well. You would be wrong. Here is just a small sample of spectacular brand failures from large companies: New Coke (Coca-Cola), Crystal Pepsi (Pepsi), Premier smokeless cigarettes (R. J. Reynolds), Maxwell House ready-to-drink coffee (General Mills), Souper Combo (a combined soup-and-sandwich meal from Campbell), and All Natural Cleaning Vinegar (Heinz).

Just having a brand means nothing. If something as simple to understand as a "brand" does not necessarily confer a competitive advantage (and even if it does, it is probably very tough to definitively say so), how do we know if a company has a competitive advantage? No prizes for guessing. Yes, a sustained high ROCE is a good *starting* point to conclude that the company may have *some* kind of competitive advantage. And if it is a consumer company like Coca-Cola, maybe it is the brand, maybe the distribution, maybe the management, and maybe some combination of these and other factors.

Once we have short-listed a company based on its sustained high ROCE, we start analyzing its competitive advantages. After weeks or months of research, we may conclude that this high ROCE is unsustainable and that the company just got lucky historically. So be it. We then choose to stay away. But taking this route—of starting our assessment of competitive advantage only for high-ROCE companies—saves us a lot of time and effort.

A Consistently High-ROCE Business Allocates Capital Well

As a (very) long-term investor, when we choose to buy shares of a business, we allocate our capital to that business. We are doing so hoping that we will earn a decent return on this capital over the long run. Hopefully, we have evaluated other options for our capital and have made the correct decision that it is best invested in *this* business. Investors who allocate capital well perform well. Those who don't don't.

Businesses are no different. They, too, allocate capital on an ongoing basis. They have many options, and they try to choose the best one. They, too, hope to earn a decent return on their investment. Some do; most don't. ROCE is an excellent measure of a company's ability to deploy capital. High ROCE implies that these businesses earn high operating profit *relative* to their capital deployed. Great businesses try neither to maximize operating profit nor minimize capital deployed; they try to earn the maximum operating profit per unit of capital deployed.

Investors may not realize it, but strategy and most capital allocation decisions are deeply intertwined. For instance, is setting up a manufacturing plant in Milwaukee versus outsourcing to China a strategic or a capital allocation decision? It doesn't matter; it is a decision that will significantly influence the company's success. And so, it is both.

Some more examples of strategic decisions that allocate capital in radically different ways are as follows: setting up one's own R&D division versus copying the best designs from the market, hiring a chief technology officer to build one's technology unit versus outsourcing it, building a manufacturing unit for critical parts versus funding a supplier, hiring young graduates and training them over many years versus hiring qualified professionals laterally, making an acquisition to enter new geography versus growing organically, funding a loss-making product in a large addressable market versus investing in profitable products in a small market, and advertising for many months on social media versus buying a single Super Bowl ad.

How does an investor know if these myriad capital allocation decisions are sensible? One way is to analyze them thoroughly. For example, one could interview the marketing head to understand why they bought the Super Bowl ad instead of spreading the same expense over many weeks or months of advertising on Google or Facebook. One could then build financial models to test the company's likelihood of success, compare its advertising strategy to other companies, and then reach a conclusion that either supports or contradicts its decision.

The second way—our way—is to select companies with high ROCE as the first filter. We assume that a company with high ROCE is, *on average*, deploying its capital well. It may make some poor decisions, but overall, we believe its capital allocation and strategic decisions are quite sound.

Also, frankly, it's just easier this way. If I were to try to build multi-megabyte spreadsheets to test various scenarios of a particular capital decision, I would fail miserably. Twice. Once in making the spreadsheet and again in reaching an erroneous conclusion.

So why try?

A Consistently High-ROCE Business Allows Companies to Take Business Risk Without Taking Financial Risk, Which Increases the Chance of Business Success

Capitalism thrives on risk-taking. And risk-taking is not limited just to teenagers starting companies in their garages in Silicon Valley. *All* companies, if they want to grow and succeed, need to keep taking calculated risks. Those that don't take risks either atrophy or remain small and irrelevant; those that venture to take bigger risks than warranted implode. It is in the Goldilocks zone of *calculated* risk-taking that most companies thrive. High ROCE allows a company to keep taking calculated business risks. This is how.

A company delivering high ROCE with modest revenue growth will generate excess cash. This is not an opinion—just a mathematical fact. For example, Company X growing its sales at 10 percent with ROCE of 25 percent can grow from zero cash to a cash balance of almost 18 percent of sales in five years (other assumptions: margin 15 percent, tax 30 percent). With an increasing cash cushion, X's management team can choose to launch new products or target new geography. Even if the new business fails, X can recover given its ability to generate cash from its core business.

Now let's look at its competitor, Y, which is growing at the same rate (10 percent) with the same margin (15 percent) but with a lower ROCE of 12 percent. In five years, Y would have a *negative* cash balance of 3 percent of revenue. In other words, Y would have to *borrow* to grow at the same rate as X. With a weaker balance sheet and a lack of spare cash, Y would be forced to either forgo new opportunities or borrow more money to launch a new product or venture in new geography. If the venture fails, Y could be in deep trouble because its core business is not generating enough cash to repay the loan and interest when due. This would *further* widen the gap between companies X and Y. Over time, X would grow larger and more successful, and Y would be just a shadow of X. We see this phenomenon play out across many industries in which a few players have tended to become more dominant given their ability to generate cash on account of high ROCE.

What happens if a company with high ROCE stumbles? Let me share the example of Havells, a Nalanda portfolio company since 2011. Havells is India's largest consumer electrical equipment business and sells fans, lights and lighting fixtures, circuit breakers, wire, water heaters, and kitchen appliances like blenders and toasters.[15]

Havells delivered 52 percent ROCE (!) from 2007 to 2017 under its exceptional leader, Anil Gupta. Its annualized revenue growth was about 15 percent during this period, and Havells was sitting on a cash balance of $230 million in March 2017. This was about 28 percent of revenue that year. In May 2017, Havells acquired the consumer business of Lloyd Electric, primarily for Lloyd's fast-growing air conditioner business.

We were not too thrilled with this acquisition. While the company was clearly not taking a financial risk with the acquisition, since its cash balance was larger than the acquisition price, it was taking a risk that was outside our comfort zone.

The biggest issue, we thought, was the difference in culture and company mindset. Havells sells high-quality products at a premium to the discerning Indian consumer. It does so by setting up high-tech manufacturing plants, customizing product features to the needs of the consumer, staying ahead of the technology curve, and creating brand pull by advertising on TV and the internet. Lloyd seemed to be the exact opposite of Havells in many ways: It had gained market share over the past decade by aggressively pushing low-priced air conditioners imported from China. While Havells "pulled" consumers, Lloyd "pushed" its products by offering large dealer incentives and product discounts. Lloyd seemed singularly focused on growth at any price, whereas Havells' growth was an outcome of delivering quality products and building the trust of dealers and consumers over six decades.

Prior to Lloyd, one of the main sources of Havells' success was its ability to launch new products through its existing sales channel. The company has built a loyal and high-performing dealership network over many decades. This symbiotic relationship has allowed Havells to manufacture and sell an extensive range of consumer durables from fans to circuit breakers to toasters. However, for the first time, with the Lloyd acquisition, Havells was unable to use the strength of its dealer network because the air conditioner sales channel was completely different from the consumer electricals channel in India.

Unsurprisingly, the company immediately began facing problems with the acquisition. It started with the resignation of the CEO of Lloyd and many senior managers within a few months of the change in ownership. Havells found that Lloyd was selling its products through only a few dealers who had grown quite powerful over the years. These dealers were demanding higher margins and a greater share of Lloyd's business. When Havells refused, many of these dealers left, adversely impacting the sales and profitability of the business. There was also some level of dissonance while the Havells management tried to reconcile two radically different brand positioning approaches: the premium positioning of Havells versus the aggressive price warrior stance of Lloyd. Within two years of the acquisition, research analysts downgraded Havells as Lloyd's numbers continued to disappoint.

At this stage, Gupta could have taken the easy route of allowing Lloyd to revert to its old business ways. This would have preserved revenue and profit momentum and created two different kinds of business under the same umbrella. But he decided to take the much tougher road of instituting long-term fundamental changes to Lloyd's organization and business model.

Gupta repositioned the Lloyd brand from being a low-priced, average-quality product that offered only basic features to a high-quality product whose features matched or exceeded the best in the market. Havells invested about $35 million to set up a new state-of-the-art air conditioner plant that is now producing high-end, feature-rich air conditioners. Over many months, Gupta gradually replaced the senior management of Lloyd with leaders steeped in the Havells culture. The company refused to be blackmailed by a few powerful dealers and built a new, more resilient distribution network despite losing sales in the short term. Lloyd is now integrated with Havells, and there is complete alignment with their strategic and organizational priorities.

One key reason Havells was able to withstand short-term pain to achieve its longer-term goals was the availability of cash on the balance sheet. And the reason it had accumulated cash was its exceptionally high ROCE over many years. It's easy for any company to claim that it is "working for long-term value creation," but these words are worthless without the courage provided by a cash cushion. We will never know what would have happened if Havells had had a lot of debt and interest to repay, but I doubt it would have had the same determination to continue on a challenging, lengthy, and uncertain path with bankers breathing down its neck.

Havells made a moderately risky acquisition, took the time and effort to integrate it despite initial hiccups, and converted what could have been a significant misstep into a strategic success. Anil Gupta rocks. Havells rocks. Because 52 percent ROCE rocks.

There Are No Guarantees in Investing

Just as selecting for tameness in silver foxes helped Dmitri and Lyudmila generate many other traits in the animals, selecting for high ROCE has ensured that we have chosen businesses with many other desirable qualities. After the companies have been through the risk filter, as I discussed in chapter 1, we reject companies with long-term historical ROCE lower than 20 percent. Our preliminary short list of about 150 companies consists *only* of those that have delivered ROCE of more than 20 percent over the past five to ten years or more.

I have not claimed that we look *only* at ROCE to arrive at our conclusion on a business. That would border on being reckless and foolish. What I have said, though, is that we *start* the evaluation of a business by studying the record of its delivered historical ROCE. If you are an investor or choose to be one, you will develop your method and style of investing. But whatever you do, *starting* with a good understanding of the historical ROCE of a business will ensure you are miles ahead of your competition.

Buy one, get many free.

As you may have guessed, there are two problems with the approach of choosing ROCE as the first filter. First, a consistently high ROCE in the *past* does not guarantee that ROCE will be high in the *future*.

For example, if a business has a monopoly in its industry, say, of operating local bus services or a copper mine, even a poor-quality management team would probably be able to earn a decent return on capital. When the monopoly ends, however, we may see ROCE trend downward. Similarly, if there is high tariff protection for a product or commodity, domestic companies manufacturing the same product or commodity may earn decent profits without breaking a sweat. And then there is luck. A company can make decent ROCE for a few years if its key competitors get in trouble of their own making.

While making the preliminary short list, we can easily eliminate these kinds of companies because they are easy to identify. However, another category of potential losers (with high historical ROCE) is tough to identify beforehand. A high-quality business can also lose its way if the founder gets distracted, the company decides to change its strategy, the management bets the company on a failed acquisition, or an aggressive new competitor makes life difficult for the company. While high ROCE can provide some cushion in the face of these mishaps, there are limits to which it can safeguard a business hell-bent on destroying itself.

But remember this chapter is about where you *start* looking for great businesses, not what *guarantees* great investment return (spoiler alert: nothing does).

The second problem with making a preliminary list of only high-ROCE businesses is that it rejects companies that may become hugely successful in the future. Take Netflix. If we had evaluated Netflix in early 2018, its median ROCE for the previous ten years (2008 to 2017) of 10 percent would have been too low for us to include it on our preliminary list. We would have missed out on a spectacular wealth-creation opportunity: Netflix's stock price jumped 2.9 times from January 2018 to December 2021.

But here is the thing. We would have looked at this lost opportunity and not regretted it one bit. I know we will lose Netflix-like businesses, and I am okay with it. Our strategy of selecting only high-ROCE companies for our initial list invariably excludes some potential winners, but it also excludes hundreds of low-quality businesses that we would never want to own. Thus, *on average*, I believe this approach works well for us.

We will not change our approach just because others have made money with a strategy that we have chosen to avoid.

C'est la vie.

* * *

In early 2022, I wrote to the Institute of Cytology and Genetics at Novosibirsk. I had two questions for them. First, was the fox experiment still ongoing, and second, was Lyudmila Trut still active? I assumed the answer to both would be an emphatic no; after all, Lyudmila had begun the experiment in 1959, more than sixty years ago.

I was surprised when Yury Herbeck, the deputy head of the Laboratory for Evolutionary Genetics at the institute promptly replied to my email. Can one be "pleasantly shocked"? If so, I was.

Not only is the experiment still ongoing, but Lyudmila Trut, who is now almost *90 years old*, is still active! And not only is she active in the institute, she is also publishing path-breaking scientific articles. Herbeck was kind enough to attach four research articles published by Lyudmila Trut (and others) in prestigious scientific journals in recent years. The latest one was published in the *Journal of Neuroscience* on July 14, 2021, and is titled "Neuromorphological Changes Following Selection for Tameness and Aggression in the Russian Farm-Fox Experiment."

I used to feel proud that we have been successfully investing for over fifteen years. No longer. After reading about Lyudmila Trut, who has maintained her passion, discipline, and excellence over more than sixty years, I am confronted with a stark and painful reality.

We have a *very* long way to go.

Chapter Summary

Evolutionary theory has taught me that . . .

. . . to avoid getting drowned by a deluge of data and information, we can reimagine investing by initially selecting a *single* business trait that brings with it many favorable business qualities.

1. In nature, selection for just one trait can influence many other behavioral and physical qualities of an organism.
2. Dmitri Belyaev and Lyudmila Trut's long-term experiment in Siberia has shown that selecting for tameness in wild silver foxes transforms them into a creature not unlike a pet dog over very few generations. The foxes become docile and crave human attention. They also develop floppy ears, a piebald coloration, and a shorter snout and can be reproductively active more than once a year.
3. Investors could benefit immensely by homing in on a business trait that, when selected, brings along many other favorable qualities with it. Some popular parameters like management quality, high growth, and high margins are inappropriate or inadequate.

4. The single business quality that correlates favorably with many other areas of business excellence is historical return on capital employed (ROCE). We start our analysis by selecting *only* those businesses that have historically delivered high ROCE.

5. High ROCE *generally* (but not necessarily) indicates that the management team is stellar, they allocate capital effectively, they have built a strong competitive advantage over their peers, and they have room to innovate and grow.

6. Selecting for ROCE is a good *starting* point of analysis. It helps us narrow down our choices. We do a lot more work to create a short list of attractive businesses after this initial filter.

7. However, not all businesses with high historical ROCE will necessarily continue to be considered good businesses. There are no guarantees in investing.

CHAPTER 3

THE PARADOX OF MCKINSEY AND SEA URCHINS

Moreover when a modification of structure has primarily arisen from the above or unknown causes, it may at first have been of no advantage to the species, but may subsequently have been taken advantage of by the descendants of the species under new conditions of life and with newly acquired habits.

Charles Darwin, On the Origin of Species, *chapter 6, "Difficulties of the Theory"*

We rarely use much debt and, when we do, we attempt to structure it on a long-term fixed basis. We will reject interesting opportunities rather than over-leverage our balance sheet. This conservatism has penalized our results but it is the only behavior that leaves us comfortable, considering our fiduciary obligations to policyholders, depositors, lenders and the many equity holders who have committed unusually large portions of their net worth to our care.

Warren Buffett, *annual letter to shareholders, 1983*

The world is shrunk into a few square miles of New York: the filth of Mumbai, the art of Berlin, the style of Paris, the food of London, the bustle of Tokyo, the gaudiness of Shanghai, the rudeness of Delhi, the shopping of Singapore, the decadence of Monaco, the chaos of Cairo, and the magnificence of its own. I love it. This is why we hold Nalanda's annual investor meeting in the city every year in late June.

When my son was young (oh, why do they grow up?), he had two favorite spots in New York. Over time, they became mine, too: the Central Park Zoo and the FAO Schwarz toy store on Fifth Avenue. Our favorite activities there were petting the baby animals and dancing on the giant piano.

I remember FAO Schwarz less for its dazzling array of toys, many of which we bought over the years, and more for being soaked in wonder and amazement. There were magicians, Rubik's Cube artists, giant cuddly pandas, otherworldly jugglers, and, on one occasion, a group of singers and dancers who rivaled Broadway performers. Growing up in semi-urban India, I had never been to a toy store before, and I am not sure to this day if our visits to this iconic institution were more exciting for my son or me.

After our ninth annual meeting in 2016, I remember walking up Fifth Avenue, waiting to be mesmerized by something new in the store. But it wasn't there. A quick Google search on my phone sank my spirits. The store had shut permanently.

How in the world could this have happened? Why would the store be closed when it was almost always teeming with customers, and there never seemed to be enough cash registers?

The Mystery of McKinsey

McKinsey, the global strategy consulting firm, decided to enter India in 1992 following the beginning of the economic liberalization of the country in 1991.[1] It decided to hire fresh interns from two MBA schools in the country. India did not have strategy consulting firms in 1992, and none of us knew anything about the industry. Remember that there was no internet then, so we could not even do basic research on the industry or the company. Our professors, too, were clueless.

I was a final year MBA student in one of those two schools. The Firm (as it is called by insiders), for some inexplicable reason, had decided to pay more than twice the next highest-paying company (Citibank). The entire MBA class applied, including me. No one cared what McKinsey did—the lure of the lucre was too strong to resist.

I happened to be at the right place at the right time (isn't that life?) and was one of five MBA graduates hired. I was there for about six years. McKinsey is a great institution. Although life was quite tough—too many PowerPoint presentations and too many Air Miles—I enjoyed the competitive camaraderie, the satisfaction of working with CXOs, and its global oneness (I worked in four different international offices in six years). Having spent many years in the outside world after my departure from McKinsey, my admiration for the Firm has grown over the years as it has continued to dominate its industry.

McKinsey was founded in 1926 by James O. McKinsey, but the man who deserves the lion's share of credit for building the Firm to its current glory is Marvin Bower, who joined in 1933. He transformed the small engineering and accounting firm into the management consulting powerhouse it is today.

In the ninety-plus years since McKinsey's founding, the Firm has suffered cataclysmic internal and external shocks. Let's start with some of the external shocks first: the Great Depression, the Second World War, rapid decolonization, the Cold War, the oil shock, multiple recessions in the United States and other major economies of the world, the population explosion, massive poverty reduction, the creation and destruction of conglomerates, the hollowing-out of manufacturing in the United States, the rise of China, the exponential increase in computing power and communications technology including the internet, the global financial crisis, and the COVID-19 pandemic to name a few.

As the external world was undergoing rapid change, McKinsey itself worked through a few internal shocks: the transfer of power from Marvin Bower to the next generation in the late 1950s, repeated internal pressures for the firm to go public (including when I was there), the imprisonment of Anil Kumar and Rajat Gupta, its massive expansion into new geographies and industry segments over the years, its dubious fees arrangement with the South African utility Eskom, and the $600 million settlement for its work with the opioid manufacturer Purdue Pharma.

Not many of McKinsey's competitors survived the rapid pace of change in the rough-and-tumble world of consulting—remember Monitor or Booz? On the other hand, McKinsey has not only survived but also continued to prosper doing exactly what it has always done: act as a trusted adviser to the CXOs. The Firm, at its core, has remained stubbornly immune to external and internal shocks.

But here is the funny—even weird—reality. The Firm, while remaining robust to change, has *also* changed dramatically over the past decades. It started in the United States but is now also in Cairo, Casablanca, and Chengdu; it primarily offered strategic consulting until the 1990s but has expanded into operational and technology consulting; it used to serve mostly manufacturers in its early days, but you will now find it crawling all over Google, Facebook, or a hot new start-up in the Valley; in my time, it rarely hired laterally, but according to friends who are now senior partners, the company now hires hundreds of experienced industry specialists.

Living Organisms Are Highly Robust

MBA degrees, management seminars, best-selling business books, and corporate titans all seem focused on ensuring that companies adapt to change and evolve into a better version of themselves. If one could bottle up corporate obsession, the label on this bottle would declare, "How do we change faster, better, and easier?"

I beg to differ. The question that should be on the minds of business leaders and investors is almost the exact *opposite*: How do we change *without* changing?

Let's turn to evolutionary biology to understand why.

Biologists have always been aware of a strange conundrum of the living world. Organisms—animals, plants, algae, fungi, and even bacteria—are incredibly complex. But they are not delicate. On the contrary, they have survived and thrived for hundreds of millions of years—and in the case of bacteria, billions of years—despite continuous assault from the turbulent and dynamic external environment. Even their *internal* environments seem to be constantly revolting against them in the form of unceasing mutations.

Despite these external and internal perturbations, not only have living things survived, but they have also successfully diversified into millions of species. They occupy almost every available niche on our planet, from icy glaciers to boiling deep-sea thermal vents. One of the greatest wonders of this world is this: Living things are highly resistant to internal and external changes while *simultaneously* possessing the ability to evolve.[2] Let me call this ability to function well despite internal and external disturbances "robustness."

If the first proto-single-celled organism were too robust, it would have remained unchanged over 3.5 billion years, and we would not have had mushrooms or meerkats or Manhattan. On the other hand, if it were not robust enough, it would have gone extinct quite quickly in the volcanic and violent days of the early earth. You and I and all the living things we see around us are here because organic life has been able to strike a delicate balance between maintaining the status quo and evolving when the need arises. How does this happen, and what can we learn from it as investors?

This dual trick—of changing while remaining unchanged—results from two separate but intimately linked phenomena. First, living systems are robust at multiple levels. Second, this robustness helps neutral mutations become the source of future innovations.

What multiple levels? And what is a neutral mutation? Does this sound like gobbledygook? Let's start at the start. Our mother, our creator. The DNA (deoxyribonucleic acid) molecule.

The DNA molecule in any organism—be it a plant or a human being—serves two key functions. It carries information to build the body parts of an organism (for example, skin, kidney, petals, leaves) and is transmitted to offspring. DNA-based genetic code determines who we are and what our children will be. The DNA molecule is shaped in the form of a double helix and consists of four types of units called nucleotides: A (adenosine), C (cytosine), G (guanine), and T (thymine). As shown at the top of figure 3.1, a gene comprises a chain of nucleotides that can number from a few hundred to a couple of million! I have shown nine nucleotides here for illustration. These DNA nucleotides always exist in pairs called base pairs. The T nucleotide always pairs with A, and the

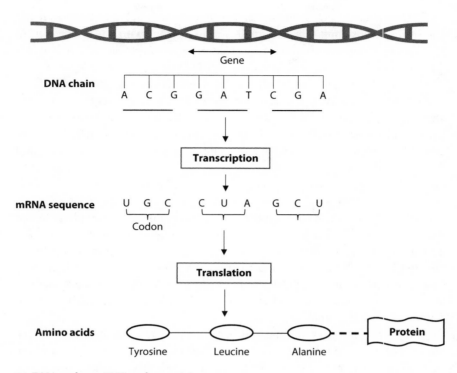

3.1 DNA makes mRNA makes protein.

C nucleotide always pairs with G. Figure 3.1 shows just one-half of a base pair with the sequence ACGGATCGA.

The DNA of all organisms comprises the *same* four nucleotides (A, C, G, and T). Just think about it for a moment: Orchids and orangutans share these same four nucleotides in their DNA code; they are just arranged differently in each. Human beings have three billion base pairs of nucleotides. Not in our whole body. In almost *every* cell of our body. I find this quite astounding. Remember that the next time you are packing a tight suitcase! And just because we rule the world does not mean we have the largest genome. The size of the human genome is quite unremarkable. The lowly *Amoeba dubia*, a single-celled organism, has 670 billion base pairs in its DNA—that makes for a genome about 220 times larger than yours and mine.[3]

For this discussion, let's focus just on genes that manufacture proteins. We are all essentially a bag of proteins. Proteins build bodies and regulate, defend, and monitor their functioning. Our body parts differ because they have different proteins. For instance, keratin makes our skin, hemoglobin carries oxygen in our blood, and proteins called immunoglobulins defend us from parasites.

DNA makes protein in a two-step process: the first being *transcription* and the second *translation*.[4] First, a single strand of DNA with a long chain of A, C, T, and G nucleotides gets *transcribed* onto a complementary messenger RNA (ribonucleic acid) sequence called mRNA (yes, this molecule is the basis of the COVID-19 vaccines made by Pfizer-BioNTech and Moderna). Thus, the DNA sequence ACGGATCGA shown in figure 3.1 will get transcribed to the mRNA sequence UGCCUAGCU. What is this new letter, U? In the transcription process, the DNA nucleotide A (adenosine) gets transcribed onto the mRNA nucleotide U (uracil), and, as described earlier, C pairs with G and T with A.

A DNA sequence has produced a *corresponding* mRNA sequence. What now? In the second step, a sequence of mRNA molecules is *translated* into a sequence of amino acids that synthesize a protein. mRNA is a single-stranded molecule, and it comprises codons made of three nucleotides that code for specific amino acids. In the mRNA sequence UGCCUAGCU shown in figure 3.1, the first codon, UGC, makes the amino acid tyrosine; the second codon, CUA, codes for leucine, and the third codon, GCU, codes for the amino acid alanine. A sequence of amino acids folds into a protein. Voilà! DNA made mRNA, which then made a protein.

If you are a biologist, I hope you haven't had a heart attack—I know that these few lines don't fully capture the complexities and nuances of the working of the universal genetic code. We haven't covered rRNA, tRNA, noncoding DNA, or enzymes. But hey, this is not a biology textbook, and I am simply trying to lay the basic groundwork to make sure we all have the same basic understanding of genetic code before moving ahead.

To comprehend the robustness of living organisms at multiple levels, let's start at the bottom: the universal genetic code.

The Genetic Code Is Robust

As mentioned, a codon comprising three bases creates an amino acid. Thus, the codon AGC creates the amino acid serine, and GGC makes glycine. Since any of the four nucleotides (A, C, U, or G) can occupy one of the three bases, there are sixty-four possible amino acids (4 × 4 × 4). However, only twenty exist in nature. How so? This is because two or more codons can code for the *same* amino acid. For instance, GGU, GGC, GGA, and GGG are all glycine. Thus, *any* mutation on the third position of the codon with the first two positions GG will always form glycine. These are called synonymous mutations. The formation of glycine is thus highly robust to mutations on the third base. Overall, the universal genetic code has funneled down sixty-four possibilities to just twenty through this type of synonymous mutation.[5]

Synonymous mutations are just the first level of robustness. Scientists have found that translation errors—errors at the point of codon formation—are most likely at the third position and least likely at the first position. Amazingly, the degree of robustness is *also* highest at the third position of the codon,[6] as in the earlier example of glycine. Thus, even though the third position is most error prone in translation, it will have no impact on the type of amino acid formed! In other words, evolution has ensured that the genetic code is extremely robust to mutations and translation errors. Isn't that cool?

Proteins Are Robust

Let's now go one level beyond the genetic code to see if proteins are robust to changes in the sequence of amino acids.

As discussed, a protein is a large molecule made up of a certain amino acid sequence. They are in all living organisms and are directly involved in all the chemical processes essential for creating and sustaining life. Thus, given the stability of life forms, one would expect proteins to show a high degree of robustness, and that is exactly what we see.

There are three types of protein robustness. First, scientists have found that the function of proteins is unaffected by the vast majority of amino acid changes. For example, the bacteria *E. coli* carries a protein called β-lactamase, which confers antibiotic resistance. This protein has 263 amino acids, 84 percent of which can experience mutation (i.e., they can be changed into another amino acid) *without* changing the enzyme's basic function. Ponder that. It would be like making 84 mistakes on a math exam comprising 100 questions and still getting an A!

The second type of robustness results from proteins with similar functions and structures being able to be made from different amino acid sequences. For example, myoglobin and hemoglobin are oxygen-binding proteins in vertebrates, and they have many distant relatives in invertebrates (like crabs and spiders) and plants. The three-dimensional structure of whale myoglobin and clam hemoglobin can be almost perfectly superimposed! Despite this uncanny structural and functional similarity, the amino acid sequences of the two are very different. Only 18 percent of the amino acids of the whale myoglobin and clam hemoglobin overlap.

Third, scientists have found that the vast majority of amino acid sequences fold into very few structures. No, I really mean it—*very* few. Let's see how few. A small protein may have 100 amino acids, and so the number of possible protein folds is 20^{100}, which is more than the number of atoms in the universe.[7] And how many proteins exist? About 10,000 (or 20^3). Thus, protein structure and function are *extremely* robust.

The Body Is Robust

Let's now go one level up from proteins to the body by taking the example of sea urchins.

Sea urchins evolved 250 million years ago and comprise about 1,000 species. For now, we will focus on just two found in shallow waters in Australia: *Heliocidaris tuberculata* and *Heliocidaris erythrogramma*. Let's call them species T and E. Their body plans are conserved; in other words, they *look* the same but have dramatically different modes of development.

T produces larvae (called pluteus) that bear no physical resemblance to the adult, and these free-swimming pluteus feed on plankton as they grow into adulthood. E, on the other hand, develops *directly* from an egg with no larval stage in between. But T and E are quite closely related and diverged only about five million years ago (almost the same time that chimpanzees and humans diverged; it would be as if chimps produced larvae that did not look like adult chimps!). The entire development programs—the shape and size of eggs, the location of cell formation for various body parts, the activation of genes that control development—of these two species differ so significantly that it is almost unbelievable that the two species have a common ancestor from only five million years ago. Despite these massive developmental changes, if you do a Google search for images of T and E, you will notice that they look almost the same.

How have the sea urchins maintained their body plans while changing many fundamental aspects of their development? And what have they achieved by maintaining highly robust body plans while evolving drastically different routes of development? We will get to these questions in a moment, but for now, let me summarize what we have learned.

We have seen that the stability of living organisms and species is maintained through robustness at multiple levels: at the levels of genetic code, proteins, and even body plan. For the sake of brevity, I have chosen to omit details of robustness at many other levels: changes in the secondary structure of RNA, changes in the regulatory regions of a gene, and drastic changes in enzyme activity, just to name a few.

A mutation changes the DNA sequence of a gene? No problem. It produces the same amino acid. The amino acid sequence changes owing to mutation or recombination? No problem. It produces the same protein. There is a change in the arrangement of proteins? No problem. The same enzyme activity continues. And so on. Living things are built to be resilient and resistant to change.

The Evolution of Evolvability

This gets us to the paradox I mentioned at the start of the chapter. Given multiple levels of robustness, how in the world do species evolve? Should they not stay fixed? What propelled bacteria to become bonobos?

The short and incredible answer is that robustness itself leads to evolvability!

We need to make a brief foray into one aspect of the history of molecular biology to unravel the paradox. In 1968, the Japanese geneticist Motoo Kimura proposed the "neutral theory" of molecular evolution.[8] Kimura contended that most changes at the level of DNA and amino acids do not impact the function of a molecule and hence the organism's ability to survive and reproduce. He contended that a small number of mutations are favorable, and natural selection preserves them. Some mutations are rejected because they are harmful, but most mutations don't really affect the organism. According to Kimura, most mutations are *neutral*, which causes robustness in the organism.

So how does neutral mutation lead to evolution? While a neutral change does not alter the *primary* function, it can alter a *secondary* function, thereby becoming the source of a *future* innovation.

Let's say gene A has primary function F. Owing to a mutation, gene A becomes gene B, but since it's a robust system, gene B continues to perform function F. But gene B affects a secondary function, F^S. F^S does not alter the fitness of the organism but can be used by the organism's descendants for a completely *new* function, thereby leading to evolution. Thus, although the genetic code was robust (because gene A changing into gene B did not affect function F), the *addition* of function F^S allowed the organism to evolve.

In a robust biological system, evolvability comes free!

Let's now return to the sea urchin example. T and E have maintained their body plans' robustness while changing their development cycle through neutral mutations over millions of years. For example, 16 of the 32 cells of the T embryo become the ectoderm (the outer layer of skin), whereas 26 of the 32 E embryo cells do so. The sea urchins' body structures have stayed robust to multiple changes in embryonic development. As a result, they have exploited a completely new ecological niche and a novel way of life. For example, E is abundant in deep seas and polar latitudes where T cannot survive—this is because E develops directly and does not need to go through the larval stage critically dependent on plankton for survival.

Something similar has been happening at McKinsey over the past century. Today's McKinsey bears no resemblance to Marvin Bower's McKinsey in terms of geographical presence, organization processes, type of client work, and breadth of expertise. But at some fundamental level of culture, oneness, problem-solving, and working with CXOs, the firm has remained stubbornly

Boweresque. It has changed without changing. This is what we seek as owners in our businesses: the ability to keep evolving while staying robust.

Businesses Must Be Robust to Evolve

Let's recap our journey until now. We have eliminated serious risks (chapter 1) and have shortlisted businesses based on ROCE (chapter 2). Now we need to select companies for their robustness.

Here are some learnings we have internalized at Nalanda.

Robustness Takes Many Forms

How does an investor measure robustness in a business? I wish I had a simple quantitative answer. I don't. Like almost everything in investing, the solution is somewhat subjective, somewhat vague, and somewhat controversial. But it works for us. The best way to understand robustness is to contrast the two extremes listed in table 3.1.

This is not an exhaustive list, but I hope you will get the general drift of what I mean when I say a business is robust. A robust business lies on a continuum between the two "poles" described in the table, with a bias toward the left side.

You will notice that, unlike in chapter 2, where we used the quantitative criterion of ROCE to select businesses, many factors contributing to robustness are qualitative. Also, almost no business falls entirely within the left or right column in my experience. Robustness is not a black-and-white measure. Thankfully. Or else, what would separate a good investor from a great one?

TABLE 3.1 **Examples of robustness in a business**

Most robust	Least robust
Has delivered high historical ROCE over a long period	Has made operating losses for most or all of its history
Has a fragmented customer base	Is dependent on very few customers
Has no debt and has excess cash	Is highly leveraged
Has built high competitive barriers	Has been unable to keep competition away
Has a fragmented supplier base	Is dependent on a few suppliers
Has a stable management team	Management turnover is high
Industry is slow changing	Industry is evolving fast

Different investors attribute different weights to the factors listed in table 3.1. For instance, many investors do not consider customer concentration to be a problem for a business. We do. We took advantage of these contrasting opinions a few months after the inception of Nalanda.

WNS is an Indian business process outsourcing (BPO) company with a U.S. listing. The leading BPO companies like WNS provide many mission-critical services to their clients of a quality and at a price that can typically not be matched by the company's internal teams. For example, they help their clients close the books of accounts, manage payables and receivables, perform timely consumer analytics, process mortgage applications, and address customer issues. We had been tracking WNS since we started Nalanda in 2007. Despite its high ROCE, zero debt, strong competitive advantage, and stable management team, we did not like the business because of its dependence on just a few customers. In 2006, WNS's top five customers accounted for 41 percent of revenue, and in 2007, this number had jumped to 55 percent.[9] We worried that the company's robustness was low and declining. But the markets did not seem to care, and WNS's stock price reached $35 by the middle of 2007.

WNS lost a major client in the latter half of 2007, and another client threatened to terminate their agreement. This wasn't great news in the short term, and the markets punished WNS severely. The stock crashed to $13 in early 2008. However, we concluded that the company would become *more* robust with a more fragmented customer base. We bought about 6 percent of the business from January to March 2008. Fast-forward thirteen years, and in 2020, WNS's top five clients accounted for only 25 percent of revenue. What was supposedly lousy news in 2007 looked pretty good in 2020!

We Assess Evolvability Indirectly by Measuring Robustness Directly

As permanent owners, we Nalanda folks are hungry for companies that can successfully implement neutral strategies to evolve and adapt to a changing environment. We want evolvability. Correction. We *need* evolvability. Having invested, we need the business to survive the onslaught of AI or other technologies, to upstage its increasing online and offline competition, to withstand multiple recessions, to conquer the adverse effects of climate change, to survive management turnover, and much more. We need it to be able to adapt.

However, just as evolutionary biologists struggle to measure evolvability,[10] I haven't yet figured out a reliable way in *advance* to directly assess a company's propensity to adapt to a changing world. Many investors contend that management interviews and discussions are an excellent way to assess the future adaptability of a business. Maybe. I consider such interviews a waste of time—but more on that later (in chapter 7).

But there is an indirect—and I would argue a reasonably reliable—path of satisfying my need. It is by measuring the robustness of an organization. Robustness lays the groundwork for evolution in living things. It does the same in businesses. Robustness is a necessary—though not sufficient—requirement for businesses to evolve successfully.

In a robust business, just as in a living organism, evolvability comes free.

Take the example of two businesses in an industry. Company A is the leader, and on sales of $100, it earns a margin of 20 percent. Let's assume its capital employed (in fixed assets, receivables, and inventory) is $50. Company A's ROCE is quite healthy at 40 percent (100 × 20% ÷ 50). If a company's growth is lower than its ROCE, it will also keep generating free cash flow, and so Company A has no debt. Company B is a weak player in the industry with half the sales of Company A, $50, and a margin of 15 percent. Since it does not have enough bargaining power with suppliers (who demand early payment) or customers (who pay late), its capital employed is the same as that of Company A ($50). Company B's ROCE is 15 percent (50 × 15% ÷ 50). Company B has a debt of $10 (which is not much, given its operating profit of $7.50), and its cost of debt is 5 percent.

Thus, both are earning decent ROCE and have a reasonably strong balance sheet—Company A is better, but Company B isn't too bad.

All seems fine. Until it's not.

COVID-19 strikes, and the country goes into a lockdown. Sales at both companies fall by half, and so do the operating margins. Company A, being a leader, can collect cash and liquidate inventory so that its capital employed falls to $25. Company B, on the other hand, while suffering the *same* drop in sales and margins as Company A, is rebuffed by its customers while asking for money and is also unable to sell its finished goods in a demand-poor environment. Its capital employed stays flat at $50. Company A's ROCE is now 20 percent (50 × 10% ÷ 25), and Company B's is 4 percent (25 × 7.5% ÷ 50).

Thus, even during the pandemic, Company A earns a respectable ROCE, allowing it to invest in growth. Fortified by its ROCE of 20 percent, Company A can also borrow in the market if it needs to, since the cost of debt is just 5 percent and the company is debt free. From being comfortably mediocre during the pre-pandemic era, Company B risks oblivion because it no longer has the money to invest in production, marketing, and distribution. At 4 percent ROCE, it would struggle to pay its debt at 5 percent. Given its precarious balance sheet and declining profits, lenders would also hesitate to lend it more money.

At least in the near term, a likely outcome is that Company A gains market share and Company B further loses its position. Since Company A had a higher degree of robustness owing to its high ROCE, it could adapt and evolve in an adverse external environment.

What I have outlined is *not* a theoretical construct. We have seen this story play out in many of our businesses. When the pandemic began, the general opinion was that all Indian businesses would suffer. Sharp stock market declines in March and April 2020 mirrored this opinion. However, as the months passed, the differences in the impact on the *business* of companies with differential degrees of robustness became quite stark. During and after the COVID crisis, we have seen these divergent outcomes play out across many of our companies and industries, be it paint, innerwear, air conditioners, tires, pipes, or batteries.

One of the best-run companies in our portfolio is Page Industries, which we were very fortunate to buy a few days after the collapse of Lehman in late 2008. Page is the exclusive licensee for the Jockey brand in India and is the largest seller of innerwear in the country.[11] Page aggressively launched new products during the pandemic and opened new stores while many of its competitors either vanished or were significantly weakened.

There are four listed innerwear companies in India, the other three being Maxwell, Rupa, and Lovable. Page's market share among its listed peers in December 2018 was already relatively high at 66 percent. However, by December 2020, Page's market share had grown to 70 percent. We don't have data for the dozens of unlisted companies, but from anecdotal evidence and feedback from industry insiders, it appears that Page's market share gain over this group during the pandemic has been even greater.

I believe Page's robustness was a significant—if not the primary or only—reason for its continued success during the crisis. Let's see how Page scores on the various factors contributing to robustness listed in table 3.1. For the year ended March 2020, Page's ROCE was 63 percent, and it was debt free. It has highly fragmented customer and supplier bases. In my opinion, it has built a deep and wide moat by investing in brand and distribution over twenty-five years. It has had the same owner since 1995. Its industry is changing very slowly, with the top players remaining the same for more than a decade.

The greater the robustness, the greater the evolvability.

We Demand Multiple Levels of Robustness in Our Businesses

There is an unbroken chain of life between us and our last universal common ancestor (scientists call it LUCA) 3.5 billion years ago.[12] Every part of this unbroken and evolving lineage has had robustness at multiple levels: genes, proteins, and body plan, to name just three. In a not dissimilar manner, I have discovered over more than two decades of investing that *more* levels of robustness lead to *more* evolvability.

Let's revisit table 3.1, which lists seven factors of robustness. As I have mentioned, there are more factors one can conjure (for example, propensity for

M&A, governance), but let's stick with these seven for now. My aim is to point you in a certain direction, not to spoon-feed.

We want our companies to tilt toward the left side of table 3.1 across all factors. Thus, we want the business to be robust at the level of ROCE *and* concentration of customer base *and* degree of leverage *and* strength of competitive advantage, and so on.

Is this asking for a lot? You bet. We are permanent owners—the key word here being "permanent." If a business can't last permanently, we don't want to own it. Without several levels of robustness, how will we be sure that the business will survive over the long term? I wish I could categorically answer the question, Is this a robust business? As a practicing investor, I know that assessing robustness is a matter of judgment and that there is no shortcut to this process. I have arrived at a certain heuristic after many years of investing. There clearly are black-and-white extremes to robustness (e.g., a business with just two customers) but in many, maybe even most, businesses, it is the gray zone that stares at us.

For example, is a company with a debt/equity ratio of 2.0 robust? Probably not. What about a ratio of 0.2 or 0.5? Maybe. For me, the answer depends on the *other* factors of robustness. Almost all the companies in our portfolio are debt free. Still, in 2010 we invested in India's leading plastic pipes business (used in homes and agriculture), Supreme Industries, whose debt/EBITDA ratio was 0.6. Not high, but not zero either. Despite the company having debt—which was small to begin with—we concluded that the company was robust because it was the clear industry leader, had been gaining market share over its competitors, had a return on capital of more than 30 percent, had successfully designed and launched many products over the past decade, had thousands of distribution points across India, was able to negotiate the best terms with its suppliers, and had not wasted time and money on unnecessary acquisitions. It was not perfectly robust, but it was resilient enough. Today, the company is debt free and continues to be the industry leader by a wide margin.

The more levels of robustness, the more we salivate.

Highly Robust Businesses Evolve by Taking Calculated Risks

As we have learned, neutral mutations make an organism robust while simultaneously planting the seeds of evolution. In the business world, neutral changes may not have a short-term impact but may be transformational over the long run. The corporate phenomenon equivalent to biological neutral mutations can be summarized in two words: calculated risks.

There are millions of small businesses across the world that are incredibly robust but will stay small. And then there are businesses that test the limits of robustness and implode. The former risk nothing, and the latter risk every-thing. The Goldilocks zone between these two extremes is what I call "calcu-lated risk." It is the degree of risk that makes managers uncomfortable, but not too much; it compels the organization to innovate, but not too much; it forces the business to invest, but not too much; and it adds areas of potential growth, but not too many.

To me, the company that best demonstrates calculated aggression and risk-taking is Walmart.

Small digression. Let's see if you know the answer to this question: What was Sam Walton's age when he founded Walmart? If your answer begins with a one or a two, your answer was the same as mine. And like I was, you are wrong. Sam Walton was forty-four when he opened his first Wal-Mart store in 1962 in Rog-ers, Arkansas (Wal-Mart became Walmart in 2018).[13] Not all the great founders of the modern era are from Silicon Valley, not all of them were hard-charging teenagers, and not all of them wanted to "change the world."

After graduating from college, Walton started in sales at J. C. Penney in 1940, then enlisted for the war in 1942. In 1945, he started managing a franchise Ben Franklin store in Newport, Arkansas (where the population was then seven thousand). By 1950 he was running two stores in Newport and had achieved reasonable success by experimenting and innovating. One of his innovative ideas that had been a massive hit with his customers was an ice cream machine. As he writes in his autobiography, "Every crazy thing we tried hadn't turned out as well as the ice cream machine, of course, but we hadn't made any mistakes we couldn't correct quickly, none so big that they threatened the business."

Could there be a better definition of calculated risk?

After Walmart's initial success in Rogers, Sam Walton opened more stores.[14] By 1967, he had opened twenty-four stores, which brought in sales of about $13 million. The company reached $1 billion in sales in 1980, by which time it had 276 stores and about 21,000 associates. Note that store openings and selling more products through the same stores propelled growth from 1967 to 1980. During these thirteen years, sales per store had increased about *seven* times. How had Walton done this? By continuously trying new things, expanding product offerings, and broadening the customer base.

Not all these experiments were successful. For example, in the early 1980s, Walton started two Hypermarts—giant stores selling groceries and general merchandise—in the Dallas–Fort Worth area. But the concept failed. He also experimented with discounted drugs (dot Discount Drug) and home improve-ment (Save Mor), both of which shuttered. One of his experiments, however, worked spectacularly well. Sam's Club, focused on retailers who buy in bulk, was launched in 1983, and within a decade, it had crossed revenue of $10 billion. The spectacular success of Sam's Club demonstrates the slight downside and colossal upside of taking manageable risks.

As discussed in chapter 1, most M&A fail, and the larger ones can destroy a business. Walmart has managed acquisitions the way they should be managed: It has kept targets small and manageable and funded them without taking on large debt. The company made its first acquisition fifteen years after inception. It was close to $500 million in sales, and by this time, as is evident from his autobiography, Sam Walton was feeling quite confident about the future of the business. Even then, he behaved prudently by acquiring a small discount store business called Mohr Value in 1977, which was about one-tenth the size of Walmart. As he says in his book, "We closed five stores and converted the remaining sixteen to Wal-Marts, and it wasn't much of a shock to our system."

By 1991, Walmart was present in forty-nine states, and the management started exploring options outside their home country. Almost two decades after the first store's inauguration, Walmart embarked on its maiden international foray by entering into a joint venture with CIFRA, Mexico's largest retailer, and by 1997 it had acquired a majority position in CIFRA. Was this a "neutral" change? It sure seems like one in hindsight—the Mexico joint venture started small and would not have impacted Walmart's U.S. operations. Also, a joint venture in a foreign country allowed Walmart to dip a toe to check the water temperature. Once the company had adjusted to the new geography, it felt confident in making a bigger commitment by acquiring the rest of CIFRA. Starting from scratch in 1991, Walmart's revenue from the international segment in 2020 was $120 billion, or 23 percent of company sales.[15]

The company did something similar—small, measured, and low risk—when it launched its web business. In 2000, Walmart joined hands with a leading Silicon Valley investment firm, Accel Partners, to launch Walmart .com. Accel, by the way, gained much fame (and a gargantuan fortune) as a result of its $12.7 million investment in an early-stage company called Facebook in 2005.[16] In about eighteen months, in mid-2001, Walmart acquired the minority stake of Accel to own Walmart.com fully. By 2020, Walmart's e-commerce sales had climbed to $24 billion and Walmart.com was approaching 10 percent of Walmart's overall U.S. sales. What had started as a "neutral" strategy in 2000 is now fast becoming the centerpiece of Walmart's approach to gaining market share.

One of our largest investors is a well-known U.S. university endowment. They have been investing in funds globally for many decades. Their CFO visited our Singapore office in 2011. After he had finished grilling us on compliance and other related matters, I wanted to know if he could share any learnings with us. He said that the one industry in which their fund managers had consistently lost money across time and geographies was retailing. In this context, Walmart's success is awe inspiring.

And how robust was Walmart at the end of 2020? Let me point to just two indicators. Its return on tangible capital employed was 46 percent. Thus, for day-to-day operations in 2020, it deployed $49.7 billion capital to earn an operating income of $22.9 billion. Its net debt level was just $26.8 billion, substantially lower than its equity value of $52 billion and EBITDA (earnings before interest, tax, depreciation, and amortization) of $38 billion. Its continued robustness has helped the management take calculated risks in the United States, as well as across the globe.

I don't want to pretend that Walmart's success is solely the result of its slow-and-steady approach to growth and expansion. Walmart has undoubtedly flourished for many reasons. Apart from Sam Walton being the founder, though, I don't know what other factors have led to its success. I can rattle off a list of things from various business books and articles written on Walmart, but I don't know if they were the cause or the effect of its success. But I *do* know that taking calculated risks and staying robustly healthy have had a strong correlation with its accomplishments over sixty years.

As it has been for almost all the Nalanda portfolio companies. When we first invested in Page Industries in 2008, it primarily manufactured and sold men's innerwear. Here are some of the milestones and neutral strategies implemented by Page since then:

2008–09: Primarily a men's innerwear company
2009–10: Launched women's leisurewear, men's sportswear
2010–11: First store for women in Delhi, first training center for production staff
2011–12: Boys' and girls' ranges, signed exclusive licensee agreement with Speedo
2012–13: Sleepwear range for women, men's performance stretch range, thermals
2013–14: New international-format retail outlets, seamless sleepwear for women
2014–15: Exclusive outlets in Dubai, Abu Dhabi
2015–16: Boys' collection (7–12 years)
2017–18: Girls' inner- and outerwear, men's and women's athleisure
2018–19: Teenage girls' range
2019–20: First digital manufacturing unit with real-time production data

The remarkable aspect of this list is what it *doesn't* include. There are no acquisitions, no unrelated diversifications, no "visionary" plans to change the world, no financial engineering. Only measured risks. For example, in 2009–10, the company launched men's sportswear. It did so through its existing distribution channel and staff, its current manufacturing units, and the same brand name. As the sportswear segment has expanded over the years, it now has its own supply chain, its own business unit, and its own advertisements.

You will notice here that the company launched a children's range in 2011–12. Page describes this natural extension of the Jockey brand in its annual report: "With the launch of Jockey Kids, the brand reaches out to the consumers of tomorrow. . . . Keeping comfort as our topmost priority, we have brought in a range using 100 percent cotton, super soft, absorbent fabric, for both boys and girls." As investors in Page, we were excited about this new target segment because it would double the Jockey brand's addressable market.

After seventeen years in India, Page had earned the right to extend its brand into a new segment. Unexpectedly, it failed. The children's range did not do well, and the company withdrew its products. Did this have any negative impact on the finance or operations of the company? No. This is because it was a calculated risk. It was a neutral strategy that did not affect the robustness of the business. Its operating ROCE in 2011–12 was 59 percent and was even higher in 2012–13 (when it realized the children's range had failed) at 64 percent. In 2012–13, overall sales grew 26 percent, and profits rose 24 percent. In both these years, the company had negligible debt. The advantage of having a solid foundation that allowed it to take small bets was evident.

Page went back to the drawing board and launched only a boys' collection in 2015–16. Even within this segment, it introduced products only for boys aged seven to twelve years. Why not five- or thirteen-year-old boys? I have no idea. I don't understand product marketing, but thankfully Page does. It launched girls' inner- and outerwear a year later. By 2020, the boys' and girls' ranges had become a hit and had started contributing to the overall sales and profit growth of the business. What had started as a small experiment in 2011–12 was finally yielding fruit.

As India went into a full lockdown in mid-March 2020 owing to the COVID-19 pandemic, the company's annual sales grew only 3 percent for the year ended March 2020. Profits fell 15 percent, but it delivered ROCE of 63 percent while remaining debt free. This robustness, we believe, should allow the company to continue to take calculated strategic bets many years into the future.

Robustness Is a Proxy for Evolutionary and Business Success but Doesn't Guarantee It

Dinosaurs, a diverse group of more than a thousand reptilian species, dominated our planet for 180 million years.[17] As a matter of comparison, we *Homo sapiens* have been around for less than 0.2 million years. Dinosaurs couldn't have survived and thrived for so long unless they were highly robust and adaptable. Molecular evidence has shown that many modern mammalian orders—Carnivora, Primata, Proboscidea—coexisted with dinosaurs for at least 30 million years during the Cretaceous period (145 to 66 million years ago), and maybe even earlier. The mammals during the era of dinosaurs were small, squirrel sized, and probably insectivores. If aliens had landed on our planet

65 million years ago, they never could have predicted that a small offshoot of the insignificant mammalians would reign supreme one day.

The cataclysmic aftermath of an asteroid strike in the Yucatan peninsula 65 million years ago wiped out the dinosaurs. But the mammals survived. No one is sure why. The extraordinary robustness of dinosaurs did not guarantee their evolvability.

In general, the greater the robustness, the greater the evolvability. But sometimes, robustness ceases to help businesses adapt. We can see this in Gap's failure to grow despite the company being very robust. Its revenue stayed flat at about $16 billion from 2005 to 2020, although it delivered ROCE of 20 percent or more for more than a decade and had no leverage. *In general*, multiple levels of robustness are better than a single level. But sometimes, even multiple levels of robustness can't safeguard the future of a business, as has been the case for thousands of newspapers across the world. *In general*, highly robust businesses evolve by taking calculated risks. But sometimes, very rarely, businesses can succeed by taking huge risks, as shown by Netflix.

We at Nalanda *never* bet against the odds. And so, despite some rare counterexamples, we have kept and will continue to keep robustness at the front and center of our investment approach. As permanent owners, we seek robustness in companies as the best *available* benchmark to assess if they are likely to adapt and survive over the long term. A better measure may exist, but I don't know what it is. We invest *only* in highly robust companies. Many of them have stayed robust and have grown their sales and profits over decades. But our track record is not perfect. We have witnessed two key problems with this approach.

First, a business can lose its robustness. We saw this happen to one of our consumer-focused companies; we still don't know how or why it lost its way. We invested in this business almost twenty years after its creation. During that period, the management had built the largest brand in its industry in the country. When we invested, the company had no debt, its sales had grown 20 percent annually for the past five years, and it had delivered ROCE of more than 50 percent. Within a few years of our investing, the company's inventory and receivables started climbing steeply, a leading indicator of potential sales issues. While the company continued to show profits, it had begun consuming cash—while having been a cash generator in earlier years. As a result, it had to start borrowing money just as its ability to repay the loans declined. Being a permanent owner, we are tolerant of declining sales or margins or market share. But we will not risk survivability. As the company's robustness nose-dived, we exited the business at a loss. The company survives but is a pale reflection of its former glory. This unexplained decline of robustness has occurred in our portfolio only once since our inception in 2007, but it *has* happened.

The second problem is *too much* robustness. One high-quality business in the Nalanda portfolio has been too robust. It has been unable or unwilling to implement any neutral strategies to expand its customer base, product segments, or geographies. As a result, the company has grown its sales at less than 5 percent annually for a decade, and its profits have stayed flat during this period. To be fair, its industry has gone through a vicious downcycle, and this business is the only one among its peers that continues to generate profits and free cash flow, and it remains debt free. It is also the only business in our portfolio that has taken robustness to its extreme by eschewing calculated risks. Maybe it is in an industry in which it can't or shouldn't. Perhaps when the industry upcycle arrives, it will finally see growth. Or maybe not. We will continue to remain owners in the business. While our returns have been positive, they have been below par. But I love them—they are a class apart in a very tough place. We are willing to sacrifice growth for robustness.

We have made almost forty investments to date, and in all of them, robustness was a primary—but not the only—selection criterion. We have worked on the assumption that robustness will lead to growth and evolution. This assumption has failed us on two occasions: one in which the company lost robustness and another in which the company's excessive focus on robustness compromised growth. I am surprised at our strategy's low failure rate. We have been quite lucky, and while robustness should continue to reward us across our portfolio, we will continue to encounter failures of the first or second kind over time.

The *Only* Way to Protect Against Loss of Robustness Is Entry Valuation

"Confronted with a like challenge to distill the secret of sound investment into three words, we venture the motto, MARGIN OF SAFETY" (emphasis in the original text). This is the best advice for investors in the best chapter of the best investing book ever written: *The Intelligent Investor* by Benjamin Graham, Buffett's actual and spiritual mentor. The chapter is titled "'Margin of Safety' as the Central Concept of Investment." Graham knew that the corporate world is highly uncertain and that the best protection offered to an investor is the price they pay for a business.

Another investment legend, Seth Klarman, offers the following advice in his book appropriately titled *Margin of Safety: Risk-Averse Value Investing Strategies for the Thoughtful Investor*: "Value investing, the strategy of investing in securities trading at an appreciable discount from underlying value, has a long history of delivering excellent investment results with very limited downside risk."

In this chapter, I have used the word "robust" to *extend* the margin-of-safety concept to many other facets of a company. We have sought a margin of safety on business quality by demanding high ROCE and a wide competitive moat, on the strength of the balance sheet by requiring it to be debt free, on the bargaining power of customers and suppliers by requiring them to be fragmented, and on the sustainability of economics by insisting that the industry be slow-changing.

But even these multiple levels of robustness or margins of safety can become compromised owing to unpredictable changes in the economy, the industry, or the company. The COVID-19 pandemic has severely impacted what had appeared to be highly robust hotel chains; Intel's erstwhile dominance in semiconductor chips has been upset by the likes of AMD, Nvidia, and Samsung; Amazon has already destroyed many small and large retail businesses; regulators in the United States and Europe appear to be threatening the very existence of Google and Facebook in their current form.

We do the best we can to choose businesses based on their current and potential degree of robustness. But bad things *will* happen—we just don't know what, when, or how. And so we turn to the one aspect of investing that is entirely within our control: the price we pay.

We know that given the nature of the businesses we are after—those with very low risk and exceptional business quality—they will almost never be available cheap. The market is not an idiot; it is almost always efficient. *Almost* always. Not always. We wait for those few occasions to pay what we call a "fair" price. Not too low but not too high either.

What is "fair"? Rather than describe it, let me state the actual number. The median trailing twelve-month (TTM) entry PE ratio for the Nalanda portfolio is 14.9. The median TTM PE for the period from 2005 to 2020 for India's primary index, Sensex, is 19.7 and for the Midcap Index is 23.8. Thus, we are buying what we think are exceptional businesses at a 25 to 30 percent discount on the index.

Over almost a quarter of a century of investing, I know I have been wrong on many occasions. The margin of safety of our entry price pays for my errors of judgment.

A Leader Is Made a Loser

Lazarus of Bethany was miraculously brought back to life by Jesus in the New Testament.[18] Charles Lazarus performed a modern capitalist miracle by making Toys "R" Us the largest and most well-respected toy business globally. Lazarus is also a beggar in a parable in the Gospel according to Luke, the third of the four Gospels of the New Testament. Once a miracle of Lazarus, Toys "R" Us suffered the same fate as Lazarus the beggar.

Charles Lazarus opened his first Toys "R" Us store in 1957.[19] In that era, parents typically went to department stores to buy toys. Toy sales were seasonal, and the six weeks leading up to Christmas made up the bulk of sales for the year. Most toy stores were small family-run shops and carried only a small number of toys. Having operated a baby furniture business from 1948 to 1957 and learned the shopping habits of parents, Lazarus decided to risk a new strategy. He wanted to sell toys throughout the year and give parents and children a novel shopping experience. His first store was 25,000 square feet in size and stocked thousands of toy varieties. The store did not keep toys in display cases as did its competitors; instead, it kept them in rows next to each other like items in a grocery store.

The store was a massive hit given its size, variety, and low prices. Despite his initial success, Lazarus moved slowly at first and opened only four stores until 1966. In 1973, Toys "R" Us started advertising on TV using its store mascot, a cuddly giraffe called Geoffrey. Lazarus also began tapping Japanese manufacturers to make inexpensive toys and negotiated attractive rates for bulk purchases. The company went public in 1978 and grew at more than 20 percent annually for the next decade. Morgan Stanley's retail analyst compared it to the venerable IBM in 1982: "I think Toys 'R' Us is a unique operation—the only proprietary merchandise company that rivals IBM as revolutionary in concept." The *Washington Post* compared it to another iconic American brand, McDonald's, by declaring, "Like McDonald's, with its regimented service and standardized burgers and fries, Toys 'R' Us has become an American institution."

Toys "R" Us kept gaining market share by opening stores slowly and steadily. It did not get enticed by "transformational" M&A, although I am sure there was no dearth of bankers paying their respects to Lazarus every week. It continued, however, to take measured risks, one of which was the opening of a Kids "R" Us clothing store in 1983. The company also started expanding overseas and, in 1984, opened its first international stores in Canada and Singapore. In 1985, the company opened five stores in the United Kingdom, and in 1991 they entered Japan in an 80:20 joint venture with McDonald's. In the United Kingdom, Toys "R" Us captured a 9 percent market share in just three years. The company continued to expand in overseas markets after its initial successes.

In 1988, the *Wall Street Journal* boldly predicted, "Toys 'R' Us, Big Kid on the Block, Won't Stop Growing." As if on cue, the problems started. In 1988, Walmart's market share at 17.4 percent came marginally ahead of that of Toys "R" Us at 16.8 percent. Toys "R" Us was in second place after being the leader for fifteen years. Toys "R" Us was being squeezed at both ends: by discount chains like Walmart, Target, and Costco, which competed on low prices, and by so-called edutainment companies like Zany Brainy, Noodle Kidoodle, and Imaginarium, which offered higher-priced specialized toys and better service.

In 1998, the company launched its website, ToysRUs.com, and its first mail-order catalog. But the company was struggling, and 1998 was the year of "restructuring," which is usually the euphemism for a business terminating its science projects and loss-making initiatives. The company announced a huge inventory reduction; the closure of fifty-nine stores in the United States, France, and Germany; the shuttering of thirty-nine Kids "R" Us stores; and a layoff of three thousand workers. The cost of restructuring was so high that the company declared its first net loss since going public.

Too often, a business in trouble tries to buy its way out. Toys "R" Us was no exception. It acquired Imaginarium Toy Centers in 1998. It also tried frequent management changes—the company had three CEOs from 1994 to 2000. But its downward slide continued with Amazon, too, muscling its way into the toy segment. The company's sales stayed flat at $11 billion from 1997 to 2004, and the operating profit fell by about 65 percent during this period. The operating ROCE was 15 percent in 1997, and it fell to 4 percent in 2004. The situation was so bad that the company shocked the world by announcing that it might completely withdraw from the toy business and focus on the Babies "R" Us chain.

Okay, let's pause here and summarize the situation in 2005.

Toys "R" Us was spectacularly successful for about four decades, from the late 1950s to the late 1990s. By the mid-2000s, however, it wasn't growing, its market share was declining, and its profitability had taken a severe beating. Whatever the reasons for its trouble, there was no doubt that it *was* in trouble. The company's robustness had suffered significantly. Maybe it was bad luck, maybe it was management missteps, or maybe it was a bit of both.

One way to think about this situation is to picture an elite marathoner whose performance has dipped in recent months. They used to be a picture of health and vigor, but nowadays, they look exhausted and cannot run even ten kilometers at their earlier marathon pace. They are now at the starting line of the Boston Marathon. What would you expect their coach to do before the race starts? If I were the coach, I would advise them to withdraw from the race, rest and recover for a few months, and slowly build their mileage back up. Maybe your advice would be different—you might counsel them to take it easy and just finish the race without worrying about a podium finish to minimize damage to the body. I assume you would be shocked if I told you that the coach not only asked them to run at full speed but also loaded a ten-pound bag on their back!

Yet this is what happened to Toys "R" Us. In 2005, the private equity giants KKR and Bain and the real estate firm Vornado purchased Toys "R" Us for $6.6 billion.[20] However, their equity contribution was only $1.3 billion, and they borrowed $5.3 billion for this purchase. And then they loaded this borrowing onto Toys "R" Us! If you know nothing about the leveraged buyout

(LBO) industry, you may be rubbing your eyes in disbelief. The private equity folks bought Toys "R" Us for a fat sum of money, borrowed 80 percent of that amount, and then burdened the *company* with this borrowing to finance their purchase? Oh, yes. Welcome to the wonderful world of finance.

While leverage may be good from a corporate finance perspective, it is bad from my point of view. But I hope all parties can agree that it is *terrible* for a struggling business. The elite but sick Toys "R" Us marathoner had just been asked to run the Boston Marathon, competing with world-class runners with a ten-pound load on its back. Remember that the capitalist world is a Boston Marathon that never ends—there is no respite at the end of a punishing two-hour race. The race goes on and on and on and on and on: 24 hours × 7 days a week × 365 days a year. It's unending, unrelenting, unforgiving.

The massive debt load meant that by 2007, 97 *percent* of the company's operating profit was consumed by interest payments. Where was the money left to innovate, invest in stores, advertise, hire and train the best people, and do all the things any business needs to do to stay on top of their game? In an *Atlantic* article on the failure of Toys "R" Us,[21] an interviewee remarks that the company was handcuffed and could not make investments. Another one rightly points out, "It's true that they could not respond to Amazon. But you have to ask yourself why." Katherine Waldock, a finance professor at Georgetown University's McDonough School of Business said in a *Wall Street Journal* article, "The $400 million a year in debt service was really constrictive as they were trying to compete."

Toys "R" Us was already *un*robust at multiple levels, and the additional leverage taken by its private equity owners proved to be the last straw. The company filed for bankruptcy in September 2017, and David Brandon, the CEO, candidly admitted, "The company's overleveraged capital structure has constrained it from making necessary operational and capital expenditures, including investing in the revitalization of stores. As a result, the company has fallen behind some of its primary competitors on various fronts." You don't say.

* * *

Toys "R" Us bought the FAO Schwarz business in May 2009. Both companies had been struggling against discount retailers and web-based sellers like Amazon. Most acquisitions compromise the buyer's robustness, and for an already weakened company like Toys "R" Us, the probability of success is even lower. Unsurprisingly, it closed Manhattan's iconic FAO Schwarz store in July 2015.[22] And left me distraught.

Dear Amazon, you have opened physical book shops in Manhattan. Time for toys?

Chapter Summary

Evolutionary theory has taught me that . . .

. . . we can reimagine investing by owning *only* robust businesses that are resilient to internal and external shocks, while continuing to evolve and grow.

1. There is a paradox in the living world: Organic life is highly complex but not fragile. Organisms have survived hundreds of millions of years despite living in constantly changing external environments and undergoing a barrage of internal mutations. This is because they are robust at multiple levels.
2. Thus, an accidental change in DNA sequence does not affect which amino acids are made; a change in amino acids or their sequence does not impact the synthesis of proteins; and a change in proteins need not affect the body plan of an organism.
3. Neutral mutations permit new functions and adaptations to arise without disrupting current functioning.
4. We want our businesses to mimic the robustness of the living world: to survive and prosper in a dynamic external environment, withstand internal strategic and organizational upheavals, *and* evolve by taking calculated risks.
5. Hence, we choose to invest *only* in businesses that are robust at multiple levels. A robust business has high ROCE, minimal or zero debt, a strong competitive advantage, fragmented customer and supplier bases, a stable management team, and is in a slow-changing industry.
6. Just because a business is robust today does not mean it will continue to be so. Our only protection against the loss of robustness of a business is to be price sensitive. We do not invest unless the market offers us an attractive valuation, which happens rarely.

CHAPTER 4

THE PERILS OF A PAVLOVIAN

As many more individuals of each species are born than can possibly survive; and as, consequently, there is a frequently recurring struggle for existence, it follows that any being, if it vary however slightly in any manner profitable to itself, under the complex and sometimes varying conditions of life, will have a better chance of surviving, and thus be naturally selected.

Charles Darwin, On the Origin of Species, *introduction*

In our view, it is folly to forgo buying shares in an outstanding business whose long-term future is predictable, because of short-term worries about an economy or a stock market that we know to be unpredictable. Why scrap an informed decision because of an uninformed guess?

Warren Buffett, annual letter to shareholders, 1994

You are going bald. Not because of age, but because you have been tearing your hair out.

A few months ago, you committed to investing $100,000 with a money manager. This fund manager did not want to raise cash and said that he would call commitments if he saw attractive opportunities to invest in the market. He made a strong pitch with a snazzy PowerPoint presentation, and, like everyone in the industry, he promised to be long-term oriented. He also claimed that he does not like to lose money (as if everyone else does!) and that he carefully assesses the quality of businesses and buys when everyone else is selling. Very Buffettesque. Very old world. You have heard the same spiel from everyone, but he seems quite sincere. Or at least he put on a good act.

A few quarters have passed, and he has called $40,000 from you. At the end of the quarter, the value of your $40,000 investment is $38,000. You know that the market has been a bit weak lately, so you ignore the minor loss. You are a patient sort and don't fret over the value of your investments daily like many of your friends.

But when you check your investments next quarter, you see that the value of your portfolio is now only $32,000. You have taken a hit of 15 percent in a single quarter. To rub salt into your wounds, the fund manager demands $15,000 more from you. He is entitled to; you have signed an agreement with him that commits you to keep investing until your $100,000 limit is reached. You invest the additional $15,000.

One more quarter goes by, and you are aghast to discover that the value of your $55,000 is now only $39,000. You are down 30 percent within six months! The fund manager repeats the same mantra, "We are long term, patient, blah . . . blah . . . blah," while asking for an *additional* $15,000! You talk to some of your friends who appear to be stock market experts. All of them advise you to stop investing more and to withdraw your remaining capital promptly. Unfortunately, your lawyer advises you that there is no way out. Not only can you not redeem your capital (because you have agreed to a lock-up for many years), but you must honor your commitment. With great reluctance, you invest an additional $15,000. Your total investment is now $70,000.

You have read Buffett's great annual letters and listened to his interviews on TV. You remember that he advises investors not to check their stock holdings obsessively. Hence, this time, you decide to wait six months before reviewing how your portfolio has performed. Kudos for your patience!

The day finally arrives. You haven't felt this nervous since the first time you used a fake ID to enter a bar. You open your account statement with increasing dread. Your worst fears are realized. Your $70,000 investment has now almost *halved* to $36,000. Your portfolio has lost about 40 percent during the past six months. Oh, and your money manager is threatening to ask for more money.

Apart from continuing to tear at your remaining hair, what should you do?

The horns of dung beetles. Maybe they have the answer.

The How Versus the Why

Dung beetles love poop. Duh. With about eight thousand species, this cleanup crew of the insect world eats poop. They build their nests with poop, live in those nests, and lay their eggs in them to sustain their larvae.[1] Check out figure 4.1 for a small sample of the astonishing variety of dung beetles. Among insects, they have the unique distinction of caring for their young: dad provides food, and mom tends to the nest.

Many years ago, while taking a poop in the open in Masai Mara in Kenya (don't ask), I *heard* them before I saw them. They scurry noisily at a surprisingly

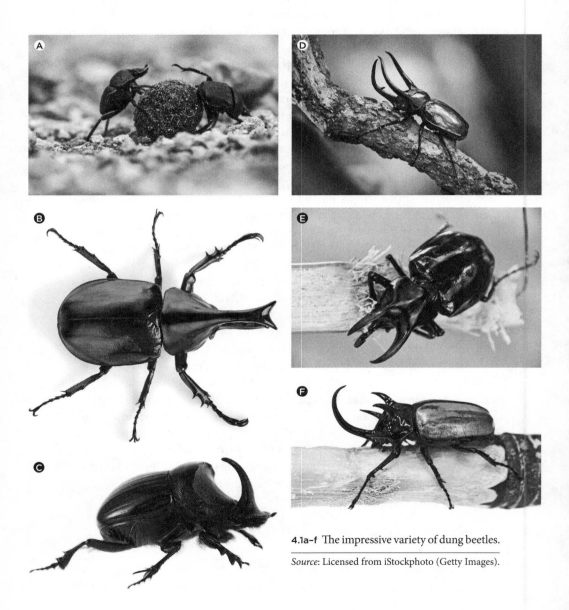

4.1a–f The impressive variety of dung beetles.

Source: Licensed from iStockphoto (Getty Images).

brisk pace. The males have impressive-looking horns, and the eight thousand species have almost as many different kinds of horns. Their shape resembles rhinoceros horns, elephant tusks, deer antlers, and even a serrated knife; their size varies from very small to massive. Some are even larger than the entire dung beetle's body.

What explains these horns? One way evolutionary biologists describe them is through hormonal, developmental, and genetic mechanisms. For example, a 2019 *Science* article provides evidence that dung beetles use wing genes to grow their horns.[2] The wing genes get turned on in the early stages of the growth of the horns. Later, these genes switch off, and a new set of genes grows and shapes the horns. An article in the *Journal of Insect Physiology* explores the types and quantities of hormones that control the length of horns in males.[3] It showed that the hormone methoprene has a significant influence on the production of horns. These scientists are asking "how" questions. How do the horns grow? How does horn length differ?

Another route of exploring the cause of horns is to understand the *adaptive* nature of them. These are "why" questions: Why did horns arise? Why do they increase the fitness of the beetle? Why can horns be considered an adaptation? The selectionist explanation contends that the horns of male dung beetles allow the bearer to garner more resources, defend their nests, and compete for the best females, thereby reproducing more than the males without horns. For example, an article in the *Journal of Insect Behavior* describes an experiment providing evidence that males with larger horns get preferential access to females and thus can be considered adaptive. The same article also describes the adaptive value of *small* horns in some males. These males have greater mobility and can sneak around the larger males to mate with the females!

The first category of explanations for the dung beetle's horns—addressing the "how" question—are called proximate causes, and the second—addressing the "why" question—are ultimate causes. Proximate mechanisms explore immediate, physical influences on a trait. The history of the organism determines ultimate causes, specifically the role played by natural selection to favor one trait versus another.

To elaborate further, let's talk about sex.

Or more precisely, polyandry in the predatory mite species *Neoseiulus californicus*.[4] Polyandry implies multiple matings by the female of a species and is the opposite of polygyny, wherein a male succeeds in mating with multiple females. Bateman's principle, named after an English geneticist, argues for the prevalence of polygyny in the animal kingdom. He contended that since females invest much more in offspring than do males, they are the limiting factor over which males compete, leading to polygyny. However, polyandry is more widespread than Bateman believed; in many species, females are not just waiting around to get impregnated—they are actively scouting for multiple partners. And one of these species is the mite *N. californicus*.

But what drives this mite to become polyandrous when the dominant trend in the animal world is toward polygyny? Peter Schausberger and his colleagues tackled this question in a *PLoS One* article, and they came up with two different sets of explanations: one "proximate" and one "ultimate."

The scientists discovered that the ultimate cause of polyandry in *N. californicus* consists of both direct and indirect fitness benefits. Females that mated multiple times produced more offspring than females that mated just once, and these offspring also survived longer. As for the proximate cause, the authors identified a key one: first mating duration. If the females' first mating period was below a certain threshold (150 minutes), the likelihood of their continuing to seek male partners increased. The immediate cause of females seeking more sex was a lack of sex. Who says science is boring?

Ernst Mayr, one of the greatest evolutionary biologists of the twentieth century, proposed the proximate–ultimate duality in a landmark article titled "Cause and Effect in Biology" in the journal *Science* in 1961.[5]

Using the example of bird migration, he posed the following question: "Why did the warbler on my summer place in New Hampshire start his southward migration on the night of the 25th of August?" He proposed four causes for this migration. First, an ecological cause: The bird would starve if it stayed in New Hampshire for the winter. Second, a genetic cause honed over millions of years that induced the warbler to respond to external stimuli and gain selective advantage over warblers that did not migrate. Third, an internal physiological cause that propelled the bird to leave once the number of daylight hours dropped below a certain level. And last, an external physiological cause that was reflected in a sudden drop in temperature on August 25. The warbler was already physiologically ready for migration, and this sudden cold wave made it leave *that* day. Mayr called the first two explanations ultimate causes and the latter two proximate causes.

Problems of Proximate Focus

Among all the philosophical issues that we have imbibed from evolutionary biology, *recognizing* the difference between proximate and ultimate causes is right on top.

We want the businesses we own to increase in value over the long run. And the *only* way for this to happen is for the company to perform well over many years, preferably decades. Investment success may not correlate with business success for a day trader or short-term investor. But for us, the ultimate success of an investment is almost entirely dependent on the ultimate success of the business.

If you accept this premise, then as permanent owners, we should focus exclusively on the quality and performance of the business over the long run. And that is what we do.

However, this is easier said than done. In today's world of Facebook, Instagram, Reddit, Twitter, WhatsApp, and other soul-destroying inventions, it is not easy to escape the din of proximate noise that can drown out the desire to seek sources of ultimate success. When there is a specter of a Greek default, an announcement of reduced jobs growth in the United States, OPEC negotiations break down, the Federal Reserve hints that the days of low interest rates are over, or company revenue falls, stocks can fall. Similarly, a bullish projection by the International Monetary Fund (IMF) on world growth, the recapitalization of banks in China, the success of a new product launch, or the increased pace of vaccination for a global pandemic can lead to higher stock prices.

All these are proximate causes of price movement. And all are divorced from what could ultimately lead to the business success or failure—and hence a higher or lower market value—of a company. The question we investors don't ask often enough but should is relatively straightforward: Does this proximate cause have *anything* to do with the cause of ultimate business success?

The interesting thing about proximate causes is that they are almost always evident in screaming newspaper headlines and hyperventilating news anchors. Ultimate causes, thankfully, are way too dull for media coverage. Why "thankfully"? I will get to it.

The sections that follow describe four categories of proximate causes of share price gyrations: macroeconomic, market-related, thematic, and company-specific factors. This list is not exhaustive; there are way too many to count. But after reading this, I hope you will be able to spot a proximate cause when you encounter it.

Proximate Macroeconomic Causes

We live in an uncertain world. But it's actually worse than that. We live in an uncertain *hyperconnected* world. On balance, hyperconnectedness has benefited humanity. (I get to eat Norwegian salmon in Singapore.) My use of the adjective "worse" here is limited to the impact of hyperconnectedness on my community—that is, fund managers. Before I became an investor in 1998, if someone had told me that inflation or U.S. employment data would affect the stock price of a paint company in India, I would have concluded that that person had no idea what they were talking about. But this is precisely what happens.

On October 27, 1997, the Dow Jones Industrial Average suffered one of its largest single-day drops in history. It fell 554 points, or 7.2 percent. For the first time in its history, the New York Stock Exchange halted trading. All major world markets were affected: Hong Kong's Hang Seng fell 6 percent, the United Kingdom's FTSE fell 6 percent, the Australian market fell 7 percent, and Germany's DAX fell almost 6 percent. In short, if you were looking for a definition of financial panic, your search would have ended here.

The proximate cause of this mayhem? The spreading of the Asian financial crisis.[6] It had all started on July 2, 1997, when the Thai government floated the baht since it did not have the foreign currency to support the baht's peg to the U.S. dollar. The currencies of Indonesia, South Korea, Malaysia, and the Philippines also suffered precipitous declines. Many companies in these countries had borrowings in dollars, and these firms started defaulting on their payments.

Table 4.1 tracks the U.S. and UK market indices at the time, along with the stock prices of a few well-known businesses. The U.S. market decline is for October 27 (Monday) relative to October 24 (Friday). The UK market reacts to the U.S. market's movement with a day's delay owing to time difference; thus, the UK market data is for October 28 (Tuesday) relative to October 24 (Friday).

Every number in the first column is negative. Why? Why did Wal-Mart, a local U.S. business, and Boeing, a global enterprise, fall on October 27? And why did Thai bond defaults impact Unilever, which earned about 70 percent of its revenue and profits from the developed world in 1997, and BP, a global oil company?

Proximate paranoia confused with ultimate reality.

TABLE 4.1 U.S. and UK market indices after October 27, 1997

Index	October 27/28, 1997	After 6 months
U.S. market		
Dow	−7%	+25%
Wal-Mart	−6%	+57%
Citigroup	−11%	−7%
Boeing	−11%	+16%
Microsoft	−5%	−35%
Exxon	−7%	+26%
UK market		
FTSE 250	−6%	+23%
BP	−5%	+14%
Rolls-Royce	−4%	+29%
Diageo	−7%	+50%
Unilever	−8%	+40%
HSBC	−7%	+23%

The evidence is in the second column, which provides the index levels and stock prices six months after October 27, 1997. The Dow, as well as the FTSE, were up 25 percent, and the dramatic upward movement of companies like Wal-Mart, Diageo, and Unilever may have led to the firing of some fund managers who had pressed the panic button on October 27.

If you want to lash out at the fund management community for being impulsive and trigger-happy, go ahead. But please don't blame us for being inconsistent. Whenever the markets get excited about a macroeconomic event, the fund managers behave predictably by riding the proximate bandwagon of stock prices. And then they repent at leisure.

Fund managers have a Pavlovian reaction to macro or market data. Will interest rates be higher? Sell. Will inflation be lower? Buy. If the fiscal deficit shoots up? Sell. Or is it a buy? Most businesses should be (and are) relatively immune to short-term macro movements. As shown in table 4.1, their stock prices, for some inexplicable reasons, are not.

Some argue that for certain types of businesses—say, banks or financial companies that rely on lending and deposit-taking—interest rates should significantly impact long-term performance. Hence, interest rate movements should be proximate *and* ultimate causes of business performance. Let's look at the following data of stock price changes for three large Indian banks over twenty years from December 31, 1999, to December 31, 2019:

HDFC Bank	81x
ICICI Bank	33x
State Bank of India	16x

During these two decades, the Reserve Bank of India had increased or decreased interest rates more than fifty times.[7] Rates varied between 5 percent and 12 percent, with wild gyrations in between. More importantly, all these banks were subject to the *same* regime of interest rates and other macro factors. If you were an HDFC Bank shareholder, did it matter what the interest rate was, or at what pace the Reserve Bank of India changed it?

HDFC Bank's business, and therefore its stock price, did spectacularly well because of its CEO, Aditya Puri, one of the most outstanding leaders in Indian corporate history. In October 2020, *The Economist* called him the best banker in the world.[8] Interest rates, current account deficits, exchange rates, and other such esoteric measures did not get in the way of Puri achieving excellence.

I am not cherry-picking here. Over the long run, well-run businesses create a lot of value irrespective of the macroeconomic environment. Do we seriously think Amazon, JPMorgan, Michelin, Nestlé, Siemens, Tesco, Walmart, Zara, and other excellent businesses are held hostage to inflation and fiscal deficit? If the business and stock price performance of exceptional *companies* is immune to macroeconomic perturbations, aren't we, as *investors* in those companies, better off ignoring the economy?

There is another big problem with considering macroeconomic data while analyzing individual businesses. Let's confront this headache through the example of tires. There are many listed tire businesses in India, so it should be a happy hunting ground for us. Let's say the World Bank announces that India will grow its GDP by 8 percent next year. This seems like good news for the country. What about tires? Someone could argue that GDP growth will lead to an increase in personal wealth, which would lead to consumers buying more cars, and hence more tires.

Should we buy a tire business then? But wait. A sales increase is not the same as a *profit* increase. The primary raw material for tire companies is rubber, which accounts for about 60 percent of revenue. What if rubber prices shoot up in anticipation that Indian tire businesses will need to buy more rubber next year? This is getting way too complicated. You need a number-crunching analyst with a lot of computing power at their disposal.

Your super-smart analyst builds their 100-gigabyte Excel model after burning the midnight oil for a couple weeks and predicts that rubber prices will be benign. Whew. Should we buy a tire business now? Hold on. How do we know what strategy or tactics the dozen or so tire companies will employ in a favorable environment? What if one of the smaller companies decides to wage a price war to shore up market share? Some have done so in the past. Or what if the dominant player increases its advertising budget significantly by sponsoring international cricket tournaments?

Let's assume the same astute analyst predicts that no company will "misbehave." (This analyst is brilliant!) OK, are we ready to invest now? Not at all. How are we to know the relative growth of various tire segments that will ultimately impact overall industry profits? The truck segment is the largest and the least profitable, whereas two-wheeler tires are the most profitable but generate only a tiny fraction of industry revenue. Thus, if the truck tire segment grows faster than the rest of the tire market, the profits of tire companies may *decline.*

You ask the analyst to forecast segmental growth. After they have come up with the answer (again!), you go back to the drawing board. And now you are perturbed by an uncomfortable realization. Since tires are highly capital intensive, they can significantly impact the debt level of a business, which could affect its robustness and the stock price. How are you to predict which tire company will invest and how much? I know. Back to our resourceful analyst!

I could go on and on. But it gets worse (or better, if you are that smart analyst on overtime pay). Note that in the tire example, I have tried to predict the performance of a business by analyzing only GDP growth. But macroeconomic data encompass a much more comprehensive range of indicators such as employment level, exchange rate, inflation, government deficit, money supply, current account balance, and many more. How can we assess all these factors in the context of a tire business? And fund managers don't invest only in tires. Are we supposed to repeat this mega-exercise across the dozens of industries and hundreds of companies we track? Also, given the connectedness of the global economy, should we also incorporate the macroeconomic data of *other* countries into our decision-making?

Are we ready to give up now?

We have seen two problems with treating macroeconomic factors as critical proximate variables. First, we noticed that even big macro events (like the Asian financial crisis) are uncorrelated with longer-term stock price performance. Second, taking the example of the Indian tire industry, we concluded that using proximate economic data to assess industry and company performance is very hard, if not impossible.

The third problem with using economic data is the most obvious of all. No one knows anything. Okay, that is exaggerating a bit. But only a bit. Since even expert economists are abysmal at forecasting the economy, why should we investors squander our time giving it any importance?

I assume you will agree that an economist's most important task is to forecast a recession. This would enable the government to take the necessary steps to prevent widespread pain and suffering. In March 2018, the IMF published a working paper titled "How Well Do Economists Forecast Recessions?"[9] The authors compared real GDP forecasts with actual growth data for sixty-three countries from 1992 to 2014. They showed that while GDP contracted by an average of 2.8 percentage points during recessions, the consensus forecast from the year before the recession was a *growth* of 3 percent! Worse, even *during* the year of the recession, the average forecast was a contraction of 0.8 percent when the real contraction turned out to be 2.8 percent.

Prakash Loungani, one of the authors of this IMF paper, told *The Guardian* in an interview that according to his analysis, economists had failed to predict 148 of the last 150 recessions! "The record of failure to predict recessions is virtually unblemished," he said. One would have thought that with a greater volume of data, more computing power, and better algorithms, our ability to forecast would have improved over the years. Yeah, right. In the same *Guardian* article, Mark Pearson, the deputy director for employment, labour and social affairs at the Organisation for Economic Co-operation and Development in Paris, said, "We are getting worse at making forecasts because the world is getting more complicated." Way to go, Mark.

I know that many investors spend a lot of time poring over economic data. Maybe they have figured out a way to factor in exchange rate movement or the external debt levels of the country in their decision-making. I am unable to do so. I do not know how to translate *any* economic indicator into the prospects of a specific business.

We ignore *every* piece of proximate macroeconomic information. We do not believe these data help us assess the ultimate success or failure of a business. We have no economic advisers, we do not talk to economists at banks or brokerage houses, and we do not discuss any economic indicators in our team meetings.

Their weightage in our investment decision is a big zero.

Proximate Market-Related Causes

I don't fraternize with folks in the financial services industry to exchange ideas or information. However, when I started my investing career with Warburg Pincus in 1998, I spent a fair bit of time with fund managers and finance professionals connected with the Indian equity markets. I had a consulting background and wanted to understand the workings of the capital market and its participants. I thought I had a lot to learn. I was right, just not in the way I had imagined.

After just a couple months at Warburg, I could predict the exact words of a finance industry professional's greeting. It wasn't "How are you?" or "How's it going?" or just "Hello." It would almost always be "*Kya lagta hai?*" Translated from Hindi, in stock market parlance, this means "What do you think the market will do?" I remember being confused. Here I was, a novice trying to understand how the markets work, while this "expert" was seeking *my* opinion? Do they not know? It took me a while to conclude that they don't. No one does.

The previous section explained market decline owing to a proximate macroeconomic problem: the Asian financial crisis. Maybe you did not notice my sleight of hand—I claimed to know the cause of market correction. The fact is that I do not know why the markets corrected, but it *looked* like the crumbling of Asian currencies played a role. I had established a connection between the market movement and economic data, however spurious that connection may have been.

But there are many other occasions when the market moves because, well, it moves. Such is the nature of markets. The proximate causes of market movements are unknown, and in my view, unknowable. Let's go back to July 24, 2002. The Dow soared 489 points, the second-best point gain ever and the best percentage gain since 1987.[10] The reason? Even after reading many news articles, I am not sure. Anyway, according to various media sources, the rally was the result of congressional negotiators reaching some kind of an agreement on corporate fraud. Also, some executives who had been defrauding the cable company Adelphia were arrested. Whatever.

Let's now look at table 4.2 on markets and how stock prices in the United States and the United Kingdom reacted to this "great" news.

TABLE 4.2 U.S. and UK market indices after July 24, 2002

Index	July 24/25, 2002	After 6 months
U.S. market		
Dow	+6%	−2%
Wal-Mart	+6%	+2%
Citigroup	+10%	+16%
Boeing	+6%	−26%
Microsoft	+7%	+11%
Exxon	+10%	+1%
UK market		
FTSE 250	+1.5%	−14%
BP	+6%	−18%
Rolls-Royce	+2%	−31%
Diageo	+9%	−15%
Unilever	+7%	+6%
HSBC	+2%	−7%

As you can see, over the following six months, the Dow in the U.S. shrugged off the gains of July 24, 2002, and *declined* by 2 percent. The significant upward moves in the share prices of large companies like Wal-Mart, Citigroup, and Boeing could not keep pace with the euphoria of this one day. Boeing declined by a fourth over the next six months.

Even more remarkable is the behavior of the markets in the United Kingdom. You would have thought that the so-called corruption investigations in the United States should not affect the UK markets. Well, we fund managers never cease to amaze. The FTSE 250 went up by 1.5 percent the day after the U.S. markets moved up 6 percent, and the stock prices of large companies, as shown in the first column of table 4.2, shot up by 2 to 9 percent. These are not small moves for companies with large market values. The euphoria did not last. Just six months after the event, Rolls-Royce was down by almost a third, and BP and Diageo had declined by 15 percent or more.

Why did fund managers in the United Kingdom start piling on to BP, Rolls-Royce, and Diageo on July 25 after a huge increase in the U.S. indices on July 24? The explanation that comes to mind was offered by the great John Maynard Keynes when he opined that the stock market players were playing a complex guessing game.[11] He asked us to imagine a game in which competitors pick the six prettiest faces from one hundred photographs. The winner is not the one who picks the prettiest faces but whose choices match the average of all the competitors.

How would you play a game like this? My approach would be to *not* choose the six prettiest faces and instead spend my time guessing which six the *other* players will select. Before I were to start feeling smug about my second-level strategy, I would realize that a more insightful competitor would go a step further to a third level. They would try to guess what the average opinion expects the average beauty to be. And so on to even higher levels.

Keynes had learned from bitter experience that this market guessing game is a colossal waste of time. In the 1920s, he used a detailed economic model to predict market levels and failed to see the Great Crash of 1929. He also underperformed the market during this period. He switched to picking stocks and, like Buffett, eschewed diversification. He declared, "The right method of investment is to put fairly large sums of money into enterprises one thinks one knows something about."

No wonder he turned out to be an excellent investor. Keynes managed the endowment of King's College, Cambridge, from 1924 to 1946. During this twenty-two-year period, he compounded the college's wealth by almost 14 percent a year. If someone had invested £100 with Keynes at the start of 1924, it would have been worth about £1,675 at the time of his death in 1946. The same money invested in the UK stock market index would have been worth only £424. Astonishingly, this period included the Great Crash of 1929, the Great Depression, *and* the Second World War.

Should the financial world not have absorbed Keynes's insights? Ha!

December 2019 looked like any other December, and the Wall Street stock market strategists were at it again—forecasting market growth for 2020. Since the year 2000, the median Wall Street forecast has *never* predicted a stock market decline in the next year. Yes, you read that right. Not once did the forecasters believe that the stock market could go down. The reality? The market fell on six occasions. The median forecasts from the year 2000 to 2020 missed the actual number by 12.9 percent points—more than *double* the average annual increase of 6 percent over these years!

Back to December 2019. Remember that no one was aware of the COVID-19 pandemic then. The median consensus among the forecasters was that the market would rise by 2.7 percent in 2020.[12] If the forecasters had known then that a pandemic would rage across the world from March 2020 until December 2020, what do you think their forecast for 2020 would have been? We will never know, but I bet they would have predicted a huge fall in the market. In any event, the S&P 500 *rose* by 16.3 percentage points in 2020. But 2020's pandemic was a once-in-a-century event, and we should not hold it against the forecasters that they were wrong by 13.6 percentage points. Fair enough.

What if we assess the forecast of an acknowledged master forecaster from early May 2020? Only eight months of the year remain, the pandemic has been raging for four months, and the dire impact on the economy seems quite evident. I would think that an "expert" *could* go wrong at this stage but probably not by much.

Harry S. Dent Jr., called by some the "contrarian's contrarian," accurately predicted Japan's economic collapse, the dot-com bust in 2000, and the election of Donald Trump.[13] After receiving his MBA from Harvard Business School, he joined Bain & Company and now runs an independent research firm. He is a regular guest on CNBC, CNN, Fox, Fox Business, *Good Morning America*, and PBS. He has also been featured in *Barron's*, *Fortune*, *Business Week*, the *Wall Street Journal*, and many other publications. He also publishes a monthly newsletter called the *HS Dent Forecast*. In short, Dent embodies as much expertise as an expert can muster.

In early May 2020, in an interview with *ThinkAdvisor*, Dent predicted that the market would peak in August 2020 and that investors might be able to make a return of 5 to 10 percent. He advised them to "get out" and counseled against buying. How wrong was he? The market kept rising until December 31, and from the time of Dent's interview in early May, the S&P 500 rose 32 percent! Even if you take the highest number of 10 percent returns in Dent's band, that is an error of 22 percentage points over eight months. Or an annualized error of 33 percent. Oops.

Before you blame me for choosing a forecaster who turned out to be egregiously wrong, I challenge you to find me an expert who asserted in May 2020 that the market would be up by 25 to 30 percent by the end of December. I could not find one. Trust me, I tried.

To be fair, I have not met a single finance professional who claims that markets can be predicted. So why do industry players spend so much time obsessing over future market levels? Why do fund managers devote enormous time and effort obsessing over what *other* fund managers think and do? Flawed incentives, false comfort, one-upmanship, you name it. It doesn't really matter.

We ignore all market forecasts. Well, maybe not entirely.

I do look at them on days when I want to have a good laugh.

Proximate Thematic Causes

At the end of annus horribilis 2020, I realized I was wrong by $6 billion.

In early September 2020, Nikola was a stock market darling. The start-up had listed barely a year earlier at a valuation of $4 billion. Its value had since quintupled to almost $20 billion. Led by its charismatic founder, Trevor Milton, who was often compared to Elon Musk, Nikola was planning to develop semitrucks powered by hydrogen fuel cells and batteries. It had just announced a partnership with GM wherein the Detroit giant would get an 11 percent stake for $2 billion in return for a contract to engineer and build Nikola's semitrucks.

On September 10, 2020, a reputed investment fund and short seller called Hindenburg Research published a scathing report titled *Nikola: How to Parlay an Ocean of Lies Into a Partnership with the Largest Auto OEM in America.* The first line of the report states that Nikola was "an intricate fraud built on dozens of lies over the course of its founder and executive chairman Trevor Milton's career."[14]

In 2017, to prove that its technology worked, Nikola shared a video titled "Nikola One in Motion," which showed its prototype semitruck speeding along a road. Hindenburg claimed that the company had simply towed an ordinary truck to the top of a hill in a remote area and had filmed it rolling down the hill. After the report was published, Nikola felt compelled to acknowledge this fact by stating, "Nikola never stated its truck was driving under its own propulsion in the video." What?! What else was a speeding truck supposed to show? The road?

The revelation of this bare-faced lie was just the start of the lengthy report. Hindenburg's research unearthed several more problems. Nikola did not have a battery technology despite Milton's claims to the contrary; it did not possess hydrogen fuel cell expertise; Milton had a history of taking technology from others and then claiming it as his own; Milton also had a track record of troubled partnerships that ended in failure, lawsuits, and recriminations; and Milton had claimed that Nikola's corporate headquarters were completely off-grid and used 3.5-megawatt solar panels, though no headquarters existed. I could list many more damning assertions made by Hindenburg in its lengthy report, but suffice to say that the future seemed bleak for Nikola.

Trevor Milton resigned within a few days of the report, and GM ended its partnership discussions with the company. The Securities and Exchange Commission and the Department of Justice launched their own investigations. Unsurprisingly, the stock price started crashing.

Here is my question for you: What do you think Nikola's market value was at the end of December 2020, three months after the Hindenburg exposé? Remember that the company had no battery or fuel cell technology, had no prototype, its founder had exited ignominiously, GM had terminated the partnership, and the government had begun investigating fraud. My answer would be close to zero.

Nope. It was $6 *billion*!

The Hindenburg report appeared to be fact based: They backed up almost all their assertions with documents, photographs, text messages, videos, and interviews. I am in no position to double-check their research. However, the facts that Milton resigned and GM terminated the partnership seem to indicate that a reasonable portion—if not all—of the report was credible. If so, how does one explain a $6 billion valuation for a company like Nikola? That's an unfair question because I doubt anyone fully understands how companies are valued. But in this case, I want to offer a two-word answer.

Thematic investing.

The theme being "new-age automotive companies will rule the world." Automotive tech start-ups have been a rage since 2020.[15] According to an article in the *Financial Times* in January 2021, these companies had amassed a market value of $60 billion, but most had not generated a single dollar of revenue. And why didn't they have any revenue? Because, like Nikola, they didn't even have a product! The popular saying "fact is stranger than fiction" is tailor made for the valuation of new-age automotive start-ups.

The *FT* article names nine listed start-ups, the largest of which was QuantumScape, valued at $19 *billion*. This company projects its first revenue of $14 *million* in 2024. In 2028, just four years after generating its first revenue, the company expects to touch $10 billion revenue! As a matter of comparison, after recording its first revenue in 2008, Tesla took nine years to cross $10 billion. And remember that Tesla had the lion's share of the market in those years. The QuantumScape website proclaims that the company's mission is "to revolutionize energy storage to enable a sustainable future." Its investors range from blue-blooded venture capital firms like Kleiner Perkins and Lightspeed to car companies like Volkswagen and SAIC.

And there were many others. Hyliion's market value was $2.6 billion, and it was planning to manufacture hybrid trucks; Velodyne Lidar, $3.9 billion, sensing solutions for autonomous vehicles; Fisker, $4.1 billion, electric cars; Luminar Technologies, $10.1 billion, object detection technology; Canoo, $4 billion, electric vehicles. You get the picture.

A foolproof method of checking the interest level in a concept or theme is to analyze Google searches using Google Trends. If you do so for the term "electric vehicles" between January 2014 and January 2019 in the United States, you will see a relatively flat trend. However, between January 2019 and February 2021, interest in electric vehicles *quadrupled*. Now, check out the dates the companies just mentioned went public:

Nikola	June 2020
Velodyne Lidar	September 2020
Fisker	October 2020
Hyliion	October 2020
QuantumScape	November 2020
Canoo	December 2020
Luminar	December 2020

I don't know if the IPOs of these companies increased the interest level in the search term or whether the increased searches of "electric vehicles" were a leading indicator of public listings. Maybe they just fed each other in a positive feedback loop. Whatever the case may be, as you can see, there is a strong correlation between the theme of electric vehicles and the IPOs of these businesses—a classic example of a strong proximate mechanism at work.

In addition, in January 2021, there were at least eight to ten more private start-ups ready to go public, all with obvious-sounding names like Charge-Point, EVgo, Lightning eMotors, Lion Electric, and Motiv Power Systems. If the market value of the listed companies holds, I bet that in the next few years, there will be dozens more listed companies with this theme.

These companies, valued at billions, with not even millions in revenue, epitomize investment strategies based on proximate themes. Like almost every proximate theme before and since, the automotive tech theme has three properties. It hypes up total addressable market (TAM), is simple to understand, and is actionable.

First, TAM. Every theme I have encountered since the start of my investing career in 1998 plays on the enormous size of the addressable market. And the size is usually so large that it dwarfs the businesses currently operating in that industry or theme. No wonder it is usually the most salient proximate cause of a theme gone wild.

In March 2021, a UBS report touted the zero-emission trucking market as potentially $1.5 *trillion* in size, and current manufacturers and start-ups raced to grab dominance. Tesla, which did not manufacture trucks in March 2021, had revenue of "only" $32 billion in 2020.

In my experience, there is only one problem with chasing a proximate theme based on TAM. It's useless. It makes astrology-based forecasts look respectable. TAM is pointless because it does not tell us whether any *profits* will be made, and even if a business can be profitable, TAM is silent on *who* will make that moolah.

One of the largest TAMs is that of apparel and footwear.[16] The U.S. market for apparel and footwear is about $370 billion. It is also one of the hardest places to make money. The lack of robustness of this industry was also evident during the pandemic when scores of apparel and footwear companies declared bankruptcies: Brooks Brothers, Centric Brands, Century 21, G-Star, JCPenney, J. Crew, John Varvatos, Neiman Marcus, Tailored Brands, and many more. Someone forgot to tell these companies that their TAM would save them.

Even prepandemic, most apparel brands struggled to grow and make a decent income. Take the example of a well-known brand like Gap. It hasn't grown in the United States since 2007, with sales almost flat at $15 to $16 billion, and it achieved its peak net income of $1.3 billion back in 2014. Guess's revenue fluctuated between $2 billion to $2.6 billion between 2009 and 2020, and its

ROCE hasn't crossed 10 percent since 2016. Abercrombie & Fitch's revenue in 2006 was $3.3 billion, and it grew to only $3.6 billion by 2019. It, too, has not earned more than 10 percent ROCE since 2014.

The global market for apparel and footwear is about $1.9 trillion, a *colossal* TAM. But the only apparel companies that seem to consistently grow their sales and churn profits are H&M, Uniqlo, and Zara. Other industries like airlines, restaurants, infrastructure, banking, and retailing are the same. Their TAMs are quite high, but most industry players don't make any money. So what use is TAM to a long-term investor?

The second reason for the seductiveness of a proximate theme is its simplicity. Even a casual reader of business news will be aware of themes like e-commerce, renewable energy, electric vehicles, fintech, food delivery, artificial intelligence, self-driving cars, infrastructure, and biotech. Unlike economic forecasting, which is full of jargon like "GDP" and "monetary supply," a layperson can relate to themes. Anyone can understand what renewable energy is and that the country needs a lot more infrastructure investment. For the automotive tech start-ups, the simple argument goes as follows. Electric and autonomous vehicles will conquer the world, and since Tesla's market value is $700 billion, shouldn't this theme capture trillions of dollars of value in the near future? And if so, why shouldn't a start-up be valued at billions of dollars? The premise is seductive because it is straightforward.

Third, it is actionable. If you believe in the theme that consumers will order more food sitting at home because it is cheaper and easier than dining out, you can invest in DoorDash or Deliveroo. Are you interested in an electric vehicle company with actual revenues? Hail Tesla. Do you believe in the providers of technology rather than the car? Velodyne Lidar beckons. Do you think trucks are a bigger opportunity? Nikola is pining for you. Why does it matter that its founder was probably a charlatan?

I don't know where the theme of automotive start-ups will end up in 2025 or 2030. What I *do* know, based on the history of capital markets and new-age technologies like railways and the internet, is that this theme will face its comeuppance someday.

Many readers will (not fondly) remember the theme ascendant in the early 2000s that home prices will rise forever. Any bank or financial company riding this theme was rewarded with increasing stock prices. Now we know that home prices *don't* keep rising, and pricier homes bought with heavy borrowing need to fall in price only slightly for panic to set in. No one investing in the theme "homes are an unbeatable investment" could have imagined that the following marquee names would go bankrupt or need a huge bailout: Lehman (assets of $691 billion), Washington Mutual ($328 billion), CIT Group ($80 billion), Thornburg Mortgage ($39 billion), General Growth Properties ($30 billion), and several more.

The Indian market is no different. At various times since the start of my investing career in 1998, I have witnessed the following themes create and then destroy billions of dollars of value in the capital markets: real estate, infrastructure, education, microfinance, consumer lending, and technology services. In addition, until early 2022, on paper, the following themes have created (but not yet destroyed) a lot of value in Indian private markets: edtech, fintech, e-commerce, software-as-a-service (SaaS), logistics, and social media. Based on history, many of these concepts will crater; I just don't know which ones or when.

How should we separate the proximate causes from the ultimate ones when there is euphoria or bearishness in a theme? Unfortunately, I am not aware of a foolproof method for doing so. But here is what we do.

We define our unit of analysis clearly as the *company*. Not the economy, not the market, not a theme. We care about the *fundamentals* of the company— nothing else. We have never invested in a theme and never will.

Again, just to be clear, I am not implying that thematic investing is flawed. Maybe some fund managers can do it successfully.

We would if we could, but we can't, so we won't.

Proximate Company-Specific Causes

In December 2016, after almost three years of Vaibhav Global's continuous underperformance, for the first time we actively debated whether we should exit entirely. Were we confusing an ultimate cause for a proximate one?

Vaibhav is a retailer of low-priced jewelry and other accessories in the United States and the United Kingdom that sells through TV and the internet. One can shop at https://www.shoplc.com in the United States or https://www.tjc.co.uk in the United Kingdom. Please do—you will find its deals unbeatable. Vaibhav competes primarily with home shopping giants like QVC and HSN, as well as hundreds of other online and offline retailers.

We invested in Vaibhav in late 2007. After underwhelming performance for a few years, the company grew its revenue and operating profit at an annualized rate of about 30 percent from the year ended March 2011 to 2014. In July 2014, the stock price hit an all-time high of INR 174; our buy price was INR 48. Sunil Agarwal, the founder and CEO, had done a stellar job in recent years.

However, from April 2014, the company's sales and profits started falling primarily owing to three self-inflicted missteps. First, Vaibhav did not respond to a significant strategic move by competition in the United States. Every major competitor of Vaibhav had started offering customers an option to pay in installments. However, Vaibhav refused to follow in their footsteps. Sunil did not want to take an unnecessary financial risk. Also, Vaibhav's average sale price is only about $20 to $25 per piece compared to $50 to $100 for competition. Sunil thought that customers would not care about installments if they got a quality product at a low enough price. It turns out that they did.

Second, the company faltered in designing and implementing a robust technology platform. The company lagged behind all its peers on the quality of its customer-facing websites and apps. Even some of its back-end technology platforms (e.g., which helped decide which products to merchandise when) were outdated and inflexible. Vaibhav's internet sales accounted for 16 percent of company revenue, whereas this number was 51 percent for QVC. The company fired its head of technology, but the new leader was taking time to fix the problems.

Last, Vaibhav lost a few key senior managers. Sunil had fired some of them, but some had left for greener pastures. He was also finding it hard to attract quality talent to fill the vacancies.

From the year ended March 2014 to March 2016, sales fell by 2 percent, but profits declined by almost 70 percent. ROCE collapsed from 55 percent in 2014 to 13 percent in 2016. The stock market had reacted appropriately: Vaibhav's stock price was INR 54 in December 2016, a fall of almost 70 percent from its previous peak in July 2014.

We were now in a dilemma. Were these problems—a delay in responding to competition, the lack of a robust technology platform, a paucity of senior leaders—proximate causes of stock price decline? Or did these headaches reflect a more fundamental and long-term issue with the company? Were these issues "fixable," or should we abandon any hope of revival? We are permanent owners in businesses and do not sell unless there is irreparable damage to a business. Were these lapses temporary, or would the company be able to overcome this adversity?

As I have discussed in this chapter, we ignore proximate problems related to the economy, the market, and even the industry. But the dilemma is much trickier to address when the proximate cause of problems relates to the company itself. Suppose the sales growth and profitability of the company has declined in the past few quarters, whereas its main competitors showed no such struggle. How would you decide if the performance issues are related to proximate (and hence temporary) causes or ultimate (and hence more permanent) causes? In my experience, developing a method and an instinct to separate proximate and ultimate causes of failure or success when they relate to a *company* event is invaluable for a long-term investor.

I have been an investor for more than two decades, and this is where I stumble most often. As usual, at the extremes, the decision is straightforward. If the share price declines owing to a downturn in one or two quarters, we ignore the decline, considering it a proximate event. But if the decline results from a loss of market share for three years in a row, we ask if there is something fundamentally wrong with the business. It is the gray area in between these extremes that creates the worst headaches for us. I do not know of any foolproof method of cracking the conundrum; the answer is almost always very company specific.

Vaibhav was in this gray zone. Maybe the proximate issues indicated ultimate problems, but maybe they didn't.

We decided to stay with the business. Under Sunil's leadership, the company had performed exceedingly well until only three years earlier, and nothing had changed in the market since then. There were no new entrants, and customer behavior remained the same. More importantly, Vaibhav's competitive position of selling jewelry and accessories in the range of $20 to $25 remained intact even during the difficult years. None of its competitors was able or willing to match Vaibhav's value proposition. Also, as time passed, we saw Sunil taking timely steps to address the issues. Late in 2014, he started offering installment plans, which put a stop to customer attrition. Despite declining profits, he invested aggressively in building the technology team and infrastructure. Finally, as he promoted some internal staff to leadership positions instead of hiring from outside, we could discern some early signs of progress.

Luckily for us, Sunil and his team did turn the business around. Sales grew by 11 percent annually from the year ended March 2016 to 2020, but, more impressively, operating profits grew almost five-fold. ROCE jumped from 13 percent to 45 percent during this period, and the annual free cash flow almost quadrupled. The stock price jumped six-and-a-half-fold from INR 54 in December 2016 to INR 352 in September 2022.

Vaibhav may have turned out well for us (for now). But this was a touch-and-go decision. It could have gone either way. Our instinct to stay in business as permanent owners helped us stay the course. Most importantly, we got very lucky.

The Pain and the Gain of Headline Harassment

Let's go back to the question I raised at the beginning of the chapter. You have sunk $70,000 in a fund that is now worth $36,000. Everything the fund manager touches seems to be heading down. Apart from continuing to tear your hair out, what should you do?

Nothing.

At the end of the anecdote, the time was March 2009. If you had done nothing and continued to hold the fund, your $36,000 would be worth a little more than $770,000 at the end of September 2022. Which is a multiple of 21.4 times over 13.5 years. In comparison, the main stock index grew six-fold during these years.

As you may have guessed, this was not a hypothetical situation. I have described what transpired at Nalanda. What you see in the numbers I've given is the result of our aggressive buying during the global financial crisis of 2008 and its dramatic longer-term impact on the fund's performance. The only change you would need to make is to switch dollars to rupees.[17] Your patience would have paid. A lot.

As the Indian market started falling from March 2008, we started buying high-quality businesses, and we did not stop until early 2009. The further the market fell, the greater our buying frenzy was. In December 2008, the fund had delivered an annualized return (called the internal rate of return, or IRR, in investing parlance) of −55 percent (!), and we continued to invest as much as we could. The fund's annualized rupee return as of September 2022 was 20.3 percent (after payment of all fees and expenses).

What allowed us to invest when the world seemed to be coming to an end? We ignored all proximate causes of stock price decline and focused *exclusively* on the ultimate sources of success of a business. Let's walk through an example.

Our most successful investment to date is Page Industries. In October 2008, the company had a stellar track record of performance over more than a decade and was the number-one innerwear brand in the country. It had overtaken competitors that had started many decades before it entered India in 1995. Over the previous five years, the company had grown revenue at 32 percent per year and had earned 57 percent ROCE.

On October 7, 2008, three weeks after Lehman's collapse, we bought 8 percent of the company for INR 455 per share. This was a 23 percent *premium* to the prevailing stock price of INR 370 per share. We took a notional loss the very next day after our purchase. In fact, the stock price did not cross our buy price for six months, until April 2009. At the end of July 2022, Page was at INR 48,873, a multiple of 107 times our buy price. During this period, the Sensex went up 5.5 times.

Our view on Page and seven other businesses we bought during the financial crisis was that global events may affect the *stock prices* of high-quality companies but not their *business strength*; the fact that investors were dumping stocks was not a problem but an opportunity; businesses' market valuations may take a hit but not their *intrinsic* value; the opportunity cost of *not* investing in troubled times far exceeds any near-term pain owing to notional losses. Our success with Page is only partly the result of our aggression at a time of market panic; it is largely the result of our unwillingness to sell a great business at any price. But more on that later.

The title of section II of this book is "Buy High Quality at a Fair Price." This is a nice-sounding strategy but far from easy to implement in practice. The problem is that high-quality businesses are seldom available at a fair price. Markets are very efficient most of the time. However, when proximate causes get divorced from ultimate ones, markets can offer even great businesses at a fair price. We took full advantage of this temporary insanity to wade in all guns blazing. Our trailing twelve-month (TTM) PE multiple for buying Page? 18 times. Can you believe it?

This undeserved luck was the direct result of what I call "headline harassment." While we were busy buying stellar businesses in 2008 and early 2009, the following headlines (and others like them) appeared in the most widely read Indian business daily, the *Economic Times*[18]:

"Mark-to-Market Losses Worry India Inc." (July 18, 2008)
"Economic Activity Is Slowing Down Fast" (August 25, 2008)
"Financial Crisis: Are MNC Jobs Secure?" (September 26, 2008)
"Sensex, Nifty Hit New 2008 Lows" (October 16, 2008)
"Economic Recession, Lay-Offs Shift Balance of Power" (November 15, 2008)
"Why Did Sensex Crash from 20K to 10K?" (December 20, 2008)

It is common knowledge that lousy news attracts way more eyeballs than good news.[19] We may blame the media for this bias, but psychologists have shown that people prefer reading bad news and remember it better. The media simply exploit an existing prejudice. In an article titled "On Wildebeests and Humans: The Preferential Detection of Negative Stimuli" in the journal *Psychological Science*, researchers showed that subjects remembered negative words faster and more often than positive ones.[20]

In times of crisis, this predisposition gets a steroid boost. Imagine reading the newspapers and watching TV in the weeks and months surrounding the Lehman collapse—headline harassment would have taken its toll across the globe. No wonder wonderful businesses were finally available at a price we could not refuse.

In sharp contrast, there was no celebration of business as usual at the high-quality companies that were becoming part of our portfolio during this period. No headlines screamed, "WNS Processes Another Mortgage Application," "Triveni's Factory Manufactures Turbine Number 39 for the Year," "Page Industries Adds Two More Retailers Today in the City of Aurangabad," or "Carborundum Factory in Chennai Finishes Another Shift."

Earlier I wrote, "Ultimate causes, thankfully, are way too dull for media coverage." Now you know why.

There is one more important reason we could embrace a diametrically opposite attitude to that of many of our peers in 2008. We are fortunate to have long-term investors—primarily U.S. university endowments and U.S. and European family offices—who have supported our aggression when the world seemed to be coming to an end. Not even one investor defaulted on their commitment. No one (I hope) tore at their hair! I know that many private equity and hedge funds could not persuade their investors to commit more capital in 2008.

We were very fortunate.

* * *

I don't make predictions, but after the global financial crisis of 2008, I told myself that I was unlikely to witness the same degree of stock market panic for decades. I couldn't have been more wrong.

At the height of the COVID-19 pandemic dread, in March 2020, the Indian market fell 23 percent. We could not stop buying, and our investment in that *single* month was 12 percent more than in the previous four years *combined*. In sharp contrast, the foreign portfolio investors in India withdrew $8.7 billion from the Indian stock market in March 2020. We continued to be hyperactive until September 2020 and then had to stop because the prices of the businesses we were interested in had increased sharply. The total amount we invested in 2020 turned out to be more than one-third of our cumulative investments over the thirteen years from 2007 until 2019.

I don't know if we made the right decision. However, I *do* know that the proximate worries of impending doom for businesses like tires, enzymes, boilers, diagnostic services, vehicle lending, and sanitaryware were divorced from their ultimate causes of success. We had been tracking many of these companies for about a decade and had great confidence that they would overcome any short-term pain over the longer run. In any event, we will know soon enough.

2030 isn't far away.

Chapter Summary

Evolutionary theory has taught me that . . .

. . . we can reimagine investing by ignoring *proximate* causes of stock price movements while focusing on *ultimate* explanations of business success.

1. Evolutionary biology explores natural phenomena by searching for proximate and ultimate causes. Proximate mechanisms explain immediate influences on a trait. The role played by natural selection explains the ultimate cause of an organism's success or failure in an environment.
2. Thus, to understand the impressive size and variety of dung beetle horns, evolutionary biologists ask the proximate question (e.g., which network of genes was switched on?), as well as the ultimate question (e.g., what is the adaptive value of the horns?). Scientists understand that these are different types of questions with different types of answers and that both types must be asked.
3. The investing world, too, must differentiate between proximate and ultimate causes. Proximate causes of share price changes can result from the macroeconomy, the markets, the industry, or the company itself. Since proximate causes are highly salient (e.g., the Fed announcing an interest rate cut or a

company announcing a slowing of sales growth), investors may erroneously overweight them in their decision-making process.

4. We ignore all proximate causes when analyzing businesses. We focus exclusively on the business fundamentals, or the ultimate causes of the success or failure of businesses.

5. We were aggressive investors during the financial crisis of 2008 and the early days of the COVID-19 pandemic because proximate worries compelled the markets to overlook the ultimate causes of the success of many high-quality businesses.

CHAPTER 5

DARWIN ATE MY DCF

When we no longer look at an organic being as a savage looks at a ship, as at something wholly beyond his comprehension; when we regard every production of nature as one which has had a history; when we contemplate every complex structure and instinct as the summing up of many contrivances, each useful to the possessor, nearly in the same way as when we look at any great mechanical invention as the summing up of the labour, the experience, the reason and even the blunders of numerous workmen; when we thus view each organic being, how far more interesting, I speak from experience, will the study of natural history become!

Charles Darwin, On the Origin of Species, *chapter 15, "Recapitulation and Conclusion"*

We prefer demonstrated consistent earning power (future projections are of little interest to us, nor are "turn-around" situations).

Warren Buffett, annual letter to shareholders, 1982

It was a once-in-a-lifetime opportunity for a trip around the world. But there was a significant hurdle.

The twenty-two-year-old man had arrived home late in the night and had been surprised to find a large envelope addressed to him. It contained two letters. One was from his college tutor and the other from his favorite teacher, Reverend John Stevens Henslow. The first informed him that a two-year voyage around the world would start in a month, and the second tried to persuade him to accept the offer.

The cost of the trip was not an issue for the young man's wealthy father, Robert. The problem was that the young man had already changed his profession twice and showed no signs of settling down; he knew that his father was frustrated with him. Robert considered his son's excitement at the global voyage as evidence of his preoccupation with entertaining but wasteful pursuits. Also, Robert demanded, why on Earth was the young man being offered a "naturalist" post on this voyage when he was qualified to be a priest? The whole scheme appeared dubious. The young man's three sisters, Susan, Caroline, and Catherine, agreed with their father, Robert, to make matters worse. With deep sadness, he declined the offer.

The next day, he carried a sealed letter from Robert to his uncle Jos. Jos was a close friend and confidant of Robert. In the letter, Robert wrote that his son's obsession with navigating the world was a mistake but added, "If you think differently from me, I wish him to follow your advice."

Fortunately for the young man, Jos disagreed with Robert and wholeheartedly supported the voyage. In his letter back to Robert, Jos argued that the trip would build the young man's character, and, far from being a waste, it would do him a lot of good. Jos's clinching argument was that the young man would be better prepared for the Church because, after all, "Natural history . . . is very suitable to a clergyman." Robert gave his permission.

On December 27, 1831, on a beautiful sunny morning, the *Beagle* lifted anchor from Plymouth. Charles Darwin's global circumnavigation would take him to Brazil, Argentina, Uruguay, Chile, Peru, New Zealand, Australia, Mauritius, Madagascar, South Africa, and the Galápagos Islands. The *Beagle*'s voyage would last five years.

It would change the young man. It would change science. It would change the world.

An Overlooked Reason for the Underperformance of Fund Managers

We encountered two harsh realities in the introduction to this book: About 90 percent of fund managers cannot beat the market, and their performance has worsened over time.

Why do fund managers underperform?

Talk to a dozen insiders, and you will get a dozen different reasons for this sorry state. One oft-repeated complaint is the misalignment of incentives for the fund manager. The fund management company gets paid based on the *size* of the fund, not on its *performance*. But over the long term, many researchers have found that an increase in fund size can lead to declining performance. For example, in a study published in 2009 in the *Journal of Financial and Quantitative Analysis*, an analysis of actively managed funds in the United States from 1993 to 2002 demonstrated a "significant inverse relation between fund size and fund performance."[1] Similarly, in a 1996 article in the journal *Financial Services Review*, the authors write, "Once large, equity funds do not outperform their peers."[2] They go on to advise investors to invest in smaller funds.

In some ways related to the problem of misaligned incentives, another reason fund managers underperform is that funds don't like to underperform the market. Yes, ironic, isn't it? In their attempt not to underperform the market, funds end up underperforming! Here is how. For simplicity's sake, let's assume there are ten stocks in an index, each with a weight of 10 percent. If the fund invests $100 in the market, with $10 invested in each business, it has perfectly replicated the index. In such a case, its active share is said to be zero. If the fund invests in none of these stocks, its active share is 100 percent.

Thus, active share is a measure of the courage and conviction of fund managers. Those unwilling to risk their careers, but happy to compromise returns for their investors, have a low active share. The daring ones willing to stick their necks out and not mimic the index have a high active share.

In a 2013 *Financial Analysts Journal* article, the author, Antti Petajisto, calculates the active share of 1,380 mutual funds in the United States in 2009 and concludes, "The performance of closet indexers has been predictably poor."[3] He also points out that funds with a high active share add value for investors. Of the mutual funds he examined, only 44 percent had an active share of more than 80 percent.

Have you heard the saying that no one gets fired for hiring IBM? Something similar seems to be going on in the fund management industry. If a fund manager has a low active share, they are unlikely to get beaten by the market by a significant margin, and since everyone else is in the same boat, their risk of getting fired is relatively low. At least one thing fund managers have learned from herbivores in the wild is that there is safety in numbers.

There are many other reasons for fund managers' underperformance. For example, poor performance also correlates with higher portfolio turnover, owning stocks with greater liquidity, investing in growth stocks, higher expense ratios, and many other factors. You can find all these and many more reasons for the dismal performance of fund managers in numerous research articles in prestigious finance journals.

What you will *not* find in these articles is the crux of this chapter. I believe a crucial reason for the continued underperformance of fund managers is their focus on *future* rewards while ignoring the treasures of the *past*.

We at Nalanda pursue the profession of investing the same way evolutionary biologists do: We interpret the present in the context of history. Evolutionary biology does not make predictions as physics and chemistry do. Nor do we. Instead, our investment approach attempts to explain the present by interpreting what occurred in the past.

In an essay on the theory of evolution, the late Harvard paleontologist Stephen Jay Gould wrote, "The present becomes relevant, and the past, therefore, becomes scientific, only if we can sum the small effects of present processes to produce observed results."[4] He could have been writing about the way we invest.

"How Extremely Stupid Not to Have Thought of That"

Let's join the young Charles Darwin, who has embarked on a life-altering journey aboard the *Beagle*.[5] Although Darwin attained fame as a zoologist and botanist, he boarded the *Beagle* as an enthusiastic geologist. Darwin's first foray as a scientist was with his professor Adam Sedgwick when they tried to map the geology of Northern Wales in the summer of 1831. He concluded after this trip that "science consists in grouping facts so that the general laws or conclusions may be drawn from them." At the end of the *Beagle* expedition, he had 368 pages of zoology notes compared to 1,383 pages of geology notes.[6]

The famous geologist Charles Lyell was a great inspiration to Darwin. He took the first volume of Lyell's book *Principles of Geology* with him on the *Beagle*. He received the second volume later in the voyage and read the third after his return home. Lyell was a strong proponent of Uniformitarianism as the core tenet of geology; Darwin would later adopt it as a guiding principle of his evolutionary theory. Uniformitarianism claims that all significant changes on Earth result from slow and steady natural processes operating over millions of years.

As a result of his interest in and exposure to geology, Darwin was preprogrammed to conceptualize very long periods unimaginable to most humans. He was the first to comprehend the importance of deep time in evolution. He wrote, "I always feel as if my books came half out of Lyell's brain, and that I have never acknowledged it sufficiently. . . . I have always thought that great merit of *Principles* was that it altered the whole tone of one's mind."

Darwin wrote more than twenty-five books,[7] and hundreds more have been written about him and his oeuvre. We can't cover even a fraction of his genius here. In this chapter, I want to focus on only one aspect of his method, which is evident in his groundbreaking book *On the Origin of Species*: his focus on *historical* information to make deductions about *ongoing* evolutionary processes.

Darwin proposed not one, not two, but *three* revolutionary theories in *Origin*: natural selection, sexual selection, and common ancestry. Let's briefly see what these theories are and how he used history in all of them to arrive at his radical explanation of all organic life.

First, let's discuss his best-known theory: natural selection.

In my layperson's view, the reason Darwin's crowning achievement—the theory of natural selection—was not discovered earlier and remained unaccepted by many stalwarts during and after his lifetime was that few understood the powerful effect of small changes accumulated over very long periods of time. But for those who understood the relevance of history, the theory was so powerful and straightforward that the famous biologist Thomas Huxley remarked, "How extremely stupid not to have thought of that."[8]

Natural selection requires three key ingredients.[9] First, there needs to be random *variation* among the progeny of an organism. Note the word "random." Variation does not seek any goal. Second, there needs to be *differential fitness* among these variants such that injurious variations get rejected and favorable ones are preserved. Last, the favorable traits must be *heritable* so that they are passed on to the next generation. Then, these three elements repeat ad infinitum over millions, even billions, of years. Resulting in a pangolin from a protozoan. In Darwin's own words, "This preservation of favorable individual differences and variations, and the destruction of those which are injurious, I have called natural selection."

Let's look at giraffes to understand Darwin's insight. They are members of the order Artiodactyla and diverged from the other members—cattle, antelope, deer, and sheep—about thirty-four million years ago.[10]

An ancestor of the current giraffe may have given birth to a baby with a slightly longer neck owing to a random mutation. There was no reason for this mutation; the animal was *not* looking to grow a longer neck. It just happened.

This long-necked creature may have had better nutrition on reaching adulthood than its herbivore competitors because it could reach taller trees to eat more succulent shoots and leaves. Better and more food could have made this giraffe healthier and more robust, helping it evade predators. Consequently, it could have mated more frequently and produced more offspring than its shorter-necked competitors. These offspring would generally have had long necks, but neck length would have varied. The longer-necked ones would be likely to have better nutrition, be subject to lower predation, and have more mates than their shorter-necked siblings. And because long necks are heritable (Darwin did not know that genes are responsible for heredity, but he knew that *something* was), some of the offspring of *these* longer-necked giraffes would also have had longer necks and continue to be more advantaged than their shorter-necked siblings and competitors, generation after generation.

This arms race for long necks has gone on for millennia, and voilà, we have the current-day giraffe.

Darwin collated a vast range of historical clues to arrive at his theory of natural selection, and this is not the place to list all of them. So instead, let me share just a few.

Darwin was a creationist when he started his journey aboard HMS *Beagle*. "Whilst on board the *Beagle*, I was quite orthodox," he writes in his autobiography.[11] At Cambridge, Darwin had studied the books of Reverend William Paley, who had made the famous watch analogy to prove the existence of God.[12] Paley's argument ran as follows. He asserted that if someone were to find a watch with all its complex machinery lying on the ground, one would conclude that someone knowledgeable had produced it. The various parts of the watch, working in perfect unison, could not have been assembled by accident. Hence, Paley argued that since nature is infinitely more complex than a watch, we must conclude that an intelligent designer is behind the universe's creation.

As Darwin sailed around the world observing nature, collecting specimens, and writing copious notes, he started harboring doubts. Then, in 1832, he found his first fossil remains in an Argentinian bay called Punta Alta. The fossilized thigh bone and teeth seemed to be from an extinct giant sloth.

Georges Cuvier, the founder of paleontology, showed that the earth had witnessed many extinction episodes and presented two indisputable facts.[13] First, the fossil remains of the past have no living peers; second, the older the fossil, the greater the divergence from living species. However, Cuvier explained these facts by invoking God, claiming that God repopulated the earth with new species after each extinction.

If this were so, Darwin wondered, why would today's sloths have a very similar bone structure to the extinct sloths of the past? If God had created them independently, why did the extinct giant sloth and the currently living sloth species appear related? He found many more fossils during the voyage, and the question continued to trouble him.

One of the core tenets of creationism is that God populated similar plants and animals in comparable climatic and physical environments. But Darwin discovered that this wasn't so. The creatures on the tropical Galápagos Islands did not resemble the flora and fauna of the tropics elsewhere in the world. Instead, they seemed closely allied with the organisms on the mainland of South America. As he wrote in *Origin*, "The most striking and important fact for us is the affinity of the species which inhabit islands to those of the nearest mainland, without being actually the same."[14]

Darwin's ornithologist friend, John Gould, informed him in March 1837 that twenty-five of the twenty-six birds from Galápagos were endemic to the islands and found nowhere else.[15] Creationism's contention had always been that God created species individually and that all species remained unchanged following their creation.[16] But then, how did one explain the diversity of the Galápagos bird species? All were similar to, but also quite different from, mainland species. Darwin reached a much different conclusion: that a species of bird from the mainland had accidentally arrived on Galápagos eons ago and had then diverged into many species occupying different niches.

To me, one of the best examples of Darwin's remarkable ability to view history in a new light is his discussion of domestic pigeons in the first chapter of *Origin*. He studied the pigeons closely for many years. He bought every breed he could lay his hands on and reared them himself. He also procured pigeon skins from as far away as Persia. He made friends with many well-regarded London breeders and joined two pigeon clubs. Pigeons were big business in nineteenth-century England, and they obsessed Darwin as well.

Over six pages of *Origin*, Darwin outlines the distinctiveness of various breeds. He starts, "Compare the English carrier and the short-faced tumbler, and see the wonderful difference in their beaks, entailing corresponding differences in their skulls." Next, he described various breeds' diversity of beaks, sizes, shapes, colors, and flight patterns. Like most naturalists of the era, he believed that all these varieties had descended from an ancestral rock pigeon (*Columba livia*). In *Origin*, he also provides ample evidence for this belief.

His friend Professor Lepsius had informed Darwin that humans had been domesticating pigeons for thousands of years—there were records of pigeons in the fifth Egyptian dynasty in 3000 BCE. Pigeons also had high prestige and monetary value in the time of the Romans and Mughals in India. It was evident that humans had altered pigeons over many years to suit their unique tastes. He called this phenomenon "artificial selection."

And then he took the bold leap that no one else had taken before him. He asserted, "Slow though the process of selection may be if a feeble man can do much by his powers of artificial selection, I can see no limit to the amount of change, to the infinite beauty and infinite complexity of the coadaptations between all organic beings, one with another and with their physical conditions of life, which may be affected in the long course of time by nature's power of selection."[17]

If humans could alter pigeons drastically, given the immensely long time at its disposal, why couldn't nature vary organic beings to create the diversity we see today? It may seem blindingly obvious to us, but no naturalist had connected the *artificially* created variety of breeds of pigeons, dogs, or plants to the ubiquitous *natural* heterogeneity of the natural world.

The Puzzle of the Peacock's Tail

Darwin's second bold conjecture in *Origin* was sexual selection.

"The sight of a feather in a peacock's tail, whenever I gaze at it, makes me sick," Darwin wrote.[18] He felt that a male ornament like the resplendent peacock's tail contradicted the theory of natural selection because it was a handicap to the peacock's survival. Why would a peacock evolve to endanger its chances of a long life? Darwin concluded that the currency of natural selection is not just survival but *reproduction.*

Any character trait that allows an animal to produce more offspring is a winner in the long run because *those* offspring, in turn, are able to produce more of themselves. A peacock with a showier tail will attract more peahens to sire more offspring over his lifetime. Consequently, there would be a race for even more elaborate tails. In *Origin* he writes, "This form of selection depends, not on a struggle for existence in relation to other organic beings or to external conditions, but on a struggle between the individuals of one sex, generally the males, for the possession of the other sex." Male peacocks struggle with each other through the beauty of their tails. The struggle is not for existence but sexual partners.

Darwin also shocked his Victorian-era readers by giving agency to the females, contending, "I can see no good reason to doubt that female birds, by selecting, during thousands of generations, the most melodious or beautiful males, according to their standard of beauty, might produce a marked effect." He was claiming that the beauty of the peacock's tail was under the control of the peahens. It was the peahens who arbitrarily decided the aesthetics of a tail.

Sexual selection is not limited to birds, of course. Like generations of naturalists before him, Darwin observed male stags, cocks, beetles, and predatory species fight aggressively over females. "A hornless stag or spurless cock would have a poor chance of leaving numerous offspring," he rightly pointed out. He compared male appendages like a lion's mane or the hooked jaw of a salmon to a sword or spear. A stag with unwieldy horns may be easier fodder for a lion but would end up fathering many more offspring than a stag with unimpressive horns.

Just as with natural selection, Darwin formulated his theory of sexual selection by examining well-established facts in a new light.

We Are One

Darwin's third assertion of common ancestry in *Origin* was his most significant intellectual leap in my layperson's view.

In his words, "I believe that animals have descended from at most only four or five progenitors, and plants from an equal or lesser number. Analogy would lead me one step further, namely to the belief that all animals and plants have descended from some prototype." Many Victorians did not even accept that Black and White *humans* descended from a common stock, and here was Darwin claiming unity across disparate *species*.

Chapter 14 of *Origin* presents copious evidence to bolster his claim that most species have evolved from very few common ancestors. He called this phenomenon "descent with modification." He starts by pointing out the obvious: Organic beings are nested within groups.[19] The hierarchy levels, in ascending order, are as follows: species, genus, family, order, class, phylum, and kingdom.

Thus, dogs are the species *Canis familiaris* and belong to the genus *Canis*. When grouped with wolves and jackals, they belong to the family Canidae. When Canidae is grouped with other families like Felidae (cats), Ursidae (bears), Mustelidae (weasels), and many others, we get to the order Carnivora. Carnivora brackets along Cetacea (whales and dolphins), Perissodactyla (horses, tapirs), Sirenia (dugongs), Lagomorpha (rabbits), and others to form the class Mammalia. Mammalia, Amphibia, and other classes merge to form the phylum Chordata. Chordates, mollusks, nematodes, and numerous other phyla cluster to create the kingdom Animalia.

Carolus Linnaeus, the Swedish botanist, laid the groundwork for this classification system in 1735 in *Systema Naturae* (*The System of Nature*).[20] Naturalists had made mutually exclusive divisions before Linnaeus; his genius was to see all of life as a nested hierarchy. Linnaeus was a highly devout man and believed that nature's hierarchical system resulted from God's plan. Amazingly, the modern organization of the living world follows Linnaeus's system with only a few modifications.

As you can see, there seems to be a particular *natural* order to this system; dogs appear rightly classified along with jackals; Canidae and Felidae are at the same level of family; and how else does one group horses and dugongs except under the class of mammals? But, as Darwin writes in chapter 14 of *Origin*, "Some deeper bond is included in our classifications than mere resemblance. I believe that this is the case, and that community of descent—the one known cause of close similarity in organic beings—is the bond, which though observed by various degrees of modification, is partially revealed to us by our classifications."

Darwin was making a strikingly original argument. The classification system seems right to us because it reflects the path of evolution of all living beings on Earth. Linnaeus demonstrated that all organic life is connected. He credited God for this natural order; Darwin concluded that it could be so only if all organisms had one or just a few common ancestors.

Darwin provides two additional pieces of proof of common ancestry. First, the early-stage embryos of seemingly unrelated groups like mammals, birds, and reptiles resemble one another so closely that it is hard to distinguish between them. I guarantee that the similarities in figure 5.1 will floor you. It is almost impossible to distinguish the five species in the figure when they are in

Human	Chicken	Turtle	Salamander	Fish

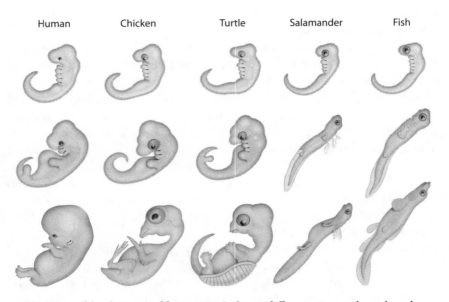

5.1 The stages of development of five species. Is there a difference among the early embryos of a fish, a turtle, and a human?

Source: Licensed from iStockphoto (Getty Images).

the early embryonic stage. In a later stage of development, a salamander resembles a fish, and a human looks like a turtle. Why should this be so? "Thus, community in embryonic structure reveals community of descent," Darwin writes.

Second, he offers rudimentary organs as evidence of the kinship of ancestral and living forms. By "rudimentary organs," Darwin meant vestigial organs that persist in an organism but have lost their function. He offered many examples: mammaries in male mammals, fused and useless wings in beetles, gills in the land-dwelling tadpoles of the common salamander, teeth in the upper jaw of calves that never cut through the gums, and rudiments of hind limbs and a pelvis in boa constrictors. Darwin opined that formerly functional parts might become vestigial if they aren't used. Ergo, vestigial body parts establish a direct line between organisms and a distant common ancestor. A tadpole that breathes on land but has useless gills should have a common ancestor with waterborne animals. The hidden hind limbs in a boa constrictor unite it ancestrally with animals that have legs; fused wings in beetles show that it has descended from an ancestor that gave rise to insects with wings, and so on.

Darwin was right, of course. Scientists have concluded that our last universal common ancestor (LUCA) arose somewhere between 3.5 and 4 billion years ago.[21] LUCA then gave rise to the six significant kingdoms of life: animals, plants, fungi, protists, eubacteria, and archaea. Although Darwin wasn't aware of four of these six kingdoms, I find it staggering that he still arrived at the correct conclusion. What a genius.

Investing as a Historical Discipline

The investment profession invites soothsayers of all kinds. Some are shady, but most are well-meaning professionals who expend enormous energy pontificating over the future. We aren't one of them.

I want to clarify an important point before we march ahead. Darwin and his theories are incomparable. In my view, no scientist comes close to him in greatness; maybe only Einstein, but probably not even him. When I compare Darwin's scientific process to what we do, I do it with full knowledge that it is markedly worse than comparing a gargantuan apple with a tiny orange. In the broad scheme of things, I think we financial investors are irrelevant to this world. Darwin wasn't.

Back to the lessons from Darwin. Like Darwin:

- We interpret the present *only* in the context of history.
- We see the same set of historical facts as everyone else.
- We have no interest in forecasting the future.

We study the history of a business to understand its financials, assess its strategies, gauge its competitive position, and finally assign value to it. So let's take them one by one.

Understanding the Financials of a Business

Those of you in the financial industry must have seen analyst reports. However, if you aren't a finance professional or haven't seen an analyst report before, here is a brief description. The brokerage firms (like JPMorgan, Morgan Stanley, and Goldman Sachs) employ research analysts who, as the name suggests, perform detailed research on publicly listed businesses and publish reports for their clients, the investors. A typical analyst report describes a company's business and financials, expresses its overall strategy and direction, and recommends that the clients buy, hold, or sell the business. Depending on the brokerage, the analysts use a wide variety of phrases—"underperform," "overweight," "accumulate," "neutral," and other esoteric terms—to make their recommendations. Still, their recommendations essentially fall into the buy, hold, or sell category.

Along with business commentary, most analyst reports typically carry the profit-and-loss account and the balance sheet of the latest fiscal year and financial projections for the next two to five years. In many of these reports, you will not find the financials of the past two to three years, let alone the last five to ten years. If you are keen to know the company's revenue growth over the past five years, the long-term historical trend of margins, or how ROCE and free cash flow have fluctuated over a decade, you are on your own.

As I write this, I have in my hand analyst reports from five brokerages for Tata Consultancy Services, India's largest technology services business with a market value of about $150 billion. They all have financial projections for the next two to three years and actual financials for the past year. Only one provides three-year historical financials. None has a five-to-ten-year financial history.

An actual incident will illuminate the reason for this state of affairs. Three of us were visiting one of our portfolio companies a few years ago. We met with the CEO and CFO for about an hour or so. As we were about to depart, the CFO received a call on his mobile phone, got visibly upset at the caller, and exclaimed, "I can't say anything; the results will be out after a few weeks." It turns out that the caller was a well-known investor who was checking to see how the quarter was progressing on the revenue and profit front.

If investors hound the company management for following quarter results, wouldn't they do the same with research analysts? So why should the analysts bother with longer-term history? Analysts produce forecasts because their clients demand they produce forecasts. I am sure many of them know it is a futile exercise. Here is why.

Let's say I need to project the following year's financials. I will need to forecast at least ten (if not more) numbers ranging from units sold, price per unit, cost of goods sold, sales expenses, receivables, capital expenditure, and so on. Let's assume that I am a great guesser and that I will correctly guess each of the ten numbers with a 90 percent probability. Hence, the chance of guessing all ten numbers correctly for next year would be only 35 percent (0.90^{10}). One may quibble that not all ten are independent variables, so we should not multiply them. True, but the number of variables is much greater than ten, and they are all at least semi-independent. Whichever way you evaluate the probability of guessing the next year's financials correctly, it is probably worse than guessing heads or tails after tossing a coin.

But this was only for next year. I also need to project for the following year and the year after that. How accurate do you think my estimates will be?

The *only* financials we prepare are for the past decade or more. Our financial trackers have no projections. Instead, we use the *same* factual financial information to which everyone else has access. Not unlike Darwin.

In developing his theories, Darwin did not have special access to any confidential data or information. The *Beagle* trip did expose him to new lands and creatures, but he did not make any discoveries. During the five-year trip, Darwin did collect 1,529 species in spirits and 3,907 samples of skin, bone, and other specimens.[22] But in all my research, I did not get the sense that he had stumbled upon anything significant unknown to science.

There were occasions when experts enlightened Darwin with *new* facts about the specimens he had collected. For example, in 1845, Darwin's botanist friend Joseph Hooker identified more than 200 plant species collected by Darwin and his team on Galápagos.[23] About 150 of these were unique to single islands, but they were also related to plants on other islands that weren't found anywhere else on Earth. Some plant ancestors, like those of the birds, had accidentally arrived on Galápagos a long time ago and had diversified into many species over time by adapting to the local environment.

Ornithologists and naturalists had been observing the mating rituals of peacocks for centuries, but no one else had given agency to the *female* for selecting male feathers. Even amateur ornithologists knew that only the male birds were adorned gorgeous plumage and that the diversity of size, shape, and color of feathers was truly staggering across all bird species. But no ornithologist interpreted their observations in the light of sexual selection the way Darwin did.

Similarly, Linnaeus's *Systema Naturae* was no secret. Its botanical classification system based on male and female sexes of plants had built Linnaeus's reputation and fame. Linnaeus modified his sexual classification system of plants in his subsequent publication, *Genera Plantarum*. *Genera* classified plants based on what he called the "natural characters" of the genera: the morphological traits of flowers and fruits. However, neither he nor anyone else could explain the source of this natural order except to claim that it was God's plan. Eighty years after Linnaeus's death, Darwin finally explained this natural order by invoking his theory of common descent.

As you can see, in every case, Darwin had the same historical facts as everyone else. It was only his *interpretations* that were radically new and different. I would like to believe our approach is no different.

If we don't forecast financials, what do we do with historical numbers? A lot. As permanent owners, we are incredibly paranoid about the financial performance of our businesses. So here is the way we use historical financials to assess our portfolio companies.

Let me take the example of Berger Paints, India's second-largest paint business. We have owned Berger since 2008. When Berger declares its quarterly results, we perform two broad historical analyses: absolute and relative.

For example, why has revenue growth declined to 10 percent over the past year compared to its longer-term average of 15 to 16 percent? What could be the reasons for high margins for the third year in a row? Has the company started spending less than usual on sales and marketing? What has led to a significant decline in receivables this quarter? Is the capital expenditure over the past year higher than usual? What has driven the increase in ROCE over the last two years versus the five years before?

We don't stop at analyzing Berger's results in the context of its long-term history. As permanent owners, we want to invest in a business that performs well on a *relative* basis; that is, one that performs better than the overall competition. We compare Berger's quarter, last twelve months, and longer-term performance against the competition on parameters like revenue and profit market share, ROCE, and free cash flow, among many others. We track Berger primarily against four competitors: Asian Paints (the industry leader), Kansai Nerolac, Akzo Nobel, and Indigo. In addition, we seek market feedback on smaller or private businesses that may have started growing aggressively. This competitive analysis through the financials can lead us to ask if Berger has lost or gained market share this quarter and last year. What has driven Kansai's increased revenue share over the past two years? Who is gaining the most from Akzo's share loss? Has Indigo been able to expand outside Kerala? What is the trend in Berger's advertising expenses relative to its competitors?

As you can see, there is a lot we do with historical financial information. What I have outlined here are the sample issues we raise for a portfolio company. The analysis is no different when evaluating a new business. We demand stellar absolute and relative financial performance based on any potential investment's actual financial track record.

Why fritter away time making useless forecasts with so much to do with the historical information we already have?

Assessing the Strategies of a Business

"Strategy" is a loaded word. For our purpose, let me just define it as "whatever companies do to achieve their goals under conditions of uncertainty." Purists will quibble on the definition of "tactics" versus "strategy." Let them. As folks investing real money, we can move on to more practical problems.

By now, I assume you can "predict" what I am about to write! Yes, we assess *historical* strategies to understand businesses. A small sample of strategic issues we focus on: Which customer segments have you targeted? How have your products or services served the needs of customers? In what ways have you been different from the competition? How have you allocated capital historically? What has been your capital structure, and why?

Two things may be evident to you as you read these questions: They are about the company's strategic steps in the past, and these are issues that even a first-year undergrad could raise. What's so great about these questions? Nothing. We ask these questions not to evaluate the answers objectively but to subjectively assess if they fit our *preexisting hypotheses* of success or failure. Yes, we know the answer we want before we have asked the first question.

If we have done a decent job over many years, it is not a result of asking these mundane questions but because our underlying bias demands the answers fit our template. We have our templates for success and failure, and we aim to assess if the company's strategy fits a pattern. Very few do—more on this in chapter 6.

This approach is not very different from Darwin's, who famously wrote in a letter to one Henry Fawcett in 1861, "How odd it is that everyone should not see that all observation must be for or against some view if it is to be of any service."[24] Darwin's unique ability was to assess objective information—available to everyone—in the light of his subjective hypothesis.

Take his view on *why* there should be a struggle for existence. In 1798, Thomas Malthus, an English economist, published an essay on the principle of population growth.[25] Malthus argued that the human population increases exponentially, whereas food resources grow linearly, so human prosperity will be impossible unless there are strict limits on reproduction. Further, Malthus wrote that unless humans started having fewer children, the inevitable food shortage would curse humanity to an eternal struggle for existence—only famine, war, and disease would check population growth. It was a dark and pessimistic view of humanity.

Darwin read Malthus's essay in 1838, and he extended the domain of applicability of Malthus's principle to the entire living world.[26] No one had done this before. I can't do better than the master's own words: "Every being, which during its natural lifetime produces several eggs or seeds, must suffer destruction during some period of its life, and during some season or occasional year[;] otherwise, on the principle of geometric increase, its numbers would quickly become so inordinately great that no country could support the product. Hence, as more individuals are produced than can survive, there must in every case be a struggle for existence. Either one individual with another of the same species, or with the individuals of distinct species, or with the physical conditions of life."

Like everyone around him, Darwin saw that no animal or plant species dominated our planet, although many produced hundreds or thousands of seeds or offspring. However, no one else interpreted history the way he did. With Malthus's inspiration, he explained the current state of the organic world by invoking the hypothesis of the unimaginable historical destruction and annihilation of organisms. His observations fit the template of the struggle for existence.

There is probably no better way to explain this than with a real example from the world of investing. We are shareholders in a company called NRB Bearings. Its owner and CEO, Harshbeena Zaveri, is an anthropology graduate from Wellesley. She is probably the best strategic thinker in our portfolio. NRB manufactures needle roller bearings for the automotive industry and has about 65 to 70 percent market share in India. The global giant Schaeffler accounts for the rest. Bearings account for just 1 to 2 percent of the cost of a vehicle but are critical components—failure can lead to severe accidents.

We avoid the automotive component space because, in general, its clients, the automotive companies, do not allow them to make money. In the United States, for example, the top five car companies controlled about two-thirds of the market in 2021.[27] This concentration allows them to drive a tough bargain with their suppliers: the automotive component companies. Unsurprisingly, not many parts suppliers can consistently earn a decent profit. India is even more consolidated than the United States—the dominant car company, Maruti Suzuki, controls half the Indian market. The Indian motorcycle market is an oligopoly of just three companies. It is not unusual for a parts supplier to have a huge customer concentration—a top customer typically accounts for 30 to 50 percent of revenues.

Hence, our bias is to reject almost every automotive component business. There *can be* an exception, though. But that exception must fit the following template. First, the parts supplier would need to manufacture a critical component requiring proprietary technology and have a low customer concentration over many years. It should have only one or two competitors, and the competitive dynamics in the industry should be stable over the long term. Finally, there should have been no new entrants to the industry for many years, and the company should have delivered good financials historically. Note that not a single criterion here is about the future.

NRB ticked every box, and so when the company valuation came to the level we liked, we swooped in to buy 10 percent of the business. We studied history, built hypotheses, did not bother predicting, and have been happy owners in the business since 2013.

Assessing the strategy of a business is useless unless we have a strategy to comprehend the strategy.

Gauging the Competitive Position of a Business

Darwin discovered that the success of a species is not dependent on its being the best but simply being better than the competition. This joke will make it more straightforward. When two friends hiking in a forest spot a lion, one starts putting on his running shoes. His friend says, "What are you doing that for? You can't possibly outrun a lion." The man replies, "I know, but I need only to run faster than you, not the lion!"

We humans do not possess an ideal body or brain design, as those with back pain, hernias, or the desire to make leveraged crypto trades will confess.

But as a species, we were undoubtedly better than tens of other sister species in the *Homo* genus, and that has allowed more than eight billion of us to rule the world.

Investors, analysts, and academics have beaten the term "sustainable competitive advantage" to death. Still, as in evolutionary theory, the real question is not just about sustainable competitive advantage but about being consistently *better* than the competition. And what is the meaning of "better"? For us, it relates to measurable parameters like ROCE, market share, free cash flow, balance sheet strength, consistency of financials, and other such measures.

We assess all these historically. So the question for us is never, "*Will* you be better than the competition," but "Have you consistently *been* better than the competition?"

Let's pick market share as an example. If a company is consistently losing market share, and if SoftBank, Tiger, Alibaba, or Naspers has not offered a billion dollars to its competitors so they can burn cash mindlessly, no one can convince me that the company has a sustainable competitive advantage. On the other hand, if a company is consistently gaining market share, isn't it highly likely that they have built a defensible moat? We want our businesses to gain market share over the long term, recognizing full well that the trend line may occasionally reverse in the short term.

In this context, it may be informative to share one of my early mistakes in the fund with you. This small-sized business was in a fragmented industry in which most businesses made decent ROCE. This business had ROCE of over 30 percent and had grown at an annualized rate of 29 percent over the previous three years. The company had no leverage. We invested at what we thought was an attractive price. After selling it at a loss of about 40 percent after five years, I concluded that price was the least of my problems. I had erred in sizing up the competitive advantage of the business.

The company had performed reasonably well in the past few years, but it had lost significant market share over the long term. The two most prominent players in the industry, founded around the same time as this company, were more than twenty times the revenue of this business. The third-largest business founded twelve years after the inception of our company was already eleven times larger in revenue.

In our diligence process, we received a lot of qualitative information from the management, customers, and even competitors about how the company's strategy and direction had started yielding fruit in recent years. The company had been performing well recently, but, with a longer-term lens, I should have seen that the company was a chronic underperformer. Moreover, the same team of founder-managers had been running the business since its inception. So how could the following five-year result be any different from the past twenty-five?

I had made a big blunder. When it comes to gauging competitive position, barring some exceptions, there is almost nothing better than measuring market share of volume, revenue, and profit over a long period.

We live and learn.

Assigning Value to a Business

A few years ago, a fund manager friend and I were meeting for coffee. He wanted to know how our portfolio was performing, and I started complaining mildly about the high valuation of our businesses. I wanted to buy more of these companies, but the prices seemed to have run up a lot. My friend was surprised and countered that the valuations weren't too high. They seemed reasonable. I would say, "Company A is at 45 PE [price/earnings ratio]," and he would counter, "No, it's only 25 PE." I would then complain about Company Y being 55 PE, and he would appear surprised and correct me that the PE for the company was only 28. I was now frustrated, and he appeared pretty surprised—did I not know the valuation of my businesses?

And then it struck me.

When I said 45 PE, I meant to say 45 times *trailing* PE. When he said 25 PE, he meant 25 times *forward* PE. His forward PE was not for the next year but for two years later! For those unfamiliar with our industry's terminology, I had valued our business based on the actual delivered earnings of the past year. On the other hand, my friend had taken the average industry estimates of company earnings two years in the *future* and calculated the PE based on these forecasted earnings.

The following example will make this clearer. Let's say that the profit after tax of a company in the past twelve months is $10 million and that its market value is $450 million. This gives a trailing PE of 45 (450 ÷ 10). If the consensus analyst estimates are that the company's earnings will be $14 million next year and $18 million the year after that, the one-year forward PE for the same business will be 32 (450 ÷ 14), and the two-year forward PE will be 25 (450 ÷ 18).

Which of these three—45, 32, or 25—is the correct PE? It depends on the investor. For us, it is the backward-looking 45, and for my friend, it is the forward-looking 25. Most discussions of PE or other valuation ratios (like price/book or enterprise value/EBITDA) are forward-looking. The *only* PE ratio we discuss relates to the delivered earnings of the past. It may be the previous twelve months or the past three years, or, for some highly cyclical businesses, even the past ten-year average PE (i.e., current market value divided by the average earnings of the past ten years). We also use other valuation metrics, but all value the current business based on its past performance.

I can understand if some investors project earnings over one or two years since that's not too far in the future. It's not ideal, but I get it. What I fail to fathom is why investors do something worse. Much worse.

It's called discounted cash flow (DCF) analysis.

Here is a simple way to understand it. Let's say it's the year 2000, and your mom promises to give you $100 a year for the next two years. You need the cash urgently, and you ask Mom to give you the cash today instead. She will not give you $200 since the value of $100 in 2001 and 2002 is lower than in 2000 (yes, Mom is a stickler and a good mathematician). How much money should she give you? You will need a DCF analysis to arrive at the answer.

For this, you will need a discount rate or cost of capital.[28] Mom decides that it should be 5 percent (maybe because this is the bank interest rate). Thus, the value of $100 in 2001 is $95 in 2000 ($100 ÷ 1.05). The value of $100 in 2002 is $91 in 2000 ($100 ÷ 1.05^2). Thus, if you choose to take all the money today, she should give you $186 ($95 + $91). This is a simple DCF analysis.

So far, so good.

The problem starts when you replace your mom with a company. Whoa! Did I just say that? But you know what I mean. If you don't, let me elaborate. As per corporate finance theory, the value of a business is simply the sum of all its *future* cash flows discounted to the present time. This makes *academic* sense. It's true mathematically. But as a *practical* way to invest, it borders on being non-sensical. Let's understand why. There are two main requirements for building a DCF spreadsheet: the discount rate and the cash flow projection.

Let's start with the discount rate.

The discount rate is the weighted average costs of debt and equity; it is equivalent to the 5 percent we used in the example with your mom. I understand the cost of debt, but what is the cost of equity? Corporate finance theory comes to the rescue and provides a clean-cut official formula. The formula is as follows: (risk-free rate) + β × (expected market return − risk-free rate). Looks neat, right? Just plug in the numbers to get the answer. Don't be fooled, though; it hides several vast issues.

Let's begin with the Greek letter β (beta), which indicates riskiness. It measures the volatility of a stock relative to the market. Thus, a stock that moves in perfect synchrony with the market will have a β of 1. But, again, isn't the notion of measuring risk by using volatility as a proxy quite silly? As I discussed in chapter 1, how does riskiness have *anything* to do with volatility? For an investor, the riskiness of a business is directly proportional to the probability of capital loss of investing in that business. The higher the potential loss, the higher the risk. I don't care about β and never will.

As you can see in the formula, we need a number for the *expected* market return. Ask ten experts, and you will get ten different answers for expected market return. What number should I pick? Average, median, whatever I like? The formula has no advice to offer.

Do you see anything in the formula about how much debt the company is carrying? Do you think a company with a considerable debt load should have the same cost of equity as a company with no debt? The formula does not believe so. It is bizarre and almost laughable. Distressed companies with high leverage get sold for a pittance because the equity investors demand a high cost of equity.

As if all this is not enough, let's look at the damaging impact of pretending that an impressive-looking math formula will protect us from egregious errors.

Let's go back to your mom. If she decides to discount cash flow by 7 percent instead of 5 percent, she will give you only $181, not $186. But if she discounts at 3 percent, you will receive $5 extra, or $191. A DCF analysis assumes cash flows in perpetuity, and so the present value of this formulation is *much* more sensitive to the discount rate than the one used by your mom. For example, assume that a cash flow of $100 grows by 10 percent over twenty-five years. Using a discount rate of 10 percent, the discounted present value of this series is $2,273. What if we reduce the discount rate by just one percentage point to 9 percent? The value jumps by 13 *percent* to $2,565. Similarly, a one-percentage-point increase in discount rate chops off 11 percent of the present value.

What's the use of fooling oneself that the mathematical precision of a discount rate with two decimal places is any better than guesswork?

And now, believe it or not, we come to the *real* problem of using DCF. Yes, we haven't even started yet!

Back to Mom. She had promised us $100 for the next two years. Can a company promise to do the same for an indefinite future? Of course not. But the DCF technique demands that we forecast cash flows. So that is what everyone does.

Theoretically, I need to make these projections in perpetuity, but for convenience, I will just use a "terminal value" at the end of the tenth year to make my task easy. Let's not wade into the problems of terminal value, which is a cesspit. Trust me; you will get indigestion.

Even if you aren't from the financial community, you may have read or heard of the stock prices of individual companies suddenly dropping or increasing massively. Let's take the example of Snapchat, an app that every teenager with a smartphone seems to be using.[29] In early May 2017, Snapchat's share price dropped almost 25 percent in a *single day* after the company declared financial results that showed slower growth than expected and a massive loss of $2.2 billion. There was a lot of public information available on the company, and since Snapchat had listed only recently, investors and analysts had analyzed its future cash flows in gory detail. They had not foreseen the abysmal financial results.

If investors can't forecast cash flows even a few days or months in advance, how can they be expected to project cash flows *years* ahead? But this is what the DCF methodology demands. Investors and analysts rarely fail to build massive, complicated financial models that assess dozens of factors to project cash flows over many years in the future. Hail Excel.

It's not that the builders of these Excel models—whether analysts, bankers, consultants, or investors—are unaware of the pitfalls. But for some reason, the deep desire to look far in the future to arrive at an *exact* number overwhelms the rational voice admonishing the person to stop pretending they are doing anything useful.

One of the best ways for you to get a sense of this future obsession is to read the transcripts of a company's quarterly results conference calls. Most companies post such transcripts in their websites' "Investor Relations" section. I analyzed three conference call transcripts—for Walmart (for Q2 2018), P&G (for Q4 2017), and General Motors (for Q2 2017)—and the results are stark.

For Walmart, analysts and investors focused twenty-eight out of forty-nine questions on the future (e.g., "implied EBIT margin direction within the guidance"). On the P&G call, fourteen out of twenty questions asked the management to make some kind of prediction (e.g., "Do you have more initiatives hitting the market?"). At General Motors, a staggering twenty-seven out of thirty-three questions were forward-looking (e.g., "What should we think about the cadence of the expected savings from the restructuring actions?").

The tug-of-war between the analyst and the management team is occasionally painful to witness: The former tries to pin down exact forecasts for revenues and margins (so that they can populate the DCF model). Knowing full well that the future is inherently unpredictable, the latter attempts to sidestep the question with some broad generic comments.

For example, on the General Motors call for Q2 2017, an analyst wanted to know the revenue projection for OnStar, an advanced communication system installed in GM cars. The answer from the CFO was, "As we have talked about before, yes, OnStar is generating revenue. We don't disclose it separately. It continues to grow." My sympathies lie with company management; they know that they don't know what the future will bring. But, on the other hand, most analysts and fund managers, having never worked in a company, think that it is the management's job to know the future; how else how will they be able to populate their DCF models?

I have been on the boards of more than twenty-five companies, and over the years I have never seen a management team meet its budgets. Some exceed their projections, and some undershoot. Occasionally, the over- or underperformance is by a wide margin. If the company management can't forecast correctly, how can investors do so? They can't. More importantly, they shouldn't try.

We have never done a DCF analysis and never will. However, I know many—if not most—investors and analysts do. Maybe they have figured out a method to look far into the future that eludes me. In any event, our approach is straightforward.

Let me take the example of a noncyclical business growing at a moderate pace. We know the market-trailing PE multiple is about 19 or 20. We pay a multiple at or below the market for an exceptional business with high ROCE, a wide moat, and low business and financial risk. Occasionally, we stretch a bit by paying a trailing multiple in the high teens or low 20s for a truly unique business, but these occasions are few and far between. The median trailing PE multiple for our portfolio when we bought the companies is 14.9.

We refine this method for cyclical businesses and those that haven't shown steady growth in earnings (e.g., if earnings stayed flat for the previous five years or doubled in the past year). But the general principle is that we assign a fair valuation based on historical, delivered financials.

Oh, one last point on valuation. It is always the last thing we discuss. When evaluating a business, risk comes first, quality second, and valuation last.

What Is Necessary Need Not Be Sufficient

In the words of Douglas Futuyma, a professor at the State University of New York at Stony Brook, "The core of evolutionary biology consists of describing and analyzing the history of evolution, and of analyzing the causes and mechanisms of evolution."[30] As a result, the natural world throws up several questions that we can't answer without drawing inferences about historical processes. For example, why do females fight over males in some species? Why are there two sexes and not five? Why does only a tiny part of our genome code for proteins? Why do lions commit infanticide? How did birds evolve from dinosaurs?

As long-term investors, we have dissociated ourselves from the "what will happen?" obsession and replaced it with "what has *actually* happened?" The former is a laundry list of conjectures and opinions, and the latter, to a large extent, consists of facts. Of course, facts in and of themselves are empty, and what matters is the *opinions* we build onto those facts, but at least they give us a foundation for a discussion.

For example, if a company has had a historical ROCE over the past decade of 40 percent, two investors could have widely different opinions of this "fact." One could assert that the company has a great future, and the other could argue that microeconomic theory demands that these returns will be competed away. Understanding that the company has had unusually high returns in the past focuses the investors' attention on the sources of these returns and their sustainability. For example, did the company earn these returns because of regulatory protection from overseas competition, and, if so, are we comfortable backing a business that has not faced genuine competition? Or were these returns earned despite fierce competition? What has the company done relative to the competition that has made it so unique?

Our focus on interpreting the present in the context of history is not free of problems. Let me share two categories of issues. Both relate to the issue of necessity versus sufficiency of track record.

The once-famous company Nokia exemplifies the first category of issues. Nokia was a high-flying company in the late 1990s and dominated the mobile phone market in the same way that the iPhone does today.[31] Large emerging markets like China and India were severely underpenetrated in the mobile phone sector in the 1990s. Based on historical performance, it appeared that Nokia would conquer the world.

Investors couldn't buy enough Nokia stock, and, at its peak in the year 2000, Nokia's market value was about $325 billion. Since then, it has lost more than 90 percent of its value. In the year 2000, all the historical signals from the company—its financial performance, competitive position, reputation, and dealer and customer feedback—would have screamed, "This is an *amazing* company." But Nokia could not compete with Apple, Samsung, or tens of local Chinese and Indian competitors over the next decade, and the Nokia phone is now a museum relic.

Anyone relying only on the history of Nokia would have suffered massive losses. Giving weight to a track record is a necessary condition for investment success, but it is in no way sufficient. We find this to be especially true in fast-changing industries that may or may not be technology related. Thus, in the case of Nokia, while most historical signals would have led one to conclude that the company had been truly outstanding, the very nature of the technology industry, in which rapid change is the norm, should have made any investor pause.

We have avoided fast-changing industries like the plague, and many are not even in the technology space. Industries like retailing, microfinance, food delivery, and e-commerce are in the early stages of evolution in India. There is way too much turmoil in these industries for us to feel comfortable using only historical information to invest.

Should an investor avoid technology companies and other rapidly evolving industries? We do, mainly because we are unable to decipher historical signals for companies in these industries. But many investors have figured out ways of assessing these industries. I don't know how to analyze fast-evolving sectors and businesses, so I don't. When encountering a Nokia-like business, I am very comfortable saying, "I can't figure this out, so thanks, but no thanks."

We can summarize the second problem of historical analysis in one word: Starbucks.

In this case, relying on history would *not* have helped us identify a spectacular turnaround, thereby depriving us of potentially a substantial money-making opportunity. Howard Schultz bought Starbucks in 1982, and from a mere four stores in Seattle, he grew it to about $2 billion in revenue by 2000. Unfortunately, he left Starbucks in 2000 owing to exhaustion, and not long after, Starbucks started underperforming.

When Schultz returned to the company in 2008, there was bad news all around.[32] Sales had been flagging for some time. McDonald's and Dunkin' Donuts had dramatically increased pressure on the company by launching their own gourmet coffee brands. As a result, the stock price had fallen by almost half over the previous year. From 2008, Schultz led a dramatic turnaround in Starbucks' fortunes by cutting back on expansion, closing hundreds of stores, creating a new instant coffee brand, and refocusing on the consumer. Investors fell in love with the company again—the stock price jumped more than eighteen-fold from December 2008 to December 2019.

Let's take ourselves back to 2008 when everything seemed to be falling apart at Starbucks. All the historical signals—customer feedback, market share, same-store sales growth—pointed to a company struggling to regain its lost glory. Schultz may have been the CEO eight years previously, but the company had changed a lot since then; there were thousands of new stores, the management was different, and customer and competitor behavior were different, too. Schultz *may* have revived the company, but there is no evidence that founders are the best turnaround artists. In 2008, given the lack of historical data pointing to a turnaround, I would not have invested in the company and lost out on a huge potential gain.

What is the solution? I don't know a way, but if you can somehow figure out a company's future in a fast-changing industry or bet on a turnaround, all power to you.

For the rest of us who are mere mortals, relying on history is a time-tested way to keep the *odds* firmly in our favor. Of course, it will not guarantee a win every time—no investment approach can—but it will allow us to win often enough.

* * *

I changed seven schools in twelve years because my father was in the armed forces, and they transferred him every two years. These were all government schools where the quality of teachers wasn't usually the best, to put it mildly. However, I doubt even the best private schools had someone like the incredible Mr. Rathod.

We had recently arrived in a small town called Jamnagar when I was in grade 7. I was miserable because I had to bid farewell to my friends in the previous town (called Dehu Road), and I found it hard to fit in socially at this new school. However, Mr. Rathod and his history class got me through that year. He refused to teach us history from the prescribed textbook. Instead, he ordered us to use the school library to read about ancient and modern Indian history from books and popular comics. And then he asked each student to pick a topic and educate the class on what they had learned. Of course, the rest of us were free to disagree with the presenter, and Mr. Rathod encouraged us to be methodical and logical in our arguments. I distinctly remember a group of twelve-year-olds almost coming to blows when debating the British influence on India.

Before meeting Mr. Rathod, history for me was objective, undisputed, unchanging. Before him, every history teacher had drilled into me that there was only one correct answer to any question. Mr. Rathod taught us that most answers to questions in a history test should begin with, "It depends." Throughout grade 7, he showed us directly and indirectly that history can teach us less about who *they* were and much more about who *we* are.

The notion that we can all be great investors just by gauging history is nonsense. It has been fundamental to *our* process, but it works for us because of who *we* are. So I bring my prejudices and biases to something as simple as a historical balance sheet. Occasionally, there are vehement disagreements on how to interpret the past. It occurs even within our small, well-knit team, which has worked together for many years. In the middle of these fiery debates, I often yearn for Mr. Rathod. Why couldn't he be here to adjudicate this?

Chapter Summary

Evolutionary theory has taught me that . . .

. . . we investors can reimagine investing by studying and understanding the *history* of a business and an industry instead of constantly obsessing over the future.

1. Darwin, the founder of modern evolutionary theory, understood better than anyone before him that the present was the result of the cumulative effect of the past.
2. He proposed his three groundbreaking theories—natural selection, sexual selection, and common descent—by construing history in a new light.
3. Unlike physics and chemistry, the science of evolutionary biology does not make predictions. Rather than answering the question, "What *will* happen to humans?" it ponders over the conundrum, "How did bipedal humans evolve from an ancestral quadruped ape?"

4. The investment world is obsessed with the future. Studying history has taken a backseat to making bold forecasts.

5. Taking a leaf out of evolutionary biology, we focus exclusively on widely and openly available historical information to analyze businesses. We spend no time building projections and forecasts.

6. We develop a point of view on company financials, strategy, competitive position, and valuation by analyzing what has *already* happened without bothering about what *will* happen.

7. However, concentrating on the past does have two main downsides. We may wrongly assume that (1) a historically successful business will continue to be so, or (2) a failed or failing business will continue to be so.

CHAPTER 6

BACTERIA AND BUSINESS
REPLAY THE TAPE

I am inclined to believe that in nearly the same way as two men have sometimes independently hit on the very same invention, so natural selection, working for the good of each being and taking advantage of analogous variations, has sometimes modified in very nearly the same manner two parts in two organic beings, which owe but little of their structure in common to inheritance from the same ancestor.

Charles Darwin, On the Origin of Species, *chapter 6, "Difficulties of the Theory"*

Charlie and I have many reasons to be thankful for our association with Chuck and See's. The obvious ones are that we've earned exceptional returns and had a good time in the process. Equally important, ownership of See's has taught us much about the evaluation of franchises. We've made significant money in certain common stocks because of the lessons we learned at See's.

Warren Buffett, *annual letter to shareholders, 1991*

Tim Cooper had no idea that that cold and windy Saturday morning in a lab at Michigan State University in January 2003 would be one of the most important of his life.

Tim started performing his well-rehearsed routine. He had done it dozens of times over the past three years, but he knew that he had to be very careful. He was. The experiment had been going for fourteen straight years, and he was not going to be the one responsible for any mishap.

First, he took a set of twelve new flasks and carefully measured exactly 9.9 milliliters of fluid into each. Next, he went to the incubator and removed the twelve old flasks housing generation number 33,127. He would inoculate the new flasks with 0.1 milliliters of fluid from each of these twelve old flasks. But he needed to check the old flasks first.

He picked up two of them and saw what he expected. The next two flasks also seemed acceptable. But in the third set of two flasks, in the flask labeled "Ara-3," he saw that the fluid had turned opaque instead of being mildly cloudy like in the other old flasks. That shouldn't have happened. The lab had seen similar problems in the past owing to contamination. There was a strict protocol for solving the issue, and Tim was well versed in it.

Tim replaced the "faulty" old Ara-3 flask and came back on Sunday to check the outcome. Of course, he expected the usual result. But he was in for the same surprise: The new Ara-3 flask, too, had turned turbid.

Something was very wrong. Or very right.

The Astonishing Anoles

Our investment strategy has an unusual feature. We don't invest in individual businesses. It may *seem* like we do, but we don't.

What in the world do we invest in then?

Let's do an evolutionary thought experiment to answer the question. Imagine another Earth-like planet that is at a similar distance from its sun-like star. This is not entirely improbable since there are a billion trillion (10^{21}) stars in the universe. Would this planet evolve the same life forms as those on Earth? How likely is it to have honeysuckles and hornbills?

Philosophers may have pondered this question for millennia, but the first modern scientist to attempt an answer was the late Harvard paleontologist and evolutionary biologist Stephen Jay Gould. In his excellent book *Wonderful Life*, Gould took the position that evolution was unpredictable: "Replay the tape a million times . . . and I doubt that anything like *Homo sapiens* would ever evolve again."

If the "evolutionary tape" were replayed a million times, each outcome would depend on two opposing forces. On the one hand, the nonrandom force of natural selection would ensure that organisms develop a small set of foresee-able solutions to the obstacles imposed on them by the environment. On the other, chance mutations and rare environmental events would make any kind of prediction impossible. Which would win? "The bad news is that we can't possibly perform the experiment," Gould mused.

The good news is that although we can't perform the experiment, nature can and has. Do you want evidence? Let's start with lizards.

More than seven hundred Caribbean islands are home to about one hundred and fifty species of lizard called anoles (genus *Anolis*). All the Caribbean species are the descendants of just two species that arrived from the mainland millions of years ago. Dr. Jonathan Losos, a professor of biology at Washington University, has been studying the anoles since the late 1980s on the four larger Caribbean islands of Cuba, Jamaica, Hispaniola, and Puerto Rico.[1]

Professor Losos discovered that the one hundred and fifty species across these four islands are broadly clustered into six groups, or "ecomorphs": Trunk, Twig, Crown-giant, Trunk-crown, Trunk-ground, and Grass-bush. This classification rests on body length, tail length, limb length, toe pad lamellae (scales on the feet of the anoles that help them stick to a surface), color, and habitat.

For example, the Trunk ecomorph lives on tree trunks, has an average body length of about five centimeters, has a short tail, and is gray. A very different ecomorph, the Grass-bush, lives in the grasses and bush, has an average body length of four centimeters, has a very long tail, and is brown.

The behavioral and physical traits of various anole ecomorphs have adapted very well to the anoles' unique local environments. Thus, the long tail of the Grass-bush ecomorph helps the anole achieve spectacular balance on narrow and unstable surfaces like blades of grass, and its brown color melds with the color of the bush and grasses. The Trunk ecomorph is very different because it has a solid tree trunk underneath its feet for most of its life—it does not need a long tail for balance. But it does need its gray color, which can provide camouflage against the gray tree trunk, thereby fooling its predators and prey. The Twig anole has short legs to help it navigate the small twigs on which it lives. Finally, the Trunk-ground ecomorph has evolved long legs to run efficiently on tree trunks and the ground.

No surprises here—Darwinian natural selection is alive and well on the gorgeous islands of the Caribbean.

What is surprising, however, is that the *same* ecomorphs are seen across the four islands. Thus, the Trunk ecomorph in Cuba looks and behaves very similarly to the Trunk ecomorph in Hispaniola, and the Crown-giant ecomorph in Puerto Rico is indistinguishable from the one in Jamaica.

I know what you are thinking: Are the Trunk anoles the same species that colonized Cuba and Hispaniola? DNA analysis has demonstrated that they aren't! The six ecomorph anoles on the island of Cuba are much more closely related to one another than they are to anoles on other islands. Thus, the Trunk anoles in Cuba are much more closely related to the Twig anoles in Cuba than to the Trunk anoles in Hispaniola. The anoles living on tree trunks on the islands of Cuba and Hispaniola are very different species but have developed the same physical and behavioral characteristics on encountering similar environments. This is true for all six ecomorphs. When presented with a specific problem, the Caribbean anoles on different islands have evolved the *same* solutions, such as tail length, body length, and color. Amazingly, they have done it independently of one another.

The anoles are a textbook example of evolutionary "convergence" wherein unrelated organisms in similar environments develop the same body form and adaptations independently.[2]

Convergence Is Ubiquitous

The fascinating example of convergence in Caribbean anoles is a rule, not an exception, in the natural world.

Dolphins are mammals just like us, and sharks are fish. But their fusiform body shapes are pretty similar, and, more interestingly, they have the same coloration. Both have a light underbelly and darker back, making them harder to spot from above and below. George McGhee, a paleontologist, claims that the reason sharks, dolphins, tuna, and the extinct ichthyosaur look alike is that there is only *one* way for a fast-swimming animal to evolve.[3]

In vertebrates, powered flight evolved in birds, bats, and (the now extinct) pterosaurs. Their common ancestor, a land-based quadruped, had no wings. Their wings *appear* to be the same, but they have evolved separately and independently. In all three, the forearms have been modified into wings, and all take (or took) to the sky in the same way: by flapping their wings downward to create upward lift and forward movement.[4]

Australia punches much above its weight in the sporting world. This nation of only twenty-five million people won 547 medals in the Summer Olympics (before Tokyo 2020), exceeding many nations much more significant in population.[5] For example, its medal tally is one-fifth that of the United States, whose population is thirteen times larger. (Now is not the time or place for me to comment on India's medal tally.)

Sport is not the only thing that makes this country, or continent if you prefer, unique. Australia was part of the supercontinent Pangea and its southern segment Gondwanaland, which started breaking apart about 180 million years ago. As a result, Australia has been a free-standing continent for about 35 million years. The mammals on this massive island have been taking a unique evolutionary path during this time.

The Australian mammals are all marsupials who give birth to undeveloped young ones and raise them in an external pouch; most of the world has placental mammals (like us) who give birth to fully developed infants. Does the dramatic difference in their life histories and development process mean that marsupials look very different from the placentals? Surprisingly not.

Compare the images of the Australian marsupials to those of the placentals in figure 6.1.[6] If we were to place them next to one another, it would not be easy to differentiate a wolf from the (now extinct) thylacine, the mouse from the mulgara, or the marmot from the wombat. They look similar despite being

6.1 The stark convergence between placental mammals—(a) wolf, (b) mouse, and (c) marmot—and marsupial mammals—(d) thylacine, (e) mulgara, and (f) wombat.

Sources: (a) and (f) courtesy of Wikimedia Commons; (b), (c), (d), and (e) licensed from Science Photo Library.

unrelated genetically because they have solved a similar problem in a similar way in vastly different regions of the world.

Now let's take the example of a niche predator that preys mainly on termites. How would you design such an organism? What traits should it possess? I assume you will agree that it should have a long and sticky tongue to trap and eat termites, it should have solid front claws for digging into termite mounds, its head should be small, and it should have a long snout that can enter termite mounds with ease. Congratulations, you have designed the marsupial anteater (called the numbat) as well as the placental anteater. As you may expect, they look surprisingly alike. Through convergence, they have developed a similar appearance and body parts without having a close common ancestor because both needed to solve the problem of how to eat termites.

Charles Darwin recognized the power of convergence when he asserted, "Animals, belonging to two most distinct lines of descent, may readily become adapted to similar conditions, and thus assume a close external resemblance."[7] Darwin was right, but not entirely so.

Convergence is ubiquitous and not limited just to the external appearance or morphology of animals. It is also widely observed and documented in animal behavior and in plants, fungi, and even bacteria.

Let's start with behavior. What do you think these four species—a cobra, a stickleback fish, an octopus, and a spider—share? There is no convergence in body form here, unlike the Caribbean anoles. But a behavior has converged among them that has led to the success of each of their species: the females of the species guard their eggs.

One of the best examples of convergent behavior is observed in humans and—hold your breath—ants! And I have witnessed this convergence with my own eyes. When I was on a family vacation in the stunningly beautiful Peruvian Amazon, I stumbled upon the tiny creatures that had beaten our human ancestors to the discovery of agriculture by many millions of years: the leafcutter ants.

I had waited years to witness the miracle, and there it was in its full linear glory. A long single column of thousands of large green leaves appeared to be miraculously moving in perfect synchrony of their own volition on the forest floor. Each large leaf was being carried by a single tiny ant, who purposefully disappeared underground to pass on the booty to her specialist sisters. These ants chew the leaves to grow a fungus garden used for food for the entire colony. Not unlike human farmers, these ants produce fertilizers (amino acids and enzymes) to aid the fungal growth, remove contaminants that can hinder the agricultural output, are highly selective in what they grow, and continuously tend to their enormous gardens.[8]

And just as agriculture helped us become the dominant species on this planet, leafcutter ants have become the dominant herbivores of the New World:

They consume close to one-sixth of all leaves produced in tropical forests. Humans and leafcutter ants have solved their food problems by converging toward a similar solution, crossing time and species boundaries.

Let's move on to plants. Most of us have had coffee, tea, and chocolate (derived from cacao). The Brazilians among us will be familiar with the drink Guaraná Antarctica, made from the guaraná plant in the Amazon rainforest. All four plants produce the same chemical desired by humans: a purine alkaloid called 1,3,7-trimethylpurine-2,6-dione—in short, caffeine.[9]

These four plants may seem to be closely related, but they aren't. The common ancestor of tea and coffee dates back a hundred million years. Cacao is more closely related to maple and eucalyptus trees than to tea and coffee. Bizarrely, the ancestor of coffee gave rise to potatoes and tomatoes but not tea! Plants have many defense mechanisms against predators, and it appears that some have converged toward the same solution: producing caffeine.

Many plants rely on birds to pollinate their flowers. So if a plant depends on hummingbirds for pollination, what should it do? Develop red flowers because red is attractive to hummingbirds. Consequently, eighteen types of plants that hummingbirds pollinate have evolved bright red flowers.

Other plants have developed a different strategy, one that exploits flies' and beetles' penchant for laying eggs on smelly decomposing carcasses. Seven types of plants—including the corpse lily and the Zulu giant (or carrion flower)—have evolved to produce a smell that resembles rotting meat. The odor fools the insects, and while visiting the plants to lay their eggs, they transfer pollen from one flower to another.[10]

I could go on and on to fill this book with examples of convergent evolution in the natural world. But scientists now agree that convergence is the rule, not an exception, in nature. This sentiment is best expressed by the most famous advocate of convergence, the Cambridge paleontologist Simon Conway Morris, who has written two books on the subject. He has explained convergence by saying, "Certainly it's not the case that every Earth-like planet will have life let alone humanoids. But if you want a sophisticated plant, it will look awfully like a flower. If you want a fly, there are only a few ways you can do that. If you want to swim, like a shark, there are only a few ways you can do that. If you want to invent warm-bloodedness, like birds and mammals, there are only a few ways to do that."

Convergence in nature symbolizes a profound fact: There is a pattern to success and failure.

What can the Caribbean anole, the crest-tailed marsupial mouse, and caffeine teach us about investing?

Convergence in business symbolizes a profound fact: There is a pattern to success and failure.

We Don't Invest in Individual Businesses

Earlier in the chapter, I made the following assertion about our investment strategy: *We don't invest in individual businesses. It may seem like we do, but we don't.*

So what in the world do we invest in then?

We invest in convergent patterns. We seek patterns that repeat. As we saw, "replaying the tape of life" often yields the same result. We operate on the principle that the business world is no different. There is a big difference between asserting "I love this business" and "I love this business *construct*." We are fans of the latter, not the former. We don't care about *a* business; we are deeply attached to a business *template*.

Not unlike the natural world, which converges toward a small subset of answers to the same questions, we have seen that companies around the globe behave in similar ways when facing a similar environment. Not always, but often enough. We have benefited enormously by asking this simple convergence question up front: "Have we seen this pattern elsewhere?"

The cost of ignoring patterns, as usual, is best demonstrated through a painful personal experience.

In 1999 or 2000, an investment bank showed us a "hot" private equity deal. There was a lot of interest from many investors (or so the bank led us to believe!). The company processed credit cards and had shown modest growth over the past few years. Unsurprisingly, the investment bank's projections showed dramatic growth starting the following year. Skeptical initially, I met the management team and talked to industry participants and investors in the business. Then, after reviewing India's low credit card penetration rates, I convinced myself that while the management's and the bank's projections were aggressive, they weren't too far off the mark. So we invested in the business at a fancy valuation.

I wasn't wrong. I was catastrophically wrong. The company did not meet its projections for more than five years. The J-curve growth never arrived. I want to emphasize that this was neither the bank's nor the management's fault. They were doing their job. But, unfortunately, I forgot to do mine.

A few years after this disaster, when I looked back at the projections, I realized that we would have saved our precious capital if I had applied the principle of convergence by asking a few simple questions. The questions I should have asked but did not were as follows: "Sure, credit card penetration is low in India, but so is penetration for every consumer product. What other consumer products in India have seen these growth rates over the long term? Do you have examples of other countries where we have seen such rapid credit card growth? If so, was their stage of development similar to India's today?" I should have demanded a convergent template, but I didn't.

Let's see what happens when we do. We invested in Info Edge in late 2013. It runs India's leading job site, Naukri.com, and is led by Sanjeev Bikhchandani and Hitesh Oberoi, two of the most well-regarded entrepreneurs in India. We did not invest in Naukri because of Sanjeev and Hitesh but because of the convergent patterns Naukri represents.

Naukri allows job-seeking candidates to post their résumés for free and charges companies a subscription fee to access these and list job vacancies. When we invested in 2013, Naukri had a dominant 65 percent traffic share and was four times larger than the second player, Monster India. Given Naukri's dominance, if you are a job seeker in India, you would almost certainly post your résumé there. If you are a company trying to hire, you are almost compelled to subscribe to Naukri because it has the most extensive and diverse pool of candidates. It is emblematic of the classic network effect: Naukri is number one because it is number one.

Our confidence in Info Edge was high because it represents not one but two convergent patterns. First, the erstwhile Yellow Pages business. Many of you have probably never heard of this life-saving invention, but they were my lifeline until the early 1990s. Yellow Pages were a fixture in every home, just like a television or a refrigerator, in the era of rotary landline phones before the age of the internet and mobile phones. Yellow Pages were ungainly, thick telephone directories usually printed on yellow paper that listed local businesses and their goods or services on offer.

Yellow Pages could give you a list of tens, even hundreds, of options, whether you were looking for a language teacher, a plumber, a wedding planner, a car dealer, or a recording studio. The directory was distributed free to the consumers, and businesses paid a fee to be listed. As a result, the largest Yellow Pages business in any city or region was usually highly profitable because of the virtual monopoly enjoyed by their network effect: Consumers went to them because they listed the largest number of businesses, and businesses subscribed to them because they attracted the largest number of consumers.

They were highly defensible businesses, and for the leading companies, the network effect ensured high profits over long periods. It was not unusual for leading Yellow Pages businesses to earn a profit margin in excess of 40 percent.[11] While Naukri operates in a different era in a different medium, our view was that it converged with many of the virtuous traits of a leading Yellow Pages business.

The second convergent pattern we noted was the performance of the leading internet job boards in other countries. This pattern was even more powerful than that of Yellow Pages. We found at least seven other job boards globally with obscenely high operating margins (more than 30 to 40 percent) and infinite ROCE, just like Naukri; for example, Seek in Australia, Dice and CareerBuilder in the United States, 51Job in China, EN in Japan, 104 Corp in Taiwan, and JobStreet in Singapore and Malaysia. These dominant franchises became more dominant each year. Their margin and return profile kept improving; they were all cash machines; the number two in any of these markets showed no signs of catching up; and LinkedIn and offline competitors had no impact on them. In other words, they were indistinguishable from Naukri.

When we first encountered a 49 percent operating margin and infinite ROCE for Naukri, we were skeptical. Who earns that kind of money? But after studying the Yellow Pages and companies in other markets, we concluded that this was no fluke. In 2021, Naukri's operating margin was 55 percent.

We invested in Naukri not just because Sanjeev and Hitesh are impressive folks (which they are), or because Naukri makes gobs of money (which it does), or because it has annihilated the competition (which it has). Instead, we invested in Naukri because the convergent models of Yellow Pages and global job board businesses gave us the confidence to believe that the Naukri *template* is tough to beat. Make that almost impossible to beat.

I will state two counterfactuals to highlight the importance of this method of investing. First, what if Sanjeev and Hitesh, impressive as they are, were operating the number 2 or 3 job board in India? We would not have touched the business. Winner takes all in the classifieds business, and we would never have bet against that pattern. Second, what if Sanjeev and Hitesh had come to us in the early days of the internet when there was no proof of concept for this business model? Again, we would have walked away because the answer to the question "Where else has this worked?" would have been "No idea."

Nevertheless, some venture capitalists did fund Naukri in its early days. Kudos to them. They recognized the genius of Sanjeev and Hitesh and deserved their mouthwatering returns.

We detest the phrases "This time, it's different" and "My gut tells me this will work." We need to see the evidence that our investment thesis has worked elsewhere. If it hasn't, we are unlikely to touch it. We are the antithesis of the venture capital community, which earns its living by betting on untested and unproven businesses. I am in awe of successful venture capital firms, but my admiration for them will never translate into a desire to emulate them.

Kahneman's Outside View and Convergence

I have learned to invest by investing and by observing other investors. I wish I could have learned from the learned finance and economics academics. Have you tried reading a finance journal or research article on economics or finance? I have, and I must admit I can't understand most of them. They are inundated with Greek symbols, complicated mathematical equations, and esoteric arguments. They leave me baffled as to their utility for actual practitioners like me. But occasionally, one of the intellectuals will take my breath away.

Daniel Kahneman is one such individual. His masterpiece *Thinking, Fast and Slow* should be compulsory reading for all investing 101 classes. If you are already an investor, there is no more valuable chapter to read (and re-read) than chapter 23, "The Outside View."

Here, Kahneman describes his experience of leading a team in Israel designing a curriculum and writing a textbook for high school students on judgment and decision-making. After a year, the team had made reasonable progress. They had prepared a detailed outline of the syllabus, written a couple chapters, and conducted some classroom lessons.

One day, Kahneman asked his colleagues to write down an estimate of the time it would take the team to submit a finished textbook draft to the Ministry of Education. Everyone on the team, including Kahneman's colleague Seymour Fox, an expert in curriculum development, estimated that it would take them about two years. Kahneman then asked Fox, who had witnessed many other teams develop similar textbooks and curricula over the years, how long it usually takes teams to finish their textbook projects.

Fox's answer stunned Kahneman. Seemingly embarrassed, Fox admitted that 40 percent of such teams never finished the task, and those who did took anywhere from seven to ten years. The actual time it took Kahneman's team? Eight years. A far cry from the two years they had estimated.

Kahneman labels the team's initial estimate of two years the "inside view." It was based on the team members' specific circumstances, their confidence in their abilities, an extrapolation based on recent goals achieved, and a hazy idea of the future. And it was wrong by a wide margin.

Kahneman calls the 40 percent failure estimate of similar projects and the completion time of seven to ten years the "outside view." As he describes, his questioning of Fox revealed two great insights. First, although Fox was aware of the outside view, he did not even consider it while initially writing down his estimate. And second, although the other team members, including Kahneman, did not have access to the information Fox did, none even attempted to understand the outside view when the project began.

But applying convergent thinking or an outside view is neither natural nor easy. As Kahneman himself states succinctly, " 'Pallid' statistical information is routinely discarded when it is incompatible with one's personal impression of a case. In the competition with the inside view, the outside view does not stand a chance."

The outside view does not have a chance in the investment community because, ironically, fund managers and analysts are savvy. Given a choice between applying their intellectual horsepower to a single business by making a ten-year projection of profits or stepping back and asking if any of it even makes sense, brilliant folks often choose the former. As I was transitioning from consulting in my early investing days, I was the biggest believer in the myth that more work produces better answers for investors. It doesn't.

Let me illustrate the power of Kahneman's outside view by outlining two ways of analyzing a potential investment in an airline.

Imagine that I have just flown to Singapore from New York aboard the über-comfortable A380 in January 2019. I have thoroughly enjoyed the legendary Singapore Airlines service. After I land, I pick up a financial newspaper and read an interesting article on the enormous potential for airlines in Asia, particularly in India and China. This article also informs me that the famous Tata Group in India launched not one but *two* airlines a few years ago. The journalist gushes about the limitless growth possibilities on the continent. Having just had a great flying experience and feeling excited about the potential of the fast-growing Asian airline market, I decide to start some serious work on the subject to evaluate an investment in an Asian airline.

If you are not from the finance industry, please do not treat this as a frivolous example. Believe it or not, this is how fund managers sometimes get interested in companies.

At first glance, there is a lot to like about the airline industry. But, to a fund manager's ears, I can describe it in two words that sound better than Beethoven's symphony: "large" and "growing." Unless you live in a monastery in a remote corner of the world, your life in the modern world, directly or indirectly, is touched by the airline industry. And the industry is beginning to impact Africa and Asia—the phenomenal growth of Dubai and Singapore as airline hubs during the last decade is testimony to the region's potential.

At this stage, I have two options:

1. Perform a detailed analysis of one Asian airline, or
2. Focus on understanding the outside view of the airline industry.

If I choose option one, which, incidentally, many fund managers choose, I will waste my time doing the following time-consuming and futile tasks.

My team and I will interview the CEO and CFO at a fancy restaurant. Then, we will visit their corporate offices, where the senior management team will wax eloquent on the culture and systems of their unique airline. Finally, we will read tens of analyst reports (most of which will be favorable; do you seriously expect an airline analyst to denigrate their industry?), and we will build a fancy Excel spreadsheet with multiyear forecasts of fuel prices, passenger miles, average ticket prices, load factors, gross margins, capital expenditures, inventory levels, lease costs, personnel expenses, marketing costs, airport charges, freight revenues, and heaven knows what else.

The result? After many weeks or months of meetings and late nights, we will either buy or choose a price at which we plan to purchase the company's shares if we think the price is too high.

Let's see what we would do if we were to choose option two instead.

We want to analyze the industry in greater depth, and so we start with an extensive study conducted by MIT on the U.S. airline industry from 2000 to 2013. The conclusions of this study are in an eighty-one-page document available for free on the internet.[12] The results are humbling.

Surprisingly, despite being a mature market, the U.S. industry grew during this period: The revenue of passenger miles grew about 20 percent from 709 million to 848 million. However, on total revenue of about $1.4 trillion during this period, the airlines made a cumulative loss of $44 *billion*. Thus, on an annual revenue of close to $100 billion, the airline industry lost about $3 billion every year from 2000 to 2013.

But these averages hide an even sorrier story. During eight of these fourteen years (or almost 60 percent of the time), the airlines made no money; that is, they declared financial losses or only a meager profit. And in the six years they *did* manage to eke out profits, their total net profit was only about $40 billion.

However, the real tragedy is that during just two bad years—2005 and 2008—the industry suffered losses of $54 billion, or $14 billion more than the *cumulative* profits of $40 billion during the entire period. It is generally assumed that the tragedy of September 11, 2001, was terrible for the airline industry, which is true; U.S. airlines suffered losses of about $19 billion in 2001 and 2002. But in 2005, four years after the tragedy and three years before the financial meltdown of 2008, the industry declared a total net loss of $28 billion, far exceeding the losses resulting from September 11.

The remarkable consistency with which airlines lose money is not a problem unique to the United States. A report from the International Air Transport Association shows that from 2000 to 2014, the industry had not earned its cost of capital for fifteen years in a row.[13] Not even in a single year!

You must now be thinking what I am thinking. The industry may be destructive overall, but what about the top airlines? Would they not be much better than the industry? Let's look at the return profiles of the top ten airlines (by revenue) in the world according to Aviation Week: Lufthansa, All Nippon, Southwest, Qantas, Air China, American, Singapore, Turk Hava, Aeroflot, and Ryanair. Using Morningstar, I calculated their return on equity (ROE) and return on assets (ROA) for ten years from 2004 to 2013, and the results are terrible. The median ROE of these airlines over ten years was 6.8 percent, and the median ROA was 2.5 percent. Scale does not guarantee success in this demanding industry.

To sum it up: It's as bad as it gets.

After studying the historical patterns in the airline industry, we can conclude the following with a high degree of confidence:

1. U.S. airlines do not make money.
2. The global airline industry does not make money.
3. The top ten airlines in the world do not make money.

The detailed and unfortunate *outside view* of the industry is quite troubling. Airlines are great for consumers, not for investors. This pessimistic view advises us to stay away from the airline industry. Instead, we should choose to invest our excess cash in a bank deposit rather than buying a single airline share.

I am sure many of you are now asking the obvious question. Can one make a decision about investing in an Asian airline based on learnings from U.S. and global airlines? If we can conclude that Asia is not dissimilar to the United States, maybe we can get comfortable with the fact that the fate of Asian airlines will be no different from their U.S. counterparts. At first glance, the industry may appear to be quite different in Asia owing to ownership and international routes. First, most airlines in Asia, including Singapore Airlines, are owned by the government, unlike in the United States, where airlines are under private ownership. Second, most of the heavy traffic routes in Asia are between international destinations, not domestic ones (there are no domestic flights in Singapore or Dubai!).

But if we dig a bit deeper into the *competitive* dynamics, we may conclude that Asia is no different from the United States. In the prepandemic days, Expedia showed that if you wanted to fly from Singapore to New York, you could choose from among twenty-two airlines! Competition is no less severe just because the flights are international as opposed to domestic. The airline rivalry in Asia may be more intense than in the United States owing to the ownership structure! Since governments care much less about economics than private investors, they may not be perturbed by continued financial losses. Moreover, most countries seem to treat their airline as a national symbol, so shutting down a national airline, as prudent as it may be for the exchequer, is unheard of in Asia. As a result, in my view, invoking convergence to understand the Asian airline industry is a legitimate investment approach.

In this case, applying the outside view to investing yielded us two significant benefits. First, we avoided investing in a company and in an industry in which the odds of making money are very slim indeed. I am not suggesting that it is impossible to make money by investing in airlines—if you bought an airline stock at a low enough price (no, I can't define what is "low enough") and then were lucky enough to sell it at some profit, good for you. But "I will find a greater fool for my crappy asset" is another way to say "speculating," not investing. It's not for us.

The second benefit was the time, money, and effort saved. Instead of conducting lengthy and unproductive management meetings, schmoozing the investor relations person, paying fat fees to consultants, and spending weeks to construct a multimegabyte Excel spreadsheet, we spent a few hours on the internet, downloaded a few reports, and made our decision within a few minutes with enough time left to go home early to our families.

Some Practical Ways of Applying the Principle of Convergence

This discussion on airlines should not lead anyone to believe that all will be well just by applying the principle of convergence or the outside view to a specific investment situation. Convergence is not a panacea, nor is it a substitute for thoughtful analysis and synthesis. But when applied wisely, it can be a powerful investment tool.

I don't know about the rest of the world, but in India, a married person inherits their spouse's family. Whether they like it or not. The likelihood of getting along with your spouse over the long term is relatively low if you don't like your spouse's first, second, and occasionally, even third cousins. For the record, my in-laws are the best.

Investing in companies is no different. Buying into a business means also buying into the *industry* of that business. For example, while I may think I am investing in a *company* that makes and sells sanitaryware, I am inheriting all the good and the bad of the sanitaryware *industry*. No company is an island. We can never ignore the kinds of businesses that surround it.

One of our principles of convergence investing is that if the *industry* allows its companies to make money consistently, we love it; if not, we better have a *perfect* reason for spending even one minute analyzing a business like an airline. Life is too short.

There are three potential answers to the question of an industry's attractiveness and profitability. First is that the companies in the industry struggle to keep their heads above water, just as we saw in the case of airlines. Industries like telecom towers, garment manufacturing, and commodity chemicals are notorious value destroyers. Most companies in these industries barely earn their cost of capital. As I have said repeatedly, one of the immensely underappreciated values of any strategy—including an investment strategy—is what it advises us *not* to do. The principle of convergence demands that I avoid investing in these industries. If most companies in the industry can't hack it, why should I believe that *this* company is unique?

The second conclusion could be that the industry is uniformly attractive for its participants. For example, companies like Accenture, Cognizant, Infosys, and TCS in the information technology (IT) outsourcing industry earn more than 40 to 50 percent ROCE and have been doing so for decades. If you accept convergence investing as we do, you should love assessing companies in the IT industry. For example, when we evaluated an investment in Mindtree, India's leading midtier IT services business, we knew that the company had been very profitable for many years. But how could we be sure that it would continue to be successful? By witnessing the convergent outcomes of other businesses in the industry, all of which had been able to scale their revenues over many decades without sacrificing profitability. In other words, it happened *there*, so all else being equal, there was a high probability that it could happen *here*.

My optimistic view does not mean that I will invest in any company in the IT services industry. Instead, my actual investment will depend on factors like valuation, financial risk, management track record, capital allocation, customer concentration, market share, and so on. But the *companies* in this industry would be right on top of my radar as Mindtree was.

You may think these industries that churn money spinners would be rare— at least that is what microeconomic theory would espouse. But they aren't. Our portfolio is full of companies in desirable industries: enzymes, paints, cookers, business process outsourcing, bearings, compressors, consumer electricals, sanitaryware, and steam turbines, to name just a few.

Last, convergence can inform us that only some companies make money in specific industries, whereas most others don't. For example, walking along Fifth Avenue in Manhattan, I am dazzled by the brilliance and splendor of fashion stores. But fashion is a brutal place to be in—very few companies grow revenues and profits steadily. Most are shooting stars that shine for a few moments and then disappear into oblivion. The same is true for retailers and restaurants. These are the trickiest companies for us to assess. Should we bet on a single business in an unattractive industry, or should we just walk away? If we evaluate a company in these industries, which we rarely do, we are exceptionally demanding—we will not invest in anyone but the undisputed leader.

We use the principle of convergence across many other areas of business apart from assessing industry attractiveness. We use it much more often to figure out what *not* to do.

I want to take you back to chapter 1, which focused exclusively on the importance of avoiding significant risks. I contended that avoiding risky investments is more important and more difficult for most investors than making good investments.

As a quick reminder, I highlighted six types of businesses we avoid at all costs:

1. Those owned and run by crooks
2. Turnaround situations
3. Those with high levels of debt
4. M&A junkies
5. Those in fast-changing industries
6. Those with unaligned owners

How did I arrive at this list? Through a combination of reliving bad experiences (1, 2, and 5), doing some factual data analysis (4, 5, and 6), watching others stumble (2, 3, and 6), and learning from owners of portfolio companies

(4 and 5). The common thread through all of these was the hunger for detecting patterns and seeking a convergence of outcomes.

Investors can detect (or manufacture) a vast range of patterns across businesses. This is not the place to discuss all of them. Instead, this chapter intends to make the simple claim that one of the most important questions an investor can ask is, "Where else has this worked?" Before moving on, let me discuss one more aspect of convergence investing that (I think) has been critical to our success.

We are price sensitive. The median trailing price/earnings (PE) ratio for our portfolio at the time of our investment is less than 15 when the Indian market has been about 19 to 20. We have rarely ever paid more than twenty times trailing PE. Most importantly, we have never said, "This is such a great business that even 30 PE is justified."

As I have made clear in previous chapters, we have no interest in investing in low-quality or mediocre businesses at any price. Our portfolio companies are truly stellar based on verifiable empirical data on historical financials, industry market share, balance sheet quality, and customer satisfaction. Moreover, the markets are generally quite efficient—businesses like these are rarely available at a throwaway price. Since we have chosen to invest exclusively in world-class businesses, we have two options:

1. Invest at a high valuation hoping that the price will rise further, or
2. Stay inactive for long periods until we get the price we want.

We have always chosen option two. Why? Convergence. Valuation matters for equity returns over the long run across years, countries, and the size of companies. The lower the valuation, the higher the prospective long-term returns. It has worked everywhere over very long periods, so who are we to defy it?

There is a lot of empirical research on equity valuation and returns. The article on this topic that I like best is "Value and Growth Investing: Review and Update" by Louis K. C. Chan and Josef Lakonishok.[14] I love this article for two reasons. First, it is a meta-research article that summarizes the conclusions of many other researchers over many years across several countries. Second, while Chan and Lakonishok are both academics (from the University of Illinois at Urbana-Champaign), Lakonishok is also the CEO and chief investment officer of a $100 billion fund called LSV Asset Management. It's always good to hear from people whose research conclusions matter to their bank balance.

The article has many tables with reams of data, and if you don't have much time, I suggest focusing on table 2. It shows returns over twenty years (from 1975 to 1995) across thirteen countries for "value" stocks (those with low valuation) and "glamour" stocks (those with high valuation) across four valuation measures. The results are stark. The value portfolio beats the glamour portfolio across almost all countries. And the outperformance is not trivial: It ranges from 1.5 percentage points for Switzerland to 6.7 percentage points for the United States (based on PE ratio as the valuation measure).

The first paragraph of their conclusion is worth repeating in full:

> A large body of empirical research indicates that value stocks, on average, earn higher returns than growth stocks. The reward to value investing is more pronounced for small-cap stocks, but it is also present in large-cap stocks. The value premium exists also in equity markets outside the United States.

Why should we risk investing at high valuations when we know that the result will be poor *on average*? Some of you may detect a paradox here. Unlike LSV Asset Management, which relies on sophisticated quantitative analysis, we do in-depth qualitative research on industries and businesses. As a result, we know a lot about our portfolio companies and their industries. Given that we have an informed view of them, should we not be willing to pay up when the opportunity arises?

No.

Why? Because I have more respect for the convergence theme with respect to valuation and potential returns than my intellect. I wish I were more intelligent. But I am not.

We now arrive at an obvious question. Under what situations should we *not* apply the principle of convergence?

Not as Straightforward as It Sounds

Someone wise—reputed to be Einstein, but there is no agreement—once remarked, "Everything should be made as simple as possible, but not simpler." Life is complicated, and so is investing. The principle of convergence may seem intelligible (I hope) and its implementation a cinch. Sorry to disappoint you, but this seemingly easy-to-use tool generates its own set of thorny issues.

Give me a conclusion you desire, and I am reasonably confident that I would rationalize it based on the principle of convergence. A couple of anecdotes may masquerade as a pattern, one pattern can be ignored in favor of another, or one can simply resort to telling a story that seems to weave in an outside view where there is none.

If you are an investor or choose to be one, you will need to learn your lessons the hard way. However, here are some pointers based on my experience.

The probability of convergent evolution is higher in living organisms if they share similarities in genetics, development, and ecology.[15] Unsurprisingly, the greater the similarity of "conditions" in businesses, the greater is the benefit of using the principle of convergence in investing. "Conditions" here could mean industry structure, geography, competitive dynamics, stage of business, the similarity of business models, and much more. For example, we saw that the Caribbean anoles were endowed with the same physical attributes when conditions were similar across the islands. Therefore, businesses should operate under the same principle.

Let me take the example of three types of businesses to explain the complications of applying the principle of convergence.

Assume that I am evaluating an investment in a company that builds residential properties in Germany. To incorporate an outside view, I would start with developing an understanding of the dynamics of the German residential property market—the industry participants, track record of growth and profitability, extent of consolidation, and anything else that would get me smart on the overall German residential market. I would prefer not to draw parallels with Germany's commercial or retail real estate market because the industry structure and types of players are usually different across these segments.

Should I study the French, Spanish, or Brazilian residential real estate market? It depends whether these other markets have a similar industry structure to that of Germany (e.g., is the industry fragmented or consolidated?) or whether the regulations are primarily comparable (e.g., if a government subsidizes mortgage payments for its citizens, it will dramatically affect consumer behavior). Intuitively, given the cultural and historical affinity of the French and Spanish residential markets, I would be more inclined to draw lessons from those markets and not Brazil's. But maybe someone can find a way to draw lessons even from Brazil. What about the U.S. residential real estate market? I am not sure. I would need to do some work to understand if there are any parallels between Germany and the United States.

Take the case of a German company manufacturing industrial robots. These robots are supplied to manufacturing businesses across the world. Since this is a global business, I would not worry too much about the German angle here. Instead, I would research enterprises supplying the same or similar equipment worldwide, whether based in China, Italy, or Singapore, to understand their growth, profitability, and trends in market share. I would also go one level "higher" to analyze the performance of global businesses that supply sophisticated industrial machinery. I may not assign as much weight to this second analysis, but I would study it to discern any apparent trends if available.

Some of you may argue that I was too quick to dismiss the German engineering businesses in general. Maybe something about German engineering strength can serve as a template for an industrial robot business. I am skeptical. But perhaps you are right. So go ahead and do the work.

Third, take the case of a German hospital business. Should we use convergent investing by assessing the economics and industry structure of hospitals in the United Kingdom, Italy, and the Netherlands? Health care in most markets is heavily regulated, and this may significantly impact the economics of a hospital. It would be too cumbersome to assess the impact of local laws on the hospitals in each country. Instead, we could use a shortcut to see if the overall hospital economics—or those of the top five to ten hospitals if industry data are unavailable—are comparable across countries. Since hospitals are a services business, can we use the information from other German services sectors (say, hotels) to refine our assessment? Think about it.

One situation in which we never apply convergence is when the industry is new or fast-changing. Convergent evolution is more evident in plants and insects since they have been around on Earth longer than birds and mammals.[16] It takes time for convergence to emerge. This fact is equally applicable to the world of business.

We have noticed greater convergence in older industries (e.g., paint, garments, engines, turbines, cars) and less in newer ones (e.g., virtual reality, robotics, electric vehicles, biotechnology). Industries converge toward similar fates after the companies have had enough time to plan and execute their strategies, after winners and losers have been (essentially) decided, and when the pace of change has declined. Thus, if we are exploring an investment in a paint company in Germany, it would be helpful to study the paint industry in the Western world. But if we were in the year 2000, drawing parallels from the U.S. e-commerce industry for an investment in a Chinese e-retailer may have been taking things a bit too far.

As you can see, convergence investing is not an objective, bias-free, mathematical endeavor that always yields the same answer. As a result, you may have a different view of one or more of my conclusions. And therein lies all the fun and frustration of investing.

This brings us back to Tim Cooper and the mysteriously turbid Ara-3 flask.

Lessons from Lenski

On February 24, 1988, Professor Richard Lenski seeded twelve sterile flasks containing ten milliliters of glucose solution with the common bacterium *Escherichia coli* (commonly called *E. coli*).

Lenski had started an experiment that continues today and has yielded hundreds of research articles, dozens of doctorates, and global acclaim.[17]

He started an experiment on long-term evolution like the one conducted on silver foxes by Lyudmila Trut and Dmitri Belyaev but with two key differences. First, he wanted to use microscopic organisms that have a generation time of only twenty minutes, thereby allowing tens of thousands of generations to evolve over a human lifetime. Second, unlike the artificial selection experiments on foxes (or dogs or wheat), in which the *experimenter* chooses who (or what) reproduces, Lenski wanted the experimental *environment* to choose.

When the experiment started, all twelve flasks had genetically the same *E. coli* since all cells came from the same mother cell. Each flask contained hundreds of millions of bacteria, so there was ample opportunity for mutations to emerge. An essential experimental twist was that food was in limited supply. Every day, the *E. coli* population increased for about six hours until the glucose was exhausted. At this point, the bacteria would stop dividing and wait. The next day, a lab member—someone like Tim Cooper—would take 0.1 milliliters out of each flask (1 percent of the flask's content) and inoculate a new flask containing 9.9 milliliters of fresh glucose solution. A new cycle would then begin until the next day, when the same procedure would be repeated. And the next day. Week after week, month after month, year after year.

Lenski was replaying Gould's proverbial tape of life simultaneously in twelve flasks. He wasn't selecting the bacteria, and he wasn't varying the medium. Instead, he was letting life run its course in parallel over thousands of generations. What he found was remarkable. In 2011, after fifty thousand generations of evolution, he said, "To my surprise, evolution was pretty repeatable. . . . Although the lineages certainly diverged in many details, I was struck by the parallel trajectories of their evolution, with similar changes in so many phenotypic traits and even gene sequences we examined."

It wasn't that the bacteria had not evolved. On the contrary, they had evolved a lot. The *E. coli* in different flasks adapted differently to the starvation diet by either growing faster or becoming more numerous than earlier generations. But the general trend was unmistakable: On average, the population grew 70 percent faster than their founding ancestors. In addition, the researchers found another example of convergent evolution. All twelve populations of bacteria had lost the ability to synthesize a sugar called D-ribose because all had undergone the *same* set of genetic changes.

Unlike Gould's prediction, the replaying of the tape of life was yielding the same result.

Until one day, fifteen years after the start of the experiment, Tim Cooper found that it didn't.

The reason the Ara-3 flask had turned opaque was that, unlike the other flasks, it had experienced a population explosion. The Ara-3 population was ten times the size of the populations in the other flasks. How could this have happened when all flasks had only a limited amount of glucose?

The Ara-3 bacteria had developed the ability to feed on some other ingredient in the solution. The only other candidate was a molecule called citrate present in all glucose solutions from day one. However, at the time of the beginning of the experiment, *E. coli* was explicitly known *not* to synthesize citrate in the presence of oxygen. Therefore, this inability was used to identify whether a type of bacteria was *E. coli* or not!

The 33,127th generation of Lenski's bacteria had deviated drastically from the clean and simple story of inevitable convergence. It was as big a case of *divergence* as biology had ever seen experimentally. Lenski's lab later found that the ability of the Ara-3 bacteria to digest citrate resulted from a series of mutations after about twenty thousand generations. Unfortunately, each mutation was rare, so no bacteria in any of the other flasks have developed this ability.

It is worth paying attention to the two critical lessons from Lenski's long-term experiment:

1. Convergence is the dominant pattern in the natural world.
2. On rare occasions, it isn't.

We can replace just one word to derive the *same* two critical lessons for us investors:

1. Convergence is the dominant pattern in the business world.
2. On rare occasions, it isn't.

I have been singing the praises of convergence as a powerful investing tool, which it is. Of course, there are only a few ways for businesses to succeed. As investors, identifying a convergent pattern of success or failure has helped us make (what we think are) some excellent investments and avoid many bad ones.

But I have also reached a painful realization that patterns can break, and a successful Ara-3-type mutant can arise occasionally. Unfortunately, we would miss an opportunity to invest in it.

If one replays the tape of business history across periods and countries, the overwhelming convergent pattern would be that business focus leads to success. Most of our portfolio comprises businesses with only one product or service or a small set of related products and services. We refuse to invest in diversified companies or conglomerates. We also express disappointment when any of our management teams try to deviate from their course.

If I were an investor in the United States, I would have missed Amazon by adhering to this investment philosophy. Amazon has a market value of about one *trillion* dollars. This business started as an electronic book retailer and diversified into an ever-growing list of offerings, many of which have almost nothing to do with one another.

You can watch a movie on Prime Video after reading its review in a magazine bought on Kindle. You can be attired in comfortable Amazon Essentials when you order milk and eggs through Amazon Fresh delivery by talking to Alexa. Amazon Logistics will deliver your groceries and announce their arrival at your doorstep via Ring. While playing Amazon Music, you can earn some money by completing a Mechanical Turk survey hosted on Amazon Web Services. And you can be a citizen of any of the fifty-eight countries globally with Amazon's presence.

If Ara-3 had a brain, it would have been intensely jealous of Jeff Bezos, who seems to have broken every business rule to out-mutate the ultimate mutant.

In 2017, Warren Buffett admitted on CNBC's *Squawk Box* that he should have invested in Amazon. I have no such qualms. I know that I would have missed Amazon in the past, and I will miss an Amazon-like business in the future. So be it.

The only saving grace of this failure? I doubt I will see another Bezos in my lifetime.

✳ ✳ ✳

When I advocate convergence investing, I admit my incompetence. I am effectively saying, "I don't know how to assess *this* particular business." Maybe this is why the approach of taking the outside or convergent view while being straightforward is not followed as widely as it should be. Yet, since 2007, we have kept doing what we love: asking questions that lead us to companies' patterns of success and failure.

In our profession, getting the correct answer is easy. But, unfortunately, asking the right question is not.

Chapter Summary

Evolutionary theory has taught me that . . .

. . . an important element of reimagining investing is internalizing the *recurring* patterns of success and failure in the business world.

1. Convergence—unrelated organisms developing the same solutions to similar problems—is ubiquitous in nature. It is seen across animals, plants, fungi, and even bacteria. In nature, every problem seems to have only a small set of solutions.
2. For example, Australia's flora and fauna has been evolving independently of those of the rest of the world for more than thirty-five million years (when Australia became a separate continent), but for every Australian marsupial, there seems to be a placental counterpart.

3. The business world, too, is convergent. There are definitive patterns to the success and failure of companies. We exploit this property of the corporate world to select outstanding businesses and reject lousy ones by asking a simple question: "Where else have we seen this?"

4. We are investors not in individual businesses but in proven and successful *templates* of businesses.

5. We are big fans of Daniel Kahneman's "outside view"—which is conceptually similar to convergence and compels us to seek similar patterns elsewhere before making an investment decision.

6. However, applying the principle of convergence is tricky because we humans can see patterns where none exist. We can also miss out on one-off opportunities like Amazon that seem to defy the convergent notion that focus is the key to success.

CHAPTER 7

DON'T CONFUSE A GREEN FROG FOR A GUPPY

The sexes of many animals incessantly call for each other during the breeding-season; and not in a few cases, the male endeavours thus to charm or excite the female. This, indeed, seems to have been the primeval use and means of development of the voice, as I have attempted to show in my "Descent of Man."

Charles Darwin, The Expression of Emotion in Man and Animals,
chapter 4, "Means of Expression in Animals"

Fechheimer is exactly the sort of business we like to buy. Its economic record is superb. . . . You may be amused to know that neither Charlie nor I have been to Cincinnati, headquarters for Fechheimer, to see their operation. . . . If our success were to depend upon insights we developed through plant inspections, Berkshire would be in big trouble. Rather, in considering an acquisition, we attempt to evaluate the economic characteristics of the business—its competitive strengths and weaknesses—and the quality of people we will be joining.

Warren Buffett, annual letter to shareholders, 1985

The Oracle from Omaha takes the crown for best investor in the world. He started managing $105,000 for family and friends in 1956 and has compounded it to half a trillion dollars today. Who is the second best?

Anthony Bolton is not widely known, but in my view, he is the sole occupier of second place in the pantheon of all-time investment greats. He was the superstar fund manager from the United Kingdom with a track record rivaling Buffett's. Bolton managed the Fidelity Special Situations Fund for twenty-eight years, from 1979 until 2007, and achieved an annualized return of 19.5 percent when the market yielded about 13.5 percent. A sum of £1,000 would have compounded to £147,000 during his tenure. If there is a better dictionary definition of "stellar," I have yet to see it.

In 2010, he came back from retirement to launch a £460 million fund. However, the fund significantly underperformed the market and lost 14 percent over the next three years. Bolton had to leave the fund in 2014.

How could a genius who had beaten the market over almost three decades suffer so dismally? Was it just bad luck, or did he slip up? If so, where? If this happened to Bolton, is anyone immune from such a fate?

The Blessings and Perils of Signals

If you are as ardent a fan of the National Geographic channel as I am, some of or all the following scenes should be familiar to you. A male lion roaring to assert his dominance over a pride; female baboons with their bright sexual swelling indicating their readiness to mate; bees performing their waggle dance to show the direction and distance of flowers; a female elephant caressing her calf to soothe him; a deep-sea squid emitting light to attract prey; and a meerkat squealing to warn her family of a predatory eagle.

All these are examples of signals, and no textbook on evolutionary theory is complete without a lengthy discussion on them.[1] Signals emitted by a "sender" have explicitly evolved to alter the behavior of the "receiver" and are used to communicate with and influence the behavior of prey, predators, mates, competitors, friends, and family. A signal can take myriad forms: touch, sound, color, motion, light, odor, or some combination of these. No organism could live without emitting and receiving signals, but a misdirected or misread signal can also lead to death. Although evolution has honed the signal emitting and receiving skills and instincts of animals and plants over millions of years, the race to deceive a predator or beat a competitor for food or a mate is never over.

This book is about an integral part of the financial services industry—an industry that deserves its reputation for dishonesty and deceit. Few have described the sad state of our industry better than Fred Schwed in his hard-hitting, timeless classic *Where Are the Customers' Yachts?* Those of you who suffered through the global financial crisis of 2008 have probably exhausted every cuss word for us finance folks. If you aren't an evolutionary biologist, you probably believe that deception is the sole preserve of our cunning species. Not so.

Let's start with green frogs.

Green frogs, like most animals, have a short window for mating. During this crucial period, males need to defend their territories aggressively to maximize their reproductive success. Larger males advertise their size and dominance by making calls (croaks, if you prefer) at a lower frequency than smaller frogs. Thus, a male green frog who is evolutionarily programmed to avoid larger and stronger green frogs will not enter a territory filled with low-frequency croaks. His brain equates low-frequency croaks with unbeatable rivals.

What do you do if you are a small green frog? Live without a mate and die a virgin? No, sir! Some small green frogs have found a way to *lower* their signals' pitch, thereby communicating that they are larger than they actually are.[2] This ability enables them to preserve their territories by fooling the larger males. Some small green frogs hijack a low-frequency croak to send a dishonest signal, thereby gaining evolutionary advantage. This dishonest signal is easy to produce and imposes a very small cost on the signaler, the small green frog.

If you think the green frogs are devious little dudes, you should be suitably impressed with the shenanigans of the fantastic fiddler crabs.

Fiddler crabs have gone one up on green frogs by dishonestly signaling their prowess to females *and* other males.[3] Male fiddler crabs have a single large claw that serves the dual purpose of fighting other males and attracting females. Researchers have found that females differentially prefer males with larger claws, and these well-endowed males also successfully deter other male rivals. When a male loses his large claw in a fight, he usually grows a new claw that is lighter in weight, slenderer, and weaker. However, its size can still be impressive, and it can *look* as potent as the previous heavier and deadlier claw.

These regenerated claws fool both sexes. The females do not differentiate between these impostors and the males with the heavier "real" claws. Even the males with the "real" claws don't pick a fight with males with lighter and weaker but impressive-looking regenerated claws. Researchers have found that up to 44 percent of males in a fiddler crab population can have regenerated claws. And you thought it was only us finance folks whom you can't trust!

If you think dishonest signals are emitted solely by animals, think again.

Plants are masters of deception. Since they can't run or hide, many of their survival strategies involve deceiving other plants or animals. Some of the best examples—or worst, if you happen to be a wasp—are certain species of Australian orchids.[4] Australia has about 1,400 species of orchids, and around 250 of these have adopted the same strategy of deceiving male wasps to enable pollination.

Here is how it works. When a female wasp, who lives most of her life underground laying eggs, is ready to mate, she emerges from the ground and emits a distinctive pheromone that attracts the males. Many males typically descend on a female and start copulating in a frenzy. Nothing out of the ordinary here. Okay, agreed, a bit disconcerting, but you know what I mean.

Enter the orchid. Many orchid species have figured out a way to emit the *same* pheromone that a female wasp emits. What is the result? The male wasps end up copulating with orchid flowers, thereby brushing against pollen, which they carry to other flowers, where the unfortunate wasps "mate" again and leave the pollen behind!

I don't want to give the impression that the living world is replete only with hustlers and cheats. Unlike green frogs, fiddler crabs, and Australian orchids, male guppies and coral snakes lead a more upright life.

Guppies populate the mountain forest streams of Venezuela, Trinidad, and Tobago. Whereas female guppies are plain and drab-looking, male guppies are quite colorful, and no two males have the same color pattern. I urge you to do a Google image search of male guppies to see how dazzlingly beautiful they are.

Scientists have experimentally demonstrated that females have a clear preference for brighter and more conspicuously red males with greater quantities of carotenoid pigments. More on carotenoids shortly. But conspicuous coloration comes at a huge cost to the males—their life.[5] More colorful guppies are also subject to higher predation. If the males have dull colors, they won't get to mate, but if they are brightly colored, they are likely to be hunted down. Talk about being between a rock and a hard place. Thus, brighter colors in a guppy are an honest signal of attractiveness to females. As Godin and McDonough succinctly state, "The viability cost associated with bright conspicuous coloration in male guppies potentially reinforces for females the reliability of this sexually selected trait as an indicator trait of male quality."[6]

While a male guppy may attract predators by honestly communicating to females, the deadly coral snake *deters* its potential predators with its bright coloration.[7] About ninety species of these fabulously colored and highly poisonous snakes are native to the tropics. They have alternating patterns of three colors: red, black, and yellow or white. This kind of aposematic (what a nice-sounding word from the world of biology!) or conspicuous coloration is quite common among many poisonous plants and animals. They are essentially broadcasting honestly to their potential predators, "Don't you dare!"

But what would evolution be if not bizarre and fascinating? Nonvenomous milk snakes kept as pets have almost the same coloration and banding pattern of coral snakes. I bet that if you put the photographs of these two species side by side, you would be unable to distinguish the poisonous one from the pet.[8] Try it.

This kind of dishonest communication is called Batesian mimicry and was first discovered in the 1860s by Henry Walter Bates in butterflies of Brazil.[9] In Batesian mimicry, a harmless species mimics the coloration of a poisonous or unpalatable species to ward off predators. Milk snakes have successfully evolved through natural selection to mimic coral snakes, thereby ensuring their survival.

I want to present a necessary qualifier here, which I will assert a few more times to avoid anthropomorphic confusion. The words "honest" and "dishonest" in the discussion so far do not communicate the *intent* of the signaler. They point to the *effect* of the signal on the receiver. When a signal fools the receiver, it is dishonest; when the receiver understands the signal for what it is, it is honest. Neither the guppy nor the milk snake possesses the ability to dictate its body color. The orchid is not deliberately releasing pheromones, nor is the fiddler crab consciously building a large fake claw. These creatures are all products of natural selection honed over millions of years.

For example, an ancestor of the harmless milk snake may have developed the coloration of the poisonous coral snake through a random mutation. These mutants would have had a higher survival rate than their nonmutated peers, thereby giving birth to more baby milk snakes with the same pattern. These babies, in turn, would have been safer from predators and would have successfully produced more offspring with the same colorful pattern, and so on. Over many generations, all milk snakes would come to have the same coloration as coral snakes. In doing so, they have perfected the dishonest signal.

The Handicap Principle Clarifies It All

While I call myself an investor, an evolutionary biologist would not be remiss in branding me a "signal decoder." The *only* things investors can rely on to assess a company are the signals emitted by it—some direct and others indirect, some comprehensible and others bizarre, some ongoing and others delayed, and some quantitative and others qualitative.

Companies relay signals in the form of press releases, media interviews, analyst meetings, earnings calls, annual reports, dividends, buybacks, acquisitions, SEC filings, newspaper boasts, and so much more. Most investors receive the same signals from companies since the capital market regulators have ensured the standardization and transparency of communication. So how is it that the long-term performance of different investors—who are all within a small band of seemingly prodigious intellectual capacity—varies significantly? Among the many reasons for this variance, one that stands out for me is an investor's ability to decode honest signals from dishonest ones (figure 7.1). Acting on a dishonest signal and ignoring an honest one can lead to hunger or death in the natural world, a fate not too dissimilar to a fund's performance.

But how is an investor supposed to distinguish between an honest signal and a dishonest one?

7.1 The strutting male: Whose signal is more honest, (a) the businessperson's or (b) the deer's?

Source: Licensed from Shutterstock.

Let's turn to the Israeli evolutionary biologist Amotz Zahavi for an exquisitely elegant answer.

But first, a brief background on signals. In the early and middle parts of the twentieth century, ethologists (ethology is the study of animal behavior) believed that signals were essentially honest indicators of senders' underlying motives. However, in the 1970s, two British scientists, Richard Dawkins and John Krebs, took an almost diametrically opposite view claiming that signals were best seen as a deceitful manipulation by a sender to alter the behavior of the receiver for the sender's benefit.[10] On the other hand, the receiver was trying to fathom the true motive of the sender and plotting its own moves. According to Dawkins and Krebs, this leads to an arms race in which the sender and receiver are constantly trying to outdo each other.

However, Amotz Zahavi rejected this pessimistic view of signals. In 1975, he proposed his famous "handicap principle," which explains how and why honest signals can evolve in the natural world where animals are presumably trying to deceive one another.[11] Zahavi's profound observation was that when signals for a particular trait are costly to produce—he rightly termed such signals "handicaps"—and cannot be matched by another with a lower quality of that trait, they can be deemed "honest." That may *sound* logical, but science, unlike the investment profession, needs empirical evidence to support its tall claims. The scientific community did not fully accept the handicap principle until fifteen years after the publication of the article in which Zahavi presented it.[12] In 1990, two articles by the Scottish biologist Alan Grafen finally turned the tide in its favor.

The best route to understanding the handicap principle is through carotenoids. Carotenoids are a class of pigments ranging from yellow to orange to red. They also provide health benefits by acting as antioxidants and strengthening the immune system. Animals can't synthesize carotenoids within their bodies and must procure them by eating plants, bacteria, or fungi. Carotenoids play a strong signaling role, and scientists have studied their effect extensively in three species: the house finch (a bird), the three-spined stickleback (a fish), and the guppy.

If the handicap principle is accurate, we should be able to confirm the following three hypotheses:

1. Females are differentially attracted to males with redder or brighter hues,
2. Males with a redder coloration are fitter than paler males, and
3. It is costly for healthy males to produce a deep red pigment.

In the species studied, researchers have shown conclusively that females react more favorably to males that display a deeper carotenoid pigmentation. Male house finches, for example, have three patches of carotenoid pigmentation on their body: on the crown, throat, and rump. Each patch varies in coloration from pale yellow to bright red. Experiments clearly show that female house finches prefer to consort with redder males whether this redness results from natural diet or artificial dyes. This finding supports the first hypothesis: receiver response.

To provide support for the second hypothesis (signal honesty), scientists demonstrated that well-fed house finches developed a deeper red coloration compared to those fed less nutritious food. When researchers exposed three-spined sticklebacks to parasites, the ones with a higher load of infectious ciliate had a significant decrease in red coloration. Other experiments like the one by Godin and McDonough described earlier have found evidence for the same phenomenon in guppies. Thus, deeper carotenoid pigmentation does seem to indicate better overall health.

Let's now deal with the last and most crucial hypothesis: whether honest signals impose a cost on the signaler. Over the years, biologists have unearthed four possible costs of deeper carotenoid pigmentation. First, carotenoid levels in fish scales or bird plumage are directly correlated with the amount of carotenoid in the animal's gut. Thus, the more time an animal spends eating nutritious food, the redder the pigment but also the greater the cost incurred. Second, since carotenoids have health benefits and are needed to ward off disease and parasites, redirecting them from the gut to dead tissues like scales or feathers for display purposes is a costly maneuver for the animal. Third, displaying carotenoid pigmentation involves the cost of processing carotenoids in the gut and then transporting them to the feathers or scales. Hence, only those animals that have eaten enough nutritious food are up to the task. The fourth obvious cost is the risk of death: A deep red coloration charms females and foes alike. In laboratory experiments, trout have been shown to be more likely to attack redder sticklebacks, and blue acara cichlids are more likely to kill guppies with greater carotenoid pigmentation.

Thus, according to the handicap principle, redder male house finches attract more mates presumably because their message to females is, "Look how healthy and virile I am; I am so darned red!" It would be very costly and potentially even suicidal for a weak or diseased house finch to produce more carotenoid pigmentation given the diversion of resources required.

Obviously, male house finches do not consciously "decide" to produce redder colors; the healthier ones simply have enough nutritional resources to produce the pigmentation, and the weaker ones don't. Ditto for the brightly colored male guppy in the example mentioned earlier. Or the dude with the shiny red Ferrari. All of them show off ornaments that are very expensive to produce or procure and hence accurately communicate the signaler's well-being.

And herein lies Zahavi's lesson for us investors: *Lend credence only to those signals from companies that are costly to produce.*

That, however, is easier said than done. What does "costly to produce" mean in the context of a corporate environment? What is the equivalent of a peacock's resplendent tail? A shiny new corporate headquarters, an industry award, a growing market value, a CEO's *Forbes* profile, or something else? I am a practicing investor, not a finance academic. I cannot offer a regression model proven to be statistically relevant, but I can offer the practical ways in which my team and I distinguish between honest and dishonest signals.

Dishonest Signals Galore

Let's start with real-life examples of dishonest signals; that is, those that do not *reliably* communicate the trait they are supposed to. A "dishonest" signal does *not* imply that the sender is dishonest, although they might be; it simply means that the *signal* may not communicate what it is supposed to. Just as in the natural world, an honest person in a business setting can send a dishonest signal *without* necessarily having a bad intention.

When we evaluate a business to make an investment or divestment, we ignore the following types of signals or assign them a *very* low weight in our overall evaluation.

Press Releases

On July 29, 2014, Apple's press release claimed that the company had updated the MacBook Pro with Retina Display (note the capital "R" and "D").[13] Should investors have cared about this news?

Maybe you would have been impressed if you were a discerning consumer, but how would this announcement have helped an investor decide if Apple was a good company to buy? You could argue that the press release indicated Apple's prowess in keeping up with the latest technology trends, and so it was, in fact, quite informative. But how many investors—or nontechies in general—even know or understand what "Retina Display" means? I don't.

Even if Retina Display, whatever it is, were to turn out to be a cool new technology, how was anyone to conclude from this information that the MacBook Pro would become a success? And to belabor the point, even if an investor did understand what Retina Display meant, and even if they concluded from various sources that it was likely to be a great success, how would this knowledge help them decide whether to buy Apple shares unless they could accurately forecast the profits and cash flows to be made from the increased sales of the MacBook Pro as a result of this technology?

A press release is probably the most used—or should I say "abused"?—signal given out by companies. The reason? It does not cost anything for the company to be in the press regularly apart from the retainer for the PR agency, which is usually an annual fixed expense. Many companies resort to regular press releases and interviews to share news of product launches, management changes, strategy shifts, and organization changes.

First, I am deeply suspicious of companies regularly in the press. (Don't they have anything better to do?) But even those that are not professionals at managing the press through their public relations consultants rarely have anything helpful to say for a long-term investor.

Second, press releases can be—and frequently are—more insidious than the harmless MacBook Pro announcement. Many press releases *appear* to reveal significant information that a long-term investor must absorb but turn out to be empty boasts at best and deliberate obfuscation at worst.

Take the example of a Unilever press release from January 20, 2015.[14] The headline states confidently, "Profitable Growth in Tougher Markets." A detailed look at the press release left me scratching my confused head. I assume you agree that developed markets like the United States and Western Europe should be classified as "tough" because they are mature, have high competitive intensity, *and* have growth challenges. But if you read the press release carefully, you will notice that sales in 2014 *declined* by 0.8 percent in developed markets. Sales did grow 5.7 percent in emerging markets (though even this growth was lower than in 2013), but I would not call emerging markets "tough."

Interestingly, the press release fails to mention which markets, according to Unilever, are "tough" and which are "easy." Maybe you disagree with me and prefer to call emerging markets tough. Alright, let's go ahead with that definition. But then how does one explain a sales *decline* of 20 percent in the fourth quarter in China? A slowdown of this magnitude, especially in a market as large as China, may be relevant information for investors, but as we saw, it is nowhere in the headlines. Unilever's overall sales in 2014, by the way, declined by 2.7 percent. Was this the cause for celebration that the press release seemed to imply?

The bottom line is that making investment or divestment decisions based on a press release can be harmful to a fund's bottom line. We treat press releases as what they are: a cheap signal given by companies to make competitors envious and to attract investors, employees, and customers.

We don't give them any importance.

Management Interviews in the Media

It was June 13, 2019. The fifty-one-year-old visionary CEO was giving an interview to *Bloomberg*'s Matt Miller on the sidelines of Europe's most prestigious digital and tech conference in Berlin. His company was a giant in payment processing, and from being a scrappy start-up in the early 2000s, its soaring market value had enabled it to win an entry into the coveted DAX index in 2018. Its stock price had tripled over the past three years, valuing it at about €18 billion. Twenty-three of twenty-nine research analysts covering the company had a "buy" rating on it.

Over the years, the *Financial Times* business newspaper and some short sellers had raised issues about its accounting practices, but the company had brushed aside all the allegations. In this context, Matt Miller was conducting an impressive interview. Rather than fawning over the celebrity CEO, Miller posed some tough questions on the sources of the company's growth, its questionable corporate governance practices, and the reasons for the persistent rumors about the company's lax compliance processes.

The relaxed and confident CEO looked Miller directly in the eyes and answered every question with remarkable clarity and precision. He assured Miller that Asia was the primary growth engine, its new sales were up 160 percent, and, contrary to the popular view, it was also witnessing growth in Europe. The CEO came down heavily on his detractors, reminding Miller that his share price had delivered a 36 percent annualized return (!) over the past fourteen years. He was confident that his compliance staff of two hundred were world class and explained that the company was investing heavily in technology to enable digital monitoring of transactions.

Almost exactly a year after this interview, on June 23, 2020, the CEO was arrested on charges of criminal fraud. The company filed for insolvency on June 25, 2020.

The CEO's name? Markus Braun. The company? Wirecard.

Braun and Wirecard had been lying for years. But Braun's hero worship was so deep and widespread in Germany that the national regulator, BaFin, filed a criminal complaint against *Financial Times* reporters in 2019, accusing them of market manipulation. Braun was a national champion, so how could he be wrong? You can watch the *Bloomberg* interview on Bloomberg TV.[15] Braun comes across as a well-meaning, smart, and thoughtful leader clearly well ahead of the competition on digital payments.

Yes, I know I am cherry-picking one management interview to show how useless they are as a species. But I hope you will not dispute that Braun showed remarkable skills as an interviewee. He reduced the complex global operations of Wirecard to sound bites like "scalable," "digital payments," "risk management," and "innovation." I am almost certain he resonated with viewers, many of whom were surely also investors in the company.

While I *have* taken an extreme example, it highlights two common features of almost all management interviews. First, they are an exercise in making the management look good. And many of them are good. But as you must know from your own experience, looking good is not the same as *being* good. Second, these kinds of interviews can provide us a lot of information about the interviewee (dog's name and favorite dish included) and the company, but not a lot that is relevant to an *investor*. For example, Braun's statements, "In many areas, we are pioneers," and "We are concentrating on technology innovations," may be of literary, academic, sociological, or cultural interest, but what do they tell me, an investor? Nothing. I should be impressed by these quotes as a viewer, but not as someone who wishes to invest in Wirecard.

Have you ever read management interviews that claim they *aren't* innovative, don't have the best business leaders, aren't "leveraging" technology, aren't customer focused, don't treat their employees well, don't listen to shareholders, make bad capital allocations, and ignore the value of making "sustainable" investments? I haven't. But the fact remains that most of the businesses I have encountered in my life as a consultant and as an investor have been deeply flawed in more ways than one. They either don't know it or won't admit to it.

Excellence is rare in this world, including the business world. You just won't know it if you are relying on management interviews.

I am not saying I don't read (or listen to or watch) interviews of business leaders. I do. But I read them for the same reason I read articles on Brexit, running, films, and the latest Trump tantrum: to gossip with friends, to pass the time on a Sunday afternoon, and for general interest in our fascinating world.

Not for investing.

Investor Conferences and Road Shows

Assume for a moment that you have had no exposure to the equity markets. The industry is facing a major problem, and you are asked to solve it. The company management teams seem to be spending too much time entertaining questions from myriad investors, and serious investors complain that their calls to companies remain unanswered because the management teams are sick and tired of answering the same questions. The investors, as well as company management, waste a lot of time and air miles meeting each other across various cities. What would be the best way to ensure that company information is shared efficiently across all interested investors?

If you are a smart person (which you are; after all, you are reading this book, right?!), you will most probably come up with the following answer. Invite many companies and investors to a single location—preferably a city with good flight connections—and let them interact formally through presentations and informally at lunches and dinners.

Well, congratulations! You have the right solution. This is exactly what the industry does by running conferences ranging in length from one to five days. Tens, sometimes even hundreds, of companies converge to make a series of presentations to visiting investors.

Road shows are a scaled-down version of these conferences during which the company management typically visits investors at their offices. Since most investors have offices in large cities like New York, San Francisco, London, and Tokyo, a company can usually meet six to eight investors in a single day.

What do you think most company managers want when they meet investors? They want the investors to buy their stock so that the share price moves up. Are they likely to present a balanced view of their business? It would be easier to believe in Santa Claus. My experience tells me that most of these conferences and road shows are an excuse for the company to show off. In a thirty-minute presentation, the company management will sing paeans of their strategy for 29.9 minutes. They will spend the remaining 0.1 minute drinking water or, if they are feeling generous, mentioning a couple of risks in such hushed tones that you will miss them if you sneeze.

I know I am exaggerating, but not by much, I can assure you. And I don't blame them. If I were them, I would behave the same way. A conference or a road show is a dishonest signal because it does not cost the management team anything to present an overly optimistic view of their company, and so that is what they do. It is a chest-thumping marketing jamboree, not a forum to evaluate investment opportunities dispassionately.

Do we at Nalanda attend conferences and meet management teams during road shows? We absolutely do. But we employ a stratospheric level of discounting to company presentations and treat these conferences and road shows as a *starting* point for evaluating interesting businesses, not as a shortcut to building robust investment theses.

One of the ways we use conferences is to meet our portfolio companies' *competitors*. Are they launching new products? Are they entering new segments? What is their approach to acquisitions? How are they planning to allocate capital? Are they becoming better than the company we own? But we *never* exit a management meeting in this kind of dog-and-pony show claiming that we have found a winner or loser and that we should place an order to buy or sell.

Investor conferences and road shows are dishonest signals not because management are dishonest—most of them are upright folks doing their job—but because it does not cost anything to spin the best story possible in a forty-five-minute presentation to an audience that is partly brain dead from rushing from one meeting to another.

Earnings Guidance

Many publicly listed companies project their profits after tax (also called earnings) over the next fiscal year. For example, in January 2019, during their earnings call, they will project their earnings for the full year of 2019. In subsequent calls (usually held after every quarter), they update this guidance depending on their recent performance and outlook. Analysts and investors follow earnings guidance quite seriously, and stock prices react promptly to the under- or overachievement of this guidance.

Investors and analysts love earnings guidance from companies. In fact, according to an article from *PR Newswire*, 77 percent of the 180 analysts surveyed wanted companies to provide guidance.[16] Analysts are smart folks, so you must be thinking that they can learn a lot from the future pronouncements of companies. Sadly, they don't.

What do you think a management team's projections for the next year are based on? In fact, on what basis does *anyone* make forecasts about the near to medium term? The recent past? A hope for a better future? Spreadsheet manipulation? All of the above? Take your pick. Earnings guidance is a dishonest signal *even though* the management may fervently believe in it. It is cheap, easy to produce, and needs little effort to deliver.

In my career spanning more than three decades, I have sat on the boards of more than two dozen companies ranging from a market value of $5 million to about $50 billion. At the beginning of every fiscal year, all these company management teams usually present their budgets for the year. And I don't remember a *single* occasion when a management team hit its target. Let me repeat that: not a single occasion. I am not kidding. The businesses either exceeded their budgets or underperformed. *And* they had no way of knowing which would happen.

There is a simple reason why earnings are so hard to predict: multiplicative probability. Earnings—or profit after tax—is the *last* line item on a company profit-and-loss statement. We can calculate profit after tax after deducting from revenues the cash expenses, noncash expenses (like depreciation and amortization), financial charges, and taxes. Thus, the management needs to hit its target on *all* these line items to hope for an accurate earnings guidance.

Many of these are not even under the management's control. For example, interest rates may change, thereby affecting the interest income or expense. A global company selling in international markets can significantly undershoot or overshoot its budget owing to currency movements.

But even the line items that you think are in management's control aren't usually so. Take revenues. Let's say the management has confidently projected a certain level of sales for next year. But what if the economy grows faster than predicted? Or slower? What if the competitor launches a price war? What if one of the factories shuts down because of a fire? What if the company's best sales manager, accounting for 7 percent of sales, falls ill suddenly? None of these "what ifs" is theoretical—they have all happened in businesses for which I have been a board member or investor.

One may now assert that the costs incurred by a business should surely be under management's control. After all, costs are all internal, aren't they? Nope. Take raw materials. A manufacturing company using a wide variety of plastics and metals is subject to commodity price fluctuations; a logistics provider is held hostage to petroleum prices; and a services company needs to bend to the vagaries of labor market prices, especially if it is using part-time staff. Sales and advertising expenses seem more controllable—a marketing manager can decide to spend $10 million on advertising next year, and that's that, right? Not so fast. If a new venture-backed competitor emerges that offers a similar product at a 25 percent discount, the marketing manager may have to react by increasing the marketing budget significantly.

Recall your basic probability class. You will remember that when many events are supposed to occur simultaneously (X *and* Y *and* Z), the cumulative probability is arrived at by multiplying all the individual probabilities. Let's assume that the management you are evaluating is truly unique in its ability to forecast, and their predictive accuracy is 80 percent. Thus, the probability of hitting the right earnings number, if it is to be broken into just five component parts (revenues, discounts, employee expenses, manufacturing expenses, and sales expenses) would be less than 33 percent (0.8^5)! In reality, the number of line items before we arrive at the earnings number is much more than five. So how would it be possible, even for a world-class management team, to keep hitting its earnings guidance numbers every quarter or every year? It is almost a mathematical impossibility. So what is the point of the financial community's laser focus on this number?

I do not blame company management or analysts for this disease. Yes, I call it a disease because it infects almost everyone in the asset management industry and prevents investors from performing to their full potential. The blame for this malady should fall squarely on *us*, the investment community, which exerts enormous pressure on businesses and sell-side firms to come up with a single earnings number.

A McKinsey analysis of earnings guidance reaches the following unflattering conclusion: "Our analysis of the perceived benefits of issuing frequent earnings guidance found no evidence that it affects valuation multiples, improves shareholder returns, or reduces share price volatility."[17] The beneficiaries of earnings guidance appear to be neither the investors nor the management—only the brokers! The reports concludes, "The only significant effect we observed is an increase in trading volumes when companies start issuing guidance."

And that's not all. The sad irony of earnings guidance is this: A company consistently meeting its earnings guidance should be seen with an even *greater* degree of skepticism.

Why? General Electric (GE).

In the latter half of the twentieth century, GE was one of the most revered companies on the planet. And under Jack Welch, the CEO of GE from 1981 to 2001, it scaled heights never seen by any company on the planet.[18] Under his leadership, the company increased its market value more than forty times over two decades. In August 2000, GE's market value was $601 billion, making it the most valuable company on Earth. By the end of 2021, it was a shadow of its former self, having lost about 85 percent of its value.

Many things went wrong at GE, and this is not the place to list them, but one of the most striking things about GE during the Jack Welch era was its ability to hit its earnings target quarter after quarter, year after year. Analysts and investors loved GE. When GE declared it would meet its earnings the next year, it always did. As Welch said in an interview with Carol Loomis of *Fortune*, "What investor would want to buy a conglomerate like GE unless its earnings were predictable?" The company had become so blasé and arrogant about "managing" its numbers that the CFO, Dennis Dammerman, was bold enough to admit to *Fortune*, "OK, we're going to take these large gains and offset them with discretionary decisions with restructurings." He was smoothening his profits in plain sight.

The managers were under enormous pressure to hit their earnings targets. When Jeff Immelt, the CEO after Jack Welch, took over the plastics division at GE and found that the previous management had been fudging the profits, he chose to keep quiet. He was a rising star within GE and knew that not meeting his budget was not an option.

GE had a special-purpose vehicle called Edison Conduit that was supposed to be independent of the company but wasn't. GE Capital guaranteed Edison's liabilities, effectively making it a GE company. Why did it exist? Its stated purpose was to issue commercial paper, but its main objective was to create profits out of thin air. It periodically bought assets from GE Capital at higher prices than the book value, thereby showing profits. But how can a company buy its *own* assets to show profits, you ask? Good question. Today it can't—it would be considered fraud. But the company was exploiting an accounting loophole of the pre-Enron era.

In 2002, the Sarbanes–Oxley Act passed, and many accounting tricks being used by GE became illegal. Jack Welch had timed his retirement almost perfectly in 2001. Jeff Immelt, the new CEO, never got the leeway from the accountants that his boss had and kept missing investor expectations. GE's stock price went into a decline that hasn't been arrested more than two decades after Welch's retirement.

I am not suggesting that all of GE's problems resulted from its guidance culture, but I think it played a significant role. When business managers are hyper-focused on meeting quarterly numbers, their long-term orientation takes a back seat; when a company is desperate to make an acquisition just to meet its earnings, it can overpay for a bad asset; when a manager is unable to speak the truth about accounting obfuscations, they pile up over time.

Last, let's assume for a moment that a company *can* accurately predict its earnings without any accounting shenanigans of the kind employed by GE. So what? Should it matter to a long-term investor that the next year's earnings will grow at 5 percent or decline by 10 percent?

We base our assessment of a company on its riskiness, competitive moat, quality of financials, and management integrity—not on its ability to forecast earnings accurately. We *know* it is very hard to predict earnings consistently, so why measure anyone on it? We have never bothered to assess earnings guidance from companies and have tried to persuade many of our portfolio companies to cease providing guidance. The results, I will admit, have been mixed. Old habits die hard.

Face-to-Face Meetings with Management

In mid-2015, Valeant, a pharmaceutical company run by a McKinsey alum called Mike Pearson, was the darling of the stock market and had a market value of about $90 billion. Just five years before, in 2010, its market value was only about $5 billion.

There was no business magazine that had not covered the stupendous success of Valeant. Nothing could stop this juggernaut acquiring pharma companies and cutting costs to the bone to enhance profits. Investors loved Mike and his seemingly unbeatable strategy, and marquee investors like Pershing Square, Sequoia, and ValueAct were big fans.

Charlie Munger, however, was having none of it. He rightly spotted that Valeant's debt-fueled acquisition spree was a recipe for disaster. Combined with Valeant's numerous unethical business practices (e.g., raising the prices of life-saving drugs many times after acquiring them), he opined that Valeant would fail spectacularly sooner or later. In a May 2016 interview with Fox Business, Munger called the company worse than a sewer![19]

Munger's views irritated some of Valeant's largest shareholders, including Bill Ackman, the CIO of Pershing Square. He wrote a lengthy letter to Munger in April 2015 requesting him to meet with Mike Pearson, but Munger refused. Munger did not need a meeting to detect the "honest" signals of Valeant's corruption and incompetence. Valeant had its comeuppance soon after and by mid-2016 had lost 90 percent of its value. Bill Ackman's Pershing Square took a loss of $3 billion on Valeant.

Why were so many experienced investors blind to the problems that Munger had highlighted publicly? Why could Munger correctly predict Valeant's demise *without* meeting Mike Pearson when many of Valeant's board members and investors continued to be passionate supporters? My hypothesis is this: Mike Pearson was a fantastic salesperson. Correction. He was probably one of the best salespeople to have enamored Wall Street.

The smartest people lost their sense of judgment when faced with Mike Pearson's persuasive skills. Valeant's honest signals of its myriad problems remained undetected or ignored in the light of the dishonest signals emitted by Mike Pearson in face-to-face meetings, which by definition were cheap to produce.

Again, I am not asserting that Mike Pearson was dishonest. Maybe he genuinely believed what he said. It doesn't really matter. The reason Munger was right was that he knew that *any* face-to-face meeting is a dishonest signal.

This claim that face-to-face meetings aren't a reliable signal may seem strange at first glance given the importance of management teams for most investors, whether they are venture capitalists, private equity funds, or mutual funds. Many investors take pride in judging management teams based on a single meeting, and if you are one such investor, good for you. I am not.

The odds are that many investors *think* they are good at judging people, but they generally aren't. Let's assume we encounter a genius who is genuinely able to judge a person's character based on a face-to-face meeting. My assertion here is *even if* they possess this rare skill, it will be useless in a management meeting and will not enable them to become a better investor. The reason is simple: *Any* signal that management gives during a meeting is a cheap signal requiring minimal effort. And since it is cheap, the *signal* may be dishonest even if the management is not.

For example, management may believe that their product is high quality, and they will say so in a meeting. Would you believe their assertion, or would you do independent checks to assess the product's quality? Management may genuinely believe that their recent underperformance relative to domestic competition is a result of their focus on overseas markets. If you are a good judge of people and conclude that management is telling the truth, would you take their stated belief to be true? Management knows what you want to hear, and quite often, that is what you *will* hear.

We do meet management teams. We use these meetings to build relationships and to understand their corporate history and some of their past decisions. We never use management meetings to build an investment case or test key hypotheses because we know we will hear what *they* want us to hear, not what *we* want to know.

Invoking Zahavi to Interpret Signals That Matter

It looks like we are in a bit of soup here. If we can't rely on press releases, investor conferences, earnings guidance, or management meetings, what kinds of signals can we, as investors, trust?

Let's go back to Amotz Zahavi, whose assertion about the natural world is highly relevant to the investing world: We should trust only *costly* signals emitted by companies because they are the only ones we can rely on. But what signals are costly to produce and hence reliable? Broadly, there are two.

We know the first one from chapter 5.

Past Operating and Financial Performance

I will not rehash the logic I outlined in chapter 5 for visiting the past to assess a business and industry; suffice it to say that we at Nalanda treat the past as one of two critical and reliable signals for our investment and divestment decisions. The past has happened. It is there for us to see. It is an undeniable signal of the company's actions and outcomes. The problem, of course, is that investors seem intently focused on receiving signals about the *future*.

Let's take the example of a ubiquitous phenomenon in the world of investing: conference calls.

I know I discussed conference calls in chapter 5, but it's important to revisit the phenomenon in the light of honest and dishonest signals. A quarterly call is a strong signal sent by the management to the broader analyst and investor community. The CEO, CFO, and some other key business leaders typically attend the calls. If there is one place where you can get all your answers, this is it. Jamie Dimon of JPMorgan, Mark Zuckerberg of Facebook, Jack Dorsey formerly of Twitter, Tim Cook of Apple, Elon Musk of Tesla—all these business leaders regularly attend their companies' quarterly calls.

Let's take a concrete example. Chevron, one of the world's largest oil companies, had revenues of about $140 billion and a market value of about $190 billion in 2019. The management held a conference call for investors and analysts on January 31, 2020, to highlight its performance.[20] The analysts and investors asked twenty-nine questions. What percentage of these do you think were about the future? More than 70 percent.

Here is a small sample of these future-directed questions:

- Can you talk a little bit more about how you think about volumes in 2020? *(Remember that this call is from the start of 2020.)*
- I was curious where else we could see some upside in the portfolio in 2020.
- As you continue to shed assets and capital intensity is lowered, just wondering how repeatable outsized dividend growth could be over the long term.

In and of themselves, the questions on volumes, potential upside, and potential dividend growth are important. But just because a question is important does not mean it has a good or reliable answer. I want to know my fund returns next year, but I would be foolish to pick a number.

Let's take the questions on volumes and potential upside. Chevron management gave a lengthy answer to these queries but essentially said that volume growth would be in the same ballpark as in previous years. Little did they—or anyone else for that matter—know that the COVID-19 pandemic would strike or that the price of and demand for oil would drop precipitously. Chevron would end 2020 with a net *loss* of $5.5 billion compared to a net profit of $2.9 billion in 2019. In the fourth quarter of 2020, revenue had dropped to $25 billion from $35 billion a year earlier, a reduction of almost 30 percent. During the conference call, management predicted capital spending of $21 billion in 2020. The actual number? $13 billion.

All the questions related to Chevron's performance in 2020 and beyond essentially turned out to be useless. I know I am being unfair because I have chosen the year of the pandemic to talk about the difficulty of making predictions. But by doing so, I want to highlight the absurdity of the financial sector's focus on a company's future. No business could have predicted the calamities of 2020, and Chevron was no exception.

We can assume that Chevron management are honest and willing to answer questions to the best of their abilities. But how can any *signal* they give about the future be anything but cheap, and hence dishonest, given that pontification of future events does not demand much effort? Any talk of the future is unreliable and just speculation.

If I were in a senior management position at Chevron and asked these questions, my replies would have been no different. The problem is not with Chevron. It is with us, the financial industry folks, who want to coerce the management of companies to do the undoable and then blame them when they don't meet our impossible standards.

An honest signal is not "our margin will be 15 percent next year" but "our average margin was 12 percent over the last ten years"; an honest signal is not "we will have robust free cash flows starting two years from now" but "we generated free cash flow only one year in the last decade"; an honest signal is not "we will launch six new products next year" but "in our recent history, we have launched an average of one product every two years."

No stories, no projections, just facts about the past.

"Because She Said So"

While most people show positive bias in evaluating themselves and their kids, they can be remarkably candid and accurate when it comes to analyzing other people and their spouses. As an investor, we have used this well-proven human quality to solicit positive and negative signals on companies. A good reputation is a *very* costly signal—and hence an honest one—because building a name for oneself in any industry consumes enormous management time and effort over many years, if not decades.

Therefore, before we make an investment, we spend many months speaking to dealers, competitors, ex-employees, suppliers, and industry experts to get a holistic understanding of a company and its industry. We consider these "scuttlebutt" signals to be sincere for two reasons.

First, in general, I have found that few people have an incentive to lie unless they bear a serious grudge against a company. If a competitor is impressed with the company you are evaluating, it will say so and give you many reasons for saying so. Second, once we have performed enough interviews with people connected to the company (but not necessarily *from* the company), we start to get a good sense of the management's reputation and quality.

I learned a valuable scuttlebutt lesson in 2008, less than a year after starting Nalanda. We had become deeply interested in a manufacturing company in India with a market value of almost $2 billion. The company had a very high return on capital over its long history, claimed to design and manufacture products that others couldn't, and had a roster of marquee clients. The financial community was all praises for the businesses. We met the management and came away suitably impressed with the articulation of its strategy and philosophy. Our analysis of past results and performance yielded only positive news.

We started talking to the company's customers, who were largely in the health care sector. We were surprised when all the customers we spoke to categorized it as a commodity supplier, not a specialist manufacturer. They told us that they were buying from this company only because it offered the lowest prices, not because it sold the latest high-tech products. It was clear to us after a few customer calls that the company had been resorting to hyperbole when it touted the quality of its products and depth of customer relationships.

We also spotted a strange anomaly in its balance sheet. A number of receivable days of 270 seemed too high for a company that claimed to have a strong relationship with its customers. Why would customers take nine months to pay? When we asked the company, their glib response was that this was customary in the health care industry. During our scuttlebutt calls, we checked with the customers, and all of them told us that they were paying the company within 90 days as per their agreement. Where was the cash hiding for the remaining 180 days?

Our third scuttlebutt signal turned out to be the most damaging. We were able to interview the company's previous head of sales who had resigned a few months earlier. When we asked him about company performance, he quipped, "You are financial sector folks. So maybe you can explain this anomaly to me. I was the global sales head and was responsible for 100 percent of company revenues. But my actual delivered sales numbers for the quarter were *always* much lower than what the company stated in its quarterly financial results. How could it be so?" We didn't need to hear any more.

The market value of this business is down 98 percent from its peak in early 2008.

If we had relied only on the company's stated past financial and operating performance and had not performed our extensive scuttlebutt research, maybe

Nalanda would not exist today. It may not have been possible to recover from making a dud investment of $150 to $200 million.

As an aside, the great investor Philip A. Fisher first popularized the scuttlebutt approach in his 1958 classic, *Common Stocks and Uncommon Profits*. In chapter 2 ("What 'Scuttlebutt' Can Do"), he asserts, "The business 'grapevine' is a remarkable thing. It is amazing what an accurate picture of the relative points of strength and weakness of each company in an industry can be obtained from a representative cross-section of the opinions of those who in one way or another are concerned with any particular company."

Truer words have rarely been uttered.

Back to Bolton

Let's get back to the mystery of the underperformance of the £460 million fund launched by Anthony Bolton in 2010. I deliberately withheld a key piece of information from you earlier: Bolton launched his fund in *China*, not the United Kingdom. I don't know what he was thinking, but having shown his mettle in the United Kingdom, I am assuming Bolton wanted a new challenge.

But China is not the United Kingdom, especially when it comes to the behavior and track record of listed companies (as an aside, India is not that different from China in this regard). You may have heard of Luckin Coffee, which was supposed to be the Starbucks of China. It claimed to have a more scalable model than Starbucks because it sold cheap coffee, primarily for takeout and delivery. It had positioned itself as a tech company because customers could order through its app. Many marquee investors, including one of China's largest venture capital firms, Joy Capital, and Singapore's sovereign wealth fund, GIC, had invested in Luckin at a valuation of $1 billion.

The company went public in the United States in May 2019, and by January 2020, its stock price had reached $50, valuing the company at more than $12 billion. In late January, the famous short seller Muddy Waters released a scathing report on Luckin alleging that its sales numbers were falsely elevated.[21] To make matters worse, Luckin's auditor, Ernst & Young, unearthed fraudulent behavior by Luckin's senior employees. By May 2020, the stock had crashed more than 95 percent.

Luckin, unfortunately, is not an exception. Chinese companies like China Agritech, China Green Agriculture, China Integrated Energy, GSX Techedu, iQIYI, Longwei Petroleum, Orient Paper, Puda Coal, and Sino Clean Energy have all been accused of accounting irregularities or outright fraud.[22]

There are probably as many explanations as there are "experts" to account for Anthony Bolton's failure in China. Mine is this: Bolton confused the Chinese signals for British ones. He did not realize that the signals from many

Chinese companies were fundamentally dishonest and that he should have been much more skeptical of their veracity.[23]

In an interview with *South China Morning Post,* the Morningstar analyst Zhao Hu pointed out that not one or two but *three* investee companies of Bolton's China fund had reeled under accounting and product recall scandals. Bolton was accustomed to honest signals from British companies, but in Zhao Hu's words, "Obviously, he had not discounted enough risk into his investments in those small, unproven Chinese firms."

Wasp and orchid redux.

* * *

There is almost never a clear winner in the arms race between the senders and receivers of signals in the natural world. You may have heard of cuckoos leaving their eggs in the nests of other bird species so that someone else can rear their chicks. The signals here are the size, shape, and color of the cuckoo egg, which match those of the eggs of some other bird species. However, scientists have found that some of the parasitized bird species have not allowed themselves to be exploited—they have evolved to produce eggs that are distinctly different, even compared to eggs of their own species.[24] As a result, they recognize cuckoo eggs as interlopers. They have evolved a way to detect the dishonest signal from cuckoos. This race has no winner, and there will probably never be one.

In sharp contrast, in the business world, the senders of signals—the companies—are clearly winning over the receivers—us, the gullible investors. No wonder our community performs poorly compared to the broader market. What should we long-term investors do?

Ignore the green frog and heed the guppy.

Chapter Summary

Evolutionary theory has taught me that . . .

. . . reimagining investing requires us to differentiate between the honest and dishonest signals of businesses.

1. In nature, the "sender" of a signal attempts to influence the behavior of the "receiver." For the receiver, differentiating between an honest and a dishonest signal can be the difference between life and death.
2. A green frog mimicking the low-pitched croak of its larger rival is a dishonest signal, whereas the conspicuous coloration of a male guppy is an honest indicator of its health and virility.

3. Zahavi's handicap principle contends that a signal that is costly to produce is honest and can thus be relied upon by the receiver. The "cost" may be in the form of additional resources required to produce the signal or an increased risk of mortality.

4. As investors, we, too, are bombarded with signals, many of which are dishonest. Examples include press releases, management meetings and interviews, investor conferences, and earnings guidance. All these signals attempt to favorably impress investors and are generally quite easy to produce. We ignore all of them.

5. We rely exclusively on honest signals from businesses that, as in the natural world, are costly to produce. These include past operating and financial performance and scuttlebutt signals from suppliers, customers, competitors, ex-employees, and industry experts.

SECTION III

DON'T BE LAZY—BE *VERY* LAZY

I f you have come this far, I hope you have been nodding your head in agreement more often than cursing the reviewers who persuaded you to buy or borrow this book. What's not to like about avoiding significant risks and buying high-quality businesses? Of course, you and I can quibble about how much weight to give management meetings, whether 20 percent ROCE is acceptable, or at which stage of a turnaround one should invest. However, suppose you are a long-term investor or desire to be one. In that case, I am assuming we agree *directionally*—taking on avoidable risks is bad, and investing in great businesses is good.

Alas, our bonhomie may not last beyond this page.

When it comes to buying and selling businesses, we are not just lazy. We are *very* lazy. We rarely buy and seldom sell. Many—probably most—long-term investors ultimately sell their investments, especially when the price is egregious. We don't. We are permanent owners. We will not sell a single share in a business we love. There are some minor caveats to this (which I will get to), but while some of you may accept the notion of buying rarely, the thought of never selling may seem wrong—even foolish—to you. That's all right. My task in this book is not to tell you what *you* should do but to share what *we* do.

Chapters 8 and 9 invoke two relatively unknown tenets of evolutionary theory to bolster the case for buying rarely and selling even more rarely. Chapter 10 focuses on selling, or rather *not* selling, by elaborating on a well-known but underappreciated concept that unites evolution and long-term investing. Finally, I conclude the book by highlighting a key lesson for investors from evolutionary theory: A simple process can lead to a stellar outcome.

I end with rabbits and honeybees. But we must begin with birds and bears.

CHAPTER 8

BIRDS AND BEARS BARE
AN ABERRATION

It may be said that natural selection is daily and hourly scrutinising, throughout the world, every variation, even the slightest; rejecting that which is bad, preserving and adding up all that is good; silently and insensibly working, whenever and wherever opportunity offers, at the improvement of each organic being in relation to its organic and inorganic conditions of life.

Charles Darwin, On the Origin of Species, *chapter 4, "Natural Selection"*

Despite the difficulties we have had in reserving and the commodity economics of the industry, we expect our insurance business to both grow and make significant amounts of money—but progress will be distinctly irregular and there will be major unpleasant surprises from time to time.

Warren Buffett, annual letter to shareholders, 1986

The island looked like a war zone. And one side had lost badly. The carcasses of dead birds were strewn everywhere.

Peter Boag and Laurene Ratcliffe returned to the island in January 1978 and found that almost 80 percent of the birds had succumbed to the drought of 1977. Only about 290 were alive. They searched for their favorite bird—a female who had followed them around the camp in 1977—but they could not find her body. Of the two main species of birds on the island, *fortis* was especially hard hit. In 1977, not a single *fortis* laid an egg or built a nest, so no *fortis* babies were born. Also, every *fortis* born the year before the drought— in 1976—had perished. Peter and Laurene took careful measurements of the dead and the living birds and went to Princeton to tabulate their findings with a heavy heart.

The results were astounding.

Had they proven Darwin wrong?

What Unites Fed Rates, Chinese Ports, and German Regulators?

One of the biggest Bollywood blockbusters of the 1970s was *Roti Kapda Aur Makaan* (*Bread, Clothes, and Shelter*). Over more than two and a half hours (yes, Bollywood movies can be lengthy) of nonstop melodrama, the film dwells on the importance of the lowest rung of Maslow's hierarchy of needs. If it were to be made today, it would be named *Wi-Fi, Roti, Kapda, Aur Makaan*. To me, the pre-internet era seems unimaginably dull. But then, there was always a lot happening in the world; the difference now is that I am made aware of it with barely a second's delay.

For a hospital nurse, a chocolate salesperson, or an automotive engineer, the flood of nonstop news can be like background noise. They have the option of tuning in or out of it depending on their mood and the amount of free time they have. Some may choose to obsess over specific topics on social media, but their jobs and the general news flow are denizens of nonoverlapping worlds for most of them.

Not so for investors. Most will tell you that the flow of news—especially business news—is a critical input for their decision-making. So it would be highly unusual not to find CNBC playing on mute in their offices or a shiny Bloomberg terminal with scrolling news stories on their desks.

Why? Let me explain by sampling some headlines from the June 22, 2021, online edition of the *Financial Times*:

"Wall Street Rebounds as Markets Adjust to Fed Rate Rise Outlook"
"Covid Outbreak at Chinese Port Exacerbates Global Supply Chain Delays"
"German Regulator Launches Antitrust Probe Into Apple"
"Emerging Markets Are Right to Worry About Capital Flows"
"Solar Power Investors Burnt by the Rise in Raw Material Costs"

Did your heart start to beat faster by the time you reached the headline on solar power? Knowing my industry, I am sure that many investors reacted to one or more of these news items by making small but significant changes to their portfolios.

Start with the first news item on the Fed rate rise outlook. Remember the discounted cash flow (DCF) models we encountered in chapter 5? I bet that most investors *worldwide*, not just in the United States, would have adjusted their DCF models to reflect the potential change in rates. The U.S. dollar is the world's currency, and any interest rate movement in the United States is vital to any country's interest rate. I don't know if this is *actually* so—the issue is too esoteric for me—but I do know that it is *seen* to be so. My inbox receives detailed commentary from Indian analysts whenever the U.S. Fed tinkers or threatens to tinker with the interest rate. And what happens when someone changes the discount rate of their model? The stocks appear cheap or expensive, which is a trigger for buying or selling.

A newspaper headline about the U.S. interest rate triggered stock market activity across the world.

Let's take the second headline about the COVID-19 outbreak at a Chinese port. The article discusses the closure of Shenzhen port in China, one of the world's largest container terminals, for a week after some workers tested positive for COVID. We learn that the container freight rate has quintupled since the previous October. A clothing factory owner in Guangzhou laments that the situation is "like a nightmare." For her, it certainly is. But should it be for investors? It almost certainly was. I would not be surprised if the shares of companies in the following industries witnessed frenetic activity after this news: container shipping companies, shopping manufacturers, ports, clothing manufacturers, logistics companies, companies anywhere in the world that import a lot of products from China—and companies anywhere in the world that *don't* import a lot of products from China (after all, wouldn't they be saving money compared to those who do import from China?).

A headline about a Chinese port triggered stock market activity across the world.

Last one. Why should a German regulator launching an antitrust probe into Apple affect the stock prices of companies other than Apple, you ask? It is not inconceivable that the stock price of quasi-monopolies like Amazon, Facebook, Google, and Twitter would have reacted to this news because fund managers in the United States and elsewhere decided that a Rubicon had been crossed owing to the action of the German regulator. And this would have led to a zillion buy or sell orders—depending on whether fund managers thought it was a good or bad thing for *their* portfolio holdings—for consumer technology and media businesses. If it could happen in Germany, why not in any other country?

A headline about a German regulator's action on a U.S. company triggered stock market activity across the world.

Alright, I know. I am on thin ice here. Without offering proof, I am claiming that fund managers bought and sold stocks globally in various businesses based on these three pieces of news. I have no idea if my *specific* claim about these three news items is valid, but there is no denying that mutual funds have become more trigger-happy over the years. According to a 2018 Morgan Stanley report titled *Long-Term Conviction in a Short-Term World*, the average holding period of mutual funds had fallen to less than one year from seven years in 1960.[1] Funds are not being bought and sold in a vacuum; fund managers decide to buy or sell based on *something*. Often that something is the latest news from a highly reputed and reliable financial newspaper.

I will let you figure out the impact of the two remaining news items on my list—they were on emerging market capital flows and the rising raw material costs in the solar power industry. It shouldn't be too hard.

Based on what I discussed in chapter 4 (proximate and ultimate causes of success) and the title of section III, which advises to be *very* lazy, you will correctly conclude that we did not react to any of these five pieces of news in June 2021. Our activity was zero.

But couldn't we have been wrong? Why should I not have adjusted my Indian portfolio based on the Fed's interest rate outlook? Many of our portfolio companies import goods from China—shouldn't we have sold them since their profits were certain to get squeezed? And why didn't we tinker with even one of our three internet businesses, which enjoy a virtual monopoly in their respective markets? After all, couldn't the Indian regulator have followed the footsteps of its German counterpart? And what could be more worrying for us than the specter of declining capital flows to India?

I will get to these answers, but before that, let's examine a different kind of news flow that hits much closer to home and is *much* harder to ignore.

Unceasing Upheavals Can Be Upsetting

We have seen the potential stock market effect of only a few news items on a single day from a single newspaper. Yet this phenomenon repeats itself day after day—actually, moment to moment—across newspapers, TV channels, social media platforms, whispers from brokers and fund managers, and heaven knows what else.

Notwithstanding special-purpose acquisition companies (SPACs) and WeWork, fund managers invest in real businesses with real money. Instead of studying generic news as we have just done, what if we track the news flow of a single company over time?

Let's do a brief thought experiment. Assume you are a long-term investor. In early January 2009, in the middle of the global financial crisis, you chose to invest in the French company L'Oréal, the world's largest and most successful cosmetics company. Your view was that a quality business like L'Oréal should be able to overcome any short-term pains owing to the financial crisis. You paid about €60 per share. Because you are a long-term investor, you plan to own the business for many years. Over the next few years, apart from the company's quarterly and annual financial results, you will also be bombarded with a wide range of news on the company. Table 8.1 provides five headlines for L'Oréal from various news sources from every year from 2009 to 2021. Before reading further, please take a quick look.

Done? OK, first question. Would you have stayed invested at the end of 2009? All five headlines look worrisome. Let's look at three of them. First, eBay

TABLE 8.1 Select news headlines for L'Oréal from January 2009 to December 2021

2009	May	Cosmetics Industry Threatened by Bee Demise
	May	eBay Wins L'Oréal UK Court Case
	Aug	L'Oréal Claims Products Were Diverted from Casinos to Pharmacies
	Nov	Denmark Declares Nivea and Biotherm Potentially Dangerous
	Dec	L'Oréal Chairman in a Legal Battle Over Gifts
2010	Feb	L'Oréal Seeking One Billion New Customers
	Mar	Nestlé Seen Seller not the Buyer of L'Oréal Shares
	Apr	L'Oréal Acquires Essie
	Jul	Police Arrest Four as L'Oréal Scandal Escalates
	Dec	Eyelash Enhancers Have Become a Booming Market
2011	Feb	Owen-Jones Ends Era as L'Oréal Chairman
	Mar	L'Oréal, P&G Fined for Cosmetics Price Fixing
	Jul	L'Oréal Adverts Are Banned for Being "Too Airbrushed"
	Aug	L'Oréal Margins Narrow on Higher Costs
	Oct	L'Oréal Beautifies Emerging Markets; the Stock Looks Pretty
2012	Mar	L'Oréal Reorganises its Luxury Division
	Aug	Jean-Paul Agon (L'Oréal), Confident About Second-Half 2012
	Sep	FDA Creams L'Oréal Over Anti-Aging Advertising Claims
	Oct	L'Oréal Gets to Know Indian Consumers
	Nov	L'Oréal to Buy Urban Decay Cosmetics
2013	Feb	After 2012 Sales Grow, L'Oréal Expected to Outperform the Market in 2013
	Apr	"Made in France" Luxury Beauty Drives L'Oréal Growth
	Apr	Savvy Social Networking Pays Off for L'Oréal China
	Aug	L'Oréal Makes $843m Bid for Chinese Skincare Brand
	Oct	L'Oréal Revenue Falls on Currency Effects, U.S. Slowdown

(continued)

TABLE 8.1 (*Continued*)

2014	Jan	L'Oréal Pulls Back from China Market
	Mar	L'Oréal Recognized as One of the World's Most Ethical Companies
	Jun	L'Oréal Outlines Plans to Double Its Consumer Base by 2020
	Jul	Nestlé Offloads Major Stake in L'Oréal
	Aug	L'Oréal's Age-Defying Claims Mislead
2015	May	L'Oréal Corners the Market on Bio-printed Skin
	Jun	L'Oréal to Lure China Shoppers with Price Cuts
	Jul	Two Scenarios That Impact L'Oréal's Valuation in Opposing Ways
	Oct	Why Is L'Oréal Increasing Its Focus on India?
	Nov	L'Oréal Sales +13.2 Percent to $20.4bn in First 9m
2016	May	L'Oréal Paris Ranked the World's Most Valuable Beauty Brand
	Jul	L'Oréal to Acquire IT Cosmetics in $1.2 Billion Deal
	Sep	Tests Show Mercury in L'Oréal Products: Maharashtra FDA
	Nov	L'Oréal Shares Surge as Demand Grows for Premium Makeup
	Dec	L'Oréal Steps Up Investments in Digital Start-Ups
2017	Jan	L'Oréal to Acquire Three U.S. Skin-Care Brands for $1.3 Billion
	Feb	L'Oréal Is Benefitting from a Higher Digital Spending
	Mar	L'Oréal Paris Launches Its Largest Loyalty Rewards Program
	Jun	L'Oréal Finalises Sale of The Body Shop
	Aug	Spotlight on Luxury: L'Oréal Results Suggest Huge Appetite for Premium
2018	May	L'Oréal Snaps up South Korean Cosmetics Firm Nanda
	Jul	L'Oréal Shares Fall as Mass-Market Drugstore Brands Struggle
	Oct	Strong Asian Demand Gives L'Oréal a Sales Bounce
	Oct	L'Oréal CEO Sees No Slowdown in China Despite U.S. Trade Tariffs
	Nov	Garnier Goes Organic in L'Oréal Bid to Lift Mass Market Sales
2019	Feb	L'Oréal Results Thrive Thanks to Strong Demand from Chinese Consumers
	Feb	Best Sales Growth Reported by L'Oréal in the Last 10 Years
	Jun	L'Oréal and Amazon Combine Artificial Intelligence and Beauty
	Sep	L'Oréal Bets on Hair.com as Its e-Commerce Home for Hair Care
	Dec	Fashion House Prada Appoints L'Oréal to Run Its Luxury Beauty Products
2020	Apr	L'Oréal Q1 Sales Shrink
	Jul	L'Oréal Sales Slump as Makeup Loses Allure During Lockdowns
	Oct	L'Oréal Sales Rebound After Lockdowns Ease
	Nov	L'Oréal Turns to Google as Coronavirus Spurs Virtual Make-Up Shift
	Dec	L'Oréal Strengthens Its Asian Business with the Acquisition of Takami
2021	Jan	Older Shoppers Are the Hot New Things for Consumer Brands
	Feb	L'Oréal Profit Falls but Sees Recovery Signs
	Apr	L'Oréal Sales Rise, Helped by Chinese Duty-Free Demand in Hainan
	Jun	Global Companies Leaving HK After Beijing's Political Crackdown
	Jun	How L'Oréal Doubles e-Commerce Growth in a Pandemic

seems to have scored a significant victory over L'Oréal in the UK courts, which ruled that eBay was not responsible for any counterfeit products sold on its website. Could this ruling lead to L'Oréal losing the e-commerce race? Second, even more worrisome, the Danish Consumer Council declared that Biotherm, a L'Oréal skin product, contained harmful substances. What kind of reputational and real damage would the company suffer in other parts of Europe? Third, L'Oréal's chair is embroiled in a legal battle among the family members who own L'Oréal. Sir Lindsay Owen-Jones, the chair, had allegedly received about €100 million from Liliane Bettencourt, who owned 31 percent of the company in return for his long service. As an investor, should we be worried that the chair might be distracted, given the public nature of the feud?

Let's examine the potentially damaging events of 2011. The regulator has fined L'Oréal for price-fixing and banned many of its advertisements, and the financial results for the second quarter clearly show that the company has been unable to pass higher costs on to consumers, thereby suffering lower margins. Does this indicate that L'Oréal is finally losing its brand power and that the competition has caught up? Owen-Jones has resigned abruptly, although his term wasn't expiring until 2014. He was widely acknowledged as the key driving force behind the company's global success and was one of France's most respected business leaders. He delivered double-digit profit growth for almost two decades when he was the company's CEO from 1988 to 2006. Should you be selling your stake in L'Oréal because it will be hard for a new leader to emulate him, or should you be buying more if the price reacts negatively?

As you glance through table 8.1, you will notice dozens of such news items that point to a potentially significant event in the company's life. Some may even seem self-contradictory. For example, in August 2013, L'Oréal made an aggressive bid to acquire a Chinese company. But by January 2014, the company appears to have pulled back from China by stopping the sale of its Garnier brand. Then, in June 2015, the company cut prices aggressively in a blatant attempt to gain market share.

We don't invest in France, but if we did, should we have reacted to these headlines? If not, why? And if so, how?

By studying Kurtén's bears and Darwin's finches.

Evolution Is Not What It Seems

The metaphor "never judge a book by its cover" should also apply to bland research articles with titles like "Rates of Evolution in Fossil Mammals." Contrary to what you would expect from this title, this article, in my layperson's opinion, is one of the most exciting in the history of the development of evolutionary theory.

In 1959, exactly a century after the publication of Darwin's *Origin*, a Finnish scientist named Björn Kurtén published this article in a biology journal.[2] Instead of celebrating Darwinism's centenary, Kurtén poked a seemingly large hole in it. To comprehend Kurtén's stunning claim, we need to revisit Darwin's assertion in *Origin*:

> I do believe that natural selection will always act very slowly, often only at long intervals of time, and generally only on a very few of the inhabitants of the same region at the same time. I further believe that this prolonged, intermittent action of natural selection accords perfectly well with what geology tells us of the rate and manner at which the inhabitants of this world have changed.

As we learned in chapter 5, Darwin was inspired by the famous geologist Charles Lyell who proposed the theory of uniformitarianism. Lyell contended that the earth has slowly and uniformly changed over the millennia and that understanding the present is key to interpreting the past. He directly contradicted the prevailing theory of catastrophism, which suggested that the features of the earth, like mountains, resulted from extensive and sudden changes or catastrophes. Darwin applied Lyell's theory of geological evolution to the biological world. He believed that just as the earth evolves slowly over very long periods, so does the world of animals and plants.

The upshot of Darwin's insight is that if we were to measure the pace of evolution, it would correlate *proportionately* with the measurement period: It would be slow over brief periods and fast over long periods. Darwin's theory stressed that species evolve slowly. This idea was gospel until Kurtén's article was published in 1959.

Kurtén plotted the evolution of the length of the second lower molar of the brown bear in Europe during the Pleistocene epoch (between 2.6 million and 11,700 years ago). Let's examine the data in table 8.2 for the rate of change of the

TABLE 8.2 The inverse relationship between measurement period and evolutionary change

Measurement period (years)	Rate of change (Darwins)
400,000	0.41
100,000	0.90
80,000	0.76
50,000	2.20
22,000	3.20
8,000	13.8

molar measured in Darwins (one Darwin is a change of 1/1000 in 1,000 years) and the period of measurement.

Do you see a trend here? Kurtén's data show that evolution appeared to occur quite quickly when measured over short periods and slowly when the measurement period was prolonged. Thus, when measured over 400,000 years, the rate of change of the molar was 0.41 Darwins, but over 8,000 years, the rate of change was an astounding 13.8 Darwins. He demonstrated a similar trend in other fossilized mammalian species, including horses.

I was incredulous when I first read about Kurtén's conclusion. Suppose we accept the Darwinian notion that the current diversity of the world is the result of species transforming slowly (but surely) throughout the eons. How is it possible that the pace of evolution is slower over more extended periods and faster over shorter periods?

Kurtén's article was not an outlier. In a 2009 article titled "Rates of Evolution," Philip D. Gingerich, a paleontologist at the University of Michigan, also supported Kurtén's claim.[3] He demonstrated mathematically and empirically that phenotypic change (i.e., changes in the bodily characteristics of a species) could be rapid from one generation to the next. In contrast, evolution can be slow on long time scales.

Does this inverse correlation between the rate of change of *bodily* parts and the time interval of measurement also apply to *genes*? It does. Simon Ho, an Australian evolutionary biologist, and his colleagues provide an excellent overview of this seemingly un-Darwinian phenomenon in their 2011 article, "Time-Dependent Rates of Molecular Evolution."[4] They summarize the research done by several scientists on the genomes of humans, insects, birds, fish, and even bacteria and viruses. Most of this research points in the same direction: Contrary to expectation, the pace of genetic evolution is *inversely* correlated with the period of measurement.

The Grants Take It One Step Further

All the research studies mentioned so far have examined evolution over hundreds or thousands of years. Do these conclusions also apply over a few years or decades?

We now return to Peter Boag and Laurene Ratcliffe, who had been stunned by the result of their analysis of Darwin's finches, both dead and living. On the small island of Daphne Major in the Galápagos, they witnessed what no one had seen before: natural selection and evolution occurring in real time in two species of finches. As Boag stated in his famous 1981 *Science* article, the intensity of natural selection in the birds was "the highest yet recorded for a vertebrate population."[5]

Fossils show that evolution has occurred, and Darwin's irrefutable logic argues that natural selection can drive evolution. However, no one had ever *seen* natural selection and evolution in action. Darwin didn't think it was even possible. In 1893, the German evolutionary biologist August Weismann wrote, "*It is very difficult to imagine this process of natural selection in its details*; and to this day, it is impossible to demonstrate it in any one point" (author's emphasis).

In their book, *The Variation of Animals in Nature*, the British evolutionary biologists Guy C. Robson and Owain W. Richards wrote in 1936, "In Darwin's treatment of the subject, no proof is adduced that a selective process has ever been detected in nature. . . . It is a very unsatisfactory state of affairs for biological science that a first-class theory should still dominate the field of inquiry though largely held on faith or rejected on account of prejudice."

The unsatisfactory state of affairs had finally ended. Boag and Ratcliffe's observations changed the field of evolution forever. They were part of a long-term project started by Peter and Rosemary Grant, a married British couple and currently emeritus professors at Princeton. The Grants wanted to study evolution in the wild and discover the key factors that lead to new species. So they decided to study Darwin's finches, also called Galápagos finches. Figure 8.1

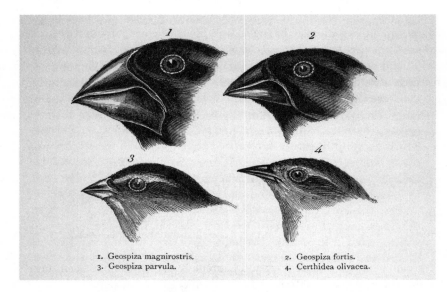

1. Geospiza magnirostris.
3. Geospiza parvula.

2. Geospiza fortis.
4. Certhidea olivacea.

8.1 Four of the fourteen species of Darwin's finches. Note the difference in the size and shape of their beaks, which have adapted to the flora and fauna of the various Galápagos Islands. This phenomenon, in which a single species evolves into many species adapted to specialized modes of life, is called adaptive radiation.

Source: Licensed from Science Photo Library.

provides illustrations of four species of finches (out of a total of fourteen) that have adapted and evolved from one mother species that landed on the Galápagos Islands two to three million years ago.[6]

The Grants landed on the island Daphne Major in 1973 to start their project.[7] As I shared in chapter 5, Darwin had visited the Galápagos in 1835. The Galápagos group of islands is almost one thousand kilometers off the west coast of Ecuador. Owing to its remote location, it is home to several endemic species (i.e., species not found anywhere else in the world). There are about a dozen central and minor islands in the archipelago.

Daphne Major is small, nondescript, and remote even by the standards of Galápagos (Darwin did not even see it) and measures barely a square kilometer in area.

The next time I feel like complaining about the firmness of the mattress or the softness of the pillows in a hotel room, I hope I remember what the Grants endured on Daphne Major for six months every year for *forty* consecutive years. Before the Grants and their research staff made it their home, no humans had lived there. How could they? There is only one way to enter the island, and that is the base of a cliff since the island has no shoreline.

To set up their camp every year, here is what the Grants had to do. They had to abandon their boat as they neared the island and approach the cliff base at low tide in a rowboat called a *panga*. A single black ledge filled with barnacles was their only landing point; it's the size of a large exercise mat. They needed to leap onto this mat while the *panga* swayed wildly in the ocean waves. From here, they had to walk up the cliff on hard, wet rocks until they arrived at another ledge that they called the Landing. Then they formed a human chain and passed up tents, poles, water, food, and everything else they would need for the next six months. Daphne Major has no water or food. They could pitch their tents only at one spot, which was the size of a table and on the rim of a volcano. They had to lug all their supplies there from the base of the cliff. They cooked their meals in a small cave protected from the harsh sun by a sheet of cloth. Once settled, they would spend the next six months measuring the body size, beak size, and beak shape of every finch on the island. They would also extract blood to do a genetic analysis.

Why would anyone in their right mind spend time on such an island? Because it offered many advantages that few other places could.

Daphne Major was so far removed from the other islands that there was only a minimal chance that the finches or other island species could escape or that new ones could arrive. It was a perfect petri dish for evolutionary studies because it would not get "contaminated." Also, the Grants realized that the Galápagos were a gold mine for testing and refining Darwin's theory. The Galápagos Islands undergo extreme climate swings—from severe drought to copious rain—thereby providing ample opportunity for natural selection. Last,

Daphne Major was small enough to track every bird that lives there over many years, which they did. From 1973 to 2012, the Grants tagged about twenty thousand birds over eight generations, and they tracked almost every copulating pair and their offspring.

In the first four years of their study—from 1973 to 1976—the island received average or excess rainfall. But in 1977, after a brief spell of rain in January, Daphne Major suffered a severe drought. Almost all the greenery disappeared from the island, and the only plants that survived the drought were cactus bushes. The finches fed on seeds of all sizes. The small and medium-sized seeds disappeared very soon, and the finches were then left with only large and hard seeds. But only the finches with larger beaks could break open these larger seeds; finches with small and medium-sized beaks could not open these seeds and so starved and perished.

The island was inhabited mainly by two species. At the start of 1977, there were about 1,200 *Geospiza fortis* and 280 *Geospiza scandens*. By the end of the year, only 180 *fortis* and 110 *scandens* were left. About 85 percent of the *fortis* and 60 percent of the *scandens* had succumbed to the drought.

The Grants' data showed that the surviving *fortis* were, on average, 5 to 6 percent *larger* than the ones that had died. The average beak length of the survivors was 11.07 millimeters compared to 10.68 millimeters for the species before the drought; the average beak depth had increased from 9.42 millimeters to 9.96 millimeters. These differences may appear small to us, but they can tilt the balance between life and death in the wild. For example, a *fortis* with a beak length of 11 millimeters can crack a seed from a plant called a caltrop, but an individual with a beak length of 10.5 millimeters will not even attempt to do so. Just half a millimeter can make all the difference.

The intensity of natural selection the Grants observed wasn't limited just to beak length and depth. At the start of 1977, there were 600 male and 600 female *fortis*. By the end of the drought, more than 150 males and only a few females were alive. The males are typically larger than the females by about 5 percent, so the males were more likely to survive. There were now six males to every female.

Natural selection can occur in a single generation, but evolution takes place only over many generations. Given the dramatic change in the beak size and sex ratio of the finches, natural selection *had* happened. But what about evolution? The Grants had to wait one more year to measure the beak size and shape of the offspring of the drought survivors of 1977. But then, they saw evolution in action, too—the new generation was 4 to 5 percent larger than the population before the onset of the drought.

They soon realized that their observation of 1977 was not a fluke. In 1983, there was a very heavy rainfall because of El Niño, and the island became lush and green. Green vines covered even the cactus bushes. This changed vegetation had a significant impact two years later when drought struck again. This time, tiny seeds were abundant (produced by the vines of 1983), and large seeds became rare. As a result, the finches with large beaks found it hard to pick up the seeds, and a large proportion of the survivors of this drought were the small-beaked finches. Their offspring, as a result, also had smaller beaks. Natural selection and evolution were evident again, except that, unlike in 1977, the beaks had evolved to become smaller.

Thus, in less than a decade, the finches' beak size increased and then decreased because of natural selection. When observed over a decade, beak size may not have appeared to change that much, but it had fluctuated significantly in the intervening period owing to the two extreme climate events.

The Grants published the results of their long-term study of the evolution of the two species of finches—*fortis* and *scandens*—in *Science* in April 2002 under the title "Unpredictable Evolution in a 30-Year Study of Darwin's Finches."[8] Before starting their research, they had hypothesized that the body traits of the finches would vary within a narrow band over the period of the study. But as they say at the beginning of the article, "The data do not support the expectation of no change."

If you examine the graphs of the body size, beak size, and beak shape of *fortis* and *scandens* in the Grants' article, you will notice the inverse correlation between the measurement period and the pace of evolution pointed out by Kurtén in brown bears. Thus, while the body size of *fortis* fluctuated a lot between the mid-1980s and the early 2000s, the overall change over those two decades was small. Similarly, the annual variation of the beak size of *scandens* appeared to be much greater than the variation from the mid-1970s until the early 2000s. The beak shape of *fortis* was practically the same when measured in the mid-1980s and the early 2000s, but its annual change was much more significant.

There is a lovely fractal-like property to this phenomenon. It does not seem to matter if the measurement period is thousands of years (bears) or just a few decades (finches). The pace of evolution speeds up over shorter periods and slows down over more extended periods.

But so what? Why should long-term investors care about Kurtén's bears and the Grants' finches?

The Grants and Kurtén Dictate When We Buy and Sell

My observations are nowhere as scientific as the Grants' or Kurtén's. However, I know that the daily, weekly, monthly, and quarterly rate of change in exceptional businesses appears *much* greater than the rate of change measured over years and decades.

This realization has helped me formulate an investing principle that I call the Grant–Kurtén principle of investing (GKPI). It goes as follows:

> When we find high-quality businesses that do not fundamentally alter their character over the long term, we should exploit the inevitable short-term fluctuations in their businesses for buying and *not* selling.

GKPI requires us to own *high-quality businesses that do not fundamentally alter their character over the long term.* "High-quality businesses" is a loaded term and can mean different things to different investors. If you have come this far, I assume you know *our* definition. For us, the critical character traits of a high-quality business are stellar operating and financial track records, a stable industry, a high governance standard, a defensible moat, increasing market share, and low business and financial risk.

How do we use GKPI for buying? By exploiting short-term fluctuations.

We are highly demanding. We want a company to be run by an honest management team, and show solid operating and financial track records over many years. It needs to stay ahead of the competition and be debt free, and we also want it to keep taking calculated risks while not unduly burdening the business. And, as if all these demands were not enough, we dare to insist on a fair price for these rare gems! How is this even possible? The market should almost never offer us an attractive price for such a business, and it doesn't.

However, on rare occasions, investors who *don't* subscribe to GKPI succumb to the pressure of temporary macro, industry, or company issues, and we can then swoop in to buy a piece of an exceptional company. It doesn't—and shouldn't—happen often, but when it does, we go all in.

Take WNS, one of our largest investments to date. It is one of India's leading business process outsourcing (BPO) companies and is listed on the New York Stock Exchange. It was set up in 1996 as a captive back office by British Airways and started serving third-party clients in 1999. In 2002, Warburg Pincus acquired a controlling stake in WNS. (I wasn't involved in the deal.) Although British Airways contributed to about 90 percent of WNS's revenues at the time of acquisition by Warburg Pincus in 2002, its revenue share had fallen to less than 10 percent by early 2008. The management at WNS had done a stellar job of diversifying away from British Airways and the travel industry. By outsourcing back-office functions like finance and accounting, mortgage processing, and customer analytics, WNS's clients typically get higher-quality service (e.g., faster turnaround times, lower error rates) at a much lower cost.

In January 2008, the stock price of WNS fell sharply from a previous high of $35 to $13. Three factors seemed to have contributed to this steep correction. First, one of its large mortgage lender clients, First Magnus, declared bankruptcy in late 2007 owing to the ongoing subprime mortgage crisis in the United

States. First Magnus had contributed to about 5 percent of WNS's revenue, so the management lowered its revenue guidance for the next year. Second, the management indicated that it may lose Aviva, a large insurance client that was contributing to about 8 percent of WNS's revenue, by May 2008 if Aviva were to acquire the WNS facility servicing it. And third, the appreciating rupee had the analysts worried since most of WNS's delivery presence was in India. (A stronger rupee could make WNS less competitive and squeeze margins.)

The question for us was this: Was this a temporary blip, or was it a more permanent decline of achievable revenue and profit growth? We decided it was the former. The loss of First Magnus wasn't WNS's fault, and even the potential loss of Aviva would be due to Aviva's change of strategy, not because WNS wasn't serving it well. Also, we didn't believe WNS's long-term competitive advantage would be adversely affected by exchange rate fluctuations. WNS's annualized revenue growth of 64 percent from 2004 to 2007 was proof that it offered high-quality back-office processing services to its clients at competitive prices.

Also, we love the Indian BPO industry. It is lucrative for well-established incumbents because it has high entry barriers for new entrants (businesses are extremely wary of outsourcing their mission critical applications to a start-up) and high exit barriers for existing clients (WNS and other leading players almost never lose a customer given the sticky nature of back-office processing). I assume you have heard the song "Hotel California" by the Eagles. The song's last line, "You can check out any time you like, but you can never leave," applies to the clients of the leading companies in the Indian BPO industry. WNS was—and is—in a great place.

The bottom line was that despite the market pessimism, we had no reason to believe that anything fundamental had changed at the company.

We bought aggressively and invested $41 million in early 2008 at an average price of $15.2 per share. By March 2022, the stock price ($85.5) had gained 462 percent, whereas the Indian indexes (the Sensex as well as the Midcap Index) had gained only 97 percent in dollars.

Then, almost exactly twelve years after our initial investment in WNS in early 2008, we got an opportunity to buy *again* during the early days of pandemic panic from March to May 2020. We invested an additional $98 million in the business at an average price of $46.1 per share just when the markets seemed to think that the world was ending. Some gifts just keep on giving.

How do we use GKPI for selling? By *ignoring* short-term fluctuations.

If we get lucky by owning a high-quality business like WNS, GKPI requires us *not* to sell. Why? Because, as shown by the Grants and Kurtén, short-term changes do not usually impact the long-term character of an exceptional enterprise. Let's revisit L'Oréal to marvel at the beauty of GKPI.

Table 8.3 provides a snapshot of the business in 2009 and 2020.[9] If you go through the annual reports for these years, you will get a sense of déjà vu—the

TABLE 8.3   L'Oréal from 2009 to 2020: Some things don't change

	2009	2020
Business	Focused on beauty	Focused on beauty
Customer segments	Mass to premium	Mass to premium
Geographies	Global	Global
Sales (bill euros)	17.5	28
Profits (bill euros)	1.8	4
Divisions	Professional Products, Consumer Products, Luxury Products, Active Cosmetics	Professional Products, Consumer Products, Luxury Products, Active Cosmetics
Consumer and luxury products	77 percent of sales	78 percent of sales
W. Europe and U.S.	66 percent of sales	52 percent of sales
Sales from Asia	13 percent of sales	35 percent of sales
Professional brands	Kerastase, Redken, L'Oréal Professional	Kerastase, Redken, Genesis, Blond Absolu
Consumer brands	L'Oréal Paris, Garnier, Maybelline	L'Oréal Paris, Garnier
Luxury brands	Lancôme, Yves Saint Laurent, Kiehl's	Lancôme, Kiehl's, Helena Rubinstein
Active brands	La Roche-Posay, Vichy	La Roche-Posay, Vichy, CeraVe
Operating margin	14.8 percent of sales	18.6 percent of sales
Free cash flow	> 100 percent of net profits	> 100 percent of net profits
Net debt	€2 billion	Net cash €3.9 billion

language, the tone, and the business focus seem eerily similar even though eleven years separate the two commentaries.

Although the company's sales grew from €17.5 billion to €28 billion during this period, it remained a global beauty business that derived most of its revenues from Western Europe and the United States. There were no unrelated diversifications, and the company did not make any significant, risky acquisitions. Its four divisions—Professional Products, Consumer Products, Luxury Products, and Active Cosmetics—remained the same during this period. Its top two divisions, Consumer and Luxury, accounted for about 80 percent of sales. Even the critical brands across divisions remained essentially unchanged. L'Oréal continued to be a cash machine, which allowed it to become a cash surplus company in 2020 after being indebted in 2009.

One significant change during this period seems to be the dramatic growth in Asia (mainly China); the revenue contribution from Asia increased from

13 percent to 35 percent from 2009 to 2020. But this was not a sudden change, as is evident from the trend of the company's Asian revenue contribution to total revenues from 2009 to 2020: 13 percent, 18 percent, 19 percent, 21 percent, 21 percent, 21 percent, 22 percent, 22 percent, 24 percent, 27 percent, 32 percent, and 35 percent. Aside from 2010 and 2019, Asia's revenue contribution inched up by only 0 to 3 percentage points every year. Steady as she went.

Let's revisit where you were earlier, back in 2009. You had bought L'Oréal stock for €60 per share. If you were a follower of GKPI, you would have ignored every piece of bad news listed in table 8.1. Instead, you would have seen these news items for what they were: unimportant and irrelevant for the long-term performance of the business. In fact, at some points in this journey, you may have chosen to load up on more shares when you found the price attractive.

Where do you think the stock price was at the end of June 2022? It was €329 per share. So your gain would have been 450 percent, which handsomely beat the French CAC 40 index, which grew only 80 percent during this period.

This is not a recommendation to buy L'Oréal. But it *is* a tribute to the proper application of GKPI. You would have done spectacularly well by doing nothing.

GKPI is our religion. And it reflects in all kinds of big and small ways in the way we work. Our office doesn't have a TV screen playing CNBC or any other news; our lone TV screen is used only for video conferencing. The only Bloomberg terminal we have is in the corner of our office pantry; it remains unused and unwatched probably 99 percent of the time. We never discuss recent company news or share prices in our team meetings. I mainly read physical newspapers, in which the information is always one day late. We have never bought or sold a single business based on news flow and never will.

GKPI demands that we be lazy when buying and *very* lazy when selling. And so we are. It has led to some decent outcomes for us.

In June 2022, excluding purchases during the previous two years, we owned twenty-eight businesses. In one of these businesses, we made more than one hundred times our money (Page); in two of them, we multiplied our money more than twenty-five times (Berger and Ratnamani); and in six of them, we made more than ten times our money (in Indian rupees). Unfortunately, all nine have suffered small but significant setbacks, some of which lasted many years (e.g., Ratnamani and Page). However, our adherence to GKPI ensured that we didn't panic, exercised patience, and stayed lazy.

Why and When We Sell

If GKPI requires that we not sell, then why do we?

We don't sell on valuation, a key reason many investors throw up their hands and exit. That is because we have no target price for selling in our portfolio. I *have* sold on valuation. Only once. I behaved foolishly and regret it even today. I will discuss this folly in chapter 10, so let's ignore it for the moment.

We sell under the following three conditions (the numbers in parentheses indicate the number of businesses sold):

1. A decline in governance standards (0)
2. Egregiously wrong capital allocation (3)
3. Irreparable damage to the business (6)

We have sold ten businesses since 2007 (the nine listed here plus the mistake). I am excluding three businesses that strategic buyers acquired. This translates to one exit every one and a half years. How's that for laziness?

As you can see, six of our nine exits occurred because we believed the business had been damaged beyond repair. And how did we come to that conclusion? An example can clarify.

We had invested in an old-world manufacturing business that was the leader in an oligopolistic industry in India. It ticked all the boxes—enviable governance standard, impeccable financials, stable industry, zero leverage, and we were able to buy at what we thought was an attractive price. Everything was hunky-dory for the first couple years. However, in the third year of our ownership, we were surprised to see that the business lost market share for two quarters in a row. We spent time with the management to understand the reasons, and after some initial resistance, they agreed that there might have been some temporary share loss. However, they were confident that this was a transitory phenomenon.

But it wasn't. The company kept losing market share, and in one of the smaller (but highly profitable) segments, its share loss accelerated over the next few quarters. Again, the management seemed to have a compelling set of explanations, all of which sounded logical. They claimed they had made many changes to their manufacturing, sales, and marketing practices and that we would see the trend reverse soon. But the loss of market share continued. We waited for *three* more years after spotting the initial trouble and finally decided to pull the plug. Since we want to be permanent owners, we demand a high performance standard in both absolute and relative terms. When we exited, this business was delivering decent results: about 35 percent ROCE with modest revenue and profit growth. But we did not want to be owners in a business that consistently fell behind the competition.

During those three years of waiting for the business to improve, several positive and negative news reports were made about the company. We ignored the news and focused on the trend in actual market share. Why did we hold the business for three more years after detecting the problem? Why did we not sell sooner? Because GKPI tells us that we should expect ups and downs in *every* business. There isn't a single business in our portfolio that has gone up in a straight line. Not one. Over the long run, most businesses in our portfolio have done well, but every business has gyrated wildly in both directions when measured over weeks or quarters. Our default option is to overlook these temporary business upheavals.

However, in some cases, like the one I've discussed here, what we think is temporary becomes more permanent. Fortunately, there have been only six such occasions in our history. Therefore, our default option will always be to continue to respect GKPI.

Remember that the maximum we can lose is our investment amount, but there is no limit to how high a share price can climb. Given the quality of businesses in our portfolio, we prefer to run the risk of selling late and losing some capital than selling early and forgoing substantial gain.

A Lot Can Happen Over Sixty Years. Or Can It?

We apply evolutionary thinking by ignoring both small and big setbacks in our businesses to focus on the long term. Despite the L'Oréal example and our experience applying GKPI, the skeptical part of your brain should raise two valid questions: (1) How long is "long term," and (2) since new businesses keep destroying old ones, won't we be left with only failed businesses after a few decades if we keep holding on?

A headline on the website of the American Enterprise Institute from October 2015 can help us answer these questions. It reads, "Fortune 500 Firms in 1955 v. 2015: Only 12% Remain, Thanks to the Creative Destruction That Fuels Economic Prosperity."[10] The article goes on to list the sixty-one U.S. companies that had survived sixty years on the list.

Contrary to the article's tone, which mourns the seemingly significant Schumpeterian destruction, I was pleasantly surprised that sixty-one companies had stayed on the list for *sixty* years. I would have guessed the number to be much smaller. The period from 1955 to 2015 was tumultuous and unpredictable for the United States and the world. Also, the world of 2015 seemed almost unrecognizable from that of 1955.

During those sixty years, we witnessed the start and the end of the Cold War, the splintering of the USSR, the advent of the space age, the U.S. Civil Rights Act, the oil shock, the savings and loans crisis, multiple crises in the Middle East, the meteoric rise of China, the formation of the European Union, the internet boom and bust, the exponential growth of mobile phones, innumerable wars across the globe, the global financial crisis of 2008, the increasing dominance of technology firms, and the rapid digitization of all businesses. I haven't stated at least a hundred more significant events that also would have impacted companies of all sizes in the United States. However, companies like 3M, Alcoa, Avon, Caterpillar, Kellogg, Pepsi, Pfizer, and many others did much better than simply endure these massive local and global shocks—they also prospered by maintaining their position in the top five hundred companies in the country.

But this number, sixty-one, was understated. First, there was a factual error. The author missed eleven businesses that appeared on both lists, companies including Colgate-Palmolive, Corning, H. J. Heinz, and PPG. It was probably just an oversight. Thus, seventy-two companies should appear on both lists.

The second reason for understatement was that the author did not count the businesses that had been acquired by a Fortune 500 business between 1955 and 2015. Let's take Gillette. In 2005, P&G acquired Gillette for $57 billion (Gillette remained a Fortune 500 business for fifty years after 1955; its rank was 215 when it was acquired). Should we consider Gillette to be a "failure"? Was it "creatively destroyed"? I don't think so. I used their overpriced blades just this morning. Since it was a part of P&G, which was ranked 32 on the Fortune 500 list of 2015, I would also consider Gillette to be on the Fortune 500 list of 2015.

United Technologies acquired Otis in 1975 (and so Otis stayed on the list for twenty years after 1955). United Technologies was ranked 45 on the 2015 Fortune 500 list, and I could reasonably argue that Otis should be counted as a continuing business as a part of United Technologies. We can reach the same conclusion for businesses like Wrigley, Quaker Oats, Carrier, Bestfoods, and McDonnell Douglas, acquired by the Fortune 500 companies Berkshire Hathaway, PepsiCo, United Technologies, Unilever, and Boeing, respectively.

There are seventy-three companies like Gillette and Otis from the Fortune 500 list of 1955 acquired by the Fortune 500 companies of 2015. Here, I have also included the larger overseas acquirers like BP and Unilever, who, if they were in the United States, would have been a part of the Fortune 500 in 2015. Thus, one hundred forty-five businesses from 1955 could be included on the 2015 list: seventy-two that survived and seventy-three that have become part of the survivors.

From 1955, sixty-three companies either went bankrupt or were untraceable (finding companies from the 1950s and 1960s is not easy). They were a part of the destruction process of capitalism.

What happened to the remaining two hundred ninety-two businesses (500 – 145 – 63) from the Fortune 500 list of 1955? They either fell out of the top 500 or were acquired by or merged with other companies. Does that mean that all of them failed? Some may not have done well, but many may have continued to survive and prosper. There are a *lot* of high-quality businesses that aren't in the Fortune 500, which, by definition, is a highly restrictive list.

For example, Eaton ranked 189 in 1955 and fell out of the Fortune 500 in 2013. In June 2021, its market value was $60 billion. So I wouldn't label it as a failure. Also, it stayed on the list for fifty-eight years after 1955, which is no mean achievement. Borden Chemical was acquired by the private equity giants KKR in 1995 and then by Apollo in 2004. Borden exists even today as part of Hexion Specialty Chemicals. USG, a building products company on the Fortune 500 list of 1955, was acquired by Knauf of Germany (revenue of €10 billion) for $7 billion in 2018.

If we assume that 20 to 25 percent of these two hundred ninety-two businesses were acquired or fell out of the Fortune 500 of 1955 but continued to successfully deliver their products and services, we get an additional sixty to seventy-five businesses from the 1955 list that have been successful.

Thus, the summary of the longevity of the Fortune 500 businesses of 1955 is as follows:

- 72 companies (14 percent) continued to be a part of the Fortune 500 for sixty years.
- 73 businesses (15 percent) became a part of a Fortune 500 business by 2015.
- 60 to 75 companies (12–15 percent) continued to do well despite being acquired or falling out of the Fortune 500.
- 280 to 295 (55 to 60 percent) of the firms on the 1955 list failed.

In chapters 9 and 10, I present the results of a study of the change in stock prices of listed U.S. firms over ninety years from 1926 to 2016. It shows that about 60 percent of the listed stocks delivered less than U.S. treasury returns over the ninety years. Hence, my estimation of a 55 to 60 percent failure rate over sixty years (as calculated earlier) is probably on the higher side. Anyway, let's stick with it.

We can safely assume that the 1955 Fortune 500 businesses were high-quality businesses. Of course, they may not have been high quality strictly according to *our* definition (e.g., some may have had modest debt levels). But there is no denying that they were extraordinary companies—they couldn't have become some of the largest businesses in the mecca of capitalism without being outstanding.

We have seen that at least 30 percent (72 + 73 = 145) of these continued to be high quality as evidenced by remaining in the top 500 for sixty years. If we include companies that may have done well over this period despite not being part of the elite 500 in the year 2015 (about sixty to seventy-five businesses), we see that 40 to 45 percent (two hundred five to two hundred twenty) of companies from the 1955 Fortune 500 list performed well over *sixty* years. This is not a small number. Capitalism and creative destruction do work well, but not *that* well.

So here are the answers to the two questions I posed at the start of this section. First, "long term" is genuinely long term: at least five decades, maybe more. And second, new businesses do replace old ones, but at a far slower rate than we think.

This brings us back to the lesson from the Grants and Kurtén. There is no point wasting time, energy, and brainpower on worrying about day-to-day upheavals in high-quality businesses. They can be highly resilient over the long term.

So why sell?

* * *

Kodak was the Facebook or Google of its day; just like these two current giants, you would not have found it easy to name the second player in photography. In 1976, Kodak held a 90 percent market share in film sales and an 85 percent market share in the sale of cameras.[11] And today? Smartphones are synonymous with cameras. Kodak is effectively dead. Ironically, an American electrical engineer at Kodak, Steve Sasson, invented the first digital camera in 1975! If we were analyzing Kodak in 1975, we would have concluded that the film industry was remarkably stable and that Kodak's dominance was unlikely to be tested for the foreseeable future. Would I have sold after witnessing the dramatic growth of digital photography? Maybe, maybe not. I am not sure. But I do know that I would have reacted late and may have lost money as a result.

Is there a solution to this problem? How do I know that ignoring *this* particular "small" event will work out in the long run? I don't.

Let me restate what I have mentioned before: *All* investing models have downsides. In my opinion, no investment strategy is foolproof. If you know of one that is, please write a book on it (or better still, email me the magic formula). Our application of GKPI will have Kodak-like downsides, but in my experience, *it works well most of the time.* And that's the best we can expect of any model.

An antelope is swift, agile, and alert and almost impossible to catch. But many do get caught and killed by cheetahs, leopards, and lions. Does it mean that the antelope's design is flawed? Not at all. The antelope is very well adapted to its environment; not all will live to old age, but enough will, thereby allowing the species to survive for millions of years.

We have applied GKPI consistently to every business we have invested in, but not all have prospered. However, as a *portfolio*, this approach has worked exceedingly well for us.

This species has survived. Very well.

Chapter Summary

Evolutionary theory has taught me that . . .

. . . we can reimagine investing by embracing the tenet that the long-term character of high-quality businesses remains unaffected by short-term fluctuations in the economy, the industry, and even the business.

1. Contrary to the expectations of Darwinism, evolution can be faster when measured over shorter periods and slower over longer periods. Björn Kurtén demonstrated this phenomenon in the evolution of the teeth of European brown bears.
2. High-quality businesses, too, seem to undergo many changes when measured over days or weeks or months but are much more stable when the period of measurement is years or decades.
3. Empirical data from the longevity of Fortune 500 businesses demonstrate the long-term resilience of exceptional businesses. About 40 to 45 percent of the Fortune 500 businesses of 1955 continued to be successful for the next sixty years.
4. We have capitalized on the inevitable short-term fluctuations in high-quality businesses to invest at attractive valuations. However, since these opportunities arise infrequently, we rarely ever buy. We are lazy.
5. After investing, we ignore near-term fluctuations because the fundamental characteristics of stellar businesses remain stable over the long term. We never sell on valuation—we are *very* lazy.
6. We have sold only when there had been an egregiously bad capital allocation or irreparable damage to a business.

CHAPTER 9

ELDREDGE AND GOULD DREDGE UP INVESTING GOLD

Why should not Nature have taken a leap from structure to structure? On the theory of natural selection, we can clearly understand why she should not; for natural selection can act only by taking advantage of slight successive variations; she can never take a leap, but must advance by the shortest slowest steps.

Charles Darwin, On the Origin of Species, *chapter 6, "Difficulties of the Theory"*

Charlie and I decided long ago that in an investment lifetime it's just too hard to make hundreds of smart decisions. That judgment became ever more compelling as Berkshire's capital mushroomed and the universe of investments that could significantly affect our results shrank dramatically. Therefore, we adopted a strategy that required our being smart—and not too smart at that—only a very few times. Indeed, we'll now settle for one good idea a year. (Charlie says it's my turn.)

Warren Buffett, annual letter to shareholders, 1993

Look back upon your life. Yes, I know you will need to stop reading to reflect on the years gone by. Please do so, and contemplate the events or moments that have made you you: life, work, business—all of it. Go ahead, take a deep breath, pause, and roll that reel backward.

Done? All right. What did you see? Let me share the snippets of my movie. Most of my five decades on this glorious planet seem to have passed in a blur. I could remember only a few moments spontaneously: when my mother cried on losing her mother, when my history teacher praised me, when my father allowed me to drive his car, when the first company I interviewed for rejected me, when a herd of elephants chased us on a safari in South Africa, when the first company I invested in had a successful IPO, when I first saw my newborn son, when I, well, you get the picture.

I may be able to list maybe thirty such events but not three thousand. It seems a bit odd since I have been alive for about thirty *million* minutes. Where are the remaining minutes? Were they all uninteresting? Is my life nothing but a long period of nothingness punctuated by moments to remember? What about your life?

And what about life on our planet? Some moments may not be forgotten even a century from now.

One came on January 11, 2020, when the Chinese media reported the first death of a person, a sixty-one-year-old man, from an unknown virus. He had been a regular at the local seafood and poultry market in the city of Wuhan. Within less than two weeks, dozens of countries across the world started reporting infections from the same virus. On January 30, the World Health Organization declared a global health emergency, and on February 11, it named the disease caused by the virus: COVID-19.

In March 2020, the world witnessed what it *never* had before: a complete global shutdown. Future generations will accuse us of photoshopping images of the empty streets of Mumbai, London, Rome, and New York in 2020. And no photograph will capture the scale or depth of human suffering and hardship.

Every equity market in the world started falling precipitously, and in the months of March and April, there seemed to be no end to the bottom. The Indian Sensex crashed 23 percent in March 2020.

What were we at Nalanda to do in these unprecedented times?

Maybe evolutionary theory could give us a hint.

The Absence of Evidence *Is* Evidence of Absence

In 1972, the paleontologists Stephen Jay Gould and Niles Eldredge published an essay that seemed to blow a reasonably large hole in the tower of classical Darwinism.

Darwin's theory of natural selection makes a robust case for "phyletic gradualism." Darwin theorized that natural selection eliminates unfit individuals so that only the better adapted will reproduce. If this continues long enough, a new species is imperceptibly created, and the original species goes extinct. He makes his view on gradualism explicit in the concluding chapter of *Origin*: "As

natural selection acts solely by accumulating slight, successive, favourable variations, it can produce no great or sudden modification; it can act only by very
short and slow steps."

If this is accurate, we should find intermediate forms of species in the fossil record providing evidence of phyletic gradualism. Let's take the example
of whales, which evolved about fifty million years ago from a four-legged,
land-dwelling vertebrate called *Pakicetus*.[1] Figure 9.1 lists some descendants of
Pakicetus, including *Ambulocetus*, *Remingtoncetus*, *Protocetus*, and *Dorudon*,
which ultimately evolved into current-day whales and dolphins. Given the large
size of whales, we should find hundreds, maybe even thousands, of intermediate forms. The problem is that we don't. For example, where are the intermediate fossils between *Remingtoncetus* and *Protocetus*? We have a decent fossil
record that helped paleontologists piece together the puzzle of whale evolution,
but we don't have most of the transitional forms.

I discussed the evolution of giraffes in chapter 5. If natural selection extermi-
nated giraffes with shorter necks over time and the longer-necked ones evolved
gradually, why have we not found giraffe fossils with necks ranging from very
short to very long? Given that we haven't, how can anyone claim that evolution
proceeds gradually and not suddenly?

Intellect and integrity are mutually exclusive traits—one does not guarantee
the other. However, Darwin was that rare genius who was also unsparingly
honest. He penned an entire chapter on the potential problems with his theory.
He starts chapter 6 of *Origin*, "Difficulties of the Theory," by stating an obvious
issue with the idea of natural selection. He argues that since natural selection gradually eliminates minor well-adapted forms, extinction and natural
selection must operate simultaneously. Hence, logic dictates that innumerable
transitional forms that were unable to adapt to their surroundings should have
existed. But, as Darwin himself points out, transitional fossils have rarely been
found. He admits that the incomplete fossil record poses a significant hurdle to
anyone trying to prove that species evolve gradually.

But he had a solution: He asserted that the geological record is incomplete.
He stated, "The geological record is imperfect, and this fact will to a large extent
explain why we do not find interminable varieties, connecting all the extinct
and existing forms of life by the finest graduated steps. He who rejects these
views on the nature of the geological record will rightly reject my *whole* theory"
(emphasis mine).

He considered the issue of a lack of transitional forms so devastating to
the theory of natural selection that he went on to devote chapter 9 of *Origin*
to a discussion of just this one problem, aptly titled "On the Imperfection of
the Geological Record." He made his case by presenting several convincing
arguments: Only a tiny portion of the earth has been geologically explored; an
organism with only soft parts cannot be preserved; if shells and bones sink to

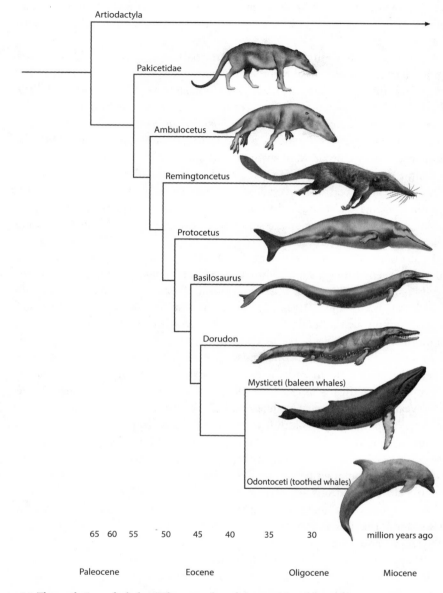

Artiodactyla

Pakicetidae

Ambulocetus

Remingtoncetus

Protocetus

Basilosaurus

Dorudon

Mysticeti (baleen whales)

Odontoceti (toothed whales)

65 60 55 ̍ 50 45 40 35 30 million years ago

Paleocene   Eocene   Oligocene   Miocene

9.1 The evolution of whales: Where are the other transitional forms?

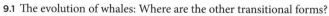

Source: Licensed from Science Photo Library.

the bottom of the sea where sediment does not accumulate, they will disappear; many species (like land shells) existed in the distant past, but hardly any fossils can be found.

If Darwin was right about gradualism, paleontologists should witness a gradual change in the fossil records over millions of years. But this is not what they find. Instead, before and since Darwin, a large number of paleontologists have found that the majority of species appear suddenly in the fossil record and then persist unchanged until they go extinct.[2]

Hugh Falconer (1808–1865) was one of the greatest paleontologists of the nineteenth century.[3] He went to India as a surgeon in 1830 but spent most of his time digging up fossils. He discovered ancient fossil beds in the southern Himalayas and excavated several extinct species like the mastodon and saber-toothed tiger. He also studied the fossils of European elephants. Darwin had colossal respect for Falconer and sent him a copy of the first edition of *Origin* in November 1859 with a personal note.

Falconer discovered that most fossil species remained stable over very long periods, even through significant environmental changes. In his 1863 monograph, after describing that the mammoths had experienced extreme changes of climate, he wonders, "If species are so unstable, and so susceptible to mutations through such influences, why does that extinct form stand out so signally, a monument of stability?"

In 1903, the famous paleontologist H. F. Cleland noted a similar stasis in Devonian fossils (from 420 to 360 million years ago). He stated, "A careful examination of the fossils of all the zones, from the lowest to the highest, failed to reveal any evolutionary changes, with the possible exception of *Ambocoelia praeumbona*. . . . The evolution of brachiopods, gastropods, and pelecypods either does not take place at all or takes place very seldom." Many other paleontologists had been making similar observations.

None of these practitioners defied Darwin's claim of gradualism, although their field observations seemed to indicate otherwise. This tension between theory and practice finally broke in 1972 when Niles Eldredge and Stephen Jay Gould published their famous essay, "Punctuated Equilibria: An Alternative to Phyletic Gradualism."[4]

They claimed that the history of the organic world could be viewed as comprising long periods of stability interspersed with brief periods during which new species emerge. In the authors' words, "As a central proposition, punctuated equilibrium holds that the great majority of species, as evidenced by their anatomical and geographical histories in the fossil record, originate in geological moments (punctuations) and then persist in stasis throughout their long durations."

Gould and Eldredge were admonishing their peers for confusing an "absence of evidence" with "evidence of absence." Gould (who died in 2002) was a paleontologist at Harvard University and conducted extensive research on West Indian land snails. Eldredge, now curator emeritus at the American Museum of Natural History, specialized in trilobites (which are now extinct). Paleontologists study fossils to learn about an organism's evolutionary history and its relationship to other organisms and its environment. In fact, until the rise of modern DNA extraction techniques, paleontology was the only science capable of studying ancient life. But even the latest and most modern DNA extraction techniques can study samples of only up to about a million years old.[5] So fossils, and hence paleontology, are our only reliable window onto the ancient past.

Gould and Eldredge's brilliant insight pointed out what may seem obvious now: The gaps in the fossil record were not a bug but a vital feature of the evolution of species. They declared that when paleontologists found a sudden change in the morphology of a particular species, they should assume that there *had been* a sudden change in morphology and *not* make the Darwinian error of trying to explain away this sudden change by invoking gaps in the fossil record.

According to them, the absence of evidence of intermediate forms *is* evidence of their absence. Therefore, there was no need to take refuge in the theory of the imperfection of the fossil record. If a brief punctuation followed a prolonged stasis, we should not find any intermediate forms because there aren't any.

In their seminal article, Gould presented evidence of sudden evolutionary change after long periods of stasis by analyzing the evolution of a Bermudan snail, *Poecilozonites bermudensis*, over three hundred thousand years into three species: *P.b. fasolti*, *P.b. sieglindae*, and *P.b. bermudensis*. He showed that sharp morphological differences in these three species, as measured by differences in color, the form of their spire, the thickness of the shell, and the shape of the apertural lip, did not arise gradually. Instead, they came about owing to a punctuation event of allopatric speciation (i.e., a new species arising as a result of the geographic isolation of a small group of individuals from their parent species). Similarly, Eldredge outlined the evolutionary history of a trilobite species, *Phacops rana*, and presented evidence for the drastic changes in eye morphology of the various subspecies of *P. rana* arising out of punctuation events, not through gradual evolution.

After Eldredge and Gould published their pathbreaking article on the fossils of snails and trilobites, scientists discovered more examples of evolution through punctuated equilibrium across all of life, including animals, plants, bacteria, and even viruses (although whether viruses are "life" is debatable).

In his research article published in 1985, A. L. A. Johnson studied thirty-four scallop species from the Jurassic period (from 200 to 145 million years ago) and found copious evidence of stasis as well as an example of abrupt speciation.[6] He concluded, "One case . . . was discovered where . . . the sudden appearance of a descendant form could fairly be ascribed to rapid evolution

---

Box 9.1: There is no contradiction here

Punctuated equilibrium seems to contradict the observations made by Kurtén and others as described in the previous chapter. Kurtén had shown that the rate of change in organisms is higher over the short term and is lower over the long term. But the theory of punctuated equilibrium asserts that living things change dramatically (i.e., create new species) after a long period of stasis. What's going on? If you read carefully, you will notice that these theories actually complement each other.

Kurtén's observations were for a single species over thousands of years, and the changes observed were within reasonable limits. The Grants' beak measurements were spread over a few decades, and the variations in beak size and shape weren't so drastic as to warrant the creation of a new species. Eldredge and Gould, on the other hand, discuss the process of the creation of a new species after the original species has been in stasis for millions of years. Both views are correct—they are explaining different phenomena over different periods.

(within no more than one million years). Inconclusive evidence of gradual change over some twenty-five million years was discovered in one of the other lineages studied. But in the remaining thirty-two lineages, morphology appears to have been static."

One of the most extensive documentations of punctuated equilibrium started as a research project to refute it! Alan H. Cheetham of the Smithsonian National Museum of Natural History in Washington, DC, is an expert on bryozoan fossils. (Bryozoa are tiny animals that look like worms and have tentacles on the outside; they live in colonies that resemble trees or flowers.) He started his work on the bryozoan species *Metrarabdotos* to illustrate gradualism.[7] Cheetham measured forty-six characters in seventeen species of *Metrarabdotos* over fifteen million years. He found that eleven of the seventeen species persisted unchanged for two to six million years, followed by a punctuational change over 160,000 years. Cheetham emphasized "the remarkably clear-cut evidence for a punctuated evolutionary pattern in these *Metrarabdotos* species."

Many such studies have found evidence of punctuated equilibrium. One of the most interesting—and conclusive—was reported in the *Proceedings of the Royal Society* in 2008 by Tiina Mattila and Folmer Bokma from Umeå University in Sweden.[8] Instead of examining fossil records, Mattila and Bokma analyzed the change in body mass of 2,143 mammal species of a total of 4,510 extant species to assess whether their evolution was punctuated or gradual. They concluded, "Our Bayesian estimates from mammals as well as separate sub-clades such as primates and carnivores suggest that gradual evolution is responsible for only a small part of the body size variation between mammal species." Their study confirmed that punctuated equilibrium played a big part in the evolution of most mammal species' body mass. Most research on punctuated equilibrium—including that by Gould and Eldredge—typically focuses on one species at a time. In contrast, Mattila and Bokma showed that the theory applied to the *entire* mammalian clade.

Gould and Eldredge's essay has turned out to be highly controversial and has many supporters and detractors.[9] Many researchers have found evidence of punctuated equilibria in species evolution, and others haven't found any. The debates are fierce and even personal—the gradualists have called the punctuated equilibria principle "evolution by jerks," and the other side has countered by calling the gradualist principle "evolution by creeps"![10] So much for scientific decency.

One of the most significant sources of controversy is their use of the words "rapid" and "sudden" when discussing the birth of new species. The critics of punctuated equilibria accuse Gould and Eldredge of reviving the discredited mutationism theory of Hugo de Vries and the macromutation theory of Richard Goldschmidt.[11] Goldschmidt, a German-born American zoologist, argued in his book *The Material Basis of Evolution* in 1940 that species were created not by accumulating minor variations but through significant mutations (called saltations) in a single generation. However, the scientific community has discredited this theory of sudden evolution, derisively termed the "theory of hopeful monsters."

Gould has rightly argued in many of his writings that punctuated equilibrium is *not* saltation. The theory was written for paleontologists who understand that "instantaneous" refers to *geological* time, spanning tens of thousands of years, and should not be confused with human time scales. In his book *The Structure of Evolutionary Theory*, Gould uses the analogy of human gestation: "As the gestation time of a human being represents 1 to 2 percent of an ordinary lifetime, perhaps we should permit the same general range for punctuational speciation relative to later duration in stasis. At an average lifetime of four million years, a 1-percent criterion allows forty thousand years of speciation."

A bizarre unintended consequence of the brouhaha among biologists was that the creationists crashed their party![12] Creationists have always used the lack of intermediate forms in the fossil record as evidence that Darwin's theory is wrong. The idea of punctuated equilibrium seemed to substantiate their claim when Gould and Eldredge emphasized that "stasis is data." Creationists believe that animals and plants emerge suddenly in the fossil record because they were created instantaneously by God; thus, they took refuge in the theory of punctuated equilibrium, which seemed to affirm the sudden emergence of species.

Gould was scathing in his takedown of the creationists with the following choice words: " . . . punctuated equilibrium provides an even easier target for this form of intellectual dishonesty (or crass stupidity if a charge of dishonesty grants them too much acumen), no one should be surprised that our views have become grist for their mills and skills of distortion."

I am not an evolutionary biologist, but as I said in the introduction, one of the skills I possess is the ability to read. I know that the famous biologists and philosophers of biology like Richard Dawkins and Daniel Dennett belittle punctuated equilibrium and claim that it's barely a wrinkle on Darwin's theory. Maybe.

The issue for me is not whether Gould and Eldredge proposed something revolutionary, but whether what they offered was a new way to look at evolution and whether it stands up to empirical analysis. A search of "punctuated equilibrium" on Google Scholar (which searches only for scientific articles) throws up more than 85,000 results. Not all may be relevant, but a glance through the first few pages of these results clearly shows that scientists have gathered enough evidence for this phenomenon over the years. To a layperson like me, it seems that the theory of punctuated equilibrium *did* move Darwin's theory forward, as the research articles described in this chapter demonstrate.

When I first read about the theory many years ago, my first thought was that life was all about not just *biological* life but *life*. No wonder a two-hour movie can capture—or seem to capture—the entire life of Mahatma Gandhi, Frida Kahlo, Muhammad Ali, or Coco Chanel. Moviemakers use punctuated equilibria to eliminate the stasis from the lives of heroes and celebrities, highlighting only the punctuations. History books apply the same technique to chronicle the life of an entire civilization over thousands of years by compressing narratives into a few hundred pages. On my desk lies a copy of Duff McDonald's book *The Firm: The Story of McKinsey and Its Secret Influence on American Business*, which compresses almost a century of the consulting firm's existence into a mere four hundred pages. Now that I have seen the theory, I can no longer *unsee* it; it seems to apply everywhere I look. But let me not get carried away.

Let's return to investing. Here are my main investing lessons from the theory of punctuated equilibrium:

1. Business stasis is the default, so why be active?
2. Stock price fluctuation is *not* business punctuation.
3. Take advantage of the rare stock price punctuations to create a new "species."

Business Stasis Is the Default, so Why Be Active?

In the business world, as in the organic world, stasis is the default.

Great businesses stay great. Bad businesses remain bad.

Yes, yes, I know. Off the top of your head, you can name an incredible business in deep trouble (so can I: SoftBank) and a lousy business that has revived from the dead (so can I: SoftBank). This assertion about business stasis is not about starting a battle of anecdotes.

My contention is not that counterexamples don't exist but that we should be more concerned about *dominant relative frequency*, an apt term I learned from Gould's magnum opus, *The Structure of Evolutionary Theory*. He argues that punctuated equilibrium "does not merely assert the existence of a phenomenon, but ventures a stronger claim for a dominant role as a macroevolutionary pattern in geological time." Similarly, my three-decade-long journey in the corporate world has led me to believe that great businesses stay great and that, *more often than not*, bad businesses stay bad.

Allow me to clarify the meaning of some words. "Stasis" does *not* mean "static." A corner store in your neighborhood selling the same products since you were a toddler is *static*. The corner store hasn't changed. Dollar General, a variety store chain that sells deeply discounted products across more than 16,000 stores and grew its revenue two and a half times between 2011 and 2021 to $33 billion, is in *stasis*. The *character* of Dollar General hasn't changed.

I am excluding industries in which "greatness" and "badness" haven't had time to settle. These include areas like AI, space travel, autonomous vehicles, food delivery, WeWork clones, quantum computing, nanotechnology, and other sectors into which substantial venture capital investments are pouring.

I wish I could apply deductive reasoning ("All humans are mortal; Socrates is a human; therefore Socrates is mortal") to prove without doubt that the great and not-so-great businesses stay in stasis over long periods. But, unfortunately, I cannot find such a route, so as usual, let me take the inductive path by presenting you with multiple strands of evidence.

I have divided this section into four parts, each of which separately asserts that great businesses remain outstanding and that inadequate businesses continue to underperform. Of course, none of these sections makes an infallible argument (hey, this is investing, not linear algebra). But, taken *together*, I hope to make a convincing case for the third leg of our investment philosophy: Don't be lazy—be *very* lazy.

Part I: Proof from Personal Experience

Don't you detest arguments that take refuge in personal anecdotes? We *Homo sapiens* can reason—rationalize—almost anything. We have spotted UFOs, witnessed election fraud, not worn masks during the COVID-19 crisis, and believed that baseball is somehow superior to cricket.

However, in this case, in which I need to show that stasis is the default for businesses, I ask that you give me some leeway for two reasons. First, I have been in the business world for almost thirty-five years, and at *some* point, anecdotes can transform into patterns. Second, this belief is not the result of armchair philosophizing but the very foundation of how we manage money for our clients and for ourselves. Almost all my wealth is in my fund. Not believing in the right way to manage money will cost me serious money.

My first job was as a production management trainee at Unilever in India in 1989. Unilever had, and I believe continues to have, an exceptional training program for its new managers. During my first year, I circulated through all the critical departments of Brooke Bond, a Unilever subsidiary that manufactured and sold tea and coffee. I remember my four-week stint at the sales office in the city of Coimbatore in South India. Every day, I went to the market with the sales officer, who should have been called the no-sales officer. On paper, his job was to sell tea, but in reality, the dominance of Brooke Bond's brands compelled him to ration the orders to the various retailers clamoring for more tea. The respect and awe he commanded would have shamed many local political leaders.

Unilever has maintained its preeminent position in tea and dozens of other consumer products in India over many decades. It was exceptional in 1989, and it is exceptional today. For example, Unilever's subsidiary listed in India, Hindustan Unilever, has a market value of almost half that of its parent listed in the United Kingdom. The same phenomenon has been confirmed across many other product and service categories in India over more than two decades: toothpaste (Colgate), chocolate (Nestlé), cars (Maruti Suzuki), innerwear (Page), consumer electricals (Havells), biscuits (Parle, Britannia), hair oil (Marico), paint (Asian Paints, Berger), tires (MRF), diagnostic services (Dr Lal), IT outsourcing (TCS, Infosys), kitchen appliances and cookware (Hawkins, TTK Prestige), herbal supplements (Dabur), and many more.

Whichever country you are in, I bet you may have noticed the same phenomenon in many industries: Most of the leading players of the 1990s or early 2000s are the leaders today. The new-age internet businesses have taken this continued dominance to a level unseen in almost any other era, whether Amazon, Facebook, Google, Twitter, or Uber. Stasis is the default.

Since great businesses remain great for an eternity, everyone knows about them. Investors bid their prices up, and rightly so. The ten-year average price/earnings (PE) multiples of some of the leading consumer businesses in India are astronomical. For example, Asian Paints, 56; Colgate India, 43; Dabur, 44; Hindustan Unilever, 51; and Page Industries, 65. As price-sensitive investors, we should not buy these businesses since their valuations would almost always be too high for us. And we don't. From the list provided two paragraphs earlier, the only companies we have been able to buy since 2007 are Page, Havells, and TTK Prestige. Our window of opportunity for buying these three was only two to three *months* over almost fifteen years—a punctuation event that lasted just 1 to 2 percent of this period.

There are very few great businesses, and they are almost always unbuyable. Hence, we buy very rarely, and when we do, we buy a lot. So, having purchased these winners, given the stasis of their success, why should we sell?

Part II: The Fate of the Fortune 500

I want to revisit the comparison of the Fortune 500 lists from 1955 and 2015 detailed in chapter 8. We saw that a plausible case could be made for 40 to 45 percent of the Fortune 500 businesses of 1955 maintaining their excellence for sixty years. Of course, this is not perfect stasis (nor is organic life in pure stasis, as we saw earlier in this chapter), but it sure is a pretty *good* case of long-term stasis.

Thus, *if* we were an owner in a collection of these excellent businesses—and I know that is a *very* big "if"—it would have made no sense to sell and leave. *As a portfolio*, not necessarily individually, the businesses in this group should have done well for us. With a reasonable degree of confidence, we *can* state that at least 40 to 45 percent of the largest five hundred U.S. businesses in 1955 performed exceptionally well over sixty years. Stasis was the default for this group of companies.

Here is another way to look at stasis. Let's shine a light on the businesses that did *not* make it. We saw that at least 40 percent of businesses (about two hundred) from the 1955 list maintained their excellence for sixty years, until 2015. How many firms, both private and public, in 1955 *could* have made it on to the Fortune 500 list in 2015 but did not? Would ten thousand be a fair estimate? That is probably a highly conservative guess because businesses would have had *sixty* years to make it onto the list, and we are not counting the thousands of businesses created *after* 1955 that could have made it to the list in 2015. Anyway, let's stick to ten thousand. Of these ten thousand in 1955 that *could* have made it to the 2015 Fortune 500 list, only three hundred did (the remaining two hundred had stayed on the list for sixty years). An apparent 3 percent "success rate." The actual number is probably closer to 1 to 2 percent or even lower. Thus, 97 to 99 percent of the not-so-great businesses could not "succeed" over sixty years. Stasis is the default.

I know I have been unfair here. To count listing among the Fortune 500 as a measure of "success" is undoubtedly an unreasonable demand. Many of the ten thousand businesses of 1955 may have achieved great success without necessarily becoming too large—they may have focused much more on profits or may have been merged or acquired, creating massive value for shareholders. My intention here was to demonstrate *directionally* that great businesses remain great much longer than we think. The probability that a not-so-great business becomes excellent over time is infinitesimal.

Our investment strategy is thus quite simple:

1. Since the vast majority of businesses do not become great, our default strategy is *not* to buy. We are lazy buyers.
2. We buy only *if* we can find a high-quality business that can stay in stasis over decades. If we believe we have such a business, we don't sell. We are *very* lazy sellers.

Part III: A Conclusion from Climbing Concentration

In an article from the July 2019 issue of *Review of Finance*, Grullon, Larkin, and Michaely ask, "Are U.S. industries becoming more concentrated?"[13] It turns out to be a rhetorical question: Of course they are. The authors demonstrate this with copious data. Their article shows two trends occurring from 1997 to 2014 that seem to reinforce each other: (1) Since the 1990s, in over three-quarters of U.S. industries, the market share of the leading players has increased, and (2) these companies show higher profit margins and provide higher returns to shareholders, which, in turn, allows them to increase their market power even more.

While the article does not state so explicitly, it is also evident that the market power of smaller and less powerful businesses has declined over this period. The authors show that not only did the revenue share of the four largest public and private companies in almost every industry increase but also that the average size of the leading companies also *tripled* in real terms during the period of measurement.

And this is not a recent phenomenon. It turns out that the specter of increasing market power among the more extensive and more successful businesses has haunted the corporate world since the beginning of the twentieth century. In 1977, Leslie Hannah and J. A. Kay published *Concentration in Modern Industry: Theory, Measurement, and the U.K. Experience*. Hannah and Kay demonstrate the inexorable rise of the biggest firms' market share in the United States and the United Kingdom from the early 1900s to the mid-1970s. The first graph in the book tracks the share of the largest hundred firms in manufacturing net output during this period. Over seventy years, the market share of these firms rose from 15 percent to 50 percent in the United Kingdom and from 20 percent to more than 30 percent in the United States. Hannah and Kay claimed increasing *market* power (which cuts across industries) and not increasing industry concentration (which measures the increasing power of companies *within* an industry). Ideally, I would like to demonstrate greater industry concentration to make my case, but it is still instructive to note the longer-term success of the largest firms in the United States and the United Kingdom.

A January 2019 OECD working paper titled "Industry Concentration in Europe and North America" presents evidence for the increasing power of more successful firms quite emphatically.[14] Between 2001 and 2012, the largest 10 percent of companies in the average industry in ten European countries increased their market share by 2 to 3 percentage points. In the United States, the increase in market share of the leading firms of the average industry between 2000 and 2014 was 4 to 8 percentage points. The paper also clarifies that the numbers were not driven by digital-intensive sectors (e.g., search engines, social media, e-commerce) but by old-world manufacturing and services firms.

In March 2016, the *Economist* magazine's cover bemoaned, "Winners Take All: Why High Profits Are a Problem for America."[15] Of course, I am not qualified to pass judgment on the appropriateness of the sky-high profits of giant corporations, but I do want to quote the magazine's view on the stasis of businesses.

The article discusses three key reasons—technology, globalization, and decline in trade union membership—for profit accumulation among the more successful firms and then follows with the following: "None of these accounts though, explain the most troubling aspect of America's profit problem: its persistence." It mentions that a highly profitable firm in 2003 had an 83 percent chance of being very profitable in 2013. A powerful visual plot of the share of the top four companies in 893 industry sectors from 1997 to 2012 clearly shows the increasing power of larger businesses.

The summary of all this research on industry and market concentration is as follows:

1. There are a few large and successful firms in most industries.
2. These successful companies are becoming even more successful.
3. Weak companies are getting weaker.

Numbers 1 and 2 are direct conclusions of the research, and number 3 is an indirect but logical outcome of 1 and 2.

As I wrote earlier, our investing experience in India is not different from what research from the United States, the United Kingdom, or Europe says. Our investee companies have been gaining share over the competition over decades. Some examples are Berger in the paint industry, Supreme in plastic pipes, Voltamp in industrial transformers, Page in innerwear, Havells and V-Guard in consumer electricals, Amara Raja in batteries, Info Edge in job boards, MRF in tires, and Ratnamani in specialty steel pipes.

In India, too, great businesses continue to be great, and poor businesses continue to suffer. The observation that "stasis is the default" does not respect national boundaries.

As permanent owners, we want to own successful businesses that will maintain their rewarding run. That sounds straightforward, but the problem is that there are *very* few successful businesses. Throwing a dart at the business landscape will land us in real trouble. So we don't. We invest rarely.

We should not sell once we own a "winner" like Havells or Ratnamani since it will likely keep gaining market share. So we don't. We sell even more rarely than we buy.

Part IV: The Narrative of a Ninety-Year Study

In May 2018, Hendrik Bessembinder of the W. P. Carey School of Business at Arizona State University published an article titled "Do Stocks Outperform Treasury Bills?"[16] He analyzed the price performance of about 26,000 common stocks listed on the New York Stock Exchange, the American Stock Exchange, and the NASDAQ from 1926 to 2016.

Unsurprisingly, 51 percent of these stocks lost their entire value over their lifetime. The majority of businesses should not be in business. Bessembinder's research demonstrates that since the average common stock will lose its value over time, owning stocks can harm one's wealth. Our default position should be *not* to buy. So we don't. We are lazy.

Can you guess the number of those 26,000 stocks, if purchased in 1926 and held until 2016 (or acquired or merged), that beat the market? The answer is about 8,000, or about 31 percent of the universe.[17] Again, I was surprised at how high this number was. Remember that we are talking about the companies not just doing well but *beating* the market over *90 years* (or until they were merged or acquired). These great businesses maintained their greatness over a *very* long period. Stasis was the default for them. Once we own such a business, selling would border on being sinful.

Stock Price Fluctuation Is *Not* Business Punctuation

A critical element of the theory of punctuated equilibrium is that fluctuation is not punctuation. During long periods of stasis, the character traits of living organisms do vary but within limits.

A critical element of our investment philosophy is that we do not confuse *stock price* fluctuation with *business* punctuation. During long periods of business stasis, stock prices vary, but the character of excellent *businesses* tends to stay within limits.

As Gould clarifies, "Stasis does not imply absolute stability, but rather directionless fluctuation that generally does not stray beyond the boundaries of geographic variation within similar species and, particularly, does not trend in any given direction, especially towards the modal morphology of descendant forms." The character traits of species *do* fluctuate while they are in stasis, but they are range bound.

There is a tendency among investors to interpret *stock price* movement as the measure of *business* direction. Shouldn't it be the other way around? Does the cart drive the horse? You bet it does, more often than you can imagine. And it does strange things to even the best of us. Our community can and does accord a level of priority to ticker symbols that they don't deserve.

Here is a true story. A venture capitalist (VC) friend and I were meeting for lunch one afternoon in Mumbai. As you may know, VCs invest in start-ups and early-stage privately held businesses. Every few minutes, he would glance at his phone and then return to our conversation. I had known him for more than a decade but had never witnessed this odd behavior before. After a few minutes, I became mildly irritated and asked him the reason for his distraction. He apologized and sheepishly remarked that two of his portfolio companies had gone public in the past two weeks. After that, he said he felt compelled to check their stock prices every few minutes. He admitted that he couldn't help himself.

My friend is an intelligent guy. He knows that the *business* of his listed portfolio companies is not changing by the minute. A few weeks earlier, when the companies were unlisted, he hardly ever thought about them. But now that they each had a stock exchange ticker that gyrated a few percentage points every day, he had gotten caught up in the action. Now imagine if he were running a public market fund like ours in which *every* portfolio company is listed. That may have driven him up the wall, which is what happens to many in our community.

A great example of stock prices getting the upper hand is provided by Amazon. The company had its IPO in May 1997 at $18. By December 1998, when dot-com mania was sweeping through the U.S. markets, the stock had climbed almost *fourteen* times to $243. The star analyst at CIBC Oppenheimer, Henry Blodget, published a price target of *$400* within twelve months.[18] The stock promptly jumped almost 20 percent to $289 in one day. In January 1999, Blodget wrote, "Unlike with other famous bubbles . . . the Internet bubble is riding on rock-solid fundamentals, perhaps stronger than any the market has seen before." Well, where was the evidence? None of the rising dot-com stars was even close to earning any profit; worse, they were burning cash as if the market faucet would remain open forever. The *only* empirical evidence backing Blodget's claim of solid business fundamentals seemed to be that the *stock prices* were rising.

By the time the dot-com bubble burst in the summer of 2000, Amazon had dropped more than 60 percent from its peak. Ravi Suria, a young Lehman bond analyst, issued a withering twenty-seven-page report predicting that Amazon was doomed and that if the company did not change its ways, it would be out of cash within a year.[19] In this highly bearish environment for all dot-coms, Amazon fell 19 percent in a single day. Bezos brushed the criticism aside, and Amazon kept doing its business the way it had always done: by caring more about cash flow than profits. Suria had predicted that Amazon would be left with $125 million in the bank at the end of 2001; instead, Amazon ended the year with $1 billion. Amazon's bonds, which Suria had predicted would collapse, were up 50 percent.

Just as Blodget had gained stardom by predicting that Amazon would keep rising, Suria became the darling of financial pundits with his prediction that Amazon would fail. The only difference? Blodget was cheerleading when all stocks were rising, and Suria predicted doomsday in the middle of a catastrophic bear market.

It is unfair to pick on only Blodget and Suria. They were two among thousands of analysts and investors who got carried away by the rising and falling stock prices of the dot-com era. The saga repeated itself during the global financial crisis of 2008 when the rising market capitalizations of highly leveraged lenders blinded most financial experts to the deepening malaise that finally brought the global economy to its knees.

In my opinion, investors can commit two types of grave errors.

First, they can treat an unfavorable stock price fluctuation as a negative business punctuation. This mindset compels the investor either to sell a good business or not to buy a good business when the price declines owing to a negative piece of news or event. I covered this first error in the previous chapter when discussing the Grant–Kurtén principle of investing (GKPI). As a reminder, GKPI says the following: *When we find high-quality businesses that do not fundamentally alter their character over the long term, we should exploit the inevitable short-term fluctuations in their businesses for buying and* not *selling.* Since chapter 8 addressed this issue, let me not dwell any more on it here.

The second error is to regard a positive stock price fluctuation as positive business punctuation. Doing so can lead to buying a lousy business (because it seems that things have permanently improved) or not selling one. Ask any long-term investor about their investment strategy, and almost all will proclaim that they buy and hold high-quality businesses. I doubt even one would admit to buying poor-quality businesses to trade later at a higher price. They are not lying. Then why is the portfolio of many funds filled with the latest Chamath SPAC? Who knows? FOMO, envy, greed, and some other quality human attributes probably play a role. It doesn't matter. These investors changed their minds about the quality of a business based on *some* positive evaluation of the opportunity.

We see the same news flow as everyone else. We often see industry brethren rake in moolah by investing in airlines, real estate, infrastructure, education, public sector banks (i.e., government-owned banks), or some other hyped-up Indian industry that does not live up to its expectations.

How have we avoided succumbing to the temptation of investing in a bad business on a stock market (or even a private market) upswing? By following three simple rules.

No Sweets in the Fridge

My wife has a sweet tooth but is also very health conscious. Over more than two decades, she has followed a simple yet powerful way of avoiding the enticement of desserts. Our fridge just doesn't have any.

In my view, the best way to avoid investing in bad businesses is to ignore them and their stock prices. We never discuss what we consider bad companies or industries in our team meetings. Never. It doesn't matter if an airline has declared spectacular results recently or if every analyst recommends buying airline shares. We are indifferent to a public sector bank that has hired a new CEO from the private sector and has pushed its stock price to an all-time high. We ignore an infrastructure business that has been awarded a new multibillion-dollar contract and a gold loan business that has announced 30 percent ROE in its latest quarterly result and is touted by the bulls to be the next billion-dollar opportunity. No one on our team is allowed to utter the famous last words of many investors: "This time, it's different." If we never discuss a business, how will we ever buy it? No sweets in the fridge: no snacking possible.

The origin of every lousy investment is a good story. Table 9.1 shows many examples of Indian industries that became newsworthy *after* rising stock prices or soaring private market valuations.

Take infrastructure. Anyone who has been to India knows that the country needs quality roads, power, ports, airports, and water. While the national highways in India are now better than highways in the United States, that's not saying much. In the mid- to late 2000s, many investors salivated at the billions (or was it trillions?) of dollars that were waiting to be made by investing in Indian infrastructure. The valuations of private and public companies were soaring, and there seemed to be a consensus that the gold rush was beginning. Amid this infrastructure mania, Reliance Power launched an IPO in January 2008 that was oversubscribed seventy-two times! It made the company's owner, Anil Ambani, the richest Indian. Despite having a power capacity of less than 1,000 megawatts at the time of the IPO, the company's value was about $35 billion. Did this lead to a large number of IPOs for infrastructure businesses that investors lapped up hungrily? Does the sun rise in the east? Both private and public equity investors in the hyped-up story of

TABLE 9.1 We ignore positive stock price fluctuations in bad places

News or event	Date
Foreign Funds Chase DLF *(India's largest real estate company)*	Jun 2007
Reliance Power IPO to Make Anil Ambani the Richest Indian	Jan 2008
Infrastructure PE: Investors Seek Returns in Mid–High Teens on Growth Potential	Dec 2009
How Gold Loans Became Popular Over the Years	Oct 2010
PEs Sharpen Focus on Green Energy	Dec 2010
PE Firms Eye to Invest in Indian Agriculture and Food Sector	Sep 2011
Three Reasons Why India Will Lead EdTech in the Twenty-First Century	Aug 2012
Benefits of Infrastructure Stimulus	Feb 2013
GoAir Joins the Profit League	Nov 2013
Blackstone Sees Indian Real Estate Turnaround	Jun 2014
How Rahul Bhatia Built InterGlobe and Its Airline IndiGo Into a Class Act	Sep 2014
Online Education: The Next Big Thing in India	Feb 2015
GSK Bets Big on Emerging Markets with $1 Billion Investment in India	Mar 2016
The Education Sector Will Grow at 7.5% to $144 Billion by 2020	Oct 2017
Health-Tech Sector Seen Generating Significant Value Over the Next Decade	Sep 2018
Jet, SpiceJet Rival Indigo Posts Profits as Fuel, Rupee Cool Off	Jan 2019
How the Airline Industry Grew Profitable Over the Decade	Dec 2019
Private Equity Firms Sense Ample Opportunity in Last-Mile Real Estate Funding	Dec 2019
Indian Healthcare Sector—A Promising $353 Billion Opportunity by 2025	Nov 2020

Indian infrastructure forgot or chose to ignore some uncomfortable truths: Every infrastructure business is held hostage to the whims and fancies of the government; the government hates to be a paying customer—underpayment and late payment are the rule, not the exception; and even if the government behaves well, the returns on these projects are capped according to law. So why would we want to spend a single minute debating if *any* power business is worth investing in?

We did not discuss a single story listed in table 9.1 in our team meetings. We ignore the stock prices and businesses of businesses we detest. By the way, that doesn't mean that we are right to do so; some investors may possess the skill to trade in and out of low-quality businesses, and that's fine. They have my admiration and best wishes.

The market value of Reliance Power at the end of 2021 was $600 million, down 95 percent from its peak.

Business Knowledge, Not Stock Price Data

As I discussed earlier, we ignore many conspicuously poor-quality industries like power, infrastructure, and airlines. But most industries and businesses don't fall neatly into this category. So what do we do when we see increasing valuation in businesses or industries that we haven't encountered before?

We ignore the hype around valuation and focus *exclusively* on business quality. I have devoted the whole of section II to this topic, so let me confine this discussion to an example.

Table 9.1 includes the news item "The Education Sector Will Grow at 7.5% to $144 Billion by 2020." This headline is from late 2017 when many new-age education companies (appropriately christened "EdTech") in India had started getting funded at unheard-of valuations in the private market.

We don't know of a single listed education business in India that has made money over the long term. However, many have had soaring stock prices over the years with the unfulfilled promise of untold riches that would accrue to an intrepid investor. One did appear to break the mold but sadly—and predictably—turned out to be a fraud. When I assess the finances of listed education businesses in a large market like the United States, I find that most don't earn even their cost of capital. For example, in 2021, the U.S. education company with the most considerable market value was Grand Canyon Education, whose market capitalization was only about $4 billion. It's a dangerous place to be.

So what should we think about the dozens of Indian EdTech unicorns or soon-to-be-unicorns? I just do not have enough information to know. At their current rate of blowing cash that would put Usain Bolt to shame, they will probably not enter our radar until 2032 (because they would need to have demonstrated at least a five-year history of being highly profitable). For us, their soaring valuation is *not* an indicator that they are great businesses but that they have mastered the art of raising capital.

Until the *business* numbers (e.g., ROCE and free cash flow, *not* revenue growth) become attractive, we refuse to engage with companies, and EdTechs are no exception.

Do We Want to Own This Forever?

Our best protection against getting swayed by a false positive—a stock price fluctuation that makes a lousy business look better than it is—is the question we pose for every investment: Do we want to be permanent owners of this business? Are we *absolutely* sure that we are willing to live with it permanently? Are we willing *never* to sell it?

We presume guilt until innocence is proven; our starting hypothesis with every business is that we *don't* want to own it. As you have seen throughout this book, a business needs to jump through several hoops before we choose to be permanent owners in it. One of India's largest real estate companies launched a $2 billion IPO in July 2007. Its stock price shot up by 70 percent before the end of the year. News anchors screamed until they were hoarse about the unlimited potential of Indian real estate; a journalist friend told me that it was easier to get an appointment with a Bollywood star than a real estate entrepreneur.

We launched Nalanda in June 2007, smack in the middle of this frenzy. We did not make a single real estate investment because we did not want to be permanent owners in a real estate business. The reasons were many, but let me just state the first one, so I don't even have to go on to the second: Real estate businesses in India aren't known for Gandhian governance, to put it mildly.

What about that company today? The stock price is down 75 percent from its peak. Given its bloated balance sheet, the company has also had to raise multiple equity funding rounds in the past few years, diluting existing shareholders. The suffering for the owners of this business seems endless.

We have saved a lot of heartburn by studying business quality while ignoring stock prices. We have stayed focused on getting married and have eschewed casual hookups, to draw an analogy from the dating world. A world intent on swiping left and right at breakneck speed probably finds it very hard to notice a marriageable candidate even when that candidate has been staring at them for decades. That gives us a competitive advantage we never asked for and probably didn't deserve.

But we will take it. Thank you very much.

Take Advantage of the Rare Stock Price Punctuations to Create a New "Species"

Eldredge and Gould's bold claim was not just that organisms changed their morphology during punctuation events but also that these events created a new *species*. As they elaborate, "The theory of punctuated equilibrium attempts to explain the macroevolutionary role of species and speciation as expressed in geological time." They disagreed with Darwin's claim of speciation through gradual change (biologists call this process "anagenesis"). Instead, they focused the minds of paleontologists and evolutionary biologists on the punctuation events that gave birth to novel species.

Suppose you agree with the premise that markets are usually quite efficient and that it is very hard to buy high-quality businesses at an attractive valuation. In that case, it should be evident that long-term investors like us must take advantage of stock price punctuation events to create a new and improved portfolio.

Let's return to the question I asked at the beginning of the chapter. As the COVID-19 pandemic created panic across the world, *what were we at Nalanda to do in these unprecedented times?* We bought. A lot.

Since our inception in 2007, we have bought *only* at times of adverse stock price punctuations. In other words, we have bought only when a stock is being abandoned by investors owing to an adverse macro event, industry troubles, or pessimism regarding a company's prospects. On three occasions (the global financial crisis, the Euro crisis, and the COVID-19 pandemic), all three combined to offer us an unprecedented buying opportunity.

Talk is cheap, so let me share some actual numbers. Table 9.2 presents the three main occasions over fourteen years, from June 2007 until June 2021, when we took advantage of stock price punctuations to dramatically alter the character of our portfolio.

There were 169 months from June 1, 2007, until June 30, 2021. We invested a total of $1.86 billion during this period. However, as you can see from table 9.2, the pace of investment was highly punctuated: We invested $851 million, or 46 percent of the total amount invested from 2007 to 2021, over only twenty-six months (15 percent of the total number of months)—months of severely damaging market punctuations.

The impact of the COVID-19 pandemic's negative punctuation on our buying behavior was even starker. We invested 22 percent of our capital in just 2 percent of the period of our existence. That is because, as shown in table 9.2, we invested $405 million (22 percent of our total capital invested over fourteen years) in only three months, from March to May 2020 (which comprises 2 percent of the 169 months).

What I have not shown in table 9.2 is our investment pace during March 2020. We invested 16 percent of our capital in 0.5 percent of working days. As the Indian Midcap Index declined 28 percent during March 2020, we invested $288 million (16 percent of the total amount invested until June 2021) over just seventeen days (0.5 percent of about 3,500 working days over fourteen years). This amount, $288 million, invested in March 2020 exceeds the amount invested in *twelve* of the fourteen calendar years since our inception—the only two calendar years during which we invested more than $288 million

TABLE 9.2 Punctuation events have helped us create new "species"

Period	Market decline	Amount invested
Jan 2008–Mar 2009	73%	$182 million
Apr 2011–Dec 2011	28%	$264 million
Mar 2020–May 2020	26% (Feb–May)	$405 million

are 2011 ($320 million) and 2020 ($486 million). Call us what you want, but scared we aren't.

I guess we can all agree that we would make a sloth envious with our rare bouts of activity. So what do we do the rest of the time? We wait. Occasionally, we have had to wait many years. For example, we invested only $34 million and $66 million in 2018 and 2019, respectively. The amount we invested in 2020 turned out to be 45 percent more than in the previous five years *combined*.

But I could have done a much better job. You may have noticed that we did invest a fair bit ($182 million) as the market panic started gathering around the global financial crisis, but we could have and should have invested a lot more. My excuse is that I had just started the fund (in June 2007) and had not done enough work on enough companies to take advantage of the panic.

The Occam's razor explanation is that I was a moron. ("Don't use the past tense," my wife reminds me dutifully.)

Table 9.2 shows the data on the overall market levels during three punctuation events. But we don't buy the market; we are interested only in quality businesses. Hence, it would be nice to find out the extent of the negative punctuation in the companies we bought. We had been tracking many businesses for years, and we were well prepared when the pandemic panic struck in March 2020.

During March 2020, we bought eight businesses and continued to buy them until May 2020. Our previous monthly record was in October 2008 when we bought six companies. (Lehman had collapsed only a few weeks earlier, on September 15, 2008, and we had started gorging on quality enterprises.) So yes, we waited almost twelve years before getting hyperactive. And you thought the comparison to a sloth was an exaggeration.

Table 9.3 lists the eight businesses we bought between March and May 2020. Four—MRF, Sundaram, Thermax, and Thyrocare—were new to the portfolio,

TABLE 9.3 The pandemic punctuation created a new species/portfolio for us (prices in INR except where specified)

Company	All-time high before Mar 2020	Date of previous all-time high	Nalanda avg buy price, Mar–May 2020	Discount to all-time high
Cera	3,796	Dec 2017	2,383	−33%
Genpact	$44.3	Jan 2020	$27.7	−37%
MRF	78,477	Aug 2018	55,487	−29%
Sundaram	2,033	Jan 2018	1,218	−40%
Thermax	1,293	Jan 2018	708	−45%
Thyrocare	753	Apr 2017	507	−33%
Triveni	151	Jul 2017	87	−42%
WNS	$73.4	Feb 2020	$46.1	−37%

and the remaining four were existing companies. We had been waiting to buy these eight for many years. For a few, our wait had lasted more than a decade.

Just as it does in nature, this rare punctuation event dramatically altered the nature of our portfolio. We were able to buy companies at prices and in quantities we never thought possible. For example, in table 9.3, check out the discount at which we bought WNS, a business we have known well (since it is in our portfolio) since 2008. In February 2020, it was trading at almost $74 per share. Within a few weeks, by March 2020, the pandemic scare had crushed the stock, allowing us to deploy almost $100 million at only $46 per share! Similarly, we bought Thermax, a business we had been tracking for more than a decade, at a 45 percent discount to its previous high in early 2018.

Remember that in March 2020, there was no discussion of vaccines, the world was reeling under a pandemic that no one had ever seen before, and it was impossible to predict how things would turn out. The world was shell-shocked, and rightly so. During this period of hyperactivity from March to May 2020 we were often asked, "Why aren't you waiting for things to get worse before buying?"

My answer was, "We can't."

We have a straightforward rule that is also easy to implement: Buy when the *price* is right. Unfortunately, not everyone follows this rule. As implied by the question, a widely practiced rule is to buy when the *time* is right. That is also a straightforward rule, but is it easy to implement? We follow the former because we know the price we want to pay for the business we want to own. It may or may not be the "right" price, but we know it for sure. We have no way of figuring out the right time. Maybe some folks do. Good for them.

There is another way to answer this question. Long-term investors, including us, always claim that we are "buying businesses, not stock prices" because this is what Buffett has been saying for decades. As a philosophical outlook, this is generally deemed a sensible strategy.

But what does that statement mean? For us, it means the following. Let's say we have valued a business at $100 per share. If the stock price falls to $100 and our business assessment remains unchanged, we buy as much of the business as we can at or below $100. We then tell ourselves that this is a private business that we will own forever, and while it happens to be listed, the stock prices quoted by the ever-fluctuating markets are irrelevant to us. As a result, we don't care if the business quotes at $50 or $75 or $500. We are public market investors, but we behave as if we are investing in private businesses for all practical purposes.

An afterthought: There is almost no business in our portfolio that we could buy at an absolute bottom, including the ones listed in table 9.3. If you are searching for an abysmal market-timer, look no further.

Our 2008/09 and 2011 investments have primarily turned out well. I don't know if our aggression in 2020 will yield fruit. But I am happy about our *process*, which was in our control; the *outcome* will be what it will be. We will know in eight to ten years if we were foolish or intelligent. Don't you love long-term investing?

* * *

A housefly lives for a month, a mosquito for one to three months, and a cockroach for up to six months. Unfortunately, most insects live only for a brief period. There is one notable exception, though. Three species of periodical cicadas found in the United States can live for up to seventeen years.

After hatching, baby cicadas, called nymphs, spend seventeen years underground feeding on the roots of plants and trees. After that time, the adults emerge together in billions (some say even trillions) beginning in the second week of May, get into a mating frenzy, lay their eggs on trees, and are dead by the end of June. The eggs hatch in about six weeks, the nymphs drop down from the trees and burrow underground, and the seventeen-year cycle begins again. This evolutionary strategy, called prey satiation, has been supremely successful for eons because no predator can consume such a large number of cicadas in just a few weeks.[20]

There are currently twelve groups, called broods, of seventeen-year cicadas. In May and June 2021, enormous broods called Brood X (meaning "ten") emerged mainly in Pennsylvania, Virginia, Indiana, and Tennessee. We will see them next in 2038.

Our patience for a punctuation event seems pedestrian compared to the remarkable restraint of the cicadas. They wait *seventeen* years for a life-changing event. We have had at least three during just fourteen years. When will we witness the next one? I have no idea. But I know this: As a *species*, we investors are nowhere as disciplined as the cicadas. Our community *will* take things to an extreme before all hell breaks loose again.

We are waiting.

Chapter Summary

Evolutionary theory has taught me that . . .

. . . reimagining investing requires us to accept the pervasiveness of business stasis. In other words, great businesses *generally* remain great, and bad businesses *generally* remain bad.

1. The theory of punctuated equilibrium contends that evolutionary change occurs quite suddenly after long periods of stasis, not through a gradual

process, as claimed by Darwin. Stasis is the default in the natural world, except when punctuations arise to create a new species.

2. Stasis is the default in the business world, too. Great businesses generally stay great, and bad businesses generally remain bad. This is evident not only from my personal experience of investing in India over a few decades but also from empirical data from the United States on the longevity of high-quality businesses.

3. Not all fluctuations in the long-term evolution of an organism are punctuations. Over a period of stasis, organisms do vary within limits.

4. We do not confuse *stock price* fluctuations with *business* punctuations. This has allowed us to be aggressive buyers three times in our history, including during the market panic of the COVID-19 pandemic.

5. We avoid investing in bad businesses when their stock prices are on an upswing by focusing on the (bad) *quality* of the business and asking ourselves if we want to own it forever.

CHAPTER 10

WHERE ARE THE RABBITS?

One of the most remarkable features in our domesticated races is that we see in them adaptation, not indeed to the animal's or plant's own good, but to man's use of fancy. . . . The key is man's power of accumulative selection: nature gives successive variations; man adds them up in certain directions useful to him. In this sense he may be said to make useful breeds.

Charles Darwin, On the Origin of Species, *chapter 1, "Variation Under Domestication"*

Despite the enthusiasm for activity that has swept business and financial America, we will stick with our 'til-death-do-us-part policy. It's the only one with which Charlie and I are comfortable, it produces decent results, and it lets our managers and those of our investees run their businesses free of distractions.

Warren Buffett, annual letter to shareholders, 1986

In October 1988, *Forbes* published a list of the four hundred wealthiest Americans.[1] Sam Walton was the richest with a fortune of $6.7 billion, and Buffett was ranked tenth with $2.2 billion. The list was full of familiar names, including Gates, Helmsley, Hillman, Kluge, Mars, Newhouse, Packard, Perot, Pritzker, and Redstone.

But who was Shelby Cullom Davis? Almost no one had heard of him. And how was he ranked as high as 197 while being a new entrant? Davis was tucked between the famous names of Joseph Albertson, the founder of the Albertsons stores, and Fritz Otto Haas, the founder of the global multinational chemical company Rohm and Haas. But what had he founded? *Forbes* mentioned that he was worth $370 million, was from Tarrytown, New York, and had created his wealth from investment banking. However, *Forbes* was not entirely correct. Shelby Davis was not an investment banker. Unlike everyone else on the list, he was not an entrepreneur and did not own a business.

He was an investor like Buffett. But the similarity appeared to stop there. First, Buffett was a professional investor managing money for others, whereas Davis invested his own money (or his wife's). Second, Buffett started investing in his early twenties, whereas Davis did not start investing until he was thirty-eight years old. Third, Buffett had studied finance and investing under the great Benjamin Graham; Davis had had no interest in economics or finance during his college days. Instead, he had majored in history and had a special love for the Russian Revolution. Finally, Buffett had spent his entire career investing; Davis had had at least five careers before age forty. He reported for CBS Radio (his first assignment was interviewing Amelia Earhart), was a freelance writer, and was a stock analyst (a "statistician"). He worked at the War Production Board in Washington during the Second World War and was a deputy superintendent in New York State's insurance department.

Even Davis's investing style was radically different from Buffett's. Buffett invested across a range of industries, whereas just one sector contributed to Davis's colossal wealth; Buffett invested in very few businesses in the United States, whereas Davis invested in at least 1,600 businesses worldwide and occasionally traded heavily.

But there was one way in which Davis and Buffett were alike. And it made Davis wealthier than most people who have ever lived on this planet.

Darwin: The Unappreciated Math Wizard

Darwin was a mathematical genius. But he didn't think so.

On July 29, 1828, the nineteen-year-old Charles Darwin wrote a letter to his close friend and second cousin, William Darwin Fox. He started with a complaint and then rued his lack of mathematical prowess: "What excuse have you to offer for not having answered my letter long before this? I hope it is nothing worse than idleness; or what would be still better, I hope it arises from your being ten fathoms deep in *the Mathematics*, and if you are God help you, for so am I, only with this difference I stick fast in the mud at the bottom and there I shall remain in status quo."[2]

Darwin reiterated his weakness in mathematics in his autobiography: "After years I have deeply regretted that I did not proceed far enough at least to understand something of the great leading principles of mathematics; for men thus endowed seem to have an extra sense." He also admitted that the subject "was repugnant to me."[3] He detested complex mathematical formulations and once wrote to a friend, "I have no faith in anything short of actual measurement and the Rule of Three." The Rule of Three is a simple mathematical calculation that answers the problem "If ten mangoes cost $8, how many mangoes can one buy for $40?"

I regard Darwin as a math genius because of his intuitive grasp of the prodigious power of long-term compounding. Most of his peers didn't understand it; in fact, neither did many of his successors. In chapter 3 of *Origin*, "Struggle for Existence," Darwin's exquisite grasp of the power of compounding is evident in his famous example of elephants. He wrote, "The elephant is reckoned to be the slowest breeder of all known animals, and I have taken some pains to estimate its probable minimum rate of increase: it will be under the mark to assume that it breeds when thirty years old, and goes on breeding till ninety years old, bringing forth three pair of young in this interval; if this be so, at the end the of fifth century there would be alive fifteen million elephants, descended from the first pair."

Like no one else before him, Darwin understood that an exponential increase of populations was theoretically possible but practically almost impossible—diseases, predators, lack of food, natural disasters, and many other factors kept populations in check. This realization led him to conclude that only the fittest variants would survive to pass on their traits to their offspring. These fitter variants would then start exponentially increasing, leading to evolution through natural selection. As he famously wrote in chapter 4 of *Origin*, "This preservation of favorable variations and the rejection of injurious variations, I call Natural Selection."

As I discussed earlier, Darwin's theory of natural selection had no place for sudden and dramatic changes. His theory required variations to be small and continuous and natural selection to work over *very* long periods through *accumulated* changes. Despite its glaring simplicity and explanatory power— or maybe because of it—his theory remained on the periphery of biological sciences during his lifetime and was not entirely accepted by the scientific community.[4]

In 1900, after the rediscovery of Gregor Mendel's work on heredity, Hugo de Vries, a well-respected Dutch botanist and geneticist, proposed a new theory of evolution called mutationism.[5] According to this theory, the slight continuous variation proposed by Darwin could not lead to the evolution and creation of species; only significant mutations could. In his *Die Mutationstheorie* (*The Mutation Theory*), de Vries claimed that new species arise suddenly owing to discontinuous alteration. He wrote, "The new species thus originates suddenly[;] it is produced by the existing one without visible preparation and without transition."[6]

Now *that* everyone could understand. Intellectually, this was a *much* simpler assertion to understand than Darwinism because it could be "visualized"—Darwin's gradualism couldn't be. The world of investing is eerily similar. Everyone seems to know that the stock price of AMC, a movie theater chain, tripled in May 2021, but how many know that Home Depot's multiplied 140 times over thirty years from 1990 to 2020?

According to mutationism, species are created not because of minor variations but because something big and strange happens that transforms the organism. The controversial debate between mutationism and Darwinism remained unresolved until the 1920s. Finally, mathematics rescued biology (who would have thought!). In the 1920s and '30s, the theoretical geneticists R. A. Fisher, J. B. S. Haldane, Sewall Wright, and a few others explained in complex mathematical language how continuous variation was compatible with Mendel's laws. Natural selection, acting *cumulatively* on minor variations, could produce significant evolutionary changes over surprisingly short periods.[7]

These acknowledged mathematical geniuses restated what Darwin had asserted almost fifty years earlier.

He was saying that if a particular variation—say color vision—could give an individual a *slight* advantage over its peers, almost the entire population would be able to see in color over many fewer generations than we would imagine. Let us assume that color vision has a "selective advantage" of 1 percent, meaning that individuals with this trait produce 101 viable offspring instead of 100 (maybe color vision allows the individuals to locate higher-quality fruits in the forest). Thus, the selective advantage here is equivalent to compound interest or annualized return. The advantage *accumulates* and grows *exponentially* over generations.

Thus, in the second generation, the 101 offspring with color vision produce 10,201 offspring who can see color (101 x 101), whereas the 100 "normal" offspring produce 10,000 "normal" offspring (100 x 100). This slight advantage compounded at 1 percent per generation yields dramatic change over time.

Suppose there are eight individuals with this trait (i.e., color vision) among a thousand individuals. Over how many generations do you think color vision would spread to 90 percent of the population? Only 3,000![8] Thus, if this were an organism with a life span of one month, most of this species would have color vision within 250 years with just a 1 percent selective advantage. In evolutionary terms, this is almost instantaneous transformation. And this is not just theory.

Scientists observed the rapid evolution of peppered moths in Manchester in Britain in the nineteenth century.[9] Peppered moths were generally white with small black splotches on their wings. They rested on lichen-covered tree trunks during the day, where they were camouflaged against birds, their main predator. The species also had a rare, black-colored mutant. But it did not survive long because it was visible to birds against the background of tree trunks. As a result, most populations of peppered moths were, well, peppered. But as Manchester became industrialized from the middle of the nineteenth century, air pollution blackened tree trunks, thereby reversing the advantage: The black mutant became invisible to birds, and the peppered form stood out. The first black peppered moth was recorded in Manchester in 1848, and by 1895, 98 percent of the population had become black. The cumulative impact of a slight advantage had converted the rare form into the dominant one. Interestingly, as Britain passed strict pollution laws in the middle of the twentieth century, trees began to lose their sooty coating. As a result, the black moth has become rare, and the peppered form is now dominant!

This kind of *microevolution* (e.g., a change in color), given enough time, can lead to *macroevolution* (i.e., the creation of a new species). There isn't a single mathematical formula in Darwin's *Origin*. Still, it captures the power and essence of long-term compounding better than the complex formulas of the geneticists.

Amazingly, a mathematically challenged naturalist could figure out what had eluded scientists over the millennia by applying a simple yet profound mathematical concept to the natural world: Compounding creates life—all of it.

But why is this relevant for us investors? Because compounding also creates wealth. Almost all of it.

The Assault on Australia

We think we understand compounding, but we don't. By "we," I mean the investment community, myself included. Although Nalanda's entire investing strategy rests on the pillar of slow and steady compounding over decades, even I am amazed at its stunning—even surreal—results when applied over long periods.

Before we proceed any further, I want you to appreciate its tremendous power. Then, I will highlight *two* surprises, one small and one big, that cumulative growth has in store for students of evolution and investing.

For this section, I will be an omniscient consultant (are there any other kinds?) in the nineteenth century, and you will be a savvy time traveler from 1925! Who said investment stories couldn't be exciting?

Let's now go back in time to Winchelsea in Australia in 1859, where I am an adviser to one Mr. Thomas Austin. Mr. Austin has imported twenty-four rabbits from England, and he wants to release them into the wild for sport hunting. He is an intelligent fellow and is wary of the rabbits' prodigious reproductive ability. As he does not wish the farmland in Winchelsea to be overrun by rabbits, he seeks my counsel.

Just as I am about to advise him to release the rabbits, I see you swooping in from the future to issue a dire warning: "I come from 1925 and see a catastrophe ahead. Don't release the rabbits." On further inquiry, you reveal that the whole of Australia is in peril because of these twenty-four creatures. I laugh at your facetious remark, ignore the warning, and ask Mr. Austin to release the rabbits. You promise to visit me every five to ten years to continue to warn me about exterminating the rabbits. You fulfill your promise, and every time you come to see me, I ask the same question. Table 10.1 captures the history of our interactions.

Thirty-five years go by, and I continue to gloat over the fact that you have been proven wrong. There are fewer than a million rabbits in about eight million square kilometers of land area, and they don't seem to pose any imminent danger. But you warn me that the historical growth rate is about 35 percent a year, and at this pace, Australia will be overtaken by rabbits in the not-too-distant future. As is my custom, I ignore the genie from the future. Table 10.2 tells the story of the next thirty-one years, until 1925.

This is a true story. Unfortunately, the twenty-four rabbits released by Mr. Austin in Australia in 1859 *did* produce ten billion rabbits by 1925 and wreaked havoc on the flora and fauna of the continent.[10] Despite more than one hundred fifty years of government efforts ranging from building fences, trapping, shooting, and conducting biological warfare (by releasing flies with the deadly myxoma virus), Australia has been unable to eliminate this pest.

TABLE 10.1 **The first thirty-five years**

Years after 1859	No. of rabbits	Your advice	My response
5	108	Kill them before it's too late.	Where are the rabbits?
10	482	Kill them before it's too late.	Where are the rabbits?
20	9,700	Kill them before it's too late.	Where are the rabbits?
35	900,000	Kill them before it's too late.	Where are the rabbits?

TABLE 10.2 **The next thirty-one years**

Years after 1859	No. of rabbits	Your advice	My response
45	17.5 million	Kill them before it's too late.	I can see some.
55	350 million	Is it too late?	No, it's not.
66	10 *billion*	I told you so.	@#$%*!

I said that there were two surprises in this story. The small surprise, at least for me, is that twenty-four rabbits became ten billion. At some intuitive level, we investors understand that compounding can lead to astronomical numbers given enough time. But even then, I doubt many of us would have been able to envision a number of ten billion rabbits in the mid-1920s when there had been fewer than a million in 1895.

The bigger surprise—which is also counterintuitive—is the *opposite* observation: *Nothing happened for a very long time!* After twenty years, not many rabbits would have been visible in Australia, and even after forty-five years, there were fewer than two rabbits per square kilometer. So Australians ignored the rabbit problem for many decades because rabbits did *not* become a problem.

This property of compounding—that its impact seemingly remains hidden for a long time—wreaks havoc on the performance of investors because most sell too soon. An investor can hold a great business for five years, multiply their money three times, and then sell off for two potential reasons. First, they think that they have made enough and that there are better fish in the sea. Second, they get tired of the slow progress. (After all, the share price of GameStop can jump seventeen-fold in a month!) Little do they realize that *if* the share price had continued to climb at the same rate, in twenty-five years, they would have made 243 times their money! I know that that is a big "if," but it isn't an insurmountable hurdle for a quality business, as we will soon see. Also, even if the *incremental* return from the fifth to the twenty-fifth year in this example falls by more than five percentage points, the investor would *still* make 100 times their money on the original investment! As I said, the bigger mystery of compounding is not that it leads to large numbers but that it doesn't do so for a long time.

The holding period of most funds is barely a few months, let alone years. If you explain this behavior to an intelligent noninvestor type (I have done so), they will find it rather odd. They say something like this: "You are telling me that it is tough to find great companies to invest in; you are also telling me that these companies can grow their profits reasonably predictably over long periods. So why would you sell such a company in a hurry after you have become fortunate enough to own it?" I haven't had a good answer to this question except, "My community is not willing to wait for the rabbits."

I have seen too many people make a profit of 50 to 100 percent on an investment in a great company and then press the exit button. We investors take pride in being math savvy. Mention the word "compounding" to us, and you will get knowing smiles. Unfortunately, most of those knowing smiles do not seem to know that what they know about compounding—that it can lead to big numbers over time—hides two great unknowns.

The first is that compounding does *not* lead to significant numbers for a *very* long time. The second is that investing would be easy if companies could compound predictably. But, alas, they don't. The real world is quite messy, and the path to long-term success is treacherous, unpredictable, and full of disappointments.

What is needed to become a successful investor is not intellect, a commodity, but patience, which is not.

Many More Reasons We Don't Sell

Are we not convinced yet? With the power of compounding in evolutionary theory as the background, let me present some more reasons we are permanent owners in great businesses. "I will never sell" would be an understandable sentiment from a passionate entrepreneur, but it is somewhat unusual—some may even say wrongheaded—coming from a fund manager. It needs a more elaborate explanation. Here we go.

Reason 1: Who Are the Richest? The Ones Who Never Sell

Have you looked at the *Forbes* list of the twenty-five wealthiest people in the world in 2022?[11] In case you are interested, Elon Musk is the leader ($219 billion), and the twenty-fifth-ranked is Zhang Yiming from China ($50 billion).

This list consists *entirely* of people who have never sold.

Even if you expand the list to the richest fifty, forty-eight are business owners (or their families) who haven't sold. So, for example, there are two money managers—Jim Simons and Stephen Schwarzman—on the list who may buy and sell shares as a part of their fund management business. Still, they haven't sold *their* businesses (Renaissance and Blackstone, respectively), which, in turn, has made them billions.

If *not* selling is creating such humongous wealth globally, why do fund managers think they can make themselves rich by trading in and out of stocks? I know that I am not smarter or better than the richest people in the world. But if holding on to great businesses has worked wonderfully for them, why should I not simply emulate them?

Many entrepreneurs on this list have had attractive offers over their lifetime. The reason for their being on the list is that they did not succumb to temptation. They intuitively understood that they were on to something quite extraordinary and that selling would have been value destroying, not value creating. For example, in 2005, Viacom offered Mark Zuckerberg $75 million for Facebook, which would have made the twenty-one-year-old a cool $35 million.[12] Within a year of Viacom's offer, Yahoo offered $1 *billion* for the company. Zuckerberg refused both these and many other offers. His net worth in 2022? More than $50 billion.

In one way, while we may not create as much wealth as these stalwarts, we are better off than them. They are betting on just one business—their own. We have the luxury of owning many great businesses. What could be better than that?

Reason 2: Empirical Evidence Shows That Owning Great Businesses Works (Oh, So Well!)

Let's go back to the Bessembinder study I referred to in the previous chapter.[13] As a reminder, Bessembinder analyzed the price performance of 26,000 U.S.-listed stocks from 1926 to 2016. He also shares the raw data from 1926 to 2019, which is available at https://wpcarey.asu.edu/department-finance/faculty-research/ do-stocks-outperform-treasury-bills.

Let's look at data from 1926 to 2019. Bessembinder defines "wealth creation" as returns earned *above* one-month U.S. treasuries. Of the 26,000 companies, about 60 percent (15,000) destroyed value. This is not surprising: Running a business is risky, and the data support this assertion.

But I *was* surprised by two facts. First, the quantum of wealth creation is almost *eight* times the dollar value of wealth destruction, although wealth destroyers outnumber wealth creators by almost 40 percent. About 11,000 companies created a wealth of $54 trillion, and about 15,000 businesses *destroyed* a wealth of $7 trillion (leading to a net wealth creation of $47 trillion). When businesses do well, the sky's the limit.

My second revelation was that only a select few companies created most of the wealth, even among the wealth creators (table 10.3).

Thus, the top 10 percent, or about 2,600 companies, account for all (actually, 10 percent more) of the *total* wealth created by the 26,000 businesses. The top 1 percent contribute to three-quarters, and just thirty firms account for almost a third of total wealth created over ninety-three years.

An even more interesting finding is shown in the last column of table 10.3. A disproportionate amount of wealth is created by businesses that have been held for longer periods. That does not mean that simply holding a business for

TABLE 10.3 **Wealth creation is highly concentrated in a few businesses held for longer periods**

	No. of companies	Wealth, $ trillion	% of total	Years held (median)
Top 10%	2,617	52	110	25
Top 1%	262	35	74	47
Top 30	30	15	32	59

an extended period creates value—it does not; the value will almost certainly go to zero for an average business. Table 10.3 shows that *if* we have a great business, on average, it is likely to generate more incredible wealth over a more extended period.

But we have one prickly issue to deal with here: How do we know what a great business is so that we can hold it for as long as possible? (I hope you did not start reading the book from this chapter—I discussed this question in chapters 1 through 7.)

We do not invest in mediocre or low-quality businesses at throw-away valuations because, as table 10.3 shows, it would be a waste of time. Only a handful of companies create wealth over very long periods, and, by definition, all need to be exceptional. Instead, we invest when we believe that the business is truly outstanding, and if it is, given the stark reality of table 10.3, why would we ever sell it?

I *have* been wrong about assessing the quality of some of our businesses. Since we hold *all* our businesses forever, the continuous compounding of earnings and value of a few businesses has taken care of all my follies. You want numbers? Comin' at you.

Reason 3: If There Is an Unbeatable Formula, Why Not Copy It?

When I was at McKinsey, we addressed client problems by sharing "best practices." These could range from advice related to post-merger integration, the process of strategy formulation, and organizational design to the allocation of marketing expenses. Of course, as a consultant, I had to account for the idiosyncrasies of a particular client. Still, I discovered that discussing "how the best businesses do it" was a great way to nudge a client toward a better solution.

Here is a puzzle for you to chew on. I assume you will agree that all fund managers want to earn decent returns while beating the market over the long run. Imagine a situation in which a multibillionaire investor shares his secret of getting rich with us every year in a detailed letter. His best practice is widely known and available to everyone, and it hasn't changed for more than fifty years. We know his advice is invaluable because he continues to amass great wealth by following his teachings over almost six decades. We also know that doing what he does is not difficult to understand or even implement, at least for the professionals. But most choose to both laud him *and* ignore him.

That investor, of course, is Warren Buffett, and his simple advice to buy exceptional businesses at a sensible price and hold them forever has made him one of the wealthiest people in the world. So then why does his advice fall on deaf ears? At first glance, this seems somewhat bizarre. Investors seem to be voluntarily giving up the chance to get rich. But if you think about it for a moment, you will realize that Buffett's advice is hard to fathom for the *same* reason that Darwin's insight was not accepted for many decades. We humans don't understand compounding. We *say* we do, but we don't.

Buffett is the Darwin of investing—he changed the field forever and for the better. But if eminent scientists in the late nineteenth and early twentieth centuries could barely comprehend the power of cumulative growth, how can investors, who by and large are much more intellectually challenged, be expected to appreciate it? But the problem is worse than you think. Not only do investors blithely ignore Buffett, their behavior over the last fifty years indicates that they firmly believe the exact opposite! The holding period of stocks by mutual funds has fallen to less than a year from seven years in 1960.

Let's return to Shelby Cullom Davis. Despite being radically different from Buffett in almost every way, how did he create his wealth? Just like Buffett, Davis held on to a select few quality businesses for decades.

Unlike Buffett, who always wanted to be an investor, Davis became an investor through a series of fortunate events. When he got married in January 1932, the Dow hit an all-time low of 41—it had fallen 89 percent from its peak in 1929. His wife, Kathryn, provided him his seed money for investing many years later; Davis was lucky that Kathryn's father, Joseph Wasserman, had kept his money in government bonds and lost nothing in the Crash.

After working as a reporter for CBS Radio, Davis earned his PhD along with Kathryn in political science at the University of Geneva (where Kathryn outscored him). In 1934, Davis was offered a job in Tokyo at the English-language newspaper, the *Advertiser*. Just as he and Kathryn were about to depart for Japan, an earthquake hit Tokyo, forcing them to cancel their trip. Also, the *Advertiser* offer fell through. Davis was now desperate for a job, but he could not find any employment in journalism in the sickening state of the U.S. economy. Kathryn asked her brother, Bill, to employ Davis in his investment firm.

Davis worked as a "statistician" in Bill's firm and traveled around the country meeting companies that looked promising for investment. But Davis and Bill did not get along, and Davis left the job to start writing full time. He published a book called *America Faces the Forties*, which explored the causes of the Great Depression and how the 1940s might lead to recovery. It was reasonably well received and caught the eye of Thomas E. Dewey, the governor of New York and Republican presidential hopeful (he lost to Roosevelt in 1944 and to Truman in 1948). In 1938, Dewey made Davis his speechwriter and economic adviser.

After losing to Roosevelt in 1944, Dewey returned to his role as the governor of New York. He unknowingly put Davis on the path to fabulous riches by appointing him the deputy superintendent of the state's insurance department. Could there be a more boring-sounding job? But Davis took it seriously. He was an outspoken advocate of insurance companies diversifying from bonds to real estate, mortgages, and stocks. Contrary to popular opinion in those days,

Davis considered bonds extremely risky. Nevertheless, he was remarkably pre-scient. Bonds went into a thirty-five-year bear market from the mid-1940s; the government bond sold for $101 in 1946 sold for just $17 in 1981.

Investors ignored insurance companies, usually quoted in the minor league of stock exchanges. Insurers were required to file their latest financials with the state agency, and Davis pored over these reports, becoming an expert at under-standing their inner workings. He discovered that a typical insurer was selling for less than its "true" book value—just the bonds and mortgages in an insurer's portfolio could be worth far more than its market value. He realized that insur-ance customers paid money up front and that insurers could deploy this "float" to buy bonds and mortgages. If customer claims weren't excessive, this hidden float could slowly and silently balloon over time. A patient investor could wait for this hidden asset to compound until the market, too, recognized it.

Davis left his job in 1947, borrowed $50,000 from Kathryn, and started investing in well-run and dividend-paying insurance companies selling for less than their book value. He also borrowed on the margin to fund some of his purchases. In a speech to the New York Insurance Brokers Association in 1952, Davis outlined his three criteria for selecting the stock of an insurer: (1) The insurer had to be profitable, (2) its assets (bonds, mortgages, stocks) needed to be of the highest quality, and (3) its market price had to be lower than its private market value. Davis was a value investor in high-quality insurers. And he held on to them.

In 1992, two years before his death, his top twelve holdings were worth $261 million—about half his total portfolio. Except for Fannie Mae, *all* were insurance companies. And he had bought each decades ago. His best invest-ment, worth $72 million, was AIG, and his third-best, worth $27 million, was Berkshire Hathaway. Once he bought a great business, he never sold it.

Why should we reinvent the wheel when we have spectacular successes like Buffett and Davis to emulate? As I will discuss, Davis's success shows that we don't even have to be *that* good to succeed. Just patient. And so we are.

Reason 4: How Else Do I Pay for My Mistakes?

Shelby Davis bought about a hundred insurers that made up three-quarters of his portfolio, and about 1,500 companies globally made up the rest. *Most* of these investments turned out to be duds! His other big mistake was to buy junk bonds worth about $23 million—almost all turned out to be actual junk.

Davis made all his wealth by investing in a few high-quality insurers and then refusing to sell them. As a result, his hundreds of mistakes became irrele-vant in the context of the exceptional long-term compounding of his winners. In his book *The Davis Dynasty*, John Rothchild states this eloquently: "In the final analysis, Davis's mistakes hindered his prosperity the way a gnat flusters a buffalo. Nevertheless, his portfolio proved once again that, over a lifetime of investing, a handful of high achievers' ideas could support a multitude of ne'er-do-wells."

I have made many mistakes, and I know I will continue to do so. This is not humility but a cold hard fact. Waiting for a few great businesses to compound has paid for these mistakes. Let me share the actual numbers with you.

Our first fund invested about INR 18 billion (about $400 million using the exchange rate prevalent at the time) in seventeen businesses from June 2007 to June 2011. In June 2022, given that enough time had passed, we could reliably assess the share price performance of individual companies in this fund. We had only one capital loss in the portfolio, so that was a failure. Let me arbitrarily label any business (or rather, the market value of the business) earning an annualized rupee return of less than 10 percent a "failure" as well. Six of the seventeen businesses had earned an annualized rupee return of less than 10 percent by June 2022. Thus, we had seven failures (one loss and six with an annualized return of less than 10 percent) out of seventeen businesses, or a "failure" rate of 40 percent.

But the overall performance of this fund has been better than my wildest dreams. So how did we get here given the underperformance of seven of our businesses? Because we did not sell our winners.

Let me call these seven "failed" businesses the "Sorry Seven." We invested INR 7.8 billion in the Sorry Seven. Let's see what happens when we hold a good business for a long time. Take Supreme, India's leading plastic products company. We invested in Supreme in 2010, and by June 2022, we had owned it for almost twelve years. We invested INR 1 billion in Supreme, which was worth INR 13.9 billion in June 2022. The *gain* of INR 12.9 billion in Supreme is *1.7 times* the *total* amount invested in the Sorry Seven (12.9 ÷ 7.8 = 1.7).

But it's much better than that. By June 2022, *six* investments had *individually* paid for the *total* amount invested in the Sorry Seven. Table 10.4 lists what I call the "Superb Six."

It's almost ridiculous, isn't it? Simply owning Page for fourteen years compensated for *seven* unsuccessful investments more than *five* times over. If the upside of holding companies for long periods is so significant, why don't investors do it? One critical reason is an underappreciation of compounding, which makes fund managers value IRR more than the multiple, instead of the other way around.

In finance jargon, IRR is the internal rate of return, or the annualized rate of return. If a stock doubles in four years, its IRR is 19 percent, and if it doubles in three, its IRR is 26 percent. For the same multiple, the shorter the period, the higher the IRR. Ignoring the beauty of compounding, investors

TABLE 10.4 **Long-term winners pay for the losers many times over (as of June 30, 2022 [in INR])**

Company	No. of years held	Multiple	Gain ÷ total investment in the Sorry Seven
Berger	13.3	32.2×	3.3
Mindtree	9.6	8.2×	1.7
Page	13.7	82.2×	5.2
Ratnamani	11.7	16.2×	1.0
Supreme	11.6	13.6×	1.7
WNS	13	10.6×	3.2

like to boast about the IRR of their investment while undervaluing the benefits of the multiple.

If we had been fans of IRR, we would have sold *each* of the Superb Six listed in table 10.4 a long time ago. The colossal downside of doing this is evident from the example of Page. In December 2012, after four years of our owning Page, it had delivered 65 percent IRR (!). For most investors, a holding period of four years seems long enough. It would not have been very intelligent to think that we could *earn 65 percent IRR incrementally* over the next five to ten years. If we were IRR fans, we would have exited Page in December 2012, crowed about the astronomical return delivered over four years, and described the return in bold in our marketing materials (actually, we don't have any marketing materials, but that is beside the point).

The multiple on Page in December 2012 was 7.8× (compared to 82.2× in June 2022), so the gain on investment was "only" INR 3.4 billion. Remember that the cost of investment in the Sorry Seven of INR 7.8 billion does not change, regardless of the holding period of Page. Thus, if we had sold Page in December 2012, we would have recouped only 44 percent (3.4 ÷ 7.8 = 44 percent) of our investment in the Sorry Seven. The remaining 56 percent burden would have had to be carried by the remaining businesses. However, since we have continued to hold Page, our gain has climbed to INR 40.8 billion, and the Sorry Seven have been paid for 5.2 times over by the gain of this single holding (40.8 ÷ 7.8 = 5.2).

Remember the example of the rare mutant with color vision (just eight in one thousand) with only a 1 percent selective advantage that overwhelmed the population in three thousand generations? Only a handful of compounders in a portfolio, growing a *little* more than the rest, achieve the same result given enough time.

We invest only in what we think are phenomenal businesses. But I also know that some may not perform and will need to be paid for. Hence, for investors like us, even *thinking* of selling our winners is worse than wrong. It's foolish.

Reason 5: The *Only* Way to Benefit from Compounding Is to Stay Invested

If we are aggressive buyers during adverse stock price movements, logic dictates that we should be aggressive sellers when stock prices rise suddenly. But, thankfully, some of the essential things in life—believing our children are unique, falling in love, being a dedicated doctor or nurse during the COVID-19 pandemic, volunteering to be a soldier—are not driven by logic.

We don't sell when stock prices rise suddenly. These nonactions during market euphoria have been as important as—actually, more important than—our acts of buying during market panics. As I wrote earlier, as of June 2022, out of our portfolio of twenty-four businesses (excluding the ones bought during the previous two years), we had multiplied our money by more than ten times in INR in nine (of these, the largest multiple, 82×, was for Page, and the smallest, 13×, was for Info Edge). In five of these nine, our holding period had been more than eleven years, and we had held the remaining ten-baggers for more than eight years.

Why do we *not* sell when stock prices rise dramatically?

The answer is shown in table 10.5. Here, I have selected two of the nine businesses whose values have multiplied by more than ten times in INR.

Let me explain what you see in Havells. As of June 2022, we had held Havells for 8.5 years, or 2,724 days of trading (not counting holidays). Our gain during this period was 1,270 percent. From table 10.5, the following facts stand out:

- 90 percent of the gain of 1,270 percent came in just thirty-five days. Those thirty-five days account for only 1.3 percent of the total number of trading days during which we held Havells. What if we had sold Havells during one (or more) of those *very* few days? Those thirty-five days are distributed across all years. For example, the top three gains for the stock came on September 20, 2019; January 21, 2021; and June 5, 2014. If, excited by the sudden price rise, we had sold our shares on June 5, 2014, we would have missed the significant jumps on September 20, 2019, and January 21, 2021. As you can see, the numbers for Page are similar: 90 percent of the total gains came in just 2 percent of trading days.
- Havells stock gained 5 percent or more on just forty-four days, or 1.6 percent of the total number of trading days during our holding period. If we add up the gains from those days, they sum to 1,800 percent, or *142 percent* of the total

TABLE 10.5 **The prodigious power of positive punctuations (June 2007 to June 2022)**

Measure	Havells	Page
Holding period		
Years	8.5	13.7
Trading days	2,724	3,586
Total gain	+1,270%	+8,890%
90% gain in		
No. of days	35	58
% of trading days	1.3	1.6
+5% gain or more		
No. of days	44	83
% of trading days	1.6	2.3
% of total gain	142	330
Days of price decline		
No. of days	1,293	1,685
% of trading days	47	47

The multiples for Page given in table 10.4 are slightly lower than those shown in table 10.5. The latter tracks the increase in stock price, whereas the former shows the appreciation of the values of our holdings. The values are marginally different because table 10.4 accounts for redemptions in the fund (which force us to sell all stocks in proportion to their value). The difference, as you can see, is very small.

gains over 8.5 years. Thus, the forty-four days of stock price gains of 5 percent or more accounted for *more* than the total gain during our entire holding period of almost nine years! The opportunity cost of *not* holding on to Havells shares during those significant days would have been egregiously high. Check out the astronomical impact of 5-percent-plus days in Page—they accounted for more than 300 percent of total gains! It would have been impossible for us to compound our capital if we had not remained invested in Page.

- Last, please look at the data from the gloomy days (i.e., days when the stock price declined). I was pretty surprised to see that the negative days account for almost half the total number of trading days across all three businesses. But, as you can see, the negative days didn't matter *because* we held on to the companies *throughout* this period.

Do you see where I am going with this analysis? If we had sold Havells or our other compounders on any day when their stock prices rose significantly, we would have been celebrated for raking in cash. Still, we would have repented at leisure as the stock prices continued to rise over the long run.

But how did I know that the Havells stock price would continue to rise? I didn't because I cannot predict stock prices. I *can* make two predictions, though. First, if we own a high-quality business, the share price will *most probably* (but not assuredly) react positively over the *long run*. Second, the share price will rarely make big moves, and if I am not invested in the stock on *those* particular days, I can bid farewell to substantial potential gains.

If we have done anything right, we have not done anything on days when selling seems to be the most logical thing to do.

Reason 6: I Love Our Entrepreneurs

I love our entrepreneurs. Behavioral economists have a quaint name for this disease: the endowment effect. It is the irrational mindset that assigns a disproportionately high value to what one owns.

Investing is supposed to be a cut-and-dried profession where, à la Mr. Spock, fund managers dispassionately enter and exit businesses based on intellect, instinct, or insight. Unfortunately, we fulfill this requirement only for entry and *some* exits.

Before investing, we base our decision *entirely* on empirical evidence, as I have shown in chapters 1 through 7. But after we have invested, and if a business continues to do well, I become emotionally attached to it. India is a tough place to do business (I am sure all countries are, but India is the only market I know), and almost every industry is fiercely competitive. In this cutthroat marketplace, any entrepreneur who stays ahead of the competition by taking calculated risks while maintaining high profitability and a clean balance sheet is genuinely admirable.

I know that new-age technology companies are in vogue, and everyone in the world seems to laud them while they blow other people's money by the millions or billions. (Where's the glory in selling a dollar for eighty cents? Maybe I am getting too old.) In sharp contrast to these cash-guzzling sinkholes, take the cases of Ahluwalia, DB Corp, Triveni Turbine, and Voltamp, four companies in our portfolio that are leaders in their field. Like clockwork, they throw up significantly more cash than they consume every year. However, our investment in them has yielded subpar returns for a decade or more. My fault, not theirs. Part of the reason for continuing to own them is that we hope the tide will turn over time (as it has for many of our other businesses). Still, an important motivation is also that I love the leaders of these businesses. They are genuinely outstanding, as shown by their operating and financial track records over *many* decades.

One of the great pleasures of our profession is that we get to know and build relationships with the likes of Shobhit Uppal, Sudhir Agarwal, Dhruv Sawhney, and K. S. Patel. I am in awe of them. So why should I give up this gratification for a few dollars?

Reason 7: Not Selling Makes Us Better Buyers

That seems like a weird assertion. How can *not* selling *cause* better buying? Here is how.

How much time do you think fund managers devote to thinking about the "right" sale price for their businesses? If you manage money, you already know the answer, but if you aren't a fund manager, please ask someone who is. The answer will probably range from 30 to 70 percent. Some fund managers argue, "If we are not a buyer, we are a seller." These people are probably contemplating a sale *all* the time.

Let's say we want to figure out whether we should exit Ratnamani, one of our portfolio companies and India's most significant specialty steel business. Ratnamani's clients are primarily refineries and petrochemical plants, both of which are cyclical industries. Hence, Ratnamani's revenues and profits, too, are cyclical.

We first need to decide upon a time frame over which we will calculate the *incremental* return. It could be one year, three years, or five years, or some other period. At the end of that time frame, we will need to forecast Ratnamani's profits and valuation multiple (PE, EV/EBITDA, or some other metric).

If we want to calculate a three-year incremental return, we will need to forecast Ratnamani's revenues, expenses, and tax rates for the next three years. This is a nontrivial exercise for a cyclical business. First, a hapless analyst in the organization will need to trash their weekends to collate the capital expenditure announcements of all the refineries and petrochemical plants that could be Ratnamani's clients. Next, they will need to assume a particular market share for Ratnamani to forecast the company revenue. ("How?" you ask? I have no idea—ask the analyst.) Finally, they will conduct a similarly detailed exercise for the significant expense lines: depreciation, raw material, employees, sales and general administration, and taxes, to name just a few. And let's not even discuss the myriad ways of projecting a valuation multiple three years from now.

Some asset managers may not resort to such a detailed exercise; they may choose to sell if the multiple or the stock price reaches a certain level. But even these professionals will need to keep track of the businesses that approach the sale price and debate whether their initial assumptions are still valid (e.g., what if the company's main competitor is in trouble?).

All this takes time, energy, and, most importantly, mind space. We do no such analyses. We buy never to sell. None of our professionals spends even a minute thinking about selling unless the business makes an egregiously wrong capital allocation or if the company (according to us) is irreparably damaged.

In the last chapter, in table 9.2, I showed you the three occasions—the 2008 financial crisis, the 2011 Euro crisis (the sovereign debt crisis in Europe that began in 2009 led to the change or collapse of the majority of euro zone governments from March 2011 to May 2012),[15] and the COVID-19 pandemic—when we were highly aggressive buyers. Given that we were inactive for many years, what allowed us to buy stocks worth $288 million (16 percent of the total amount invested since our inception in 2007) in just seventeen days in March 2020? We acted decisively and disruptively because we were well prepared. We are *always* well prepared to buy because we have been freed of the concerns of selling.

Just because I have time to think does not mean I will think correctly; I have made buying mistakes and will continue to do so. But freed from the worries of selling, our buying *process* is highly focused and disciplined. What more can I ask?

"It Does Not Make Any Sense"

It seems too easy, isn't it? Buy a great business. Sit tight. Watch the moolah roll in.

It is, and it is not. Over my decades of investing, I have heard many objections from my fund manager friends and investors who have refused to give us money because they were uncomfortable with our permanent owner approach. "It does not make sense" is a common refrain after I reveal that we plan to be permanent owners.

Let me share with you some of these objections and my responses to them.

Objection 1: Why Should I Hold On to 60 PE?

We are price sensitive; we do not invest if the valuation is high. A logical question, then, is, Why aren't we sellers when the valuation is high?

Take a concrete example of a business that went from a PE multiple of 15× to a PE multiple of 60× over five years of our holding period. Let's say that earnings doubled during those five years. We would be sitting on a multiple of eight times our initial investment: four times from multiple expansion and two times from earnings growth.

Many investors would justify selling at this point with the following calculation. Let's say the business doubles its earnings over the next five years (the same as over the last five years). If the PE multiple stays the same, we will only double our money, and if it halves to 30 PE (which is possible because the long-term market PE is 19 to 20), we will not make *any* return for the next five years. So shouldn't we be sellers?

It's a logical and fair question. It is so logical and fair that most fund managers *will* sell and exit at this point. We won't. The reasons are three-fold.

First, I have found that great businesses usually surprise on the upside. What if the earnings triple or quadruple in the next five years? Remember that we buy *only* phenomenal companies. They stand out because they are much better than the competition and usually keep gaining market share and, more importantly, market power. We saw evidence of the increasing concentration of leading businesses across most industries in the previous chapter.

Second, valuation multiples generally don't stay benign for great businesses. As I write this, Walmart, with a market value of $400 billion, has a PE of 33; L'Oréal, with a market value of $260 billion, has a PE of 61! We are interested *only* in stellar businesses. Their valuation multiples likely stay elevated over very long periods.

Third, why should I limit my calculation to only the next five years? Let's say I am wrong on earnings growth *and* PE multiple over the next five years. Assume that the earnings stay flat and the valuation multiple halves. I will be sitting with a loss of 50 percent over five years. So what? What if the business continues to perform for a decade *after* five years? After five years, I will fail to capture the value from years five to fifteen by selling at a high multiple. Let me share a theoretical case and a real case to make my point.

Let's go back to the example from the beginning of this section. I buy shares of Company A for $1 in the year 2000 for a PE multiple of 15. In 2005, the earnings have doubled, and the PE multiple has expanded to 60. The share price is now $8. If I sell, I will make eight times my money at an annualized return of 52 percent. *Very* nice, right? But I choose to hold.

In the next five years, the earnings stay flat, and the valuation halves to 30 PE. The stock price is $4 in 2010. So I have lost half the capital relative to 2005. I look like a fool. But wait.

If the business does well, and if the earnings quadruple over the *next* ten years, from 2010 to 2020 (this is an annualized growth of 15 percent, not an aggressive assumption for a great business), and if the multiple increases by 50 percent to 45 PE, the stock price would be $24 in 2020. It thus has an annualized return of 17 percent over twenty years. I have made twenty-four times my money in twenty years, which, for me, is a much better outcome than eight times my money in five years. Why? Because I would have made mistakes in between, and as I discussed earlier in this chapter, *someone* needs to compensate for it. As Shelby Davis has shown us, not all the businesses in our portfolio need to work from year five to year fifteen; a handful will be more than sufficient.

Now let me share an actual example from our portfolio. We bought Ratnamani for INR 128 per share from late 2010 to early 2011. The price did not move for the next three years, and in January 2014, the stock price was INR 135. We stayed calm and continued to hold our shares because the company was doing fine. However, in January 2015, the share price jumped to INR 700, a *five*-fold increase in just one year. The earnings had expanded suddenly, and so had the valuation multiple.

Should we have sold? We didn't. Why? Because the *business* continued to be stellar. The price stayed around the same level of about INR 700 for the next two years until January 2017 before slowly moving upward. In January 2021, the price was INR 1,600. If we had sold our shares for INR 700 per share in 2015, we would have missed the run-up to INR 1,600 over the next six years. More importantly, what matters to us is our *buy* price of INR 128, and, relative to this price, INR 1,600 for a ten-year hold does not seem bad at all (an annualized return of 29 percent). Some may argue that we should have sold in January 2015 to make more than a 50 percent annualized return. That makes sense, but I prefer a 29 percent return over ten years (a 12.5× multiple) compared to a 53 percent return over four years (a 5.5× multiple). We continue to own Ratnamani.

The answer to the objection "Why should I hold on to 60 PE?" is straightforward. Because, *on average*, over the long run, great businesses have a way of making us more prosperous than we ever thought possible.

Objection 2: My "Incremental" Return Will Be Low from Now On

I have gotten over my buying mistakes but will never forgive myself for my only selling blunder. I made it because I feared that our "incremental" return would dissipate.

We invested in a company called Shree Cement in late 2011 for INR 1,700 per share. Shree is the best cement business in India and is probably one of the best in the world. Cement is a highly cyclical business, and we bought Shree when the sentiment in the cement industry seemed to have reached its nadir. Within a few months of our investing, to our great surprise, the cement cycle turned, and the stock price more than doubled.

While I did believe that we should own businesses forever, I mistakenly thought we should make an exception for highly cyclical businesses. I assumed that we would "play" the commodity cycle by buying when the sentiment was weak and selling when the mood turned positive. I knew we could not time the cycle perfectly, but I thought we could do reasonably well. I sold Shree for about INR 3,800 per share in October 2012 because I thought our "incremental" return over the long run would be underwhelming. Instead, we made about 2.2 times our money in less than a year. We returned the proceeds of $80 million to our investors and felt proud to have trounced the market.

It was the stupidest decision I have ever made. The cost to the fund? Four hundred million dollars and counting. The stock price of Shree Cement in June 2022 was about INR 19,009, or more than *five* times the selling price ten years ago. It hurts. Badly.

Having learned the expensive Shree lesson, my response to this objection is, Incremental over what period? One day, one month, one year, three years, twenty years? And why bother if it's a stellar business?

The rule for selling a great business is simple: Don't. You. Dare.

Objection 3: There Is a Better Opportunity to Deploy Capital

The holding period of stocks has kept falling over the past few decades. Investors aren't trading for the sake of trading (I hope). They sell X to buy Y because they assume Y is a better prospect than X. Shortly after that, they get rid of Y to buy Z for the same reason. There *always* seems to be something better out there. One justification for this hamster-on-a-wheel behavior is that it is prudent to sell a business with 50 PE to buy a business with 15 PE. Not for us.

We never indulge in "sell-high-to-buy-low" activity. We *only* sell if we have lost confidence in a business, and when we do, we return the money to our investors. The opportunity to own an outstanding business comes along *very* rarely, and if we have won this lottery, why should we kill the goose laying golden eggs? (Yes, yes, I know. I sold Shree Cement. Do I have to be reminded?)

Look at it differently. I assume many of you own a home or know someone who does. Do you know of any homeowner who trades in and out of their home at frequent intervals? Does a homeowner check the price of their house every day, every month, or even every year to sell it at a high price and buy another one at a lower price? If not, I see no reason to treat holding shares in a business differently.

And empirical evidence shows that this strategy does not work.[16] As discussed earlier, there is a strong correlation between a fund's underperformance and its portfolio turnover. I don't know what causes what, and frankly, I don't want to know.

We are happy owning a great business and treating it as our home.

Objection 4: What Should I Do the Whole Day?

Believe it or not, a friend who used to work at a hedge fund told me many years ago, "But that is a lazy way to make money!" He is a rational fellow and did not disagree that money could be made by allowing a few quality businesses to compound. But he considered it almost immoral to make money with no hyperactivity involved. It takes all kinds. He has since left the hedge fund business because he got burnt out staring at his Bloomberg screen twelve to fourteen hours a day while worrying about his daily P&L.

Another fund manager asked, "If I don't trade, what should I do the whole day?" This person claims to have made all his money by owning a few high-quality businesses but wants to stay busy during the day! I wanted to say, "Take a vacation." But I didn't—different strokes.

Investing is a unique profession in which inactivity can be hugely rewarding. It has been so for us. We will continue to be lazy. *Very* lazy.

* * *

Mahabharata is one of two great epics of ancient India (*Ramayana* being the other one). It was written over a few hundred years, starting about 400 BCE. At about 1.8 million words, it is the longest poem known to humanity and is seven times the length of the *Iliad* and the *Odyssey* combined. The epic describes the struggle for dominance between two groups of cousins but is a treatise on moral philosophy and the psychology of human behavior.

There is a famous section in *Mahabharata* called *Yaksha Prashna*. The spirit or demigod (*Yaksha*) poses a series of questions (*Prashna*) to Yudhishthir, the eldest and wisest among the cousins. The stakes are high because giving correct answers will revive one of Yudhishthir's four brothers killed by the *Yaksha*.

One of the most famous questions posed by *Yaksha* is, "What is the greatest wonder in this world?" Yudhishthir's reply is, "Everyone sees countless people dying every day, but they act and think as if they will live forever." Yudhishthir's insight was that we are strangely blind to a fact that is blindingly obvious.

For us, the *Yaksha Prashna* would be, "What is the greatest wonder in the world of investing?" With due apologies to Yudhishthir, my answer is, "Everyone sees immeasurable wealth being created by people who never sell, but they think and act as if it is selling that creates wealth."

Chapter Summary

Evolutionary theory has taught me that . . .

. . . reimagining investing requires me to be *very* patient and not to sell an outstanding business at almost any price.

1. Darwin laid the foundation of evolutionary theory by asserting that if an organism has a small advantage over its peers (say, the ability to run faster), then given enough time, this favorable trait will spread across the entire

population. Darwin understood, like no one else before him, that compounding can create *macroevolution* through *microevolution*.

2. Investors, proficient in mathematics, think they understand compounding. But the evidence suggests otherwise—the holding period of stocks is barely a few months. Investors are unable or unwilling to exercise patience and typically press the exit button after meager gains or losses.

3. We have internalized the lessons of long-term compounding from Darwin, and if a business is performing well, we refuse to sell it at any price.

4. Some of the key reasons to stay invested forever are that the richest people in the world are the ones who refuse to sell; empirical evidence from a ninety-year-long study shows that great businesses create enormous wealth; Buffett has shown that the strategy of holding forever works beautifully; fund managers can pay for their mistakes by allowing the good businesses to multiply; and only those who stay invested can benefit from compounding.

5. Most investors refuse to subscribe to the philosophy of owning businesses forever. This, in my opinion, is a big mistake.

6. We have been successful not because we are better at buying, but because we refuse to succumb to the temptation of selling.

CONCLUSION

Honeybees Win by Repeating a Simple Process. So Can We

He must be a dull man who can examine the exquisite structure of a comb, so beautifully adapted to its end, without enthusiastic admiration. We hear from mathematicians that bees have practically solved a recondite problem, and have made their cells of the proper shape to hold the greatest amount of honey, with the least possible consumption of precious wax in their construction.

Charles Darwin, On the Origin of Species, *chapter 8, "Instinct"*

Your goal as an investor should simply be to purchase, at a rational price, a part interest in an easily understandable business whose earnings are virtually certain to be materially higher five, ten and twenty years from now. Over time, you will find only a few companies that meet these standards— so when you see one that qualifies, you should buy a meaningful amount of stock. You must also resist the temptation to stray from your guidelines.

Warren Buffett, annual letter to shareholders, 1996

e started our journey with bumblebees, so it's only fair that we end with honeybees.

Making Sense of an Uncertain World

The field of biology, particularly evolutionary biology, took a giant leap forward in 1953 with one of the most significant discoveries of the twentieth century: the molecular structure of DNA. This Nobel Prize–winning effort of Watson and Crick unraveled the mystery of how genetic information is encoded and transmitted through the double helix.

Or did it?

Even decades after this seminal event, scientists do not agree on the definition of what constitutes a gene.[1] We are endowed with 22,500 genes; some scientists think that less than 2 percent are helpful, whereas others assert that more than 50 percent are. As a result, we do not know what most of our DNA—comprising more than six billion letters—does. More surprisingly, even when there is agreement on the function of a particular bit of DNA, it is still a mystery how this DNA translates into a phenotype, or observable trait.

The plain truth is that despite hundreds of millions of dollars being spent every year by dedicated researchers globally, we don't understand how evolution works at the molecular level.[2] And this is a good—no, great—thing. It allows scientists to ask the right questions to explore the unknown further. Most scientific articles in biology discuss what has been discovered or proposed and what further questions or doubts should be explored. Unfortunately, it appears that these researchers never get to a definitive answer to any question; the best they do—and boy, do they do it well!—is to raise even more questions.

As investors, we are supposed to have deep insights into our companies and industries. We are required to understand the business of the companies we invest in, with the implicit assumption that the individual who can comprehend a business better will become a better investor. Of course, we are also required to answer all the questions anyone might pose on the businesses we have invested in. But the problem is that if brilliant biologists are still struggling to unravel the mysteries of a lowly, discrete, organic molecule after seventy years of research, how can we think that an entity as amorphous as a company can be analyzed by investors in seventy days, or even seven hundred?

A consistent pattern was present throughout all ten chapters of this book. Did you detect it? Our entire investment approach at Nalanda admits to, and hence compensates for, our profound ignorance:

- We avoid many categories of risks because of the wide range of possible outcomes in these situations.
- We invest only in exceptional businesses because most businesses fail, and we want to reduce uncertainty.

- We buy at an attractive valuation because, while we don't know *what* will go wrong, we assume that *something* will.
- We rarely buy, and sell *even more* rarely, because every activity may have unintended consequences we can't foresee.

In this complex, unknowable, and uncertain world, we are not trying to make the best investments since we are in the dark about most things. We don't know what the best investment would be. Instead, we are simply trying to invest well. These are very different ways of investing and lead to radically different investment models. Our model—that of investing well—tries to achieve just one objective amid uncertainty: increase the *predictive accuracy* of our investments.

How have we done this? By emulating honeybees.

She Dances Her Way to Eternal Success

Apis mellifera, the honeybee, weighing one-tenth of a gram, has existed for thirty million years. She has faced multiple ice ages, thousands of environmental catastrophes, an unending stream of macro- and microscopic predators, and the arrival of the most destructive beings in the history of the planet: *Home sapiens*.

The most consequential decision in the life of honeybees is the choice of their home. I call it a "decision" because that is what it is: It seems to follow a process, it can take many hours or even days, and every honeybee in the colony appears to have a say. Unlike eating, mating, or fighting, choosing a home appears to be a deliberate and "thoughtful" process for honeybees. Let me explain.

Honeybees are highly social and live in colonies of thousands in very close proximity. A beehive typically has a single queen fed and protected by worker bees, all of whom happen to be sterile females.[3] A single colony typically splits into a few colonies (called swarms) at the end of winter. Each of these swarms needs to find a new home to construct beeswax combs, raise worker bees, and build a store of honey for the following winter.

Hence, as the bees create a new swarm, their most important task is finding a suitable nesting location for their hive. Their home needs to have a cavity volume to accommodate enough honey to last the entire winter. In addition, the entrance needs to be high enough above the ground to prevent land-based predators from targeting the bees. The entrance should also be small to ensure secrecy and warmth so that the bees' home can be protected from the elements, such as extreme winds.

So, how do honeybees select their home? By dancing.

Let's say you have decided to study how honeybees choose their nesting site. Here is what you will observe. When the bees from the mother colony split into a swarm, a few dozen scouts fly away in different directions to inspect nesting sites within a five-kilometer radius. When a scout encounters an attractive site, she returns to the swarm and performs a waggle dance to communicate the site's distance, direction, and quality to her sisters. (The males are lazy bums and don't do any work; their only job is to impregnate the queen.) The duration of the dance is proportional to the distance to the new site, the angle at which the bee waggles represents the angle of the outward run relative to the sun, and the vigorousness of the waggle (the number of dance circuits) denotes the quality of the new site.

Since the scouts have flown over a large area, they advertise many widely separated locations to their hive mates. The honeybees in the swarm follow the lead of various scouts to check out the widely dispersed sites and return to the swarm to perform their waggle dance.

Thus, initially, the scouts advertise several possible nesting sites, seemingly trying to recruit their hive mates to each of the chosen sites in what appears to be a quite chaotic scene. However, after a few hours or days, all of the bees begin to dance in favor of just one location. Once a consensus has been established, the swarm flies to the chosen location. But, of course, the bees don't have a leader. (The queen bee is just a reproduction machine and is entirely dependent on the worker bees for her food and welfare.) So you will (rightly) conclude that the choice of nesting site is accomplished through a democratic process in which all the honeybees have participated.

Once you have observed this phenomenon, here are some of the questions you will probably ask: How does this democratic process of building almost 100 percent consensus work? How does *dancing* lead to consensus over time? Do the bees reach the "right" decision? Is this decision-making a simple or complex process? Let's proceed step by step.

As I mentioned earlier, honeybees need to select a high-quality dwelling place to ensure their survival. But what is not apparent is that if they are given a choice of multiple high-quality sites, they will almost *always* choose the best possible site. "Good enough" is not acceptable to these discerning bees. When scientists artificially create a number of good nesting sites within the flying range of honeybees, they find that the bees almost always converge on the best possible site. Even more surprisingly, the bees seldom find the best nesting site first. But over time, even if the bees discover the best site much later than other slightly inferior sites, consensus is ultimately built around the best site.

Researchers have conclusively proven that honeybees have an absolute standard for assessing the quality of a nesting site. The vigorousness of their waggle dance, translated into the number of dance circuits, indicates the quality of a *particular* site. A honeybee takes between fifteen minutes and an hour to evaluate a potential site. She inspects the cavity's outside and spends a lot of time inside walking around and taking short flights. If the bee finds the nesting site desirable on first inspection, she returns to the swarm and advertises the site with a waggle dance. If another bee follows her to this site, she will perform almost the same waggle dance (in terms of duration and intensity) when she returns to the swarm. Honeybees have a universal standard for assessing nest quality.

All honeybees have a congruent interest while choosing a nesting site. Their consensus is built over time so that eventually, all bees support just one site, and this almost always happens to be the best possible site. But how?

Initially, scientists hypothesized that a honeybee scout compares her old nesting site with a new site (to which other dancing scouts recruited her). If she finds that the new site is of higher quality, she ceases support for the old site and dances more vigorously to demonstrate support for the new site. Thus, more dance circuits implies that the new site is better than the last one. This process builds consensus over time since the bees keep comparing the various nest sites, and the best site wins in the end. This hypothesis made perfect sense. But it has turned out to be wrong. Most honeybees visit just one nesting site, and very few visit two or more.

So what's going on? Painstaking work by Thomas Seeley and others revealed the mystery behind the consensus-building process.[4] It has just two elements. First, as we already know, the bees dance more circuits for a better-quality site. Second, the bees in the swarm attach themselves *randomly* to a dancing honeybee to explore a new site.

But how do these two simple actions lead to a consensus of nearly 100 percent over the best possible site? First, let's look at a simplified version of what happens in the wild.

Let's assume there are three scouts to begin with, and they evaluate three possible new nesting sites—A, B, and C—of varying quality. Let's assume site A is the best and site C is the worst. After assessing site A, the first scout returns to the swarm and performs twenty dance circuits. The second scout evaluates site B and performs ten dance circuits. Finally, the third scout performs only five dance circuits after evaluating site C.

Let's assume there are one hundred bees in the swarm waiting for their scout sisters to return. Remember that they will attach themselves randomly to any bee dancing and will then go and explore the site that this bee is excited about. Since the first bee contributes to 57 percent of the dance circuits (20 ÷ 35), fifty-seven of the one hundred bees in the swarm will attach themselves to the first bee. By the same logic, twenty-nine bees will end up assessing site B, and only fourteen will assess site C. What happens when these one hundred bees return to the swarm?

57 honeybees from site A perform 20 dances each = 1,140 dance circuits
29 honeybees from site B perform 10 dances each = 290 dance circuits
14 honeybees from site C perform 5 dances each = 70 dance circuits

Thus, site A now contributes 76 percent (1,140 ÷ 1,500) of the total number of dance circuits performed by the bees compared to 57 percent in the first round. In the next round, the bees attach themselves randomly to any of their dancing sisters. And so, 76 percent of the waiting bees will go and explore site A.

If this process keeps going, you can see that the support for the best site, A, will keep increasing exponentially—in the third round, following the same logic, support for site A will increase to 88 percent—until almost all the bees are supporting only site A.

Are you as gobsmacked as I was when I first read about this process? Do you see what has happened here? The honeybees have an extraordinarily complex and challenging decision to make. Yet, they make it through a very straightforward process: Dance harder for a better site, and attach yourself randomly to a dancing sister. That's it.

We Follow a Simple and Repeatable Process Like the Honeybees

The investment community ties itself up in knots over finding the "best" investments. I have seen extraordinarily complex algorithms and multigigabyte spreadsheets to assess the value and quality of a business. On the other hand, we are interested only in executing a sound investment *process*.

Our algorithm, while nowhere near as elegant as the honeybees', has only three steps:

1. Eliminate significant risks.
2. Invest *only* in stellar businesses at a fair price.
3. Own them forever.

The honeybee algorithm does not lead to 100 percent success, and it need not. Some swarms are unable to find a suitable dwelling location and perish. But so what? It is a *statistically* robust process in which, *on average*, the simple nest-seeking model works beautifully. And the reason it is robust is that in addition to the algorithm being sound, it is *repeatable*. Deviations from this simple model are neither required nor allowed. A honeybee colony sticks to its nest-seeking process season after season, year after year, millennium after millennium.

The failure of most investors does not lie in pursuing a wrong model but in failing to repeatedly pursue a good model. It does not take a genius to theorize that investing in quality management teams running excellent businesses should lead to success over the long term, but how many can translate this theory into practice day after day and year after year?

I believe we at Nalanda have, and you probably do not vehemently disagree, a sound investment model. While we strayed on a few occasions in the first few years (selling Shree Cement), we have primarily been able to stay on the straight and narrow. Obviously—and sadly—this does not guarantee investment success. Some investments haven't worked, and many more will not. But we will not second-guess our investment process. We will keep repeating it, whatever the outcome.

We have always tried to be, although we know we never will be, like the honeybees.

* * *

Investors, unlike biologists, are rarely filled with doubts and uncertainties. I am not talking about a typical television "expert" here—who is meant to entertain, not educate—but about self-perception and actual behavior. A scientist may spend her life working on the genetics of a maize plant (Barbara McClintock, winner of the Nobel Prize in Physiology or Medicine, 1983), deciphering the organization of the olfactory system (Linda Buck, cowinner of the Nobel Prize in Physiology or Medicine, 2004), or inventing a gene-editing technique (Jennifer Doudna and Emmanuelle Charpentier, winners of the Nobel Prize in Chemistry, 2020) and still admit that she has barely scratched the surface of what is knowable. In contrast, an investor, at the end of a one-hour group meeting with a company he has never met before, confidently declares that he has found the next P&G.

My circle of ignorance has expanded in lockstep with my age. As a young McKinsey consultant, I thought I had all the answers. As an older investor, I have only questions. I wish I had ready solutions for them, but I don't. So my only option is to internalize and implement a process that can simplify the world's complexity in a way that my intellect can't.

If we are surviving and outperforming the market many years from now, it will not be because we know a lot. Instead, it will be because we know that we don't.

Chapter Summary

Evolutionary theory has taught me that . . .

. . . we can reimagine investing by executing a simple and repeatable investment process.

1. The honeybees' choice of a new nesting site is extremely consequential (a suboptimal site can lead to death) and seemingly complex.

2. Honeybees don't have a leader; they make their decision through a consensus-building process that is surprisingly simple. This process does not lead to the best nesting site every time, but on average, it has served honeybees extremely well for more than thirty million years.

3. The business and investing worlds are highly complex, and I know that my limited intellect is incapable of fully comprehending them.

4. Hence, we at Nalanda have no interest in finding the "best investment" but in executing a sound investment process.

5. Our three-step investment process is simple and repeatable:

    a. Eliminate significant risks.
    b. Invest *only* in stellar businesses at a fair price.
    c. Own them forever.

6. We know this process does not guarantee investment success every time, but *on average*, it has worked out quite well for us.

7. We always have and always will stick to our process irrespective of individual outcomes.

NOTES

Introduction

1. 2/20 is the compensation structure of most hedge funds: They charge 2 percent of assets and 20 percent of a fund's profits as management fees (oddly termed "carry").
2. Tsuyoshi Ito, Sreetharan Kanthaswamy, Srichan Bunlungsup, Robert F. Oldt, Paul Houghton, Yuzuru Hamada, and Suchinda Malaivijitnond, "Secondary Contact and Genomic Admixture Between Rhesus and Long-Tailed Macaques in the Indochina Peninsula," *Journal of Evolutionary Biology* 33, no. 9 (2020): 1164–79, https://doi.org/10.1111/jeb.13681.
3. Andrea Rasche, Anna-Lena Sander, Victor Max Corman, and Jan Felix Drexler, "Evolutionary Biology of Human Hepatitis Viruses," *Journal of Hepatology* 70, no 3 (2019): 501–20, https://doi.org/10.1016/j.jhep.2018.11.010; Robin M. Hare and Leigh W. Simmons, "Sexual Selection and Its Evolutionary Consequences in Female Animals," *Biological Reviews* 94, no. 3 (2019): 929–56, https://doi.org/10.1111/brv.12484; Sarah M. Hird, "Evolutionary Biology Needs Wild Microbiomes," *Frontiers in Microbiology* 8 (2017): 725, https://doi.org/10.3389/fmicb.2017.00725; Andrew Whitten, "Culture Extends the Scope of Evolutionary Biology in the Great Apes," *Proceedings of the National Academy of Sciences* 114, no. 30 (2017): 7790–97, https://doi.org/10.1073/pnas.1620733114; Norman C. Ellstrand and Loren H. Riesberg, "When Gene Flow Really Matters: Gene Flow in Applied Evolutionary Biology," *Evolutionary Applications* 9, no. 7 (2016): 833–36, https://doi.org/10.1111/eva.12402.
4. Berlinda Liu and Gaurav Sinha, *SPIVA U.S. Scorecard: Year-End 2021* (New York: S&P Dow Jones Indices, 2021), https://www.spglobal.com/spdji/en/documents/spiva/spiva-us-year-end-2021.pdf.
5. Liu and Sinha, *SPIVA U.S. Scorecard*.

6. Akash Jain, *SPIVA India Scorecard: Year-End 2017* (New York: S&P Dow Jones Indices, 2018), https://www.spglobal.com/spdji/en/documents/spiva/spiva-india-year-end-2017 .pdf?force_download=true.

7. Akash Jain and Arpit Gupta, *SPIVA India Scorecard: Mid-Year 2020* (New York: S&P Dow Jones Indices, 2020), https://www.spglobal.com/spdji/en/documents/spiva/spiva -india-mid-year-2020.pdf?force_download=true.

8. Krissy Davis, Cary Stier, and Tony Gaughan, "2020 Investment Management Outlook," Deloitte, November 17, 2021, https://www2.deloitte.com/us/en/insights/industry/financial -services/financial-services-industry-outlooks/investment-management-industry -outlook.html.

9. Mary Jane West-Eberhard, *Developmental Plasticity and Evolution* (Oxford: Oxford University Press, 2003), viii. West-Eberhard's expertise is in the natural history and behavior of social wasps, but her book raises important issues related to the core tenets of evolutionary theory. She argues that since she can read, her narrow expertise in one subject does not preclude her from developing a point of view on a much different and broader issue.

10. Paladinvest, "Wesco Meeting," Motley Fool (forum), May 7, 2000, https://boards.fool .com/wesco-meeting-12529248.aspx; Ikoborso, "Re: Wesco Meeting," Motley Fool (forum), May 7, 2000, https://boards.fool.com/here-are-neuroberks-notes-from-the-wesco-12529644 .aspx.

11. To learn more about evolutionary theory and related subjects, here are several I have found useful:

   - A popular book that got me started on evolutionary theory: Richard Dawkins, *The Selfish Gene* (Oxford: Oxford University Press, 1989).
   - Before you move ahead, please do read the greatest book of all: Charles Darwin, *On the Origin of Species* (London: John Murray, 1859).
   - A classic: Carl Zimmer, *Evolution: The Triumph of an Idea* (New York: HarperCollins, 2001).
   - A graduate-level book that covers most topics of evolutionary theory quite well: Mark Ridley, *Evolution* (Hoboken, NJ: Blackwell Scientific, 1993).
   - One of my favorites on the general theory of evolution (it's a big book, but its value far exceeds its weight!): Stephen Jay Gould, *The Structure of Evolutionary Theory* (Cambridge, MA: Harvard University Press, 2002).
   - A highly accessible book on genetics for laypeople: Siddhartha Mukherjee, *The Gene: An Intimate History* (New York: Scribner, 2016).
   - If I had to choose one book to get started on the philosophy of evolution, it would be this one: Elliott Sober, *Evidence and Evolution: The Logic Behind the Science* (Cambridge: Cambridge University Press, 2008).
   - My favorite on human evolution and the science and controversy behind biology (e.g., does defining human "race" make any sense?): David Reich, *Who We Are and How We Got Here: Ancient DNA and the New Science of the Human Past* (Oxford: Oxford University Press, 2018).

12. The opinion that biology has almost no laws is expressed well in this essay: Pawan K. Dhar and Alessandro Giuliani, "Laws of Biology: Why So Few?," *Systems and Synthetic Biology* 4, no 1 (2010): 7–13, https://doi.org/10.1007/s11693-009-9049-0.

13. On scientists' disagreement regarding the definition of what constitutes a species, see Ben Panko, "What Does It Mean to Be a Species? Genetics Is Changing the Answer,"

Smithsonian Magazine, May 19, 2017, https://www.smithsonianmag.com/science-nature/what-does-it-mean-be-species-genetics-changing-answer-180963380/. On the evolution of the term "gene," see Petter Portin and Adam Wilkins, "The Evolving Definition of the Term 'Gene,'" *Genetics* 205, no. 4 (2017): 1353–64, https://doi.org/10.1534/genetics.116.196956.

1. Oh, to Be a Bumblebee

1. A type I error occurs when we reject a null hypothesis that is true. For an investor, the null hypothesis should be that an investment is bad. This is because most investments *are* bad. Now, let's say we encounter a bad investment. If we mistakenly assume that this investment is good, we would have rejected the null hypothesis that the investment is bad. Thus, in this case, rejecting the null hypothesis would mean that we would make a bad investment. We would have lost money. Now, let's look at a good investment. In this case, a type II error occurs when we accept a null hypothesis that is false. Here, the null hypothesis is false because the investment is good. But we have accepted the null hypothesis, thereby branding the investment as bad and not making the investment. Thus, a type I error occurs when I commit money to a bad investment, and a type II error occurs when I choose to omit putting money into a good investment. See "What Are Type I and Type II Errors?," Minitab 21 Support, accessed January 2021, https://support.minitab.com/en-us/minitab-express/1/help-and-how-to/basic-statistics/inference/supporting-topics/basics/type-i-and-type-ii-error/.

2. For a description of the inverse relationship between type I and type II errors with an example, see "What Are Type I and Type II Errors?"

3. For a brief explanation of deer evolution, see "Deer (Overview) – Evolution," Wildlife Online, accessed January 2021, https://www.wildlifeonline.me.uk/animals/article/deer-overview-evolution.

4. A good description of the breeding behavior of deer can be found at "Red Deer Breeding Biology," Wildlife Online, accessed January 2021, https://www.wildlifeonline.me.uk/animals/article/red-deer-breeding-biology.

5. For more on dodo extinction, see Editors of *Encyclopaedia Britannica*, "Dodo," *Encyclopaedia Britannica*, May 17, 2022, https://www.britannica.com/animal/dodo-extinct-bird.

6. For more on the cheetah's size and prowess, see Warren Johnson, "Cheetah," *Encyclopaedia Britannica*, August 26, 2021, https://www.britannica.com/animal/cheetah-mammal.

7. For a history of plants, see James A. Doyle, "Plant Evolution," McGraw Hill, last reviewed August 2019, https://www.accessscience.com/content/article/a522800. See also Rebecca Morelle, "Kew Report Makes New Tally for Number of World's Plants," BBC News, May 10, 2016, https://www.bbc.com/news/science-environment-36230858.

8. Abdul Rashid War, Michael Gabriel Paulraj, Tariq Ahmad, Abdul Ahad Buhroo, Barkat Hussain, Savarimuthu Ignacimuthu, and Hari Chand Sharma, "Mechanisms of Plant Defense Against Insect Herbivores," *Plant Signaling & Behavior* 7, no. 10 (2012): 1306–20, https://doi.org/10.4161/psb.21663.

9. Mike Newland, "When Plants Go to War," Nautilus, December 14, 2015, http://nautil.us/when-plants-go-to-war-rp-235729/. The section "Spy Games" describes how plants mimic the predators of their predators.

10. Janet Lowe, *Warren Buffett Speaks: Wit and Wisdom from the World's Greatest Investor* (Hoboken, NJ: John Wiley, 2007), 85.

11. Sergei Klebnikov, "Warren Buffett Sells Airline Stocks Amid Coronavirus: 'I Made a Mistake,'" *Forbes*, May 2, 2020, https://www.forbes.com/sites/sergeiklebnikov/2020/05/02/warren-buffett-sells-airline-stocks-amid-coronavirus-i-made-a-mistake/?sh=4da74fc15c74.

12. For the classic definition of "risk," see James Chen, "Risk," Investopedia, last updated September 20, 2022, https://www.investopedia.com/terms/r/risk.asp#:~:text=Risk%20is%20defined%20in%20financial,all%20of%20an%20original%20investment.

13. "Listed Domestic Companies, Total," World Bank, accessed February 2021, https://data.worldbank.org/indicator/CM.MKT.LDOM.NO.

14. KPMG, *Returns from Indian Private Equity: Will the Industry Deliver to Expectations?* (Mumbai: KPMG, 2011), https://spectruminvestors.files.wordpress.com/2011/12/return-from-indian-private-equity_1.pdf, 2.

15. For a discussion of the poor returns delivered by the PE industry in India from 2001 to 2013, see Vivek Pandit, "Private Equity in India: Once Overestimated, Now Underserved," McKinsey & Company, February 1, 2015, https://www.mckinsey.com/industries/private-equity-and-principal-investors/our-insights/private-equity-in-india. While this article does not discuss real estate or infrastructure specifically, it does provide data on the poor returns delivered by these sectors. On the subpar performance of the Indian PE industry, see Neha Bothra, "With Poor Returns, India Loses Sheen for Private Equity Firms," *Financial Express*, last updated April 5, 2015, https://www.financialexpress.com/market/with-poor-returns-india-loses-sheen-for-private-equity-firms/60582/. For data on the share of the Indian real estate and infrastructure, see Vivek Pandit, Toshan Tamhane, and Rohit Kapur, *Indian Private Equity: Route to Resurgence* (Mumbai: McKinsey & Company, 2015), https://www.mckinsey.com/~/media/mckinsey/business%20functions/strategy%20and%20corporate%20finance/our%20insights/private%20equity%20and%20indias%20economic%20development/mckinsey_indian_private%20equity.pdf, 19. See also exhibit 2.10, which shows the PE returns across sectors.

16. Lou Gerstner's turnaround of IBM is described in the following: Shah Mohammed, "IBM's Turnaround Under Lou Gerstner, Business and Management Lessons, Case Study," Medium, May 29, 2019, https://shahmm.medium.com/ibms-turnaround-under-lou-gerstner-case-study-business-management-lessons-a0dcce04612d; "Lou Gerstner's Turnaround Tales at IBM," Knowledge at Wharton, December 18, 2002, https://knowledge.wharton.upenn.edu/article/lou-gerstners-turnaround-tales-at-ibm/; Sabina Gesmin, Bernard Henderson, Syed Irtiza, and Ahmed Y. Mahfouz, "An Analysis of Historical Transformation of an IT Giant Based on Sound Strategic Vision," *Communications of the IIMA* 11, no. 3 (2011): 11–20, https://core.ac.uk/download/pdf/55330343.pdf; Louis V. Gerstner Jr., *Who Says Elephants Can't Dance? Inside IBM's Historic Turnaround* (New York: HarperCollins, 2002).

17. For JCPenney's historical stock prices, see "J. C. Penney" at Trading Economics, https://tradingeconomics.com/jcp:us. For the company's 2006 and 2010 annual reports, see JCPenney, *Annual Report 2006* (Plano, TX: JCPenney, 2006), https://www.annualreports.com/HostedData/AnnualReportArchive/j/NYSE_JCP_2006.pdf, and JCPenney, *Summary Annual Report 2010* (Plano, TX: JCPenney, 2010), https://www.annualreports.com/HostedData/AnnualReportArchive/j/NYSE_JCP_2010.pdf. On Ron Johnson's achievement at Target, see Adam Levine-Weinberg, "Target Corporation Should Give Ron Johnson a Chance at Redemption," *Motley Fool*, May 14, 2014, https://www.fool.com/investing/general/2014/05/14/target-corporation-should-give-ron-johnson-a-chanc.aspx. On Johnson's success at Apple, see Adria Cheng, "Ron Johnson Made Apple Stores the Envy of Retail and Target Hip, but This Startup May Be His Crowning Achievement," *Forbes*, January 17, 2020, https://www.forbes.com/sites

/andriacheng/2020/01/17/he-made-apple-stores-envy-of-retail-and-target-hip-but-his-biggest—career-chapter-may-be-just-starting/?sh=44edc5c60bbb. For more on Johnson's failures at JCPenney, see Margaret Bogenrief, "JCPenney's Turnaround Has Already Failed," *Insider*, December 30, 2012, https://www.businessinsider.com/jc-penney-the-turnaround-disaster-2012-12; Aimee Growth, "Here's Ron Johnson's Complete Failed Plan to Turn Around JCPenney," *Insider*, April 8, 2013, https://www.business insider.com/ron-johnsons-failed-plan-to-turn-around-jcpenney-2013-4; Nathaniel Meyersohn, "How It All Went Wrong at JCPenney," CNN Business, September 27, 2018, https://edition.cnn.com/2018/09/27/business/jcpenney-history/index.html; and James Surowiecki, "The Turnaround Trap," *New Yorker*, March 18, 2013, https://www.newyorker.com/magazine/2013/03/25/the-turnaround-trap. On JCPenney filing for bankruptcy, see Chris Isidore and Nathaniel Meyersohn, "JCPenney Files for Bankruptcy," CNN Business, May 16, 2020, https://edition.cnn.com/2020/05/15/business/jcpenney-bankruptcy/index.html.

18. For a discussion of leverage, see Troy Adkins, "Optimal Use of Financial Leverage in a Corporate Capital Structure," Investopedia, last updated April 30, 2021, https://www.investopedia.com/articles/investing/111813/optimal-use-financial-leverage-corporate-capital-structure.asp#:~:text=In%20essence%2C%20corporate%20management%20utilizes,financial%20distress%2C%20perhaps%20even%20bankruptcy.

19. Katherine Doherty and Steven Church, "Gold's Gym Files for Bankruptcy Protection Amid Fitness Closures," Bloomberg, May 4, 2020, https://www.bloomberg.com/news/articles/2020-05-04/gold-s-gym-files-for-bankruptcy-protection-amid-fitness-closures#:~:text=Gold's%20Gym%20International%20Inc.,liabilities%2C%20according%20to%20court%20papers; Robert Ferris, "Why Hertz Landed in Bankruptcy Court When Its Rivals Didn't," CNBC, August 17, 2020, https://www.cnbc.com/2020/08/17/why-hertz-landed-in-bankruptcy-court-when-its-rivals-didnt.html; Debra Werner, "Intelsat Reveals Plan to Reorganize and Trim Debt," *SpaceNews*, February 14, 2021, https://spacenews.com/intelsat-files-reorganization-plan/#:~:text=Intelsat%20filed%20for%20bankruptcy%20court,U.S.%20Federal%20Communications%20Commission%20auction; "Fact Sheet: J. Crew Succumbs to Bankruptcy After Private Equity Debt, Finance Looting," Americans for Financial Reform, May 4, 2020, https://ourfinancial security.org/2020/05/jcrew-private-equity-fact-sheet/; Reuters, "J.C. Penney Rescue Deal Approved in Bankruptcy Court, Saving Close to 60,000 Jobs," CNBC, November 10, 2020, https://www.cnbc.com/2020/11/10/jc-penney-rescue-deal-approved-in-bankruptcy-court-saving-close-to-60000-jobs.html#:~:text=J.C.%20Penney%20filed%20for%20bankruptcy,protection%20amid%20the%20coronavirus%20pandemic; Lauren Hirsch and Lauren Thomas, "Luxury Retailer Neiman Marcus Files for Bankruptcy as It Struggles with Debt and Coronavirus Fallout," CNBC, May 7, 2020, https://www.cnbc.com/2020/05/07/neiman-marcus-files-for-bankruptcy.html; Rami Grunbaum, "Sur La Table Creditors Signal Doubts About the Seattle Kitchenware Retailer's Financial Outlook," *Seattle Times*, May 13, 2020, https://www.seattletimes.com/business/retail/sur-la-table-creditors-signal-doubts-about-the-seattle-kitchenware-retailers-financial-outlook/.

20. Jeff Desjardins, "The 20 Biggest Bankruptcies in U.S. History," Visual Capitalist, June 25, 2019, https://www.visualcapitalist.com/the-20-biggest-bankruptcies-in-u-s-history/.

21. Prerna Sindwani, "No Layoffs, Asian Paints Will Give Salary Increments to Boost Employees Morale," *Business Insider: India*, May 15, 2020, https://www.businessinsider.in/business/corporates/news/asian-paints-will-hike-salaries-and-not-lay-off-to-boost-employee-morale/articleshow/75754451.cms; Drishti Pant, "Asian Paints Raises Pay to Boost

Employees' Morale," People Matters, May 15, 2020, https://www.peoplematters.in/news/compensation-benefits/asian-paints-raises-pay-to-boost-employees-morale-25685.

22. Kala Vijayraghavan and Rajesh Mascarenhas, "Asian Paints Raises Staff Salaries to Boost Morale," *The Economic Times*, last updated May 15, 2020, https://economictimes.indiatimes.com/news/company/corporate-trends/asian-paints-raises-staff-salaries-to-boost-morale/articleshow/75746239.cms.

23. Rita Gunther McGrath, "15 Years Later, Lessons from the Failed AOL-Time Warner Merger," *Fortune*, January 10, 2015, https://fortune.com/2015/01/10/15-years-later-lessons-from-the-failed-aol-time-warner-merger/; Marvin Dumont, "4 Biggest Merger and Acquisition Disasters," Investopedia, last updated February 21, 2022, https://www.investopedia.com/articles/financial-theory/08/merger-acquisition-disasters.asp#:~:text=America%20Online%20and%20Time%20Warner,combination%20up%20until%20that%20time; Kison Patel, "The 8 Biggest M&A Failures of All Time," DealRoom, last updated November 8, 2021, https://dealroom.net/blog/biggest-mergers-and-acquisitions-failures; "Verizon to Acquire AOL," Verizon News Center, May 12, 2015, https://www.verizon.com/about/news/verizon-acquire-aol.

24. Clayton M. Christensen, Richard Alton, Curtis Rising, and Andrew Waldeck, "The Big Idea: The New M&A Playbook," *Harvard Business Review*, March 2011, https://hbr.org/2011/03/the-big-idea-the-new-ma-playbook#:~:text=Executive%20Summary&text=Companies%20spend%20more%20than%20%242,and%20how%20to%20integrate%20them; George Bradt, "83% of Mergers Fail—Leverage a 100-Day Action Plan for Success Instead," *Forbes*, January 27, 2015, https://www.forbes.com/sites/georgebradt/2015/01/27/83-mergers-fail-leverage-a-100-day-value-acceleration-plan-for-success-instead/?sh=647b5a765b86; Linda Canina and Jin-Young Kim, *Commentary: Success and Failure of Mergers and Acquisitions* (Ithaca, NY: Cornell School of Hotel Administration), July 2010, https://ecommons.cornell.edu/bitstream/handle/1813/72320/Canina12_Success_and_Failure.pdf?sequence=1; Toby J. Tetenbaum, "Beating the Odds of Merger & Acquisition Failure: Seven Key Practices That Improve the Chance for Expected Integration and Synergies," *Organizational Dynamics* (Autumn 1999): 22, https://go.gale.com/ps/anonymous?id=GALE%7CA56959356&sid=googleScholar&v=2.1&it=r&linkaccess=abs&issn=00902616&p=AONE&sw=w; "Why M&A Deals Fail," Great Prairie Group, June 2018, https://greatprairiegroup.com/why-ma-deals-fail/#. See also Shobhit Seth, "Top Reasons Why M&A Deals Fail," Investopedia, last updated May 25, 2021, https://www.investopedia.com/articles/investing/111014/top-reasons-why-ma-deals-fail.asp.

25. "Railways in Early Nineteenth Century Britain," UK Parliament, accessed January 2021, https://www.parliament.uk/about/living-heritage/transformingsociety/transportcomms/roadsrail/kent-case-study/introduction/railways-in-early-nineteenth-century-britain/; "Railroad History," *Encyclopaedia Britannica*, last updated September 4, 2020, https://www.britannica.com/technology/railroad/Railroad-history; Gareth Campbell and John Turner, *"The Greatest Bubble in History": Stock Prices During the British Railway Mania*, MPRA Paper No. 21820 (Belfast: Queen's University Belfast, 2010), https://mpra.ub.uni-muenchen.de/21820/1/MPRA_paper_21820.pdf.

26. Michael Aaron Dennis, "Explosive Growth," *Encyclopaedia Britannica*, last updated September 12, 2019, https://www.britannica.com/place/Silicon-Valley-region-California/Explosive-growth; Brian McCullough, "A Revealing Look at the Dot-Com Bubble of 2000—and How It Shapes Our Lives Today," Ideas.Ted.com, December 4, 2018, https://ideas.ted.com/an-eye-opening-look-at-the-dot-com-bubble-of-2000-and-how-it-shapes-our-lives-today/; Adam Hayes, "Dotcom Bubble," Investopedia, last updated June 25, 2019, https://www.investopedia.com/terms/d/dotcom-bubble.asp; Chris Morris,

"Failed IPOs of the Dot-Com Bubble," CNBC, last updated September 13, 2013, https://www.cnbc.com/2012/05/17/Failed-IPOs-of-the-Dot-Com-Bubble.html; Jean Folger, "5 Successful Companies That Survived the Dot-Com Bubble," Investopedia, last updated August 15, 2021, https://www.investopedia.com/financial-edge/0711/5-successful-companies-that-survived-the-dotcom-bubble.aspx; Jake Ulick, "1999: Year of the IPO," CNN Money, December 27, 1999, https://money.cnn.com/1999/12/27/investing/century_ipos/#:~:text=Initial%20public%20offerings%20raised%20more,s%20record%20first%2Dday%20gains.

27. Wayne Gretzky, "Wayne Gretzky Quotes," Goodreads, accessed January 2021, https://www.goodreads.com/author/quotes/240132.Wayne_Gretzky.

28. Ganga Narayan Rath, "Loan Waivers Are a Double-Edged Sword," BusinessLine, last updated June 9, 2020, https://www.thehindubusinessline.com/opinion/loan-waivers-are-a-double-edged-sword/article31789331.ece; Anjani Kumar and Seema Bathla, "Loan Waivers Are No Panacea for India's Farmers," International Food Policy Research Institute, January 22, 2019, https://www.ifpri.org/blog/loan-waivers-are-no-panacea-indias-farmers.

29. "Group Companies," Tata, accessed January 2021, https://www.tata.com/investors/companies#:~:text=ten%20business%20verticals-,Founded%20by%20Jamsetji%20Tata%20in%201868%2C%20the%20Tata%20group%20is,30%20companies%20across%2010%20clusters.

30. Lijee Philip, "Meet Siddhartha Lal, the Man Who Turned Around Royal Enfield Into Eicher Motors' Profit Engine," *Economic Times*, last updated September 9, 2015, https://economictimes.indiatimes.com/meet-siddhartha-lal-the-man-who-turned-around-royal-enfield-into-eicher-motors-profit-engine/articleshow/46461712.cms?from=mdr.

31. "What Is a Bumblebee?," Bumbleebee.org, accessed February 2021, http://bumblebee.org/; "Artificial Meadows and Robot Spiders Reveal Secret Life of Bees," *ScienceDaily*, September 7, 2008, https://www.sciencedaily.com/releases/2008/09/080902225431.htm.

2. The Siberian Solution

1. Buffett provides his advice to individual investors on index funds in his 2013 annual letter. He writes, "The goal of the nonprofessional should not be to pick winners—neither he nor his "helpers" can do that—but should rather be to own a cross section of businesses that in aggregate are bound to do well. A low-cost S&P 500 index fund will achieve this goal." He has repeated this advice in many other letters as well. See Warren Buffett, Berkshire Hathaway 2013 annual letter (Omaha, NE: Berkshire Hathaway, 2013), https://berkshirehathaway.com/letters/2013ltr.pdf.

2. Nathan Gregory, "Analyst's Conference January 2000 Pt 1," YouTube video, 1:32:36, uploaded 2017.

3. Biography.com editors, "Jeffrey Skilling Biography," Biography, last updated May 10, 2021, https://www.biography.com/crime-figure/jeffrey-skilling.

4. David Kleinbard, "The 1.7 Trillion Dot.Com Lesson," CNN Money, November 9, 2000, https://money.cnn.com/2000/11/09/technology/overview/.

5. Alex Castro, "This Is What Really Brought Down WeWork," *Fast Company*, December 20, 2019, https://www.fastcompany.com/90444597/this-is-what-really-brought-down-wework; Jonathon Trugman, "WeWork IPO Fail Is Unique," *New York Post*, October 5, 2019, https://nypost.com/2019/10/05/wework-ipo-fail-is-unique/; Statista Research Department, "Revenue of WeWork Worldwide from 2016 to 2020 (in Million U.S.

Dollars)," Statista, July 6, 2022, https://www.statista.com/statistics/880069/wework
-revenue-worldwide/. See https://statista.com for financial information for WeWork
and IWG.

6. "Lehman Brothers Holdings, Inc. Form 10-K for Fiscal Year Ended November 30, 2007,"
EDGAR, Securities and Exchange Commission, https://www.sec.gov/Archives/edgar
/data/806085/000110465908005476/a08-3530_110k.htm.

7. "Bear Stearns Companies Inc. Form 10-K for Fiscal Year Ended November 30, 2004,"
Filings.com, 2004, http://getfilings.com/o0001169232-05-000947.html; "Schedule I:
Condensed Financial Information of Registrant the Bear Stearns Company Inc. (Parent
Company Only)," EDGAR, Securities and Exchange Commission, January 28, 2008,
https://sec.edgar-online.com/bear-stearns-companies-inc/10-k-annual-report/2008
/01/29/section27.aspx.

8. Derek Lidow, "Why Two-Thirds of the Fastest-Growing Companies Fail," *Fortune*,
March 7, 2016, https://fortune.com/2016/03/07/fast-growth-companies-fail/.

9. The operating margin, ROCE, and number of inventory days for Costco and Tiffany
come from thirty-year financials available at https://gurufocus.com.

10. Editors of *Encyclopaedia Britannica*, "Collectivization," *Encyclopaedia Britannica*, last
updated May 20, 2020, https://www.britannica.com/topic/collectivization.

11. Dmitri Belyaev and Lyudmila Trut's long-running experiment is detailed in Lee Alan
Dugatkin and Lyudmila Trut, *How to Tame a Fox (and Build a Dog): Visionary Scientists and a Siberian Tale of Jump-Started Evolution* (Chicago: University of Chicago
Press, 2017). On melatonin impact, see 116–20; gene expression, 124–25; the HTR_2C
gene, 188; oxytocin release in humans and dogs, 114; the role of serotonin in early
development, 166; changes in reproductive cycle, 167; similarities among domesticated
animals, 162. On method of handling fox pups and assigning classes, see Lyudmila
N. Trut, "Early Canid Domestication: The Farm-Fox Experiment," *American Scientist* 87, no. 2 (1999): 163, https://www.jstor.org/stable/27857815?seq=1. The experiment
is also well described in Jason G. Goldman, "Man's New Best Friend? A Forgotten
Russian Experiment in Fox Domestication," *Scientific American*, September 6, 2020,
https://blogs.scientificamerican.com/guest-blog/mans-new-best-friend-a-forgotten
-russian-experiment-in-fox-domestication/.

12. Trut, "Early Canid Domestication," 160–69.

13. Baijnath Ramraika and Prashant Trivedi, "Sources of Sustainable Competitive Advantage," *SSRN* (January 5, 2016), https://papers.ssrn.com/sol3/papers.cfm?abstract_id
=2713675.

14. Matt Haig, *Brand Failures: The Truth About the 100 Biggest Branding Mistakes of All
Time* (London: Kogan Page, 2003); Kurt Schroeder, "Why So Many New Products Fail
(and It's Not the Product)," *Business Journals*, March 14, 2017, https://www.bizjournals
.com/bizjournals/how-to/marketing/2017/03/why-so-many-new-products-fail-and-it
-s-not-the.html.

15. On Havells' acquisition of Lloyd, see Ashutosh R. Shyam and Arijit Barman, "Havells
Acquires Consumer Biz of Lloyd Electric for Rs 1600 cr," *Economic Times*, last updated
February 19, 2017, https://economictimes.indiatimes.com/industry/indl-goods/svs
/engineering/havells-acquires-consumer-biz-of-lloyd-electric-for-rs-1600-cr/articleshow
/57233192.cms?from=mdr#:~:text=Read%20more%20news%20on&text=ADD%20
COMMENT-,MUMBAI%3A%20Havells%20India%2C%20India's%20leading%20
makers%20of%20branded%20electrical%20products,%2415%20billion%20consumer
%20appliances%20market. On Havells' founding and history, see Havells, *Deeper Into
Homes: Havells India Limited 34th Annual Report 2016–17* (New Delhi: Havells, 2017),

https://www.havells.com/content/dam/havells/annual_reports/2016-2017/Havells%20 AR%202016-17.pdf. On Havells' new air conditioner plant, see Havells, *The Future Has Already Begun: Havells India Limited 35th Annual Report 2017–18* (New Delhi: Havells, 2018), https://www.havells.com/HavellsProductImages/HavellsIndia/pdf/About-Havells /Investor-Relations/Financial/Annual-Reports/2017-2018/Havells_AR_2017-18.pdf. On the downgrading of Havells by research analysts, see ET Bureau, "Analysts Downgrade Havells as Lloyd Numbers Disappoint," *Economic Times*, last updated October 26, 2019, https://economictimes.indiatimes.com/markets/stocks/news/analysts-downgrade -havells-as-lloyd-numbers-disappoint/articleshow/71770087.cms.

3. The Paradox of McKinsey and Sea Urchins

1. The history of McKinsey is well summarized in Duff McDonald, *The Firm: The Story of McKinsey and Its Secret Influence on American Business* (New York: Simon & Schuster, 2013). McKinsey is also well profiled in this obituary for Marvin Bower: Douglas Martin, "Marvin Bower, 99; Built McKinsey & Co.," *New York Times*, January 24, 2003, https://www.nytimes.com/2003/01/24/business/marvin-bower-99-built-mckinsey -co.html. McKinsey's cozy relationship with Eskom blew up in its face in 2018; see Walt Bogdanich and Michael Forsythe, "How McKinsey Lost Its Way in South Africa," *New York Times*, June 26, 2018, https://www.nytimes.com/2018/06/26/world /africa/mckinsey-south-africa-eskom.html. In early 2020, McKinsey agreed to pay about $600 million to settle claims related to its work with Purdue Pharma, the company primarily responsible for the opioid epidemic in the United States. See Chris Hughes, "McKinsey's Opioid Settlement Is a Warning to All Consultants," Bloomberg, February 5, 2021, https://www.bloomberg.com/opinion/articles/2021-02-05/opioid -epidemic-mckinsey-s-settlement-is-a-warning-to-all-consultants.
2. Andreas Wagner, *Robustness and Evolvability in Living Systems* (Princeton, NJ: Princeton University Press, 2005).
3. Wagner, *Robustness and Evolvability*.
4. Mark Ridley, *Evolution*, 3rd ed. (Hoboken, NJ: Wiley, 2003). See in particular chapter 2, "Molecular and Mendelian Genetics," and table 2.1 on mRNA codons.
5. Wagner, *Robustness and Evolvability*, chapter 3, "The Genetic Code."
6. Stephen J. Freeland and Laurence D. Hurst, "The Genetic Code Is One in a Million," *Journal of Molecular Evolution* 47 (1998): 238–48, https://doi.org/10.1007/pl00006381.
7. John Carl Villanueva, "How Many Atoms Are There in the Universe?," Universe Today, July 30, 2009, http://www.universetoday.com/36302/atoms-in-the-universe/. The universe has 108 atoms, and 209 is equivalent to 1010.
8. Douglas J. Futuyma, *Evolutionary Biology*, 3rd ed. (Sunderland, MA: Sinauer, 1997), chapter 11.
9. "WNS (Holdings) Limited. Form 20-F for Fiscal Year Ended March 31, 2007," EDGAR, Securities and Exchange Commission, 2007, https://www.sec.gov/Archives/edgar/dat a/0001356570/000114554907002102/u93119e20vf.htm#104; "WNS (Holdings) Limited. Form 20-F for Fiscal Year Ended March 31, 2020," EDGAR, Securities and Exchange Commission, 2020, https://www.sec.gov/Archives/edgar/data/0001356570/00011931252 0131094/d863476d20f.htm.
10. Stephen Jay Gould, *The Structure of Evolutionary Theory* (Cambridge, MA: Belknap, 2002), 1270–71; Michael E. Palmer and Marcus W. Feldman, "Survivability Is More Fundamental than Evolvability," *PLoS One* 7, no. 6 (2012): e38025, https://doi.org/10.1371

/journal.pone.0038025; Joseph Reisinger, Kenneth O. Stanley, and Risto Miikkulainen, *Towards An Empirical Measure of Evolvability* (Austin: University of Texas at Austin Department of Computer Sciences, 2005), http://nn.cs.utexas.edu/downloads/papers /reisinger.gecco05.pdf. Reisinger, Stanley, and Miikkulainen state, "Currently no benchmarks exist to measure evolvability."

11. "Corporate Information," Page Industries Limited, accessed March 2021, https://pageind .com/corporate-information; "Annual Reports," Page Industries Limited, accessed March 2021, https://pageind.com/annual-reports.

12. Keith Cooper, "Looking for LUCA, the Last Universal Common Ancestor," Astrobiology at NASA, March 30, 2017, https://astrobiology.nasa.gov/news/looking-for-luca-the -last-universal-common-ancestor/.

13. Sam Walton with John Huey, *Made in America: My Story* (New York: Doubleday, 1992). On Walton's early years and for his quote on calculated risk, see chapter 2. On Hypermart and other failures, Sam's Club, and the acquisition of Mohr Value, see chapter 13.

14. "History," Walmart, accessed March 2021, https://corporate.walmart.com/our-story /our-history.

15. "Walmart Inc. (WMT)," Yahoo! Finance, https://finance.yahoo.com/quote/WMT/financials ?p=WMT; Walmart Inc., *Walmart Inc. 2020 Annual Report* (Bentonville, Arkansas, 2020), https://s2.q4cdn.com/056532643/files/doc_financials/2020/ar/Walmart_2020_Annual _Report.pdf.

16. Michael Arrington, "Accel Partners' Extraordinary 2005 Fund IX," TechCrunch, November 22, 2010, https://techcrunch.com/2010/11/22/accel-partners-fund-ix-facebook -extraordinary/?guccounter=1.

17. Carl Zimmer, *Evolution: The Triumph of an Idea* (New York: HarperCollins, 2001). On the era of dinosaurs and their extinction, see 84, 190. On the evolution of mammals 225 million years ago, see 166. On the molecular evidence for the coexistence of mammals with dinosaurs, see Ridley, *Evolution*, 671–72.

18. "Chapter 43: Jesus Brings Lazarus Back to Life," Church of Jesus Christ of Latter-Day Saints, accessed March 2021, https://www.churchofjesuschrist.org/study/manual/new -testament-stories/chapter-43-jesus-brings-lazarus-back-to-life?lang=eng. See also the Gospel according to Luke in the New Testament.

19. Joan Verdon, "Toys R Us Timeline: History of the Nation's Top Toy Chain," *USA Today*, last updated March 15, 2018, https://www.usatoday.com/story/money/business /2018/03/09/toys-r-us-timeline-history-nations-top-toy-chain/409230002/; Barbara Kahn, "What Went Wrong: The Demise of Toys R Us," Knowledge at Wharton, March 14, 2018, https://knowledge.wharton.upenn.edu/article/the-demise-of-toys-r-us/#:~:text =Though%20Toys%20R%20Us's%20business,an%20Era%20of%20Endless%20Disruption; *Entrepreneur* staff, "Charles Lazarus: Toy Titan," *Entrepreneur*, October 10, 2008, https://www.entrepreneur.com/article/197660; Erin Blakemore, "Inside the Rise and Fall of Toys 'R' Us," History, March 19, 2018, https://www.history.com/news/toys-r-us -closing-legacy; Dave Canal, "Frank Thoughts: The Retailing Genius," Contravisory, June 16, 2015, https://www.contravisory.com/blog/posts/frank-thoughts-retailing-genius; Merrill Brown, "Shop on 18th Street Grows Into a Giant," *Washington Post*, November 14, 1982, https://www.washingtonpost.com/archive/business/1982/11/14/shop-on-18th -street-grows-into-a-giant/cba05ab5-28aa-46a4-8faa-9a230cb3f7f2/; Ed Bruske, "Play Merchant to the Masses," *Washington Post*, December 18, 1981, https://www.washington post.com/archive/local/1981/12/18/play-merchant-to-the-masses/afdba3a4-a483-4bc7 -91cd-716b0707459a/; Rachel Beck, "Wal-Mart Dethrones Toys R Us," *AP News*, March 29, 1999, https://apnews.com/article/6e6082b522082a0d782052046c75b0b2; Julia Horowitz,

"How Toys 'R' Us Went from Big Kid in the Block to Bust," CNN Business, March 17, 2018, https://money.cnn.com/2018/03/17/news/companies/toys-r-us-history/index .html; "Toys 'R' Us, Inc. History," Funding Universe, accessed March 2021, http://www .fundinguniverse.com/company-histories/toys-r-us-inc-history/; Joseph Pereira, Rob Tomsho, and Ann Zimmerman, "Toys 'Were' Us?; Undercut by Big Discounters, Toys 'R' Us Is Indicating It May Get Out of the Business," *Wall Street Journal*, August 12, 2004, http://www.homeworkgain.com/wp-content/uploads/edd/2019/08/20190603204438 bus520articletoysrus.pdf.

20. Mark Dunbar, "How Private Equity Killed Toys 'R' Us," *In These Times*, October 10, 2017, https://inthesetimes.com/article/how-private-equity-killed-toys-r-us; Toys "R" Us, "Toys 'R' Us, Inc. Announces Agreement to Be Acquired by KKR, Bain Capital and Vornado for $26.75 per Share in $6.6 Billion Transaction," press release, EDGAR, Securities and Exchange Commission, March 17, 2005, https://www.sec.gov/Archives/edgar /data/1005414/000119312505057773/dex991.htm; Jeff Spross, "How Vulture Capitalists Ate Toys 'R' Us," *The Week*, March 16, 2018, https://theweek.com/articles/761124/how-vulture -capitalists-ate-toys-r; Michael Barbaro and Ben White, "Toys R Somebody Else," *Washington Post*, March 18, 2005, https://www.washingtonpost.com/wp-dyn/articles/A45446 -2005Mar17.html; Nathan Vardi, "The Big Investment Firms That Lost $1.3 Billion in the Toys 'R' Us Bankruptcy," *Forbes*, September 19, 2017, https://www.forbes.com/sites /nathanvardi/2017/09/19/the-big-investment-firms-that-lost-1-3-billion-on-the-toys -r-us-bankruptcy/?sh=3eb163f2308f; Miriam Gottfried and Lillian Rizzo, "Heavy Debt Crushed Owners of Toys 'R' Us," *Wall Street Journal*, September 19, 2017, https://www .wsj.com/articles/heavy-debt-crushed-owners-of-toys-r-us-1505863033; Bryce Covert, "The Demise of Toys 'R' Us Is a Warning," *The Atlantic*, June 13, 2018, https://www.the atlantic.com/magazine/archive/2018/07/toys-r-us-bankruptcy-private-equity/561758/.

21. See Covert, "The Demise of Toys 'R' Us."

22. Drea Knufken, "Toys 'R' Us Buys FAO Schwarz," *Business Pundit*, May 28, 2009, https:// www.businesspundit.com/toys-r-us-buys-fao-schwarz/; John Kell, "Exclusive: Toys 'R' Us Is Selling Off Iconic FAO Schwarz Brand," *Fortune*, October 4, 2016, https://fortune .com/2016/10/04/toys-r-us-sells-fao-schwarz/.

4. The Perils of a Pavlovian

1. Christian Cotroneo, "10 Divine Facts About Dung Beetles," Treehugger, last updated December 4, 2020, https://www.treehugger.com/dung-beetles-facts-4862309; Editors of *Encyclopaedia Britannica*, "Dung Beetle," *Encyclopaedia Britannica*, last updated April 19, 2020, https://www.britannica.com/animal/dung-beetle; Erica Tennehouse, "Dung Beetles Borrowed Wing Genes to Grow Their Horns," *Science*, November 21, 2019, https://www.sciencemag.org/news/2019/11/dung-beetles-borrowed-wing-genes-grow -their-horns; Roberta Kwok, "Little Beetle, Big Horns," *Science News Explores*, May 14, 2007, https://www.sciencenewsforstudents.org/article/little-beetle-big-horns; Douglas J. Emlen and H. Frederick Nijhout, "Hormonal Control of Male Horn Length Dimorphism in the Dung Beetle *Onthophagus taurus* (Coleoptera: Scarabaeidae)," *Journal of Insect Physiology* 45, no. 1 (1999): 45–53, https://doi.org/10.1016/S0022-1910(98)00096-1; Martha Cummings, Haley K. Evans, and Johel Chaves-Campos, "Male Horn Dimorphism and Its Function in the Neotropical Dung Beetle *Sulcophanaeus velutinus*," *Journal of Insect Behavior* 31 (2018): 471–89, https://doi.org/10.1007/s10905-018-9693-x.

2. Yonggang Hu, David M. Linz, and Armin P. Moczek, "Beetle Horns Evolved from Wing Serial Homologs," *Science* 366, no. 6468 (2019): 1004–7, https://www.science.org/doi/abs/10.1126/science.aaw2980.

3. Douglas J. Emlen and H. Frederik Nijhout, "Hormonal Control of Male Horn Length Dimorphism in the Dung Beetle *Onthophagus taurus* (Coleoptera: Scarabaeidae)," *Journal of Insect Physiology* 45, no. 1 (1999): 45–53, https://www.sciencedirect.com/science/article/abs/pii/S0022191098000961.

4. Peter Schausberger, J. David Patiño-Ruiz, Masahiro Osakabe, Yasumasa Murata, Naoya Sugimoto, Ryuji Uesugi, and Andreas Walzer, "Ultimate Drivers and Proximate Correlates of Polyandry in Predatory Mites," *PLoS One* 11, no. 4 (2016): e0154355, https://doi.org/10.1371/journal.pone.0154355.

5. Ernst Mayr, "Cause and Effect in Biology: Kinds of Causes, Predictability, and Teleology Are Viewed by a Practicing Biologist," *Science* 134, no. 3489 (1961): 1501–6, https://science.sciencemag.org/content/134/3489/1501; Bora Zivkovic, "The New Meaning of How and Why in Biology?," *Scientific American*, December 15, 2011, https://blogs.scientificamerican.com/a-blog-around-the-clock/the-new-meanings-of-how-and-why-in-biology/; Kevin N. Laland, Kim Sterelny, John Odling-Smee, William Hoppitt, and Tobias Uller, "Cause and Effect in Biology Revisited: Is Mayr's Proximate-Ultimate Dichotomy Still Useful?," *Science* 334, no. 6062 (2011): 1512–16, https://doi.org/10.1126/science.1210879.

6. Malina Poshtova Zang, "U.S. Stocks Whipped by Losses," CNN Money, October 27, 1997, https://money.cnn.com/1997/10/27/markets/marketwrap/; Into the Future, "The October 27th 1997 Mini-Crash," *Know the Stock Market* (blog), May 31, 2009, http://stockmktinfo.blogspot.com/2009/05/october-27th-1997-mini-crash.html; Edward A. Gargan, "The Market Plunge: The Asian Crisis; Hong Kong's Slide Goes Deeper," *New York Times*, October 28, 1997, https://www.nytimes.com/1997/10/28/business/the-market-plunge-the-asian-crisis-hong-kong-s-slide-goes-deeper.html?searchResultPosition=1. Stock price data is from Bloomberg.

7. Deepak Shenoy, "Chart of the Day: Bank FD Rates from 1976," Capitalmind, September 30, 2020, https://www.capitalmind.in/2020/09/chart-of-the-day-bank-fd-rates-from-1976/; Shankar Nath, "RBI Interest Rates & Its Evolution Over 20 Years (2000–2019)," Beginnersbuck, accessed April 2021, https://www.beginnersbuck.com/rbi-interest-rates-history/.

8. "Who Is the World's Best Banker?," *The Economist*, October 29, 2020, https://www.economist.com/finance-and-economics/2020/10/29/who-is-the-worlds-best-banker.

9. Zidong An, João Tovar Jalles, and Prakash Loungani, "How Well Do Economists Forecast Recessions?," IMF Working Paper 18/39 (Washington, DC: International Monetary Fund, 2018), https://www.imf.org/en/Publications/WP/Issues/2018/03/05/How-Well-Do-Economists-Forecast-Recessions-45672; David Floyd, "Economists Seriously Can't Forecast Recessions," Investopedia, March 7, 2018, https://www.investopedia.com/news/economists-seriously-cant-forecast-recessions/; Adam Shaw, "Why Economic Forecasting Has Always Been a Flawed Science," *The Guardian*, September 2, 2017, https://www.theguardian.com/money/2017/sep/02/economic-forecasting-flawed-science-data.

10. Alexandra Twin, "Raging Bulls Propel Dow: Dow Soars 489 Points in Second-Best Point Gain Ever, Best Percentage Gain Since 1987," CNN Money, July 29, 2002, https://money.cnn.com/2002/07/24/markets/markets_newyork/index.htm; Jonathan Fuerbringer, "The Markets: Stocks; Battered for Weeks, Dow Enjoys Its Biggest Daily Gain Since '87," *New York Times*, July 25, 2002, https://www.nytimes.com/2002/07/25/business/the-markets-stocks-battered-for-weeks-dow-enjoys-its-biggest-daily-gain-since-87.html?searchResultPosition=1.

11. Richard Thaler, "Keynes's 'Beauty Contest,'" *Financial Times*, July 10, 2015, https://www .ft.com/content/6149527a-25b8-11e5-bd83-71cb60e8f08c; David Chambers, Elroy Dimson, and Justin Foo, "Keynes the Stock Market Investor: A Quantitative Analysis," *Journal of Financial and Quantitative Analysis* 50, no. 4 (2015): 431–49, https://papers.ssrn.com /sol3/papers.cfm?abstract_id=2023011; Joan Authers, "The Long View: Keynes Stands Tall Among Investors," *Financial Times*, July 6, 2012, https://www.ft.com/content/813a7b84 -c744-11e1-8865-00144feabdc0; Zachary D. Carter, *The Price of Peace: Money, Democracy, and the Life of John Maynard Keynes* (New York: Random House, 2020), 116–18.

12. Jeff Sommer, "Clueless About 2020, Wall Street Forecasters Are At It Again," *New York Times*, December 21, 2020, https://www.nytimes.com/2020/12/18/business/stock-market -forecasts-wall-street.html; Jane Wollman Rusoff, "Harry Dent Predicted 'Once-in-a-Life time' Crash by 2020. What Now?," ThinkAdvisor, May 4, 2020, https://www.thinkadvisor .com/2020/05/04/harry-dent-predicted-once-in-a-lifetime-crash-by-2020-what-now/; Shawn Tully, "Why the Stock Market Probably Won't Get Back to Even This Year," *Fortune*, March 9, 2020, https://fortune.com/2020/03/09/stock-market-outlook-2020/.

13. Wollman Rusoff, "Harry Dent Predicted." For more information on Harry Dent, see https://harrydent.com.

14. Neal E. Boudette and Jack Ewing, "Head of Nikola, a G.M. Electric Truck Partner, Quits Amid Fraud Claims," *New York Times*, September 21, 2020, https://www.nytimes .com/2020/09/21/business/nikola-trevor-milton-resigns.html#:~:text=Hindenburg %2C%20a%20short%2Dselling%20firm,after%20the%20company%20and%20G.M.&- text=On%20Monday%2C%20the%20shares%20lost,deal%20was%20announced; Hindenburg Research, *Nikola: How to Parlay an Ocean of Lies Into a Partnership with the Largest Auto OEM in America* (Hindenburg Research, September 10, 2020), https://hindenburg research.com/nikola/; "Nikola and General Motors Form Strategic Partnership; Nikola Badger to Be Engineered and Manufactured by General Motors," news release, General Motors, September 8, 2020, https://investor.gm.com/news-releases/news-release-details /nikola-and-general-motors-form-strategic-partnership-nikola; Noah Manskar, "Nikola Shares Pop 53 Percent After GM Takes $2B Stake in Tesla Rival," *New York Post*, September 8, 2020, https://nypost.com/2020/09/08/gm-takes-2-billion-stake-in-nikola-electric -rival-to-tesla/; Andrew J. Hawkins, "GM Pumps the Brakes on Its Deal with Troubled Electric Truck Startup Nikola," *The Verge*, November 30, 2020, https://www.theverge.com /2020/11/30/21726594/gm-nikola-deal-equity-badger-truck-hydrogen.

15. Ortenca Aliaj, Sujeet Indap, and Miles Kruppa, "Automotive Tech Start-Ups Take Wild Ride with Spacs," *Financial Times*, January 12, 2021, https://www.ft.com/content/688d8472 -c404-42d6-88b7-fbd475e50f7c; "Nikola Sets the Record Straight on False and Misleading Short Seller Report," press release, Nikola, September 14, 2020, https://nikolamotor.com /press_releases/nikola-sets-the-record-straight-on-false-and-misleading-short-seller -report-96; Hyliion (website), accessed April 2021, https://www.hyliion.com/; Fisker (website), accessed April 2021, https://www.fiskerinc.com/; Luminar Technologies (website), accessed April 2021, https://www.luminartech.com/; "About Us," Canoo, accessed April 2021, https://www.canoo.com/about/; Mark Kane, "The List of EV SPACs: Completed and Upcoming," Inside EVs, January 23, 2021, https://insideevs.com/news /481681/list-ev-spac-completed-upcoming/; Jack Denton, "Watch Tesla, Nikola and These Other Stocks as Change Comes for a Trucking Market Worth $1.5 Trillion, Says UBS," *MarketWatch*, March 20, 2021, https://www.marketwatch.com/story/watch-tesla -nikola-and-these-other-stocks-as-change-comes-for-a-trucking-market-worth-1-5 -trillion-says-ubs-11616099185; Shanthi Rexaline, "Nikola Skyrockets After IPO: What to Know About the EV Truck Manufacturer," *Benzinga*, June 9, 2020, https://www.benzinga

.com/news/20/06/16212027/nikola-skyrockets-after-ipo-what-to-know-about-the-ev-truck-manufacturer; "Velodyne Lidar Goes Public," Velodyne Lidar, September 30, 2020, https://velodynelidar.com/blog/velodyne-lidar-goes-public/; Kara Carlson, "Electric Trucking Company Hyliion Goes Public Through Merger," *Austin American-Statesman*, October 6, 2020, https://www.statesman.com/story/business/technology/2020/10/06/electric-trucking-company-hyliion-goes-public-through-merger/42729399/#:~:text=The%20resulting%20combination%20is%20named,at%20about%20the%20same%20level; Nicholas Jasinski and Al Root, "EV Battery Maker QuantumScape Just Went Public. Its Stock Soared 55%," *Barron's*, November 27, 2020, https://www.barrons.com/articles/ev-battery-maker-quantumscape-went-public-its-stock-soared-55-51606513410; Stephen Nellis, "Luminar Technologies Becomes Public Company as Lidar Race Builds," Reuters, December 3, 2020, https://www.reuters.com/article/luminiar-gores-metro-idINL1N2IJ00F; David Z. Morris, "Electric-Vehicle Startup Fisker Inc. Shares Jump 13% on Stock Market Debut," *Fortune*, October 30, 2020, https://fortune.com/2020/10/30/fisker-inc-stock-fsr-shares-ipo-spac-ev-electric-vehicle-car-startup/; Viknesh Vijayenthiran, "EV Startup Canoo Goes Public with Nasdaq Listing," Motor Authority, December 22, 2020; "Electric Vehicles" (search term), Google Trends, January 1, 2014, to April 10, 2021, https://trends.google.com/trends/explore?date=2014-01-01%20 2021-04-10&geo=US&q=electric%20vehicles.

16. P. Smith, "Apparel and Footwear Market Size in the United States, China, and Western Europe in 2019 (in Billion U.S. Dollars)," Statista, January 13, 2022, https://www.statista.com/statistics/995215/apparel-and-footwear-market-size-by-selected-market/; Layla Ilchi, "All the Major Fashion Brands and Retailers Severely Impacted by the COVID-19 Pandemic," WWD, December 24, 2020, https://wwd.com/fashion-news/fashion-scoops/coronavirus-impact-fashion-retail-bankruptcies-1203693347/; P. Smith, "U.S. Apparel Market – Statistics & Facts," Statista, June 2, 2022, https://www.statista.com/topics/965/apparel-market-in-the-us/#dossierSummary__chapter2.

17. In INR, the fund multiplied 19.6 times from March 2009 to March 2021, whereas the main index multiplied 5.1 times. In the same period, in USD, the fund multiplied 12.6 times, whereas the main index multiplied 3.6 times.

18. V. Raghunathan, "Why Did the Sensex Crash from 20K to Under 10K?," *Economic Times*, last updated December 28, 2008, https://economictimes.indiatimes.com/why-did-sensex-crash-from-20k-to-under-10k/articleshow/3901597.cms; Shreya Biswas and Prashant Mahesh, "Economic Recession, Lay-Offs Shift Balance of Power," *Economic Times*, last updated November 15, 2008, https://economictimes.indiatimes.com/the-big-story/economic-recession-lay-offs-shift-balance-of-power/articleshow/3715185.cms?from=mdr; Moinak Mitra, Priyanka Sangani, Vinod Mahanta, and Dibeyendu Ganguly, "Financial Crisis: Are MNC Jobs Secure?," *Economic Times*, last updated September 26, 2008, https://economictimes.indiatimes.com/financial-crisis-are-mnc-jobs-secure/articleshow/3529077.cms?from=mdr; "Sensex, Nifty Hit New 2008 Lows," *Economic Times*, last updated October 16, 2008, https://economictimes.indiatimes.com/sensex-nifty-hit-new-2008-lows/articleshow/3602137.cms?from=mdr; Vinay Pandey, "Economic Activity Is Slowing Down Fast," *Economic Times*, last updated August 25, 2008, https://m.economictimes.com/news/economy/indicators/economic-activity-is-slowing-down-fast/articleshow/3404817.cms.

19. Tom Stafford, "Why Bad News Dominates the Headlines," BBC, July 28, 2014, https://www.bbc.com/future/article/20140728-why-is-all-the-news-bad.

20. Ap Dijksterhuis and Henk Aarts, "On Wildebeests and Humans: The Preferential Detection of Negative Stimuli," *Psychological Science* 14, no. 1 (2003): 14–18, https://doi.org/10.1111/1467-9280.t01-1-01412.

5. Darwin Ate My DCF

1. Xuemin (Sterling) Yan, "Liquidity, Investment Style, and the Relation Between Fund Size and Fund Performance," *Journal of Financial and Quantitative Analysis* 43, no. 3 (2008): 741–67, https://doi.org/10.1017/S0022109000004270.

2. Conrad S. Ciccotello and C. Terry Grant, "Equity Fund Size and Growth: Implications for Performance and Selection," *Financial Services Review* 5, no. 1 (1996): 1–12, https://doi.org/10.1016/S1057-0810(96)90023-2.

3. Antti Petajisto, "Active Share and Mutual Fund Performance," *Financial Analysts Journal* 69, no. 4 (2013): 73–93, https://doi.org/10.2469/faj.v69.n4.7.

4. Stephen Jay Gould, *Hen's Teeth and Horse's Toes* (New York: W. W. Norton, 1983), 124.

5. John Gribbin and Michael White, *Darwin: A Life in Science* (London: Simon & Schuster, 1995), 80, 96, 97, 125; Adrian Desmond and James Moore, *Darwin: The Life of a Tormented Evolutionist* (New York: W. W. Norton, 1991); Charles Darwin, *The Autobiography of Charles Darwin*, ed. Nora Barlow (London: Collins, 1958).

6. Gribbin and White, *Darwin*, 80.

7. "Darwin's Book Publications," American Museum of Natural History, accessed March 2021, https://www.amnh.org/research/darwin-manuscripts/published-books.

8. Joe Cain, "How Extremely Stupid: Source for Huxley's Famous Quote," *Professor Joe Cain* (blog), accessed March 2021, https://profjoecain.net/how-extremely-stupid-thomas-henry-huxley/.

9. Mark Ridley, *Evolution*, 3rd ed. (Hoboken, NJ: Wiley, 2003).

10. Lory Herbison and George W. Frame, "Giraffe," *Encyclopaedia Britannica*, last updated September 2, 2021, https://www.britannica.com/animal/giraffe.

11. Darwin, *Autobiography*, 71.

12. "William Paley, 'The Teleological Argument': Philosophy of Religion," P.L.E., accessed March 2021, https://philosophy.lander.edu/intro/paley.shtml.

13. Editors of *Encyclopaedia Britannica*, "Georges Cuvier," *Encyclopaedia Britannica*, last updated August 19, 2022, https://www.britannica.com/biography/Georges-Cuvier.

14. Charles Darwin, *On the Origin of Species* (1859; repr., New York: Random House, 1993), 537.

15. Frank J. Sulloway, "The Evolution of Charles Darwin," *Smithsonian Magazine*, December 2005, https://www.smithsonianmag.com/science-nature/the-evolution-of-charles-darwin-110234034/.

16. Gribbin and White, *Darwin*, 33.

17. Darwin, *Origin*, 108.

18. Charles Darwin to Asa Gray, April 3, 1860, Darwin Correspondence Project, University of Cambridge, letter no. 2743, accessed March 2021, https://www.darwinproject.ac.uk/letter/DCP-LETT-2743.xml.

19. Diana Lipscomb, *Basics of Cladistic Analysis* (Washington, DC: George Washington University, 1998), https://www2.gwu.edu/~clade/faculty/lipscomb/Cladistics.pdf.

20. Staffan Müller-Wille, "Carolus Linnaeus," *Encyclopaedia Britannica*, last updated May 19, 2022, https://www.britannica.com/biography/Carolus-Linnaeus (on Linnaeus's reputation being built on his botanical classification system, see section "The 'Sexual System' of Classification"); Ken Gewertz, "Taxonomist Carl Linnaeus on Show at HMNH," *Harvard Gazette*, November 1, 2007, https://news.harvard.edu/gazette/story/2007/11/taxonomist-carl-linnaeus-on-show-at-hmnh/#:~:text=A%20highly%20religious%20man%20(although,God%20created%2C%20Linnaeus%20organized).

21. Madeline C. Weiss, Martina Preiner, Joana C. Xavier, Verena Zimorski, and William F. Martin, "The Last Universal Common Ancestor Between Ancient Earth Chemistry and

the Onset of Genetics," *PLoS Genetics* 14, no. 8 (2018): e1007518, https://doi.org/10.1371
/journal.pgen.1007518.

22. Gribbin and White, *Darwin*, 80.

23. Sulloway, "The Evolution of Charles Darwin."

24. Charles Darwin to Henry Fawcett, September 18, 1861, Darwin Correspondence Project, University of Cambridge, letter no. 3257, accessed April 2021, https://www.darwin project.ac.uk/letter/DCP-LETT-3257.xml.

25. Donald Gunn MacRae, "Thomas Malthus," *Encyclopaedia Britannica*, last updated April 25, 2022, https://www.britannica.com/biography/Thomas-Malthus.

26. "Darwin and Malthus" (video), PBS.org, 2001, https://www.pbs.org/wgbh/evolution /library/02/5/l_025_01.html.

27. "Passenger Car Market Share Across India in Financial Year 2022, by Vendor," Statista, July 27, 2022, https://www.statista.com/statistics/316850/indian-passenger-car-market -share/; "Estimated U.S. Market Share Held by Selected Automotive Manufacturers in 2021," Statista, July 27, 2022, https://www.statista.com/statistics/249375/us-market -share-of-selected-automobile-manufacturers/; "Share of Visteon's Sales by Customer in 2015 and 2016," Statista, January 31, 2020, https://www.statista.com/statistics/670526 /visteon-sales-by-customer/.

28. CFI team, "Cost of Equity," CFI, last updated January 25, 2022, https://corporatefinance institute.com/resources/knowledge/finance/cost-of-equity-guide/; "5 Major Problems in the Determination of Cost of Capital," Accounting Notes, accessed April 2021, https:// www.accountingnotes.net/financial-management/cost-of-capital/5-major-problems -in-the-determination-of-cost-of-capital/7775; "Problems with Calculating WACC," Finance Train, accessed April 2021, https://financetrain.com/problems-with-calculating -wacc/; Charles W. Haley and Lawrence D. Schall, "Problems with the Concept of the Cost of Capital," *Journal of Financial and Quantitative Analysis* 13, no. 5 (1978): 847–70, https://doi.org/10.2307/2330631.

29. Olivia Solon and agency, "Aw Snap: Snapchat Parent Company's Value Plummets After Earnings Report," *The Guardian*, May 11, 2017, https://www.theguardian.com /technology/2017/may/10/snap-inc-first-quarter-results-share-price-drops.

30. Douglas J. Futuyma, *Evolutionary Biology*, 3rd ed. (Sunderland, MA: Sinauer, 1997), xvii.

31. "Why Did Nokia Fail and What Can You Learn from It?," *Medium*, July 24, 2018, https:// medium.com/multiplier-magazine/why-did-nokia-fail-81110d981787; James Surowiecki, "Where Nokia Went Wrong," *New Yorker*, September 3, 2013, https://www.newyorker .com/business/currency/where-nokia-went-wrong.

32. Daniel Liberto, "Investors Rush to Short Starbucks as Howard Schultz Mulls 2020 Run," Investopedia, February 8, 2019, http://www.investopedia.com/ask/answers/033015/why -did-howard-schultz-leave-starbucks-only-return-eight-years-later.asp.

6. Bacteria and Business Replay the Tape

1. Professor Jonathan Losos has been studying *Anolis*, or Caribbean lizards, since the late 1980s. See *The Origin of Species: Lizards in an Evolutionary Tree* (Chevy Chase, MD: HHMI BioInteractive, 2018), https://www.biointeractive.org/sites/default/files/LizardsEvoTree -Educator-Film.pdf.

2. Jeff Arendt and David Reznick, "Convergence and Parallelism Reconsidered: What Have We Learned About the Genetics of Adaptation?," *Trends in Ecology & Evolution* 23, no. 1 (2008): 26–32, https://doi.org/10.1016/j.tree.2007.09.011.

3. Jonathan B. Losos, *Improbable Destinies: Fate, Chance, and the Future of Evolution* (New York: Riverhead, 2018), 14.

4. Losos, *Improbable Destinies*, 89–90.

5. "All-Time Olympic Games Medal Table," Wikipedia, accessed April 2021, https://en.wikipedia.org/wiki/All-time_Olympic_Games_medal_table.

6. Editors of *Encyclopaedia Britannica*, "Placental Mammal," *Encyclopaedia Britannica*, last updated February 19, 2021, https://www.britannica.com/animal/placental-mammal; Editors of *Encyclopaedia Britannica*, "Marsupial," *Encyclopaedia Britannica*, last updated August 19, 2021, https://www.britannica.com/animal/marsupial.

7. Quoted in Jonathan B. Losos, "Convergence, Adaptation, and Constraint," *International Journal of Organic Evolution* 65, no. 7 (2011): 1827–40, https://onlinelibrary.wiley.com/doi/10.1111/j.1558-5646.2011.01289.x.

8. Editors of *Encyclopaedia Britannica*, "Leafcutter Ant," *Encyclopaedia Britannica*, last updated October 15, 2018, https://www.britannica.com/animal/leafcutter-ant.

9. Losos, *Improbable Destinies*, 29–31.

10. George McGhee, *Convergent Evolution: Limited Forms Most Beautiful* (Cambridge, MA: MIT Press, 2011).

11. Michael Isikoff, "Yellow Pages Battle Begins," *Washington Post*, June 4, 1984, https://www.washingtonpost.com/archive/business/1984/06/04/yellow-pages-battle-begins/9096ae78-3100-475c-91ad-6d92979fa348/.

12. MIT International Center for Air Transportation, *An Introduction to the Airline Data Project* (Cambridge: Massachusetts Institute of Technology, June 2014), http://web.mit.edu/airlinedata/www/2013%2012%20Month%20Documents/ADP_introduction.pdf.

13. International Air Transport Association (IATA), *IATA Annual Review 2014* (Geneva: IATA, 2014), https://www.iata.org/contentassets/c81222d96c9a4e0bb4ff6ced0126f0bb/iata-annual-review-2014.pdf, 15.

14. Louis K. C. Chan and Josef Lakonishok, "Value and Growth Investing: Review and Update," *Financial Analysts Journal* 60, no. 1 (2004): 71–86, https://doi.org/10.2469/faj.v60.n1.2593.

15. Losos, *Improbable Destinies*, 334.

16. Editors of *Encyclopaedia Britannica*, "The Rodent That Acts Like a Hippo," *Encyclopaedia Britannica*, December 7, 2001, https://www.britannica.com/topic/The-Rodent-That-Acts-Like-a-Hippo-753723.

17. Losos, *Improbable Destinies*, chapter 9.

7. Don't Confuse a Green Frog for a Guppy

1. Many books discuss signals. The main ones I referred to are as follows: Mark Ridley, *Evolution*, 3rd ed. (Hoboken, NJ: Wiley, 2003), chapter 12; Edward O. Wilson, *Sociobiology: The New Synthesis*, twenty-fifth anniversary ed. (Cambridge, MA: Belknap, 2000), chapter 8; Jonathan Losos, ed., *The Princeton Guide to Evolution* (Princeton, NJ: Princeton University Press, 2014), section 7; William A. Searcy and Stephen Nowicki, *The Evolution of Animal Communication: Reliability and Deception in Signaling Systems* (Princeton, NJ: Princeton University Press, 2005), chapters 1–5; David Sloan Wilson, *Evolution for Everyone: How Darwin's Theory Can Change the Way We Think About Our Lives* (New York: Delta, 2007), chapter 15; Richard O. Prum, *The Evolution of Beauty: How Darwin's Forgotten Theory of Mate Choice Shapes the Animal World* (New York: Anchor, 2017), chapters 2–4; Adam Nicholson, *The Seabird's Cry: The Lives and Loves of Puffins, Gannets, and Other Ocean Voyagers* (New York: Henry Holt, 2018); Laurent

Keller and Élisabeth Gordon, *The Lives of Ants* (New York: Oxford University Press, 2009), chapter 10; Thor Hanson, *Feathers: The Evolution of a Natural Miracle* (New York: Basic Books, 2011), chapter 10; Thomas D. Seeley, *Honeybee Democracy* (Princeton, NJ: Princeton University Press, 2010). See also Jack W. Bradbury, "Animal Communication," *Encyclopaedia Britannica*, last updated April 8, 2022, http://global.britannica.com/EBchecked/topic/25653/animal-communication.

2. Searcy and Nowicki, *The Evolution of Animal Communication*; Carl Zimmer, "Devious Butterflies, Full-Throated Frogs and Other Liars," *New York Times*, December 26, 2006, https://www.nytimes.com/2006/12/26/science/26lying.html.

3. Patricia R. Y. Backwell, John Christy, Steven R. Telford, Michael D. Jennions, and Jennions Passmore, "Dishonest Signaling in a Fiddler Crab," *Proceedings of the Royal Society B: Biological Sciences* 267, no. 1444 (2000): 719–24, https://doi.org/10.1098/rspb.2000.1062.

4. Anne C. Gaskett, "Floral Shape Mimicry and Variation in Sexually Deceptive Orchids with a Shared Pollinator," *Biological Journal of the Linnean Society* 106, no. 3 (2012): 469–81, https://doi.org/10.1111/j.1095-8312.2012.01902.x.

5. John A. Endler, "Natural Selection on Color Patterns *Poecilia Reticulata*," *Journal Evolution* 34, no. 1 (1980): 76–91, https://doi.org/10.2307/2408316.

6. Jean-Guy J. Godin and Heather E. McDonough, "Predator Preference for Brightly Colored Males in the Guppy: A Viability Cost for a Sexually Selected Trait," *Behavioral Ecology* 14, no. 2 (2003): 194–200, https://doi.org/10.1093/beheco/14.2.194.

7. Editors of *Encyclopaedia Britannica*, "Coral Snake," *Encyclopaedia Britannica*, last updated May 2, 2022, https://www.britannica.com/animal/coral-snake.

8. James Venner, "Animal Communication: Honest, Dishonest and Costly Signalling," Zoo Portraits, July 24, 2018, https://www.zooportraits.com/animal-communication-honest-dishonest-costly-signalling/.

9. "Henry Walter Bates Describes 'Batesian Mimicry,' " Jeremy Norman's HistoryofInformation.com, last updated July 6, 2022, https://www.historyofinformation.com/detail.php?entryid=4277; Wolfgang J. H. Wickler, "Mimicry," *Encyclopaedia Britannica*, last updated February 7, 2019, https://www.britannica.com/science/mimicry.

10. Jack W. Bradbury and Sandra L. Vehrencamp, "Honesty and Deceit," *Encyclopaedia Britannica*, last updated April 8, 2022, https://www.britannica.com/science/animal-communication/Honesty-and-deceit.

11. On Zahavi's handicap principle, see Searcy and Nowicki, *The Evolution of Animal Communication*, introduction; Laith Al-Shawaf and David M. G. Lewis, "The Handicap Principle," in *Encyclopedia of Evolutionary Psychological Science*, ed. Todd K. Shackelford and Viviana A. Shackelford-Weekes (Cham, Denmark: Springer, 2018), https://doi.org/10.1007/978-3-319-16999-6_2100-1. On carotenoids, see Searcy and Nowicki, *The Evolution of Animal Communication*, chapter 3. While the handicap principle seems to provide a logical explanation for assessing the reliability of signals, scientists have proposed other mechanisms, too; see Searcy and Nowicki, *The Evolution of Animal Communication*, chapter 6: "In summary, the reliability of some classes of signals seem best explained by the handicap principle, in the sense of signal costs that act differentially on different categories of signallers." Note the qualifier "some classes of signals." The authors describe the following four alternatives to the handicap principle: (1) Signals can be honest without the signaler incurring a cost if the receiver and the sender have the same interest; for example, alarm signals given by birds when they see a predator. (2) When the benefit to the signaler (as opposed to the cost) varies with the attribute of the signal, honest signals may arise; for example, when offspring solicit their parents for

food. (3) The "constraints hypothesis" states that a signal can be honest when bodily or other constraints force the signal to be reliable; for example, carotenoid pigmentation in red-shouldered widowbirds (see chapter 4). (4) The theory of "individually directed skepticism" states that receivers remember the honesty or dishonesty of signals emitted from a certain signaler in the past and adjust their response to the signaler accordingly. Thus, a habitual deceiver will become unable to generate the desired response in the receiver; for example, signals given by domestic chickens for food.

12. Amotz Zahavi, "Mate Selection: A Selection for a Handicap," *Journal of Theoretical Biology* 53, no. 1 (1975): 205–14, https://doi.org/10.1016/0022-5193(75)90111-3.

13. Monty Solomon, "Apple Updates MacBook Pro with Retina Display," press release, Mail Archive, July 29, 2014, https://www.mail-archive.com/medianews@etskywarn.net/msg17476.html.

14. Unilever, *2014 Full Year and Fourth Quarter Results: Profitable Growth in Tougher Markets* (London: Unilever, 2015), https://docplayer.net/2815586-2014-full-year-and-fourth-quarter-results-profitable-growth-in-tougher-markets.html.

15. Markus Braun, interview by Matt Miller, Bloomberg TV, "Wirecard Concentrates on Innovation, Not 'Controversy': CEO Braun," Bloomberg, June 13, 2009, https://www.bloomberg.com/news/videos/2019-06-13/wirecard-concentrates-on-innovation-not-controversy-ceo-braun-video; Olaf Storbeck, "BaFin Boss 'Believed' Wirecard Was Victim Until Near the End," *Financial Times*, January 24, 2021, https://www.ft.com/content/a021012e-bd2e-44d5-a160-96d997c662f1; Liz Alderman and Christopher F. Schuetze, "In a German Tech Giant's Fall, Charges of Lies, Spies and Missing Billions," *New York Times*, June 26, 2020, https://www.nytimes.com/2020/06/26/business/wirecard-collapse-markus-braun.html; Olaf Storbeck, "Wirecard: A Record of Deception, Disarray and Mismanagement," *Financial Times*, June 24, 2021, https://www.ft.com/content/15bb36e7-54dc-463a-a6d5-70fc38a11c81.

16. "Sell-Side Analysts Strongly in Favor of Companies Providing Earnings Guidance," *PR Newswire*, accessed April 2021, http://www.prnewswire.com/news-releases/sell-side-analysts-strongly-in-favor-of-companies-providing-earnings-guidance-57993442.html.

17. Peggy Hsieh, Timothy Koller, and S. R. Rajan, "The Misguided Practice of Earnings Guidance," McKinsey & Company, March 1, 2006, https://www.mckinsey.com/business-functions/strategy-and-corporate-finance/our-insights/the-misguided-practice-of-earnings-guidance.

18. Don Seiffert, "GE Is No Longer the Most Valuable Public Company in Massachusetts," *Boston Business Journal*, October 30, 2018, https://www.bizjournals.com/boston/news/2018/10/30/ge-is-no-longer-the-most-valuable-public-company.html#:~:text=In%20August%202000%2C%20GE%20was,run%20into%20myriad%20financial%20problems; Thomas Gryta and Ted Mann, *Lights Out: Pride, Delusion, and the Fall of General Electric* (New York: Houghton Mifflin Harcourt, 2020), 35 (Immelt's discovery of fudged profits at GE Plastics), 58 (Edison Conduit accounting lie), 59 (Dammerman's quote), 60 (Welch's interview with Carol Loomis).

19. Fox Business, "Charlie Munger: Sewer Too Light a Word for Valeant," YouTube video, 4:37, uploaded May 2, 2016, https://www.youtube.com/watch?v=yxMZM_63Fpk; Matt Turner, "Here's the Email Bill Ackman Sent to Charlie Munger to Complain About Munger's Valeant Comments," *Business Insider*, May 9, 2016, https://www.businessinsider.com/bill-ackman-email-to-charlie-munger-2016-5; Svea Herbst-Bayliss, "Ackman's Pershing Square Sells Valeant Stake, Takes $3 Billion Loss," Reuters, March 3, 2017, https://www.reuters.com/article/us-valeant-ackman-idUSKBN16K2KT.

20. Chevron, *4Q19 Earnings Conference Call Edited Transcript* (San Ramon, CA: Chevron, January 31, 2020), https://chevroncorp.gcs-web.com/static-files/3436e36f-bf60-4466 -b550-b4f88d60a893.

21. Selina Wang and Matthew Campbell, "Luckin Scandal Is Bad Timing for U.S.-Listed Chinese Companies," Bloomberg, July 29, 2020, https://www.bloomberg.com/news /features/2020-07-29/luckin-coffee-fraud-behind-starbucks-competitor-s-scandal.

22. Zhang Rui, "Misbehaving US-Listed Chinese Enterprises and Their Gambler Attitudes," trans. Grace Chong and Candice Chan, ThinkChina, May 6, 2020, https://www.thinkchina .sg/misbehaving-us-listed-chinese-enterprises-and-their-gambler-attitudes; *The China Hustle*, directed by Jed Rothstein (New York: Magnolia Pictures, 2017), 82 min. The list of companies involved in the scandal can be seen at 1:23 in the film's trailer: Movie Coverage, "The China Hustle Trailer (2018) Documentary," YouTube video, 2:37, uploaded December 28, 2017, https://www.youtube.com/watch?v=DxbX5Dfk4b4. See also the following news articles: Arjun Kharpal, "Chinese Netflix-Style Service iQiyi Tanks by 18% After U.S. Regulators Investigate Fraud Allegations," CNBC, August 13, 2020, https://www .cnbc.com/2020/08/14/iqiyi-sec-investigation-into-fraud-allegations-shares-plunge .html; Sissi Cao, "Famed Tesla Short Seller Says This Soaring NYSE-Traded Chinese Company Is a Fraud," *Observer*, August 11, 2020, https://observer.com/2020/08/tesla-short -seller-citron-andrew-left-gsx-techedu-fraud-chinese-ipo/; Anna Vodopyanova, "Orient Paper to Change Its Name to IT Tech Packaging, Symbol to 'ITP,'" *Capital Watch*, July 19, 2018, https://www.capitalwatch.com/article-2506-1.html; "China Agritech (CAGC US)," GMT Research, last updated August 2021, https://www.gmtresearch.com/en /about-us/hall-of-shame/china-agritech-cagc-us/; U.S. Court-Appointed Receiver for Sino Clean Energy Inc., "U.S. Court-Appointed Receiver for Sino Clean Energy Inc. (Nasdaq 'SCEI') Files Criminal Charges in Hong Kong against Chairman of Nas- daq-Listed China Energy Company Accusing Him of Fraud on U.S. and Chinese Investors," *Cision PR Newswire*, June 23, 2015; Dena Aubin, "Judge Recommends $228 Mln Damages in Puda Coal Fraud Lawsuit," Reuters, January 9, 2017, https:// www.reuters.com/article/puda-fraud/judge-recommends-228-mln-damages-in-puda -coal-fraud-lawsuit-idUSL1N1F002L; Scott Eden, "SEC Probing China Green Ag," *TheStreet*, January 12, 2011, https://www.thestreet.com/markets/emerging-markets/sec -probing-china-green-10971670; T. Gorman, "SEC Charges Another China Based Firm with Fraud," SEC Actions, June 27, 2016, https://www.secactions.com/sec-charges -another-china-based-firm-with-fraud/; Lucy Campbell, "China Integrated Energy, Inc CBEH Securities Stock Fraud," BigClassAction.com, March 28, 2011, https:// www.bigclassaction.com/lawsuit/china-integrated-energy-inc-cbeh-securities .php.

23. Ed Monk, "Fidelity Star Fund Manager Anthony Bolton Retires and Calls Time on Trou- bled China Adventure," *This Is Money*, June 17, 2013, https://www.thisismoney.co.uk /money/investing/article-2343119/Fidelity-star-fund-manager-Anthony-Bolton-retires -calls-time-troubled-China-adventure.html; Jonathan Davis, "Farewell to the Harry Potter of Investment," *Independent Advisor*, July 30, 2006, https://web.archive.org /web/20060828135414/http://www.independent-investor.com/stories/Farewell_to _Bolton_438.aspx; Patrick Collinson, "Fidelity Star Fund Manager Anthony Bolton to Step Down," *The Guardian*, June 17, 2013, https://www.theguardian.com/business/2013 /jun/17/fidelity-anthony-bolton-steps-down-china; Jeanny Yu, "Famed British Fund Manager Anthony Bolton Meets His China Match," *South China Morning Post*, June 19, 2013, https://www.scmp.com/business/money/markets-investing/article/1263890 /famed-british-fund-manager-anthony-bolton-meets-his.

24. Mary Caswell Stoddard, Rebecca M. Kilner, and Christopher Town, "Pattern Recognition Algorithm Reveals How Birds Evolve Individual Egg Pattern Signatures," *Nature Communications* 5, no. 4117 (2014), https://doi.org/10.1038/ncomms5117.

8. Birds and Bears Bare an Aberration

1. Kristian Heugh and Marc Fox, *Long-Term Conviction in a Short-Term World* (New York: Morgan Stanley, 2018), https://www.morganstanley.com/im/publication/insights/investment-insights/ii_longtermconvictioninashorttermworld_us.pdf.
2. Björn Kurtén, "Rates of Evolution in Fossil Mammals," *Cold Spring Harbor Symposia on Quantitative Biology* 24 (1959): 205–15, https://doi.org/10.1101/SQB.1959.024.01.021.
3. Philip D. Gingerich, "Rates of Evolution," *Annual Review of Ecology, Evolution, and Systematics* 40 (2009): 657–75, https://doi.org/10.1146/annurev.ecolsys.39.110707.173457.
4. Simon Y. W. Ho, Robert Lanfear, Lindell Bromham, Matthew J. Phillips, Julien Soubrier, Allen G. Rodrigo, and Alan Cooper, "Time-Dependent Rates of Molecular Evolution," *Molecular Ecology* 20, no. 15 (2011): 3087–101, https://doi.org/10.1111/j.1365-294X.2011.05178.x.
5. Peter T. Boag and Peter R. Grant, "Intense Natural Selection in a Population of Darwin's Finches (*Geospizinae*) in the Galápagos," *Science* 214, no. 4516 (1981): 82–85, https://doi.org/10.1126/science.214.4516.82.
6. Hanneke Meijer, "Origin of the Species: Where Did Darwin's Finches Come From?," *The Guardian*, July 30, 2018, https://www.theguardian.com/science/2018/jul/30/origin-of-the-species-where-did-darwins-finches-come-from.
7. Jonathan Weiner, *The Beak of the Finch: A Story of Evolution in Our Time* (New York: Vintage, 1994); Emily Singer, "Watching Evolution Happen in Two Lifetimes," *Quanta Magazine*, September 22, 2016, https://www.quantamagazine.org/watching-evolution-happen-in-two-lifetimes-20160922; Joel Achenbach, "The People Who Saw Evolution," *Princeton Alumni Weekly*, April 23, 2014, https://paw.princeton.edu/article/people-who-saw-evolution.
8. Peter R. Grant and B. Rosemary Grant, "Unpredictable Evolution in a 30-Year Study of Darwin's Finches," *Science* 296, no. 5568 (2002): 707–11, https://doi.org/10.1126/science.1070315.
9. L'Oréal, *2009 Annual Results* (Clichy, France: L'Oréal, 2010), https://www.loreal-finance.com/eng/news-release/2009-annual-results; L'Oréal, *2020 Annual Results* (Clichy, France: L'Oréal, 2021), https://www.loreal-finance.com/eng/news-release/2020-annual-results.
10. Mark J. Perry, "Fortune 500 Firms in 1955 v. 2015: Only 12% Remain, Thanks to the Creative Destruction That Fuels Economic Prosperity," American Enterprise Institute, October 12, 2015, https://www.aei.org/carpe-diem/fortune-500-firms-in-1955-vs-2015-only-12-remain-thanks-to-the-creative-destruction-that-fuels-economic-growth/.
11. Andrew Hudson, "The Rise & Fall of Kodak: A Brief History of The Eastman Kodak Company, 1880 to 2012," August 29, 2012, https://www.photosecrets.com/the-rise-and-fall-of-kodak.

9. Eldredge and Gould Dredge Up Investing Gold

1. "Macroevolution Through Evograms: The Evolution of Whales," Understanding Evolution, University of California Museum of Paleontology, last updated June 2020, https://evolution.berkeley.edu/evolibrary/article/evograms_03.

2. Stephen Jay Gould, *The Structure of Evolutionary Theory* (Cambridge, MA: Belknap, 2002), 749. Many observations in this chapter come from chapter 9, "Punctuated Equilibrium and the Validation of Macroevolutionary Theory."

3. "Palaeontological Memoirs and Notes of the Late Hugh Falconer," Jeremy Norman's HistoryofScience.com, accessed April 2021, https://www.jnorman.com/pages/books /40957/hugh-falconer/palaeontological-memoirs-and-notes-of-the-late-hugh-falconer. See also Gould, *Structure*, 745.

4. Niles Eldredge and Stephen Jay Gould, "Punctuated Equilibria: An Alternative to Phyletic Gradualism," in *Models in Paleobiology*, ed. Thomas J. M. Schopf (San Francisco: Freeman, Cooper, 1972), 82–115, https://www.blackwellpublishing.com/ridley/classic texts/eldredge.pdf.

5. Jonathan Chadwick, "World's Oldest DNA Is Extracted from the Tooth of a Mammoth," *Daily Mail*, February 17, 2021, https://www.dailymail.co.uk/sciencetech/article-9270399 /Worlds-oldest-DNA-extracted-tooth-mammoth.html.

6. Gould, *Structure*, 826.

7. Gould, *Structure*, 827.

8. Tiina M. Mattila and Folmer Bokma, "Extant Mammal Body Masses Suggest Punctuated Equilibrium," *Proceedings of the Royal Society B: Biological Sciences* 275, no. 1648 (2008): 2195–99, https://doi.org/10.1098/rspb.2008.0354.

9. "Repeat After Me," *The Economist*, December 16, 2004, http://www.economist.com /node/3500219.

10. Jonathan Rée, "Evolution by Jerks," *New Humanist*, May 31, 2007, https://newhumanist .org.uk/articles/598/evolution-by-jerks.

11. Mark Ridley, *Evolution*, 3rd ed. (Hoboken, NJ: Wiley, 2003), 17, 266.

12. David H. Bailey, "Does the Punctuated Equilibrium Theory Refute Evolution?," SMR Blog, April 21, 2019, https://www.sciencemeetsreligion.org/blog/2019/04/does-the-punctuated -equilibrium-theory-refute-evolution/.

13. Gustavo Grullon, Yelena Larkin, and Roni Michaely, "Are US Industries Becoming More Concentrated?," *Review of Finance* 23, no. 4 (2019): 697–743, https://doi.org/10.1093 /rof/rfz007.

14. Matej Bajgar, Giuseppe Berlingieri, Sara Calligaris, Chiara Criscuolo, and Jonathan Timmis, "Industry Concentration in Europe and North America," *OECD Productivity Working Papers*, No. 18 (Paris: OECD Publishing), https://doi.org/10.1787/2ff98246-en.

15. "Winners Take All: Why High Profits Are a Problem for America," *The Economist*, March 26, 2016, https://www.economist.com/weeklyedition/2016-03-26.

16. Hendrick Bessembinder, "Do Stocks Outperform Treasury Bills?," *Journal of Financial Economics* 129, no. 3 (2018): 440–57, https://doi.org/10.1016/j.jfineco.2018.06.004.

17. Bessembinder, "Do Stocks Outperform," table 2A, panel D.

18. CNET News staff, "Blodget and Amazon: A Long History," CNET, January 2, 2002, https://www.cnet.com/news/blodget-and-amazon-a-long-history/.

19. James Surowiecki, "Doom, Incorporated," *New Yorker*, May 12, 2002, https://www .newyorker.com/magazine/2002/05/20/doom-incorporated.

20. "Brood X Periodical Cicadas FAQ," National Park Service, last updated September 1, 2022, https://www.nps.gov/articles/000/cicadas-brood-x.htm.

10. Where Are the Rabbits?

1. Associated Press, "Forbes List 400 Richest Americans: Sam Walton of Wal-Mart Stores Is No. 1 with $6.7 Billion," *Los Angeles Times*, October 11, 1988, https://www.latimes.com

/archives/la-xpm-1988-10-11-fi-3693-story.html; John Rothchild, *The Davis Dynasty: Fifty Years of Successful Investing on Wall Street* (New York: John Wiley, 2001).

2. Charles Darwin to W. D. Fox, July 29, 1828, Darwin Correspondence Project, University of Cambridge, letter no. 45, https://www.darwinproject.ac.uk/letter/DCP-LETT-45.xml.

3. Julie Rehmeyer, "Darwin: The Reluctant Mathematician," *Science News*, February 11, 2009, https://www.sciencenews.org/article/darwin-reluctant-mathematician.

4. Mark Ridley, *Evolution*, 3rd ed. (Hoboken, NJ: Wiley, 2003), 10–13.

5. David T. Mitchell, "Mutation Theory," *Encyclopaedia Britannica*, last updated March 21, 2016, https://www.britannica.com/science/mutation-theory.

6. Francisco Jose Ayala, "Evolution," *Encyclopaedia Britannica*, last updated August 22, 2022, https://www.britannica.com/science/evolution-scientific-theory. See in particular subsection, "The Synthetic Theory," https://www.britannica.com/science/evolution-scientific-theory/Modern-conceptions#ref49842.

7. Douglas J. Futuyma, *Evolutionary Biology*, 3rd ed. (Sunderland, MA: Sinauer, 1997), 24.

8. Sean B. Carroll, *Making of the Fittest: DNA and the Ultimate Forensic Record of Evolution* (New York: W. W. Norton, 2007), 49–51.

9. Stuart Read, "Peppered Moth and Natural Selection," Butterfly Conservatory, https://butterfly-conservation.org/moths/why-moths-matter/amazing-moths/peppered-moth-and-natural-selection.

10. Ping Zhou, "Australia's Massive Feral Rabbit Problem," *ThoughtCo*, last updated November 22, 2019, https://www.thoughtco.com/feral-rabbits-in-australia-1434350. I am not sure if the number of rabbits provided in table 10.2 for the years *between* 1859 and 1925 are correct since all data sources point to the number ten billion in the 1920s, but they are presented to marvel at the power of exponential growth.

11. Richard Mille, "Forbes World's Billionaire List: The Richest in 2022," ed. Kerry A. Dolan and Chase Peterson-Withorn, *Forbes*, https://www.forbes.com/billionaires/.

12. Nicholas Carlson, "11 Companies That Tried to Buy Facebook Back When It Was a Startup," *Insider*, May 13, 2010, https://www.businessinsider.com/all-the-companies-that-ever-tried-to-buy-facebook-2010-5.

13. Hendrick Bessembinder, "Do Stocks Outperform Treasury Bills?," *Journal of Financial Economics* 129, no. 3 (2018): 440–57, https://doi.org/10.1016/j.jfineco.2018.06.004.

14. This is cash-to-cash annualized return, which accounts for all cash movements in and out of the fund. It is a better way to measure returns than simply annualizing 12 times the money over the period.

15. Michael Ray, "The Euro-Zone Debt Crisis," *Encyclopaedia Britannica*, last updated September 3, 2017, https://www.britannica.com/topic/European-Union/The-euro-zone-debt-crisis.

16. Claudia Champagne, Aymen Karoui, and Saurin Patel, "Portfolio Turnover Activity and Mutual Fund Performance," *Managerial Finance* 44, no. 3 (2018): 326–56, https://doi.org/10.1108/MF-01-2017-0003; Laura Cohn, "The Case for Low-Turnover Funds," *Kiplinger*, March 28, 2010, https://www.kiplinger.com/article/investing/t041-c009-s001-the-case-for-low-turnover-funds.html; Pedro Luiz Albertin Bono Milan and William Eid Jr., "High Portfolio Turnover and Performance of Equity Mutual Funds," *Brazilian Review of Finance* 12, no. 4 (2014): 469–97, https://doi.org/10.12660/rbfin.v12n4.2014.41445; Diego Victor de Mingo-López and Juan Carlos Matallín-Sáez, "Portfolio Turnover and Fund Investors' Performance" (paper presented at the Management International Conference, Venice, Italy, May 24–27, 2017), https://www.hippocampus.si/ISBN/978-961-7023-12-1/146.pdf.

Conclusion: Honeybees Win by Repeating a Simple Process. So Can We

1. Christopher D. Epp, "Definition of a Gene," *Nature* 389, no. 537 (1997), https://doi.org/10.1038/39166.
2. Philip Ball, "DNA at 60: Still Much to Learn," *Scientific American*, April 28, 2013, https://www.scientificamerican.com/article/dna-at-60-still-much-to-learn/.
3. The fact that evolution had produced females that seemed to have given up the right to reproduce and were therefore apparently violating the law of natural selection baffled Darwin, and he could not crack the conundrum in his lifetime. W. D. Hamilton's kin selection theory famously solved the problem in the 1960s.
4. Thomas D. Seeley, *Honeybee Democracy* (Princeton, NJ: Princeton University Press, 2011), chapters 5, 6.

INDEX